What's Wrong With Wende?

WINDELL YVETTE BEAIRD

Copyright © 2020 Windell Yvette Beaird

All rights reserved. No part(s) of this book may be reproduced, distributed or transmitted in any form, or by any means, or stored in a database or retrieval systems without prior expressed written permission of the author of this book.

ISBN
978-1-5356-1770-3 - Paperback
978-1-5356-1772-7 - Hardcover

I'M DEDICATING MY BOOK TO these people
who helped my dreams come true….

To my father, John Milton Beaird Jr., the greatest man I ever knew…

To the 'ONE OF A KIND' country music artist who
"… lit a fire down in my soul" and made me believe I could achieve my
dreams against all the odds…

To Pamela Allison for paving the road,
which changed the course of my life…

Lastly, this book is dedicated to all those who suffer in silence for any reason.

Turn the page; this story is for you…

Contents

Preface 8

1. Introduction 11
2. Roots… 13
3. Childhood Memories 19
4. The most magical time of the year 29
5. Innocence Lost 37
6. Lone Star Donuts 41
7. SAM 47
8. Momma's broken heart 51
9. One lie too many 55
10. Double-dog-dare 61
11. I didn't mean to rob 7-11! 65
12. Delaware and drug dealers 73
13. CLARK 79
14. Sex Skeletons 85
15. Rats, Roaches, and Asthma 91
16. Reflection and leaving Georgia 99
17. Sam, Special Deliveries, and Violence 103

18. Abilene and Methamphetamine 109
19. In the Navy… 115
20. BOOT CAMP 123
21. Pregnancy and Terror...131
22. High-Risk pregnancy ward 137
23. Welcome to the world Scuter!..143
24. Floodgates, Bulimia, and things you can't take back.................149
25. Pregnant again… 155
26. Welcome to the world Patrick!..159
27. Just rewards and spirits 165
28. Final goodbye, cabbie and rape 171
29. Divorce, loneliness, and one night stands.................................177
30. August 1982 183
31. Visions, telethons, and burning bushes 189
32. Goodbye Momma… 197
33. Reflections and acid trips!...203
34. Revelations, college, and prison penpals..................................207
35. Smuggling drugs into prison 213
36. It's time to meet the man you married!!!..................................219
37. SERIAL-RAPIST-MURDERER 225
38. I'm going to kill you! 233
39. Dealing drugs… 237
40. Lethal bumps, and kind-hearted cop from New York!..............243
41. Buried fortunes, Ted, and boys come home! 251
42. Cottonwood Park and Skating Rinks… 257
43. College, Sam, and rehab… 265
44. Last rape and Cancer...269
45. MIRACLES REALLY DO COME TRUE............................275
46. Momma Beatrice and Covington, Louisiana............................283

47. Poor choices, and the Undercover Narc!...................291
48. Incarceration and Intimidation.................................299
49. Donut shop and the old GEEZER! 305
50. End it all and Rescues! 311
51. Hep C, SWAT, and Grandma Georgia Bell 317
52. Maw-Maw's Promise and Paw-Paw's Demise 323
53. James, Andy, and Negotiations..................................329
54. Twelve steps, and another death…...........................337
55. Facebook and Maw-Maws..345
56. Maw-Maw Cruse's Rose Bush 351
57. Last donut shop, and who's that country singer?....355
58. Concerts, grandbabies, and true Christian friends!......363
59. Bubba the wild-man, child custody, and Hair Loss......369
60. Meeting Keith Urban...375
61. China..385
62. Broken promises and forgotten dreams…...............393
63. Flying high and Crashing low....................................401
64. Waterworks forever… 405
65. "Revealing Conversations" 409
66. Hit by a train!...417
67. Inspirations and shocking requests..........................423
68. Daddy Dimes and Little Sister...................................427
69. Promises Kept and Dreams Come True...................435
70. Epilogue 439

SPECIAL MESSAGE JUST FOR YOU!...............................443

Preface

Dear Readers,

This book is my original, unedited work. It is the true story of my life.

It would have been impossible to tell the story of my life using grammatically correct language because my family are, and were, simple country folks. I am well aware of the many syntax errors you will find within the pages of my book. The grammar I chose to use was deliberate and with intent. I have done my best to make sure that punctuation inaccuracies were kept to a minimum. Since it is the first time I've ever written a book, you may find other mistakes I've made as well.

I chose not to have it professionally edited because I wanted to tell my story, my way. I did not want an editor to chop it up and decide what needed changing. If it was important enough for me to write about, then I saw no need to have it removed by someone who had no way of understanding it's relevance to my story.

The only apology I offer is for the times I may have repeated myself. I admit I have that habit in life at times, but just like I tell my family when they catch me, if I mentioned it twice, then it must be important to me.

I have nothing to hide; my life is an open book. I have left no stones uncovered in my quest to share my experiences truthfully and accurately. Yet having said that, there is no way I could detail every instance of my life within the pages of one book.

Many of the names used in my book are pseudonyms out of respect for others' privacy.

There are a few people I want to thank for helping me on my journey to write this book:

Bobbi-Jo Davis, Thank you for being my proof-reader and helping me with technical assistance. Thank you for always being my friend and helping me walk through painful memories as only a friend can do.

Robin Fedrick, Thank you for being my hairdresser for the past fifteen years and for being my pseudo/therapist. Your honesty helps me more than you'll ever know.

Facebook friends, Thank you all for your encouragement and feedback on the chapters I shared.

To my family, thank you for always believing in me, even when I drive you crazy!

Lastly, to my readers, I hope my book encourages you to believe in miracles and know that it's never too late to chase your dreams.

As always I remain,
WINDELL YVETTE BEAIRD

Chapter 1

Introduction

September 2016

THE CANCER IS BACK. I didn't have much time left to begin with, according to the top heart, lung, and thoracic surgeon from East Texas. He gave me five to seven years before my lungs start hardening three years ago. Cancer may take part of that time away sooner. I reckon it's time to share my life, my way, and on my terms.

I've always wondered if there was something wrong with me; cause to save my soul; I can't help but tell on myself. Good, bad, or ugly; I sugarcoat nothing. I'm gonna tell it. My stepmother used to get on to me all the time for it.

She'd say, "Wende, some things are better kept to yourself!"

When I was younger, my parents would tell folks that they didn't have to worry 'bout me going behind their backs. If I did anything wrong, I'd soon tell on myself.

I learned to hate deceit as I grew older. I'd be told things by others then sworn to secrecy. Depending on who it was or what was said became a great burden on me. Perhaps my transparency was a self-defense mechanism, or maybe it was a case of an overactive conscience getting to me. At this point, it's merely a matter of me being a grown-ass woman with nothing left to hide.

Funny thing, honesty. You can tell the truth 'til you're blue in the face, but there's always gonna be that one person who'll never believe you. I finally realized that folks like that don't believe themselves either, and it's best to move on and stop wasting time trying to convince them otherwise.

I suppose I ought to pay heed to what the surgeon told me three years ago, but I don't know if I believe him. After the life I've lived, it's hard to know what to think. And what a life it's been! If I hadn't lived it, I'm not sure I would believe that so much could happen in one person's lifetime.

Not that I'm some saintly, unique person destined for fame and fortune. On the contrary, I will be the first person to admit here and now, that a great many of my downfalls and misfortunes in life were consequences of my own making. In my defense, I'd like to state for the record that I've always been an overachiever. When I've done well, I've done very well. Likewise, when I've been bad, I've been very bad.

Of course, I've been ashamed for some of the stunts I've pulled in my past. There were always reasons and excuses, I told myself, to excuse my conscience for stepping to the side long enough to screw my life up once again. Boy did that have detrimental effects. Ashamed as I was, I was also proud of myself. I learned to forgive myself and realize no one is perfect. I am the sum total of all my parts: good, bad, and ugly.

I've never stopped telling on myself. I share stories about my life all the time. Nearly every time, folks ask me why I haven't written a book about my life. Seriously? I don't want to get locked up in a funny jacket or go to prison for one or more of my past criminal transgressions!

Somewhere along the way, I've come to a conclusion that perhaps their right. I never murdered anyone, and I'm pretty sure that's the only crime that isn't covered by the statute of limitations. If nothing else, I'd be leaving behind my own account of this crazy; wild; miraculous life I've led for my ancestors. No one can tell our tale like ourselves, right? Lord knows how "screwy" the re-tellings can be, so I best tell my side while I have the chance!

I'm gonna do my best to tell the absolute truth, but there will be those who saw my life from a different angle. They may believe whatever they'd like; I can only tell my story as I lived it. I offer no apologies to anyone for the life I've led. Those whom I've wronged have already received apologies, and I've forgiven myself as well.

So, if you're easily offended, my story may not be for you. It's certainly not for the faint of heart. They say that life is stranger than fiction. Well, whoever "they" are, I'm bound to agree with them. Not sure I'd call my life strange, but what do I know? It is, after all, the story of my life.

Chapter 2

Roots...

THE EARLIEST MEMORY I RECALL is not a pleasant one.

We were sitting at the dinner table at Maw-Maw Lummus', Daddy's mother, house when I blurted out my scary dream. Momma turned white as a sheet, and Maw-Maw covered her mouth with her hand. The event had taken place when I was two and a half, and I had near-perfect recall through my dream.

Momma had set the alarm clock ahead by an hour so she could surprise Daddy with breakfast. She had it all laid out across the coffee table when she woke him up. Daddy panicked that he was late for work, got up in a frenzy. He couldn't hear what Momma was saying he was so mad. With one hand, he flipped the coffee table up, sending dishes and food flying. In the process, Daddy knocked over the birdcage, killing Momma's lovebirds. Momma screamed as he drew back to hit her. To this day, I remember standing on my tippy toes, grabbing Daddy's back pants pockets and saying, "Don't hurt Mommy!" Daddy was so enraged he didn't realize it was me as he grabbed my arm and slung me across the room. I don't recall flying through the air, but they said I did. I vaguely remember bouncing on Daddy's shoulder as he ran down the steep stairs of our apartment with Momma following close behind. I remember it was raining as Daddy gently laid me in the car.

They said that I was taken to an emergency room to get checked out since I passed out and had a goose egg on my head. I know Daddy never meant to hurt me that morning. He just couldn't control his temper and often *'blacked out.'* I've experienced the same things, so I know it's true.

When Momma was pregnant with me, she used to pick Daddy up from work.

"John, what are you gonna do when that little boy you call Windell turns out to be a girl," his co-workers often asked.

"I'm gonna name her "Windell" just for being a girl!"

"Oh yea, bet you fifty dollars, you don't!"

Hmph! I was named Windell after my Aunt Windelyen, Daddy's oldest sister. Daddy was so mad I turned out to be a girl that he never came to the hospital 'til it was time to pick Momma and me up. It was love at first sight.

Daddy was overwhelmed, thinking everyone was breathing germs on me. He took a box of surgical masks home and tried to make everyone that held me wear one. Aunt Windelyen told how she cried and cried cause Daddy hurt her feelings by making her wear a mask. Her and Maw-Maw Lummus, finally convinced Daddy that his baby sister Ida Mae's kids had survived "family" germs, and so would I.

My father was illiterate and came from a backwoods Louisiana, dysfunctional family. Yet, despite my father's disability, he managed to raise his kids and be the backbone for all who knew him. Not one welfare benefit was ever drawn on Daddy's family. Us kids were grown before Daddy chose the only out he saw... It was the greatest regret he ever had, more 'bout that later.

All Daddy ever wanted was someone to love him for himself and for his kids to get an education and not be like him. As I recall childhood memories of Daddy's family, all I remember is love. Simple country folk who provided for their own.

Laura Belle May, aka Maw-Maw Lummus, came from a family of eleven children. Pretty sure they were dirt poor from the pictures I have. You could see in her features, from childhood pictures, that she was part Native American. I don't recall a lot of her early years, but she was fourteen when she married Paw-Paw John. He was her first husband. Maw-Maw promptly had three children after marrying, a baby raising babies.

John Milton Beaird Sr., Daddy's father, was a big 'ol man. He served in the Army during WWI. I have a picture of him in his dress uniform in France while he was fighting overseas.

Paw-Paw was twenty years older than Maw-Maw. He was a quiet, settled man, and unfortunately, Maw-Maw was young and liked to drink. They parted ways when Daddy was still in grammar school. Daddy joked about going in the front door of the school and straight out the back.

It must have been true in part due to his illiteracy. I heard stories 'bout Maw-Maw being at the honky-tonks, and so drunk Daddy would have to go get her and drive her home at times when he could barely reach the foot pedals. I can't remember who said the kids at school shamed Daddy for it. In a small town, everyone knew everyone else's business.

Maw-Maw met a man named Jack Lummus and followed him from her little town to Dallas, Texas, when Daddy was nine. Daddy told how he got his first job pulling golf bags on the golf course by their home when they got to Texas. He caddied up to age sixteen when he started working for Dallas Morning News.

Maw-Maw went to work at the Hormel Meat Packing plant after she married Paw-Paw Jack, her second husband. I have vague memories of him though I was very young when he died. The strongest memory I have is lying next to him on one of those old black couches that had the silver thread running through it. I liked curling up next to him and going to sleep. Maw-Maw Lummus 'bout fainted at Paw-Paw Jacks' funeral when I crawled up in the casket and laid down next to him.

Everyone that knew Jack Lummus thought the world of him. Maw-Maw even quit the honky-tonks and toned down her drinking for him. When he died, she was back at it again.

Longhorn Ballroom was the place to be back in the day. Maw-Maw met Paw-Paw Ernest there. He might have been my step-grandfather, but to me, he was Paw-Paw, and I couldn't have loved him more. Pictures of him and Maw-Maw sitting at the table with Momma and Daddy showed him thin as a rail. It didn't take long for Maw-Maw to fatten him up after they got married.

Maw-Maw slowed her drinking here and there, but God forbid she take a swig of anything but beer. Maw-Maw always had a case of beer stored at the bottom of her icebox. If she got down to a six-pack, someone was carrying her across the river for some more. She drank beer like some folk's drink water. The craziest I ever saw her was when we all lived in the Piedmont Apartments out in Pleasant Grove. They were fourplexes. Least, that's what I called them cause there were four apartments in each building. I heard recently they've been torn down now.

I don't remember too many times that Aunt Windelyen and her son Clinton didn't live near Maw-Maw Lummus, or with her. Might as well say Maw-Maw raised Clinton Ray. Auntie had an apartment at the Piedmonts as well, right above Maw-Maw's.

Auntie always worked as a seamstress, and once worked with Maw-Maw Cruse, Momma's mother, at Stockton's Manufacturing in downtown Dallas.

Thinking about that reminds me of the time Maw-Maw Cruse got into it with her boss Bessie. Bessie had pushed timid little Maw-Maw around for years.

One day, Maw-Maw had her fill and told Bessie off when Aunt Windelyen walked into the lunchroom. Maw-Maw had made sure everyone knew that she and Aunt Windelyen were family from the start. Aunt Windelyen was a tall, strong, country gal that not many folks crossed. Not that she was mean, but because she was the real deal.

Bessie looked from Maw-Maw to Aunt Windelyen and left the room without saying a word. Aunt Windelyen would always laugh, re-telling her tale. She said Maw-Maw Cruse got downright cocky for a while after that. She said she told Maw-Maw, "Miss Cruse, you might want to slow down a bit in case I don't come to work one day!"

Back to my story. I don't remember what Maw-Maw Lummus drank that night at the apartments, or what started it. All I know is the call came for Daddy to get over there and in a hurry. We all followed but kept our distance.

Maw-Maw Lummus was chasing Aunt Windelyen all over the apartment with a butcher knife. Must have been something to see a little woman of 4'11 chasing a 5'8 amazon. Guarantee you one thing, Maw-Maw was the only person in this whole world Auntie was afraid of. Not that I believe for a moment that Maw-Maw would have hurt her. I'll always hold to the notion that Maw-Maw got a hold of some firewater, which turned her loose. It took Daddy a skinny minute to calm Maw-Maw down and take the knife from her. I really wish I could remember more of that story, but I don't.

Maw-Maw Lummus took a big chunk of my heart to heaven with her.

I get my love of dancing from Maw-Maw Lummus. Truth be told, there's a lot of that 'ol woman in me. On the weekends, I wasn't at Maw-Maw Cruse's; I was at Maw-Maw Lummus's. Maw-Maw might've had her faults, but I guarantee you, poor housekeeping wasn't one of them.

For starters, if you weren't sick, once that bed was made, you didn't sit on it. She kept her kitchen sparkling clean, washing up after every meal. I would spend many hours learning, on my hands and knees, how to make hardwood floors shine like they were wet. You never went to Maw-Maw's table before scrubbing your hands either. Children and menfolk always ate first. She was real particular 'bout her laundry too. I can still feel Maw-Maw's crisp, from the line, sheets after a nice warm bath.

Saturday nights, right after dinner, Maw-Maw Lummus would move the coffee table into the kitchen. When she did that, everyone knew what time it was! Porter Waggoner & Dolly Parton, Hee-Haw, and The Grand Ol' Opry was about to come on. I learned to waltz, two-step, and shake a leg in that living room on Ramsey Ave.

Maw-Maw taught me to dance, but more importantly, she taught me how to cook. The first thing I learned to make at six years old was home-made biscuits. My first batch was a mess. I forgot to add baking powder to the biscuits, and my cream gravy resembled the glue that came in a jar with a brush. Daddy suffered through them anyways, chipping a tooth on those flat, hard biscuits. He was so proud of me. She taught me many more dishes, but those biscuits are all Maw-Maw. She would quit drinking one day, but that's another story.

Maw-Maw Cruse, aka, Mae Belle Hodges,[1] was born in Hahira, Georgia. She came to Dallas by way of the Social Services when she was two. Her mother had taken ill and couldn't support all six of her children. They lived in a shotgun house on the Suwanee River. Times were hard, back in 1914, after Maw-Maw's father ran off and deserted his family. A family adopted Maw-Maw in Dallas, Texas.

Maw-Maw grew up with a gift of playing the piano by hearing. She used to pick out commercial jingles and play them for me; to make me laugh. Maw-Maw married; had a boy and divorced; by the time she met my Paw-Paw Bodiddle[2], Momma's father.

Paw-Paw Boddidle was born Louis Roscoe Cruse. He claimed he was quite the ladies' man, yet to look at him, you had to wonder why? He was a short, balding; Irishman who drove a truck all his life. I can't recall how they met, but Paw-Paw Bodiddle didn't stay with Maw-Maw Cruse long after she had Momma. Mamie, Maw-Maw's adopted mother, took over the raising of my half-uncle, Thomas. Maw-Maw had her hands full raising Momma. Imag-

---

[1] I believe my grandmother's surname at birth was Hodges; however, I haven't been able to verify that information. Early census records In Dallas, Texas show her adopted surname as Graham.

[2] Bodiddle was a nickname

ining Momma growing up from the stories I remember and understanding bi-polar as I do breaks my heart for Momma and everyone around her.

Maw-Maw Cruse was the church pianist for nearly twenty years when it happened. Momma was always running around the neighborhood, telling *'whoppers'* to anyone who would listen. One morning as Maw-Maw made ready for her day of hosting the church choir social, the police came knocking on her door. Momma in tow; they explained a neighbor had called to complain that a child was being abused and starved. Maw-Maw very politely asked if they could see any bruise's on Momma as she ducked behind one of the officers. Maw-Maw then escorted them into a well-stocked pantry. One of the officers tipped his hat at Maw-Maw and suggested she get a *'handle'* on Momma as they left the house.

When the officers left, Momma began kicking and screaming when Maw-Maw tried asking her why she'd *'storied.'* Maw-Maw sorrowfully told how she dragged Momma to a closet and locked her in.

Then it dawned on Maw-Maw that the ladies would be there soon. Off she flew in a hurry to finish her preparations. Sometime later, she heard the door chimes and was glad she'd just been able to finish. Unfortunately, she'd forgotten about Momma. She'd left Momma kicking and screaming in the closet, and after a while, Momma had quieted down.

Just as Maw-Maw opened the door to allow the lady's social group in, Momma began screaming and pounding again. One of the more *'busy body'* ladies of the group stepped forward, opening the coat closet. Momma rushed out and into the woman's arms accusing Maw-Maw of abuse.

Poor Maw-Maw was shamed and shunned from attending church again after the scandal that ensued; though, she never gave up on her Savior. "I can't wait to meet my maker someday," was a phrase Maw-Maw often said.

I learned that families come from all walks of life, and despite how they were, I loved my family. It was the only family I knew.

Chapter 3
Childhood Memories

When 9/11/2001 occurred, I sat for days in front of the T.V. paralyzed by the tragedy. My beloved New York City, which held some unknown mystery for me, had been attacked. Like the rest of the world, I too felt its sorrow.

Thinking back to the last of my childhood memories, I realize why national tragedies always immobilize me. Naturally, it was something I learned from Momma.

We were living at the same house where Bubba and Jack burnt down the shed on Maryland Ave., only many years later did they pull their stunt. I vividly recall where all the furniture was, and how the T.V. sat diagonally in the corner of the room. Looking out through the dining room and kitchen was a clear shot to the back door. I could see Momma hanging sheets on the clothesline through the screen door. I was watching Cartoon Carnival after lunch when the news cut in with an important announcement. I was only four years old, but I remember it like it was yesterday.

The date was November 22, 1963.

Walter Cronkite appeared on the screen. Not the kind man I often saw on the nightly news, but a solemn man was saying, "The president has been shot!" I don't know how Momma heard it, but here she came through the back door.

I remember hearing the name, 'John Fitzgerald Kennedy', for the first time that day. Momma sat in front of our T.V. for days glued to every word that was said, crying and crying. It was so bad that I remember Daddy telling Momma she was acting as if she was his long-lost lover, but at the time, I didn't understand what he meant. She acted the same way when Martin Luther King was assassinated. Both their funerals are forever etched in my mind. Momma was just that way. She'd get all worked up over something and couldn't let it go.

I became fascinated with everything about John Fitzgerald Kennedy as I grew older. But I couldn't have told you why.

Thinking of music as I end this chapter, and of President Kennedy, puts me in mind of my favorite Frankie Valli and the Four Seasons song, 'December 1963'. I just loved that song! In fact, I was obsessed with it though I never knew why.

One day it would take on a very different meaning for me and make perfect sense!

I was reading by age four and remembered being pulled from under the kitchen table with the newspaper on more than one occasion. Momma said it made me ask too many questions. "But I wanna know 'bout the war. Why are people killing each other?" I still have that habit. I want to know why? I wanted to know why there were signs that said coloreds had to sit at the back of the bus. Momma said it was cause some folks were ignorant.

Maw-Maw Cruse, took me to downtown Dallas on the bus most every Saturday morning. Always the same routine. Up with the roosters' crow before the crack of dawn. Maw-Maw lived in the city but hosted all manners of wildlife in need of refuge. Corn flakes and milk in front of the small black and white T.V.; watching the roadrunner best poor ol' coyote was a prerequisite to our day. We'd walk to the bus stop, and it always appeared right after we got there. Maw-Maw said it was magic. Off we'd go on our adventure past the Dallas Zoo and across the viaduct. The bridge with the fancy glass globes is there to this day amongst the new mega highways. I never pass by it that I don't think of Maw-Maw Cruse. If she ain't in heaven, then no such place exists! Across the viaduct, over the Trinity River, were the largest buildings in Dallas. To a young girl, they represented excitement with endless possibilities. Years later, when "That Girl" hit the airwaves, I understood how she felt when she stood among all the tall buildings.

Off to Kress' department store, we headed. Down the escalator, to the basement, we'd go. I loved their mashed potatoes, and our waitress always put extra butter in them for me. Maw-Maw and I would *'piddle around'* as she said in Kress' then head off to pay her bills. Maw-Maw worked for Stockton manufacturing as a seamstress as long as I can remember. She retired from there at age sixty-two. As I was cleaning out her home when she passed away and found paycheck stubs from Stockton's in the early sixties, I was flabbergasted! For a forty-hour workweek, Maw Maw's net pay was forty-nine dollars and fifty cents.

My birthday came late at the end of September, so by the time I started school, I was seven years old. Shortly after school began, they gave us a booklet called the Iowa tests, or something such as that. Our teacher instructed us to go through and answer as many questions as we could.

Many years later, as I watched the movie "Short Circuit" with my sons, reminded me of that morning long ago when they handed me my test. I zoomed through the test as fast as Johnny 5 did when he read the dictionary, flipping the pages in a frenzy! Input, input. I finished the whole booklet a short time later it seemed while the others were struggling to get past the first part. My teacher saw me looking around and came to stand beside my desk.

"Have you gone as far as you can," Mrs. Mosemiller asked?

I still remember the incredulous look on her face as she turned page after page. She took my test and left the room. When I got home, later that afternoon, Momma cornered me.

"What in heavens have you done," Momma asked? "The school called and requested your Daddy, and I come in for a conference first thing tomorrow morning."

I assured Momma I had been a good girl all day, and I didn't know why they did that. Daddy wasn't too happy cause he had to take off work, but he did.

I didn't understand what was being said other than I was really smart the next morning as my parents listened to the principal and school administrator. According to the test I took, I had the I.Q. of an average third grader in the middle of third grade. The principal beamed as he suggested my parents allow them to double-promote me into the third grade on the spot.

My parents were allowed to discuss their thoughts before the principal and administrator returned to the room.

"Thank you, but we prefer our daughter to remain with children her age," said Momma.

I was kind of sad but didn't know why.

I rushed through my booklets so fast each day; I had nothing left to do. Mrs. Mosemiller would shake her head, bring me to sit by her desk, and let me be her helper. I graded papers and ran office errands.

My classmates shunned me. I was called the teacher's pet. I felt isolated as if I'd done something wrong. As time went on, I came to realize it was probably a good thing because I would have been afraid to invite a classmate home to my house as I often heard others do. I never knew what I was going home to each day. I never knew if I was going to find Momma sleeping, and the house a wreck, or not. I knew if Momma had slept the day away, with nothing done, Daddy would come home in a *'rage.'* I learned to rush home and wake Momma up to help her clean and start dinner before Daddy got there. Momma said she had a *'sleeping sickness,'* and although she felt terrible about it, she couldn't help herself.

The day that the school called Daddy to complain that me and my brother had shown up in wrinkled, soiled clothing, and late more often than not, is one for the books. I came in from school that day, shocked to find the house in sparkling clean condition. I could smell dinner cooking from the kitchen. I was so proud of Momma. I thought to myself, "Boy, Daddy is gonna be so happy!"

When Daddy stormed through the door later, just as Momma sat the last bowl on the table, I knew something was wrong. I saw that look on Daddy's face and knew it was coming. He was across the room in a flash. With one arm, he cleared the whole table sending everything crashing to the floor. He nearly choked Momma to death, or so it seemed to poor little Bubba and me.

I snuck the phone into the bathroom and called Maw-Maw Lummus. I asked her to call me extra early every morning, so I could jump up and make sure our clothes were clean and pressed. I could make our breakfast and make sure we got to school on time from then on. This way of life was to be my childhood.

Back in the early sixties, bipolar disorder was often tagged as hysteria. Poor Momma… She was such a confused young woman. I have no doubt she suffered from full-blown bipolar disease. Momma only had a tenth-grade education, but it wasn't cause she was unable to excel in her classes. It was her behavior that got the best of her. She was a little too smart for her own good! I recall memories of Daddy telling me my mouth was gonna be my downfall, just like Momma. I remember that as a loving thought sitting here on this beach watching the sunrise over the ocean, and reflecting on life past, present, and future. Watching the waves roll in takes me back to my childhood memories.

Of all the things Momma got wrong, taking me to Vacation Bible School when I was five, was something she got right. I don't remember her ever attending church except for that one week and never sat inside a church with my Daddy until a few short months before his death. Except for funerals, but that's another story.

I was very attentive as I listened to the folks talking 'bout Jesus and how he'd hung on a cross for our sins. By the end of Vacation Bible School that week, I was hooked.

Hillcrest Baptist Church was a few blocks from Maw-Maw Cruse's house at 2330 South Ewing Ave. It was a huge, imposing sight to a little girl of five, but I knew the people inside were kind and loving. Maw-Maw would get me all prettied up and walk with me each Sunday morning. She'd always be waiting to walk me back to her house when church let out. At least 'til I turned seven cause, then I was a big girl and could walk by myself. Everyone in that big 'ol church knew who I was. I was the child who asked lots of questions. I was also the one who won award after award for various events from Sunday school. From remembering all the books of the Bible to quoting scripture verses, I was that child. I constantly craved attention. I always pushed myself to be the *'best of the best.'* It didn't always win the approval of my peers, but I had very few friends my age anyways. Thinking about that reminds me of a very enlightening incident with one little friend I had from the church.

I seldom got to spend the night with friends, mostly cause I didn't have any. My little friend from church invited me to spend the night with her one Saturday and attend church with her the next morning. It was to be followed by Sunday dinner at her grandmother's house. I was used to Sunday dinner at Maw-Maw Lummus' cause every Sunday; my parents would pick me up after church to go to Daddy's mothers' house.

I noticed right away when I got to my friend's house that there was something different between my home life and hers. Everyone seemed like they'd stepped right out of the *'Leave it to Beaver'* sitcom, which was another favorite of mine. Her family was very reserved, as I recall.

Everything was going smoothly until I started telling some of my stories at the supper table that Saturday night. Me and my friend were excused from the table the instant we finished our dessert though I didn't understand why.

We got to church the next morning, and church just flew by. I could hardly wait to taste all the goodies my friend had bragged that her grandma made.

I'd never heard of some of 'em, and being the curious little girl I was, I loved trying out new stuff. I was in awe as she showed me around her grandma's mansion, or so it appeared to me having never stayed overnight with anyone but family I'd never seen anything so grand. Unbeknownst to me at the time, it would be the last time I stayed with my friend or was allowed to associate with her other than Sunday school after that day.

We were told we could get a soda pop out of the refrigerator, which sounded odd to me cause I'd always heard them called iceboxes. Anyways, off we went. My friend's grandmother was at the sink when we opened the door to get our pops out.

"Where's your grandmother's beer at," I asked my friend matter of factly.

"My Maw-Maw Lummus saves the whole bottom shelf for her beer, and let me tell you there'll be hell to pay if anyone messes with it!"

I was mocking Maw-Maw's words she repeated to us kids all the time, mimicking her country accent, and thinking it was funny.

My friend's eyes grew wide as we heard the glass shattering on the floor, which her grandmother had been holding. Needless to say, we were ushered out of the kitchen, and my mother was called to pick me up. I didn't understand why I wasn't allowed to stay for lunch, but Momma gave me a stern lecture 'bout my *story-telling* when we left. I was grown by the time I understood what she meant by "raised in different social circles."

I usually stayed at Maw-Maw Cruse's on weekend's cause after our adventures on Saturday's came church on Sunday mornings.

Maw-Maw hardly ever went unless I had some award to receive, or if it was a particular holiday service cause of all that mess with Momma years ago. She just didn't have the heart to go, she'd say. I always invited her, though. In fact, I was always telling anyone who'd listen about God and explaining how they ought to go learn about him.

The details of the morning I was baptized have long since been forgotten except for the overwhelming feeling I got when I was plunged beneath the water. With my eyes closed as I went under the water, I saw Jesus standing there waiting for me to run into his arms.

My saving grace has always been my relationship with My Lord.

He is my true hero! I would not be alive to tell my story without him. I give all the glory in my life to my Lord and Savior, Jesus Christ. Not that I'm some perfect holy-roller, but I could never make a day without him by my side. God loves me right where I'm at, and often reminds me that I'm still a work in progress.

I believe one of the reasons I've drug my feet in beginning my book was because I want to honor God in all I do. The telling of my life isn't always gonna be pretty. At times, downright evilness will jump off the page at the reader. The only way to portray how things really were is to tell it like it was. At least that's what I've finally determined. I've prayed long and hard about this to God and begged his forgiveness if I'm wrong. I apologize for the cursing, and filthiness that will eventually spill out onto these pages. I just don't know how else to tell my story truthfully without evoking evilness. If I'm gonna say it, I might as well tell the whole truth, so help me God. I hope you continue reading past those ugly stories. I want to share how awesome my God is. He carried me through some hard times, and to this day hasn't left my side.

I also have many happy memories from childhood.

Daddy made time for his kids every night when he got home from work. As always, when Momma wasn't creating havoc. We'd often get in the middle of the floor and wrestle with Daddy. We were so loud one night; a neighbor called the police. They showed up at the front door just in time to see Bubba hit Daddy over the head with a coke bottle. They were made of thick glass back then, and Daddy had a nice goose egg for days to prove it.

One vacation that I remember well was the summer we went to Galveston. We got to stay in a motel with a kidney-shaped pool and colorful outdoor furniture. We had our rubber duck floaties, and life was wonderful. Daddy was a big old kid at heart when Momma wasn't driving him crazy.

Everyone wanted my Daddy to be theirs. Most Friday nights, he'd load us up in the car, and off we'd go to the drive-in movies. Momma always brought dinner for us wrapped in foil. Us kids couldn't wait to get there, cause down at the front and beneath the big picture screen, was the best playground ever. No one worried 'bout their kids being safe. The only thing we paid attention to were the goofy intermission ads.

I only remember one time that Daddy and Momma went to the drive-in without us kids. I remember saying, "But I'm big enough to watch 'Bonnie and Clyde'!" When I got older, I watched the early version over and over.

My parents couldn't have been more ill-suited if they wanted to, but in their own way, they mustered through seventeen years best as they could, I guess. Life is life, and people are people. Life happens sometimes. No sense in hating on folks for who they are. I, in no way, wish ever to convey the impression that I don't love my family or where I came from. I used to blame my parents for all my misfortunes, but luckily, I grew up. I'm very proud of my roots. As horrible as my life has been at times, I wouldn't trade one moment of those cherished memories. Crazy as it sounds, I'd go back and suffer every tragedy again, just to relive the good times once more.

I've had trouble sleeping all my life, and often would go get a drink or use the restroom when I woke from scary dreams.

One such night which remains forever etched in my memory was the time we lived on Ann Arbor St. Don't ask me how I can remember so much from my childhood at such early ages, I don't know, but I remember details as if they're snapshots in my mind.

I had walked into our kitchen and opened the icebox door causing the light to shine toward our kitchen door, illuminating it. Standing there on the other side of the door was a huge, dark figure jiggling our kitchen doorknob. I stood transfixed, for I don't know how long before running and screaming into my parents' bedroom. I grabbed Daddy's arm, and of course, that was a mistake. Daddy didn't ever wake up well from a dead sleep, and I soon learned like everyone else already knew, to stand way back if you was gonna wake Daddy up. I flew back against the nightstand as Daddy's arm swung out in reflex. He came awake instantly, hearing me scream that a man was trying to break in our house through the kitchen door. The man was long gone by the time Daddy, shotgun in hand, made it to the back door.

This reminds me of the one other time I saw a burglar during my childhood. It was on a weekend night I had been at Maw Maw Cruse's house. Maw Maw's bed was in her living room, pushed right up next to the window. Folks slept with their windows open and screens on the windows to keep the bugs out. She bought an old swamp cooler that she used to cool the house after that night.

I always curled up next to Maw-Maw and slept when I stayed at her house. We were two peas in a pod she'd say. All except the fact that as hard as I tried, I couldn't sew a lick. I'd sit for hours watching her peddle her Singer sewing machine while she talked to me. I still have that Singer Sewing machine. I've been offered a nice sum for it a time or two as it is now an antique. I wouldn't part with it for a million dollars, and God knows that's the truth! Later, she bought me a Learn How to Crochet book, and I taught myself to work that needle and thread fast as lightning. Maw-Maw would peddle sew while I crocheted. Mostly lopsided pot holder's back then, but everyone I gave one to sure loved them.

We'd just settled into bed that night, and Maw-Maw's snoring told me she was fast asleep when for some reason, I opened my eyes. I just happened to be sleeping next to the window and facing the street. Standing there, bent down with a knife glinting off the street lamp, was the biggest man I ever saw fixing to cut the window screen. I shoved my elbow into Maw-Maw's ribs, waking her at once. She looked up at that man, and I'll never forget what happened next! She never reminded me more of granny from the *'Beverly Hillbillies,'* as she did that night! She flew out of bed, grabbed the broom sitting by the front door, and tore the cheap lock off as she ran out yelling, "Get your ass off my porch!" She then proceeded to chase the man down the middle of the street with that broom! I'm not sure what happened afterward, as the last thing I recall is her running with that broom held high like a banty rooster.

Man, how I miss her! She sure was a mess. Trust me; there'll be more on Maw-Maw Cruse later.

I rarely hung out with other kids except for watching specific television programs. I always wanted to be in the middle of the adults. Maw-Maw Lummus was very old-fashioned about letting kids in her kitchen, but eventually gave up on me and made me an apron to wear when I was helping her. She had Paw-Paw Ernest make me a stool to stand on so I could see what she was doing.

Paw-Paw Ernest.

He was Maw-Maw's third husband, and also a truck driver. He and Paw-Paw Bodiddle drove for A.J. Miller's trucking company for years together. I remember one time they tried going out on a run together, which ended out in the middle of Arizona somewhere in a comedy of errors. Though, as I recall, it wasn't too funny when it happened. They'd gotten into an argument at a truck stop, which resulted in a threatening match.

"Well, I'm gonna call my son-in-law, and he'll come out here and whip your tail," Paw-Paw Bodiddle exclaimed.

"Is that so? He's my step-son, and we'll just see about that," Paw-Paw Ernest threatened.

Daddy got so tickled when they both called him on the phone. Daddy managed to calm them down and talked Pawpaw Ernest into catching a bus home. They didn't speak to each other at family get-togethers for a long time after that until one day they caught Bubba and my cousin Jack mocking them. Jack was my Aunt Ida's youngest son, and him and Bubba was always up to something. Like the time they almost gave a very pregnant, Aunt Windelyen a heart attack when they set our shed on fire.

She was babysitting us kids and noticed that Bubba and Jack was missing about the same time she smelt the smoke. Here they come a running through the back door. By the time the fire truck got there, the old shed had burned to the ground. Maw-Maw Lummus swore that Aunt Windelyen's baby was gonna be marked from her going through this so close to her due date. You know old wives' tales. My family had a bunch of them.

So, back to my story. Paw-Paw Ernest and Paw-Paw Bodiddle saw Bubba and Jack mocking them about the same time. I don't remember who laughed first at the silliness of the situation, but afterward, they shook hands and let bygones be bygones.

They both continued working for A.J.'s for a long time after that. They decided that driving together was not a good idea for two old farts who were both stubborn 'ol mules as Maw-Maw Lummus said. Both their lives would end tragically one day, but we'll get to them later.

Paw-Paw Ernest was a tough old bird, and most of the family steered clear of him. If you look in the dictionary under *ornery,* you'd find Pawpaw Ernest. To his credit, Paw-Paw Ernest had a very abusive childhood from his stepfather. I learned one sad facet of it one day when I was sweeping Maw-Maw's kitchen floor with her old straw broom. When I went toward him with the broom and told him to raise his feet, he got a strange look on his face, threw his arms up as if to shield himself, and jumped up so quickly he sent the chair flying backward as he ran from the room. Maw-Maw explained after she got Paw-Paw calmed down that he was regularly beaten with a broom as a child and had scars on his back to show for it. I felt so bad for Paw-Paw and was very careful when I swept around him from then on out. I loved and adored him to the end. Me and Maw-Maw Lummus were the only ones who mourned his passing, but I'm getting ahead of myself.

Chapter 4

The most magical time of the year

I GET MY LOVE OF driving from Momma. She loved road trips; that's for sure. I always think about Momma when I'm driving. I even talk to her when I'm on my own. Headed back up north to see the doctor, I'm taking a different route to avoid tolls.

Texas very rarely displays the change in seasons the way the northeastern states do. The bright, vivid orange, red, and yellow foliage is breathtaking. The mountains, valleys, and many bridges are welcome distractions for me as I cruise down the road listening to my music. Funny how each song evokes memories past. As the song begins to play, I am transported back in time to specific events, causing familiar feelings to stir inside of me.

Not all welcome, but today, I am grateful for anything that gets my mind off what lies ahead. Having escaped death many times, I can't help but wonder if my time on earth is drawing to a close. On top of that, I am faced with some tough choices.

I would have to say the hardest decisions since I got clean many years ago. Difficult choices are hard for anyone, but being a recovering addict complicates matters. Uppermost in my mind is to run away, but that's not really an option anymore.

Bing Crosby's 'White Christmas' pops up from my playlist, and although it's mid-October, I let it play.

No matter what Momma was up to the rest of the year, holidays brought out the best in her. I don't remember one fiasco occurring during a holiday. That is except for the year my baby sister Shelley was born.

Momma, Maw-Maw Lummus, and Aunt Windelyen started our Thanksgiving dinner early Thanksgiving eve 1965. All the baked goods were prepared first, saving the oven for Mr. Turkey on Thanksgiving morning.

Thank God everyone was still there late that night when Momma's water broke. Daddy was a nervous wreck and wouldn't have remembered everything he was supposed to do. Maw-Maw Lummus went with Momma and Daddy while Aunt Windelyen stayed behind with Bubba and me to continue our meal preparation. Momma always kidded Shelley about having to eat nasty hospital food that Thanksgiving Day.

My sweet baby sister.

She was special from the day they brought her home. The nurses nicknamed her 'Tinkle' and it stuck for years until she got old enough to understand what it meant. Then she demanded we call her Shelley. We'd slip up from time to time, but she'd just grin and shoot us a look that clearly stated we better cut it out.

Shelley nearly died when she was four weeks old.

I recall Momma and Daddy loading us in the car late one night and Daddy driving like a race car driver to Dr. Shoecrafts' office. Back then, family doctors were very accessible. Dr. Shoecraft told my parents to meet him at his office when they called. Shelley was running 104° by the time they got her there. Me and Bubba stayed in the car huddled in blankets as Momma and Daddy rushed in through the backdoor. I can see that the back door illuminated by one small light. I stared at it for what seemed an eternity waiting on someone to come out and tell me my baby sister was ok.

Daddy was a wreck when he came out to check on us. He said they had packed my baby sister in ice and was waiting on an ambulance. Daddy waited for Momma and Shelley to be safely tucked in the ambulance before he took off like a madman racing to drop us off at Maw-Maw Lummus' house. Shelley's was the second case of Spinal Meningitis to occur in Dallas at that time. The first person had not survived. By the grace of God, Shelley survived after days and days of treatment. Just as on holidays, any time one of the family was seriously ill or was facing hardship, the whole family gathered for the vigil. By the time Shelley got home, she had attained her status. She would grow on the hearts of all who met her. Let me tell you; she could do no wrong, regardless if she was guilty or not.

When she started talking, her lisp only added to her charm. Eventually, they had her tongue clipped as she was tongue-tied, but she'd already endeared herself to all who knew her. Shelley was the baby and got her way until the day she died. But that's another story I'm not ready to tell just yet.

Hearing ol' Bing, brings back so many cherished memories. Christmas was the most magical time of the year. It was extra special for me cause everyone seemed to go out of their way to be kind to one another. Thanksgiving signaled the start of the holiday season.

Everyone would gather at the hosts' house, bringing their additions to the meal along with them. The host always cooked Mr. Turkey, and the minute you stepped in the house, you could smell him wafting through the air. Us kids would make a beeline for the television, and Macy's Thanksgiving Day Parade. I always begged Momma to take us to Macy's as she did to the parades in downtown Dallas. She'd just laugh and say New York City was a little too far to drive. I'd get frustrated and tell everyone that someday I was gonna go to New York City to see Macy's parade even if I had to go by myself!

After the parade, the menfolk always commandeered the television for the big football game. My love of football grew from being forced to watch it on the TV. No one had more than one TV back then, if you wanted to watch TV, you watched what the grown-ups chose. Of course, me being me, I was always asking questions about the plays I heard my Daddy and uncles talking about.

"Why'd they do that Daddy," I seemed always to be asking.

Daddy would humor me and try to explain unless the Cowboys were in a tight situation, then he'd get after me saying I asked too many questions. Later, he'd apologize if he'd been too hard on me. Then he would try to explain what I'd asked to begin with.

In a lot of ways, I was a tomboy growing up. I was up under my Daddy's butt as much as I was the womenfolk when they were cooking. I never was a normal child. Maybe cause of the role I was thrust in with Momma, I don't know. Perhaps I'll ask, 'Dr. Phil' someday if I ever finish my book. Ain't that a lofty dream? Perhaps my grandiose thinking is a result of my disease. I've never been diagnosed as such, but I am my mother's daughter, so I wonder. I have been able to notice certain mood swings at times since I've gotten clean, but due to certain circumstances, I won't discuss that now. I, in my own way, have learned over the years to cope with whatever it is and carry on.

After everyone stuffed themselves with turkey dinner, and once the football game was over, outside, we all went. Daddy and the other menfolk always organized a football game between them and us kids. About the time the menfolk got tired, one or more of us kids commenced to wrestling.

"I had the ball first!"

"No, you didn't!"

And here we'd go. I was always besting Bubba, until the day he called me out. We'd barely finished turkey dinner that year 'til Bubba announced to everyone he had something to show them. It had always been a running joke on Bubba that his older sister could make him cry 'Uncle.' Well, that day, he boasted he was ready to show everyone how he was gonna make me cry uncle for a change. I believe I was ten, and he was eight that year. I just laughed and said, "Let's go!"

Out the door, we went with everyone laughing and taking bets as they came out behind us. All of a sudden, before I had a chance to stop him, Bubba had me pinned on the ground. I screamed for Daddy to get him off me.

"Not 'til you say 'Uncle' I won't," Bubba said.

"Fair is fair. Don't you think it's time for you to say 'Uncle,'" Daddy said, trying hard not to bust out laughing.

That was the last time I ever wrestled with my brother. He let me up, and with his smug little grin walked off like a prize champion fighter. However, I still recall many times being accosted in the hallways, or on the playground at school by kids who said my little brother had threatened them with his big 'Sissy.'

With Thanksgiving's passing, the magical world of Christmas time began. Everyone hung Christmas lights back then. Christmas lights and yard decorations were everywhere you looked.

Seeing a white Christmas in Texas, rarely, if ever happened. But not to worry, spray snow decorated our windows, so that looking out gave that wintry feeling. Our tree always went up the day after Thanksgiving, and Momma could make it come alive like no other. She'd first wrap the trunk with bright, white lights, following with strand upon strand of colored lights. You could easily see the treasured ornaments she carefully hung inside the branches so they wouldn't get broke. I loved staring at my reflection in the bright gold, red, and blue balls. It was distorted like the images of ourselves when we looked in the mirrors at the funhouse each year when Momma and Daddy would carry us kids to the State Fair of Texas.

Us kids weren't allowed to hang ornaments on the tree, so we sat and made colored paper-chain wreaths, and strung popcorn with a needle and a thread while watching Daddy help Momma. Bless his heart; Daddy always seemed to hold his temper with Momma when she'd have him redo a strand of lights because they weren't even. All the while we were decorating, we were drinking hot chocolate with the little marshmallows in it and eating Christmas cookies from the special tin cans Momma loved. The white powdered sugar ones are my favorite to this day.

My favorite Christmas movie has always been the early, black and white version of 'Miracle on 34th Street'. I just knew in my heart that New York held the key to some great mystery, and someday I was gonna find out what it was.

Of course, everyone who knows me can tell you in a *'New York skinny minute'* (my favorite saying) what my most beloved Christmas cartoon is! I've got many, many replicas I sit out at Christmas every year. I even have my own miniature village, which tells the tale. Oh, how I love 'Rudolph'!

As an adult, I can only suspect the deeper meaning of my attachment to 'Rudolph' having to do with him being the underdog who rose above to become a hero. My obsession with fictional characters continued throughout my childhood. I never shared these obsessions with others before now as I tell the story of my life. I've always had a wild imagination but kept some things to myself. Looking back at my childhood, I kinda believe they were my *'go-to'* fixes when I was faced with tragedies. I learned to look to my 'heroes' and how they'd respond to the situation.

Us kids spent a lot of time watching TV when Momma would have her *'sleeping sickness'* bouts. My all-time favorite TV character was, and is, *'Lucy Ricardo,'* my so-called alter ego.

I must admit, I'm often guilty of coming up with some hilarious, and sometimes irrational, hair-brained ideas. "What's Lucy up to today?" I'm frequently asked when I come out with, "I've got this great idea…" It has been a running joke on me for as far back as I can remember.

One of my favorite things to do at Christmas time involved the annual Christmas parade, and 'Titche's Department Store' in downtown Dallas. Momma and Maw-Maw Cruse would gather me, Bubba, and Shelley, and together we'd ride the bus downtown. We'd find a perfect spot to watch the parade, and anxiously wait to see Santa. Next, we'd walk around and see all the gay, festive sights. We would eat lunch at Kress' and then head over to 'Titche's Department Store.' There was an area set up, called Santaland, for the kids to ride a miniature train around brightly animated scenes, which ended at Santa's workshop. After our time on Santa's knee, one by one, we were allowed to push a button on a machine that spat out our own unique gift. Hot chocolate with miniature marshmallows at the drug store counter at Woolworth's always ended our day before taking the bus back to Maw-Maw's house.

Christmas Eve always found us eating dinner in a rush before heading to Aunt Ida's house. The whole family always gathered there to exchange gifts. I mainly looked forward to what Aunt Ida had for me. We all knew we'd get the customary offering of 'Lifesaver's,' which looked like a book until you opened it to see it was ten rolls of different flavored 'Lifesaver's.' But Aunt Ida always picked out girly stuff for us girls like scented bubble bath and such as that. Once we were all done, Daddy would load all seven of us cousins in the car with him and Momma, and off we'd go for the ultimate Christmas light show. We all knew we were headed for the 'Singing Hills' neighborhood. Interlochen, in Arlington, is very similar to what we saw back at Singing Hills, but it's just not the same to me.

Block after block after block; the cars crept up and down the streets. The folks who lived in this very exclusive neighborhood went above and beyond to create a magical Christmas wonderland. Momma always played Christmas music until we got to Snuffy Smiths' block. Snuffy Smith owned a car dealership best as I recall and went all out on Christmas eve. He had an old jalopy which he decorated like a sleigh. He even had Santa's helper hand out candy canes for everyone in each car as it stopped. He would always remind us kids to hurry up and go to sleep as soon as we got home cause Santa was on his way from around the world to our house, and any kid worth his salt knew Santa wouldn't come 'til he was fast asleep.

Down the block and around the corner from Snuffy Smiths' was the prettiest girl I'd ever seen. Each car would pause briefly in front of the house with the huge window which ran the length and height of the mansions living room. Everything was bathed in white. From the furniture to the shag carpet, all you saw was pristine white. The beautiful girl who looked like an angel always wore a stunning, floor-length white gown with flowing sleeves, and she sat at a pearl white, grand piano. The music she played for all to hear was piped outside so that each passerby could listen to it. I think of that young woman from time to time and wonder how her life turned out. Pretty sure it was nothing like mine, but what do I know. I've long since found out that addiction doesn't discriminate, and that it crushes and destroys families despite their socio-economic status.

The '*angel's*' house was 'bout near the last stop we made before heading home to await Santa. Daddy always stopped at the Dairy Freeze on the way home for treats and snacks before dropping off my cousins. Us kids would stare out the window on the drive home, searching the sky for any sign of Santa. One year we finally saw Rudolph's bright red nose blinking in the sky.

"Look, Momma quick! Is that Rudolph?"

"Well, look a there! I do believe that's him," she said, winking at Daddy.

They never had any problem getting us kids to hurry through our baths for bed on Christmas Eve. Wearing the new pajamas, we always got on Christmas Eve, off to bed we flew. The night we saw Rudolph, Momma barely got to the end of reading 'Twas the Night Before Christmas' when we heard bells jingling outside. You never saw three kids fall asleep so fast. Momma and Daddy couldn't wait to see our faces on Christmas morning, so it was their tradition to wake us up the minute that Santa came and went from our house. We'd be woken up in the middle of the night to see all that Santa had brought. Best as I can figure, they did that cause a lot of our larger presents were never wrapped, and they wanted to make sure we didn't catch a glimpse of them if we woke during the night on our own.

Chapter 5

Innocence Lost

Momma began going to doctors to get help for her *'sleeping sickness'* around the time I turned ten. She'd go to one doctor to get her *'wake up'* pills and another doctor to get the pills, which helped her sleep at night so Daddy wouldn't know what she was doing. Momma took me to the doctors with her; this was our 'big secret.' Momma said I must never tell Daddy cause we know what happens when Daddy gets mad.

Momma started working at the Dunkin Donut shop at Illinois and I-35 as a counter girl to help with the bills. Daddy always picked her up a little early cause he was fascinated watching the man behind the big window making donuts.

Daddy had found his niche!

It wasn't long before Daddy trained to become what would become his passion in life. Offered a chance to become a manager, Lone Star Donuts, stole him away from Dunkin. Of course, Daddy worked extra hard, putting in long hours to excel. He soon became one of their top distributors. Everyone knows when *'it's time to make the donuts.'* Daddy worked the graveyard shift, driving across town to work and leaving Momma alone with us kids. Like a snapshot from my memory banks, again, I recall one of those nights in vivid detail.

Momma's piercing screams woke me from a dead sleep. I ran to her bedroom to see what was wrong. I saw the cut screen, and Momma's shaking hand as she held the phone, crying and begging them to send the police in a hurry. I heard our dog barking loudly.

It seemed like forever before we heard the police at the front door. Strangely, not long before they showed up, our dog had stopped barking. The police looked around and found nothing amiss. They seemed to think it was a fabric of my mother's imagination as though she had cut the screen herself.

Momma kept trying to get me to stay awake with her after the police left. Try as I might, I couldn't hold my eyes open. Momma was so desperate for me to stay awake that she gave me one of her *'wake up'* pills. Before I knew it, I was wide awake and talking to Momma non-stop.

The next morning when Daddy came home, he found our dog hanging from the garage rafters. I shudder to think what might have happened if the police hadn't shown up and scared the prowler away. Too bad, our little dog had to die first. Who knows, he probably saved our lives.

And so, it began. Every time Momma got scared, she would give me one of her *'wake up'* pills. I would stay awake with Momma all night, then go to school the next morning. It wasn't long before the school called Momma, saying I was falling asleep in my classes. Momma began giving me one of her pills to take at school when I would get sleepy. It was another 'big secret' me and Momma kept between us...

Not long after Momma started sharing her *'wake up'* pills, Daddy bought a donut shop in Ft. Worth. It was Daddy's dream to own his own business. Daddy was a hard worker and excelled at everything he did. I'm more than a little proud of my Daddy! I remember many times where Daddy worked two jobs at the same time. I've seen Daddy go to work sick as a dog running a fever and throwing up.

Momma babysat for this lady and her husband around the time we moved to Ft. Worth. Momma stayed in touch with her after the move. She drove the distance to bring her little boy for Momma to watch sometimes.

I was eleven years old when my parents were invited for a weekend getaway to tour some property. Horseshoe Bend offered the luxury outdoor life young families were looking for to escape the city. Horseback riding, archery, swimming, fishing, and other activities constituted an outdoor overload. Along with our family, Momma was encouraged to invite another couple. The lady Momma babysat for happened to be sitting there when Momma got the call.

"Why don't y'all come along," Momma asked the young mother?

"We'd have to get a sitter for the baby, but it sounds like fun," she replied.

Another Saturday I'll never forget began with the biggest breakfast buffet I'd ever seen. Next was a tour around the property, which ended at the horse stables. Everyone wanted to go horseback riding. I was the last one to get my horse and equipment. For the life of me, I can't remember his name, but the sitter's husband hung out waiting on me. The others were way ahead as we guided our horses out of the stables. As scared as I was of the big ol' horse I was on, I found myself laughing as I bounced up and down on the horses back. My long hair kept getting in my face until he stopped us and tied my hair back. I remember thinking how nice he was to stick around at the back of the pack with me. He just kept smiling that funny smile and telling me what a pretty young woman I was.

I don't remember a lot about the rest of that fun-filled day, but later that evening, I realized I had lost my watch[3] and figured it had been on the horseback ride. It was special to me, so I took off down the trail looking for it just as the sun was setting. I became startled about ten minutes into my search.

"Oh, it's you," I said as the lady's husband came up beside me.

"What are you doing out here by yourself," the man asked, looking around.

"I'm looking for my watch. I think I lost it when we were riding the horses," I answered while continuing to search the ground.

"C'mon, I'll help you look for it," he said, falling into step beside me.

I don't know how long we walked before he started talking to me as if I was someone else. "When a man sees a beautiful woman, certain things happen to him that he's unable to control. All-day long, I watched a beautiful young woman coming alive."

Something in his manner frightened me, but I couldn't figure out what it was. I turned around and started to head back toward our tents. Before I could take a step, he grabbed me from behind and pulled me toward a cluster of trees.

"I'm not really worried 'bout my watch. Let's come back tomorrow," I offered, yet fearing nothing I said mattered.

He backed me against a tree and began touching me all over. I was so afraid my voice wouldn't connect to my vocal cords. Paralyzed, I couldn't mouth a word as he kept telling me he couldn't help himself and that he had to have me now. It was like everything happening to me was happening to someone else until I felt the piercing pain between my legs, which sent him into a frenzy. He kept it up until he screamed out and became oddly still. I

---

[3] The picture of me on the cover of this book shows me wearing my 'cherished' watch. The picture was taken not long before we went to Horseshoe Bend.

was beyond feeling anything at this point, just grateful he'd stopped. After what seemed a lifetime, he moved away from me. He pulled his shirt off and began wiping the blood from himself and then me. I had no clue where the blood came from since no one had ever talked to me about sex or the birds and the bees. Crying, the man told me how sorry he was. He said he couldn't help himself because I was so beautiful and that he'd been watching me from the time Momma began babysitting his son. He said he was in love with me, and now he was gonna go to prison because of it. Then his mood changed. He became angry, and the look on his face scared me so much I couldn't breathe. He started telling me that I couldn't tell anyone cause they'd know I'd been a bad girl. He said it was my fault for teasing him the way I had. I promised that I was good at keeping secrets and wouldn't tell a soul. He must have believed me cause he turned and walked away.

"Wait a while before you come back. We can't be seen together," the man warned menacingly.

Momma and Daddy were in their tent and didn't see me slip back into the kids' tent. I was terrified that he was hiding in the bushes watching to see if I would tell on him. I don't remember much about the rest of that night. Other than the pain that kept aching between my legs; and wondering if the toilet paper I stuffed in my underwear would stop the bleeding that still trickled down my legs. I have no other memories from Horseshoe Bend. Whatever happened after I finally fell asleep is gone to me.

Returning home Sunday evening, I had another one of those, "*I gotta tell*" moments. Like a snapshot in my mind, I remember my parents' room the way it was as I blurted out what had happened to me. I remember feeling confused when I saw Momma raise her hand.

"How dare you accuse that man of something so horrible," Momma said in disgust, slapping my face hard enough to spin my head to the side.

I stood as if stuck to the floor. Looking at my father, I knew what the man had said was true. The look on my father's face is one burned in my memory. He hated me.

I walked back to my room, feeling lower than dirt on the ground. Maybe it was my fault. The incident wasn't mentioned after I left my parents' bedroom. Not one word said.

It would be nearly forty years before I found out what Daddy had really been thinking that night so long ago.

Chapter 6
Lone Star Donuts

Going into the donut shop years brings back a flood of memories. I believe I could write a whole sitcom based on those years. One of my fondest memories of my baby sister happened at that shop.

Shelley did her own thing, always.

She played by herself and meddled all the time. Back in the early seventies, no one had their eyes on their children all the time. It's a good thing too cause you never knew what Shelley was up to.

Lone Star Donuts sat in the middle of the Wedgwood Shopping Center right across from the Wedgwood Theatre. If only those walls could talk! I drive by there occasionally for nostalgia's sake. Not too long ago, the insurance agent who is leasing the building happened to be there and let me walk through it. It's been changed up quite a bit, but the backroom and bathroom where I had many firsts are still the same. I applied my first make-up, saw my first monthly, and downed my one and only cup of moonshine there, so many memories.

Out in front of the shop, and throughout the shopping center are neon lights above the walkways. Well, let me tell you, in the springtime and summertime, those lights attract insects. One year the crickets were there by the thousands. Shelley just loved playing with crickets.

We were all working in the shop when I looked up and saw Shelley with two empty milk jugs. I heard Daddy ask her what she was up to now, and Shelley replied, *"Jus' playin' wid my cwickets Daddy."*

Nothing else was said as we went through the mornings' work. Ours was a family run business. Me and Bubba worked there from the start. We did so cause we wanted to, and Daddy paid us the same as everyone else. Bubba would often go to sleep halfway through the night, but Momma was still sharing her *"wake-up"* pills with me, so I always stayed up. The rest of the day passed by uneventful as I recall.

Coming into work the next morning started off bad because Daddy had overslept. Daddy hated being late. It meant he would miss his early morning sales. We were all standing behind Daddy as he opened the front door of the shop.

Oh my! The instant he pulled the door open and flipped the light switch, a symphony of crickets could be heard. Alfred Hitchcock's *'The Bird's'* had nothing on these crickets. They were everywhere!

In the showcase, on the showcase, on the tables, on the walls, and they covered the floor so well, you couldn't take a step without killing a few. Daddy went to cussing like I never heard before. He rushed into the donut making area to find them blanketing it as well. We cautiously followed, knowing at any minute, Daddy was gonna blow his lid. I hurried to grab a broom and was standing next to the fryer when Daddy came out of the backroom. He was holding two milk jugs, which still held crickets. Momma and Bubba were standing next to the icebox. Daddy screamed, *"Shelley!"* She peaked her little head around the icebox and looked up at Daddy with huge eyes.

"What is this, and why are they in my shop," Daddy demanded.

"I wanned ta keep dem safe Daddy, so I bought dem inside fore we weft," with that lisp of hers, she said.

Big 'ol tears welled up in her little eyes cause Daddy'd never raised his voice at her. It was the only time I ever saw my Daddy back down when he was that mad. He shook his head and held out the jugs for her to come and get. When he bent down to hand them to her, she jumped up and threw her arms around his neck and gave him a big kiss! Taking advantage of Daddy's calmness, the rest of us scurried around rounding up crickets with Shelley.

It took a good two hours to get started that morning. Needless to say, the donuts were late coming out. For years after that, Daddy would tell the tale 'bout *Shelley's crickets*.

There were other crazy openings that are memorable. One time, Daddy had turned on the fryer as he always did while the rest of us went about our morning routine. He loaded the cake hopper and was just about to start pumping the batter into the shortening when he shouted, "*Everyone out!*" When Daddy yelled, we moved. Daddy barely made it to the front before the shortening exploded into a beautiful golden fountain.

As soon as it stopped, Daddy went to see what happened. He shut the fryer off, and once it cooled, he found three bullets in the bottom of the fryer. We later found out that one of his employees' boyfriend was upset with her and had dropped a handful of the bullets into the fryer. Daddy didn't press charges, but that kid never showed his face around there ever again.

So much has happened these past few weeks.

Staring out across the lake, I'm grateful Texas is experiencing this almost tropical weather in November. My youngest stepsister Lynn has the most awesome back yard. It slopes down, giving access to the lake. The lake itself shapes into a U, with houses surrounding it, each having access to the lake.

Lynn has named most of the ducks that live on her portion of the lake. They flock here at feeding time, or as is the case with Margaret, I met her this morning when she came up for her private feeding. Watching the ducks going about their day, and the water ripple from their movements have a calming effect as I hear God whisper, "I got this."

I know he does, and I have faith that no matter what, he knows better than me. I want to say I wished I had listened to him when I was younger, but ya' know, I like me today, or should I say, I like who I've become.

Folks can say what they want about a separation from God when you're out there sinning against him, but they'd be wrong. It was in the midst of my deepest, darkest days that he carried me. The poem "Footprints" is all about that very thing. God never left my side. It was me who chose not to listen.

I tried over the years to have my sons in church, and given the circumstances, I believe I at least introduced them to God. Being in church provided sanctuary for us between the chaos that was our lives.

Not long after Horseshoe Bend, I became obsessed with true crime magazines. At first, it was a little scary for me to read those stories and caused nightmares, where I became the victim in the story. Momma forbid me to read them after waking her one night by my screams. She threw the magazine away, but I dug it out of the trash and hid it. I was intrigued by the stories I read. I wanted to know why people murdered each other. I wanted to know what the person did to become murdered. I wanted to make sure I didn't do anything to get myself killed. It's only by the grace of God I'm here today cause

I shouldn't be by the law of averages.

Maw-Maw Cruse, was Paw-Paw Bodiddle's first wife. His second wife was named Georgia Bell. Georgia Bell gave Paw-Paw Bodiddle a daughter named Juanita. She was Momma's half-sister whom I'd come to know as Aunt Nita. Paw-Paw Bodiddle's wives couldn't have been more different if they'd have wanted to.

That Paw-Paw Bodiddle!

I was with Momma and her best friend Tressie, the night she went to clear out Paw-Paw Bodiddle's room at the old Lawrence Hotel in downtown Dallas after he died.

Momma was beside herself with grief as she opened the door to his room. She sat on the bed for a few minutes looking around the room. I was feeling guilty for all the times I had laughed at him being a short, bald-headed, Irishman.

Sitting at the foot of the bed was a huge black trunk.

I can't help but chuckle every time I think of that moment. Momma stood up and braced herself for what she might see. I know she was expecting to find an artifact or such as that which would make her cry. Lifting the lid of the trunk, Momma's expression, went from sorrow to confusion and ending with shock!

The trunk was stuffed with women's underwear from across the United States. I would say that ninety percent of those undies had notes attached containing names, addresses, and phone numbers. After all, he'd been a long-haul trucker his whole life.

I busted out laughing as I fell to my knees at the expressions on Momma's face. It wasn't long till Momma was laughing too. I remember thanking God for sparing my mother and letting her laugh instead of cry. I don't care what mistakes she made; I loved my Momma fiercely. I still do. The older I get, the more I realize I got a whole lot of Momma in me.

I wish Momma could have found what she searched for during her life. Must be pretty sad to never be satisfied. I wish I'd lived enough to tell her before she died that true happiness must come from within. I have lots of happy memories with Momma. I never judged her. I loved her no matter what anyone said.

In a way, Momma treated me more like a friend than anything else. When I was a little older, Momma let me skip school and go running around with her. We'd go looking at garage sales, then have lunch before resuming our rat-killing.

My first concert was a brainchild of Momma's. Her and Daddy had tickets to see Tom Jones, but the show was canceled at the last minute. Instead of getting a refund, Momma chose to take my oldest cousin and me to see Bobby Sherman. I was star-struck after that, buying up every issue of "16" the teen magazine in search of his pictures.

Momma was also behind the next concert I went to, which will reign forever as the best concert I ever went to. I remember the day I found out I was going with her. I had just walked into the donut shop when I heard my name.

Momma was talking to Daddy about the tickets she managed to get for them to see Elvis Presley in concert. It was a pretty big thing since both shows he was scheduled to do had sold out in less than an hour. Momma was telling Daddy that Elvis had agreed to do two additional shows the next day and that I was throwing a fit for her to take me to see Elvis too.

"When did I do that," I asked?

Momma poked me in the ribs when Daddy wasn't looking, and I suddenly found my memory.

"Oh yea, that would be so cool," I said to Daddy, who had a look on his face that clearly stated he knew what Momma was up too.

"You'd better get y'all a couple of tickets before they run out," Daddy said, winking to let me know he understood.

By the day of the concert, I was pretty excited even though our seats were in the nosebleed section. I remember that day like a movie replaying in my mind. I got so tickled watching them old lady's acting like teeny boppers.

The minute the lights went out, and 2001 Space Odyssey began playing; I knew there was something special happening. The electricity in the air was palpable. The hairs on my arm and neck stood on end. Once the lights came back on, Elvis strutted across the stage, and time seemed to stand still. Whatever else might be said of him, Elvis Presley was the ultimate entertainer!

I cherish the memories from that afternoon with Momma. Me and Momma would be sharing lots of fun times again in the not too distant future, but not before Momma got her heart broke.

The first time Momma ran off from Daddy was something else. Somehow or another, she managed to get the donut shop bank account overwrote to nearly two-thousand five-hundred dollars. Back then, that was a lot of money.

Momma was terrified of what Daddy would do when he found out. Momma begged several people to help her but got no takers. So, she did the only other thing she knew to do, and that was to run off with us kids and Maw-Maw Cruse to Georgia.

Momma, Shelley, and Maw-Maw rode in the front seat. Momma had half the back seat filled with clothes covered by an old quilt. Me, Bubba, and the dogs rode on top of the quilt in the back seat. There were no seat belt laws back then. You know it's a wonder us kids ever survived.

Maw-Maw had a sister, Mattie Lou, who lived in Columbus, Ga. I remember her being very stern and harsh. Momma called Daddy after a couple of weeks, and of course, he forgave her. He'd worked things out with the bank, and all he wanted was us to come home. We drove to New Orleans, where we picked Daddy up at the airport so he could drive us the rest of the way home. He was so happy to see us! We went home, and things went well for a year or so after that.

Momma's half-sister, Nita, came to work at the donut shop around this time. I really loved her and my cousins. Momma and her sister looked a lot alike. It was uncanny!

I forget what tragedy occurred, but once again, Momma was ready to hit the road. This time she asked her sister to help Daddy when we left. Bubba put his foot down and refused to leave Daddy. I remember crying and looking out the back window at Bubba standing next to Aunt Nita and wondering when I'd see him next.

A few weeks later, Daddy sent Momma the money for us to come back home. Aunt Nita married a cop and moved to Colorado with my cousins.

Things were different, but I couldn't figure out what it was. Daddy was on top of everything that was going on at the shop, and Momma was staying home more.

Chapter 7
SAM

I WAS TWELVE WHEN "SAM" came into my life. It's not my intention to disrupt Sam's life, but his involvement with me had an immense impact on mine. Sam isn't his real name, nor will I share the details of his involvement with my family. He's now an international businessman involved in high-level politics, and I see no need to throw him under a bus.

I know that what he did to me wasn't right when it started, but at some point, I had to accept the role I played as well. I recently had an opportunity to see him one last time, and gave him a letter absolving him of all guilt.

I'd shoved the Horseshoe Bend incident into the far reaches of my mind the night I left my parents' room. I guess I was traumatized to the point that pretending it never happened was the only way my eleven-year-old self could cope. It never dawned on me to tell anyone about what was taking place with Sam and me. I had learned my lesson.

I was like any other twelve-year-old girl back then where boys were concerned. I had every forty-five record that Donny Osmond ever cut. It was around that time when Sam entered my life with a haircut similar to Donny's.

Sam was a cocky fellow who was always getting under my skin and always pushing my buttons. Remember, I said I was part tomboy; well, Mr. Sam was always challenging me. One day when he was around, he came up and informed me that my problem was that I needed to be kissed!

"Oh, yea? And just who do you think is gonna get by with that," I asked. I'd never actually been kissed, nor had I ever had a boyfriend other than elementary child play.

"I believe I am the man for the job," Sam said as he dramatically grabbed me and bent me backward as he laid one on me.

I was taken by surprise and pretty shook up when he released me. So many emotions ran through me at once. I grabbed the acrylic brush, which always hung out my back pocket, and very forcefully hit him over the head with it, breaking my brush into.

"Ouch!!! What'd you do that for," a very startled Sam cried?

All I could do was sit and stare at the 15-year-old boy who would change my life forever and become my first love!

I followed him around like a love-sick puppy! I was convinced everyone was wrong that teased me with Donny's song "Puppy Love."

Sam strung me along for several years just enough to earn my undying devotion. He was around a lot. I hero-worshipped him to the point I believed every word he said.

A few months into the necking which he introduced me to, he told me a story which I bought hook line and sinker. He said that boys were different than girls, body-wise.

He said that when young men get excited, their "*balls*" swell up with fluid. He said that if their "*balls*" aren't relieved, it caused a serious condition called "*blue balls*." He told me that every time he got around me, he got excited. Wow, I thought to myself, I guess that means he likes me! Just the thing my crushing heart needed to hear.

He said he needed help to release the fluid, which he called '*cum*.' He undid his pants and pulled out his erect penis. He took my hand and placed it on him. At twelve, I had never touched a boy's privates and was very worried cause I knew it was wrong. Sam assured me that it was okay between two people who loved each other. I went stone still thinking how he'd said in a roundabout way that he loved me. My poor heart was doing somersaults! He showed me how to pleasure him, and there it began. It wasn't long until he introduced me to oral sex.

The difference is that other than fondling me, he never reciprocated. He never touched me down there, which suited me just fine until I was older and wanted him too. As much as I pleaded with him, he never gave in. I think somewhere in his mind he was afraid of Daddy, at least that's what I told myself.

I asked Sam one time if all young men got "*blue balls*" as much as he did cause he sure had a problem. He'd pick me up several times a week to go and take care of it. Wherever we were at times, he would pull me to the side and have me relieve him. Most of the time, he'd take me to his bedroom when his mother wasn't around. Speaking of his mother, if she only knew what happened the night her and Sam's father picked us up at the emergency room after a minor car wreck, she would have had a heart attack.

Sam and I got in the back of his parent's luxury vehicle, and off we went across town, back where we lived. Sam got that look that said he needed me now, as he grabbed me and laid me across his lap. He already had it pulled out as he shoved me down on him.

"Oh well, it's his parents," I thought to myself, finishing in record time.

Sam began bringing high school girls around about a year after he and I became a *'secret couple.'* Everyone knew I crushed on him, but he said it was best if he treated me like a kid sister in front of folks that way they wouldn't know about *'our secret.'* He said these girls were just friends, and I wanted to believe him.

The more girls he brought, the more upset I became. For all the good, it did me. I guess I went for several years without looking another boy's way.

I met a boy in the eighth grade who I really liked. There was another girl who liked him too. I decided I would win his devotion by showing him what I could do. If Sam could have other girls, I could do the same.

I was two months into the eighth grade when all hell broke loose. My new friend had a big mouth, and the whole school soon knew what I had done. The other girl was upset and decided I needed a butt whipping.

She challenged me to meet her at the Whataburger parking lot after school. Word spread about the upcoming fight so that by the time I got there, a crowd had gathered.

"Whore; Slut," shouted the crowd.

I felt like a piece of trash on the ground because I knew what I'd done was wrong. The girl who challenged me, and her friend, jumped me, but before they could hurt me, the management of Whataburger stopped them.

According to the school, since we were on the way home from school, we were subject to disciplinary measures. We were all given alternative school assignments, and as it happened, me and one of the girls were going to the same school. I was mortified at the thought that the whole school knew what I had done. Momma solved it all. She withdrew me from school and said she was sending me to California to live with an aunt. Just like that, in the middle of the eighth grade, I was out of school.

Sam had awakened something inside of me yet avoided giving me release. He made me feel ugly and unattractive. He made me feel like I was lucky I got to relieve him.

I remember thinking once that I was gonna pleasure him so well that he'd never be able to forget me. Must have worked since every few years we seemed to run into each other. Regardless of our respective marriages, we'd meet for '*old times*' sake.

Thinking back to my youth, I distinctly recall the passionate love scene I had worked up in my mind the many times I dreamt of Sam making love to me. The funny thing is, I barely remember the details of the first time we had sex, not of the act itself. I was eighteen at the time it happened, on my second marriage, and had my first child when Sam suggested it was time for him to take me all the way. Of course, I said yes, since I never could tell him no.

My conscience couldn't take it, so I told *hubby* two the truth not long after it happened. Sam happened to show up one morning at the donut shop, not long after I told on myself. *Hubby* two barely let Sam step from his car before punching him three times in the jaw. He lifted Sam a bit off the ground with one of his punches.

Sam got back in his car, and it was quite a few years before I saw him again. I'm getting ahead of myself, but I wanted to describe the relationship with Sam and me. Our relationship continued throughout the years until recently, but that's another story.

I'm not proud of my many failed marriages. Nor am I proud of my promiscuity over the years. Marriage, to me, was a means to an end. "Lucy" always had logical excuses for the outrageous ideas she came up with. Getting a divorce was easier than continuing on in a bad situation.

In my mind, one day, Sam would realize the errors of his ways and rescue me.

Chapter 8
Momma's broken heart

Around the time I turned thirteen, I found out that Daddy was smoking marijuana. I don't know how or why he started that because Daddy had always been strait-laced. He never cared for alcohol, and I'm pretty sure that was cause of Maw-Maw and her drinking. I suspect it was that long-haired hippie Daddy hired.

Anyways, Daddy had it in his mind that me and Bubba was gonna end up smoking marijuana on our own. To his way of thinking, he figured he would smoke it with us first to make sure we were safe. I found out later that Bubba had already tried it with his little friends. The first time Daddy smoked a joint with me was on the way back from Lake Benbrook. I was so paranoid by the time Daddy pulled the truck up to the shop that all I wanted to do was run and hide in the bathroom.

Daddy had heard you could make brownies with marijuana, so he came up with the bright idea to make some cake donuts with it. Unfortunately, he tried it out one Sunday morning.

Once Daddy finished pumping out the apple-spice cake donuts for the customers that morning, he added a bag of marijuana to the rest of the batter and pumped them out. You could smell marijuana throughout the cooking area. Thank God it was early in the morning. Daddy was pretty worried about it until the smell dissipated. As usual, once the yeast production started, it was game on and no stopping. I soon forgot about the "*special*" donuts.

Daddy had customers that drove in from all over to get his donuts, some as far as Burleson. It was nothing for Daddy to run a seven-hundred dollars day on the weekend. In the early seventies that was a lot of donuts. People would line up all the way around the corner, waiting on Daddy's delicious, mouthwatering sweets.

He had his regulars that came early to sit and read their newspaper while having their coffee and donuts. One such customer was a very devout minister who came early to avoid the rush. Every Sunday morning, without fail, he had two apple-spice donuts and a large coffee.

Everything was going good that morning, right up until I heard the minister start laughing himself silly. In the two years he'd been coming there, he'd barely uttered a word; he was so reserved. I looked at Daddy, and then at Bubba when he stepped up to the counter and said he wanted a half dozen more apple-spice donuts to go. He said he didn't know what we'd changed in the recipe, but they sure were good!

Then it dawned on me! I raced to where I'd stashed the "*secret recipe donuts,*" and to my great horror, they were gone. Someone had put them in the showcase. I rushed out there with the right tray of apple-spice just in time to stop the counter girl from sacking up the pot-laden donuts.

I don't guess that minister ever knew what he ate that morning. Although he did mention a time or two, how he wished we'd try '*our special recipe*' again. What I wouldn't have given, to be a fly on that ministers' pulpit that Sunday morning.

Barely a year after moving to Colorado, Aunt Nita and my three cousins had moved back to Texas. Momma let them move in with us. Aunt Nita was going in to work with Daddy, and Momma was taking care of us kids at home.

Momma started confiding in me that she thought there was something going on between Daddy and Aunt Nita. "Of course, they're not Momma," I promised. I knew that would never happen, and me saying so made Momma feel better.

Not long after Aunt Nita was living with us, the movie "*Jaws*" hit the theatres. Momma didn't want to go and encouraged Daddy and Aunt Nita to take us kids. After the movie was over, we all went across the street to have donuts and chocolate milk. I didn't see where Daddy and Aunt Nita went but hurried to the back room of the shop to use the restroom.

Opening the door and stepping into the back room, I stopped dead still. Locked in a passionate embrace was my Daddy and Aunt. I turned and ran from the shop. I ran 'til I couldn't run anymore. When I finally went back, I refused to talk to anyone. The next day my aunt and cousins moved out of our house.

Later that evening, I told Momma what I had seen. Daddy agreed to cut all communication with my aunt, but Momma couldn't let it go. Daddy and Bubba moved in with Aunt Nita a few days later.

Before the next six months passed, Momma let Shelley go live with Daddy, and they got divorced. Daddy married Aunt Nita shortly after. I wouldn't have left Momma's side for love nor money. She needed me now more than ever.

Me and Momma moved to Maw-Maw Cruse's house cause Momma was a mess. Momma must have slept for a solid month around the clock. I just let her sleep. Every time she was awake, she just cried and cried.

I woke Momma up a couple of times a day and coaxed her to eat. I sat in front of the TV for the rest of the time. At that moment in time, I despised both my Daddy and Aunt Nita.

One day out of the blue, Momma seemed to snap out of it, stating we were going to get our hair fixed, go shopping for new clothes, and hit the honky-tonks.

The lady at the beauty school gave me an updo, piling curls on top of my head. Next, Momma took me shopping. I can still see the cute mini dress with bloomers hanging on the rack that Momma bought me. By the time we got to the *"It'll Do Club,"* no one had bothered asking how old I was. I was nearly fifteen when we started *"bar hopping."* The first time I heard Reba McIntyre's song, "Fancy," my first thoughts were of that day.

It started out as one or two nights a week. Eventually, Momma got to going so much that I was in her way. Right before I got shipped off to Daddy, I got married.

This obnoxious guy I'd met at the bar just couldn't take "No" for an answer. I told him I was a virgin and was saving myself for my husband. As far as I was concerned, it was true. We even double-dated with his father and Aunt Windelyn a couple of times. All I can say is, my aunt Windelyn sure could cut a rug!

One night, Mr. Obnoxious came up with a plan. Right around midnight, he asked me to marry him. I was excited and saw my way out, so I asked Momma if she would sign for me. Pretty soon, everyone was caught up in the excitement.

Unfortunately, we were gonna have to wait 'til the following morning before we could get a 'Justice of the Peace.' Mr. Obnoxious convinced me it was time, and that we were getting married the next morning after all, so I agreed to go to a motel with him and meet Momma in the morning. Mother nature was visiting, so we would have to wait, but I took care of his problem anyway. It was the first time I had shared my experience with oral sex with him, and needless to say, he acted as though I had railroaded him. He married me the next morning and took me to his parents' home. I helped cook dinner that evening and felt like I was finally on my own.

Sunday evening, he dropped me at my mother's house to gather my clothes, promising to pick me up soon. I was just finishing up packing when his sister called. She told my mother that he thought I had tricked him into marriage, and he'd changed his mind. She assured Momma that he would have it annulled immediately.

I was saddened, realizing he had planned to use me from the start. I wasn't in love with him; I just wanted to be on my own. I shook him off pretty easy and was sent to live with Daddy.

It took some time, but I forgave Daddy and Aunt Nita. I didn't know what to call her at first, but by the time she died, she was Mom Nita. She had helped Daddy learn to control his temper, and put her foot down 'bout marijuana. She wasn't havin' drugs under her roof. Daddy even lost a lot of weight with Mom Nita standing beside him and supporting him. She loved Daddy with all her heart and wanted only the best for him.

Momma, God rest her soul, had been terrible to Daddy. She took advantage of the fact he couldn't read, she cheated on him, and eventually pushed him into the arms of the woman who would love him till the day she died. I think Momma eventually realized that everything happens for a reason.

As a matter of fact, the day before Momma died, years down the road, Daddy and Mom Nita spent the entire day with Momma, and they made amends between them. In the end, Momma was grateful that the other woman was her sister because she already loved us kids. She was a petite, little woman, but she ramrodded every one of us. We had our moments over the years, but I guarantee you, I never deliberately crossed her.

Chapter 9

One lie too many

THERE WERE TIMES WHEN I had mixed emotions regarding Daddy growing up. I was afraid of him when he was mad, though he only whipped me once. It was after he divorced Momma when I had another *'I gotta tell'* moments. I would have been somewhere around fifteen at the time this occurred.

Daddy was a bowling fool. In fact, he was offered a spot on a professional bowler's tour. He was that good! Of course, Daddy turned it down. Daddy said he would never take a chance when it came to supporting his family. His love of bowling continued throughout his life, and he bowled on leagues as far back as I remember. He even taught us kids to bowl when we got older.

I remember that Saturday as if it were yesterday. I had been over at a girl's house that morning hanging out, trying out different ways to wear make-up. There was one eyeshadow that made my eyes look cool, or so I thought. This girl's mother had a basket full of eyeshadow, and I thought, "Hmmm, she won't miss this one." Later, as I was sitting on the steps leading to our upstairs apartment, I saw my friend and her father barreling across the courtyard. For whatever reason, I got up and walked towards them. The man looked at me like he was gonna beat me.

"I'm giving you one chance to hand over my wife's make-up, or else I'm calling the police," my friend's father threatened.

I remember thinking that I wanted to be anywhere but there, as he kept yelling for the whole complex to hear, what a low-life, cowardly thief I was. Out of nowhere, my father appeared next to me.

"This is my daughter you're yelling at. I'd suggest you tell me what the hell is going on," Daddy said, trying to hold back his anger.

When the man explained what a thief I was and how I had disrespected his home, Daddy turned to me and asked if it was true. I looked at my friend, and then at her father with the smug look on his face, and finally back at Daddy who I'd never lied to, except for keeping Momma's secrets that is.

"No, Daddy, I didn't steal anything."

"You little liar," the man spat out vehemently

"My daughter has never lied to me," Daddy roared!

The man never saw it coming as Daddy punched him right square in the mouth. It didn't take that man no time to turn around and head for his own apartment, putting plenty of distance between him and my father. Daddy looked at me and forbade me to go near that man's house again.

Later that evening, as I stood watching my father bowl one of his best sets ever, my conscience came alive. Daddy had just bowled eight strikes in a row when he stepped away to relax before his next ball. I couldn't help myself; I had to tell him now before I lost my nerve. He'd been bowling so good; surely, he'd go easy on me. Daddy had turned every shade of red imaginable by the time I finished telling on myself for lying.

"Get the hell out of my sight. Now!"

The sound of Daddy's voice sent shivers up my spine. I felt fear as I'd never felt in my life as I turned and walked away. Mixed in with that fear was shame. I remember the next time my father bowled and still recall the sick feeling in my stomach as I watched that ball hook so hard it struck dead center of those ten pins: four, seven, ten split. Daddy didn't recover it.

The ride home seemed to take forever yet was over too soon. The looks on the faces around me, and the ensuing silence, told the tale. Reaching the apartments, Daddy pulled the car to an abrupt stop. Daddy jumped out of the vehicle without delay dragging me behind him. It seemed like forever before we got to my friend's apartment. Daddy knocked on the man's door so hard it shook. The man jerked his door open and stopped in the middle of a curse as my father spoke. "My daughter has something to give you."

I opened the hand that clenched the make-up case, dropping it into the man's hands. I remember thinking how odd to see pity instead of anger coming from the man's eyes.

"I apologize for doubting you, sir," my father said. Daddy unbuckled his belt from his pants, and in one fell swoop, the belt flew from Daddy's pants.

I'll never forget the sick feeling I felt as it dawned on me what was coming. My father had never laid hands on me, never, not once in my whole life. He pointed in the direction of our apartment, and I took that first step.

Yes, indeed, every step I took felt the sting from Daddy's belt. From my ankles to my butt, no space was left untouched. Wouldn't you know it, we lived in one of those multi-unit complexes and the two apartments couldn't have been further apart. People looked away as we made our way across the complex. Unbelievably, no one called the police.

Up the stairs we went, my God, what was he going to do when he got me inside our home, I feared. Mom Nita met us at the top of the stairs and motioned for me to go to my room, stepping between Daddy and me. I heard her scream as I ran into the apartment.

"John, John, it's me," Mom Nita shouted as Daddy hit her twice with his belt before coming to his senses.

Mom Nita came in a short while later and helped me pull the jean material from the bloody mess that was my legs. She gave me some aspirin and gently wiped the blood away. She promised me with all her heart that Daddy *'blacked out'* and never meant to hurt me that way. Later, I heard my father cry for the second time in my life. He never laid hands on me again.

At 15, I was bored to tears, and everyone I knew was in school. Sam was in the service, so I decided I would join too. How to do it become my mission.

One of Daddy's long-time employees and I were sitting around brainstorming one day when we came up with a plan.

It just so happened that if you turned the nine, in fifty-nine upside down on my birth certificate, it became a six making my birth year fifty-six. So, we got a box knife and cut perfect squares around all the nines on my birth certificate and turned them upside down and taped them from the back. Next, we made a copy of it. There were a few spaces where the squares weren't joined, so we covered them with copy fluid. Then we made the final copy. I folded and re-folded it until it looked worn. I took it to the newest driver's license office on I-30 in Garland and watched the desk clerks. Sure enough, there was one who was not as strict with the applicants. When she got to me, she briefly looked at my birth certificate before asking about the seal. I explained my apartment had burned down a couple of weeks ago, and this copy was one I had given to my Maw-Maw to save. The girl took it without another question. I took my tests and passed them. Within an hour, I went from age fifteen to eighteen. Back then, the legal age was eighteen. I was an overnight sensation. As I recall, the only booze I bought for my new best friends and me was Boonesfarm Strawberry-Hill wine, and Schlitz beer. Today, the mere thought of *Strawberry-Hill* makes me want to puke.

I went and took my GED not long after I got my license. I'd never stepped a foot inside a high school but passed the GED with high scores. Wow! I didn't understand the implications of my scores but just took it for granted that I was still pretty smart. I took the ASFABS and passed them with high scores too, but I got cold feet thinking the military would find out my actual age and didn't go back.

Before I came to live with Daddy, he and Mom Nita had given me a yellow VW beetle. Momma took it over and left me with no vehicle. When I went to live with Daddy, he bought me another *"bug"* that was OD green. Olive drab wasn't my color, but I didn't care. I was fifteen and had my own car.

I'd always considered myself privileged. I got just about anything I ever wanted.

Just like the time my father had promised me a motorcycle for my twelfth birthday. Unfortunately, times were tough, and Daddy didn't have the money to get my bike. The manager at the motorcycle shop he went to had been trying to buy Daddy's motorcycle forever. Daddy's bike was his pride and joy.

Daddy always sacrificed for his kids. When he couldn't figure out any other way, he traded his bike for mine and a little cash. I told him he didn't have to do it, but Daddy prided himself on never breaking his word to us kids.

I had ridden many miles behind Daddy on his bike. We tore up I-20, between Arlington and Wedgwood, when it was being built. Back then I-20 was surrounded by fields and fields. Now all you see are businesses and homes lining the interstate. Daddy taught me where the brake was, where the gas pedal was, and how to work the clutch and gears. I was confident I could manage my motorcycle on my own.

The donut shop sat on a hill surrounded by parking spaces in the shopping center. You had to drive down the hill and turn onto the street to reach the rest of the shopping areas. I got on my Honda ninety that was bored out to a one twenty-five, and down the hill, I went. I was feeling pretty cocky as I turned and headed back up the hill. Somehow, I lost my balance and pulled back on the right handle pretty hard. Up came the front wheel, and all of a sudden, I was nearly standing. Bubba and Daddy came running toward me, telling me to let go of the throttle, but I couldn't for the life of me remember what the throttle was.

Later, after we tended to the road rash I had, they said I did a perfect cross-over. I didn't care what they said I did; I wasn't ever riding another motorcycle as long as I lived. That lasted about thirty minutes before Daddy had me back on my bike. He would never let us kids get by with walking away from anything. When Bubba's horse threw him off, Daddy made him get right back in that saddle. Or the times we fell, learning to roller skate, he made us get up time and again 'til we got the hang of it. Daddy might not have been educated in the academic world, but he was sure smart when it came to other stuff.

Chapter 10
Double-dog-dare

SEEMS LIKE A WHOLE BUNCH of stuff happened in my fifteenth year. Around the time Momma slept so long at Maw-Maw Cruse's, I had become pen pals with this guy who was in the Air Force with an adopted cousin of mine. I was mainly just passing the time exchanging letters. It was suggested that I ought to come for a visit some time. The thought hung in the back of my mind teasing me to go. The idea came and went until one day I, or should I say "Lucy," decided it was time to go.

Me and my oldest stepsister, Renee, was always *double-dog*-daring each other. I have to say we were unstoppable. Or else she was pulling pranks on me with Bubba.

One time she *double-dogged*-dared me to go skinny dipping out at Lake Benbrook. I didn't understand why she backed out at the last minute. I'd already enlisted a couple of friends to go, so we decided to go on without her.

We waited till almost sunset, and off we went. One by one, we stripped down to what the good Lord gave us and dove into the water. We'd left our clothes thrown across my *bug* with our towels and was having ourselves a good ol' time. That is until the headlights shone on us. Under the water, we went. I picked out Bubba and Renee's laughter first! Unbeknownst to us, Renee, Bubba, and one of my friend's brother had followed us out there.

"Daddy's gonna tan your hides when he finds out what y'all did to us," I threatened.

"Not before the snakes and snapping turtles get to y'all," Bubba spit out between his guffaws!

We splashed and made sounds like some wild-banshees when he mentioned critters in the water with us. I was screaming, cussing, and threatening all manners of revenge on Bubba and Renee when the lights finally went off, and they disappeared. They took off with all our clothes leaving only towels behind. Have you ever tried to drive a stick shift wearing only a towel?

All I talked about back then was flying off in a big plane to Delaware to meet my pen pal. I fancied myself infatuated with this guy, who knew, maybe he was "*the one*" who would erase Sam from my heart

Airfare must have been for the rich and famous cause I never could raise it on my own. "Lucy" wasn't accepting defeat. It wasn't long before I got the brilliant idea to drive to Delaware. Renee wasn't about to let me take off on my own. She decided that she needed to go with me.

We grabbed some clothes, sold a few of our belongings, and off we went with fifty-three dollars and a tank of gas.

Everyone had CB's back then, including me. My handle was "*Blue-jean Baby.*" We were having the time of our lives driving east up Interstate 30. Passing the truckers, Renee always gave the blow-your-horn hand signal, and nearly every time, she got a response. We were talking to this pair of truckers when we were invited to stop for coffee. It was almost 3 am when we pulled off the interstate. The looks on those old men's faces when they saw me and Renee was priceless.

"Just how old are you youngsters," one of the old men asked.

"I'm eighteen, and my sister is seventeen," I lied.

I was afraid if I told them I was fifteen, and Renee was thirteen, that they would call the police. They bought our breakfast and lectured us while we ate it. I promised I would stop at a payphone down the road and let our families know we were safe. Renee tried her best to talk me out of calling, but I had to call my Daddy. The truckers had got to me. The minute I told Daddy we were okay, he told me the one thing I couldn't ignore.

"Either turn that car around and come back home right this minute, or else I am gonna stop being your father," Daddy swore. I started crying and said we'd head right home. Beside me, Renee was throwing a wild-eyed, conniption fit.

"Oh no, we're not 'til I talk to Mom," Renee screamed, grabbing the phone from me. Renee made Mom Nita promise we wouldn't get a whooping or grounded before she agreed to go home. I talked to Daddy after Renee finished talking and told him I didn't know if we had enough money to get back. Daddy said he would send the money through Western Union.

I learned something from Momma on our road trips. Historical markers, scenic routes, and slightly re-routed directions could be interesting and fun. We stopped at a truck stop in Nashville, where I planned our adventure home. We wasn't gonna get in any more trouble than we were already in. The closest place I found on the way home that sounded cool was Hot Springs and the Ouachita Mountains. Off we went. We gave a hitchhiker a ride but then ditched him at the motel in Little Rock, where we stopped for the night. He got his own room, and we were supposed to wake him up the next morning, but we didn't.

Getting ready for bed that night, I couldn't figure out why I was itching like crazy in a place I shouldn't be until I went to the toilet. There was a bug crawling on me, but I couldn't catch it. I hollered for Donna to bring me a razor! Best we could figure, there was one time where she couldn't wait to go and used the Men's Room. I waited and went to the Women's Room. Later as I re-told the story, Maw-Maw Lummus laughed herself silly bout what I'd done. How was I supposed to know some ointment would have done the trick? To this day, I don't sit on public toilet seats.

We got to Hot Springs and checked out the points of interest. I saw a cheap souvenir place where we found stuff for everybody. I figured nobody would be mad if we took them souvenirs.

We made it to the mountain range when the clutch started slipping. I called Daddy, but he said I better figure it out, or else I would have to leave my car behind. I knew Daddy wouldn't really leave us stranded. He just wanted me to "*stew in my mess*," so maybe I'd think twice before pulling another stunt. We finally limped my *bug* back home. We didn't get whipped, but Daddy promptly took my keys.

Unfortunately, I hadn't learned my lesson. My wanderlust had only just begun.

Chapter 11

I didn't mean to rob 7-11!

I NEVER COULD TYPE! I have two left hands. Not to mention the fact that I'm not the greatest with word processing. When I set out to edit my original Chapter 21, instead of deleting one word, I deleted the whole chapter! I didn't know there was an undo button as I saw the entire chapter vanish before my eyes. I found that out a little too late. I worked so hard on this chapter. It was very painful to relive as I put it on paper. I became so disheartened that I quit writing for the past year. I had just about given up telling my story at all.

I began questioning my motives for wanting to write a book to start with. I became convinced that no one would read it. I am nobody. Who cares enough about my life to read about it? As I researched how to get my book published, I found that there are thousands of people, much like myself, who have the same ideas and lofty dreams. Others have suffered tragedies that they, too, hoped to share with the world and become noticed. Perhaps to become rich and famous, or to inspire hope to other lost souls searching for answers. I've done a lot of soul-searching this year, and I think I know why I need to finish this book to the end. It won't be easy by a long shot. I know that now. Those lofty dreams I had when I began Chapter One, fell by the wayside. Who wants to be rich and famous, anyway? Come to think of it; I treasure my anonymity more than dollar signs any day of the week.

As I push forward on my journey to put pen to paper, I thank God that I haven't died yet and that I've accomplished much of what I sat out in life to do. Daddy always said the only thing standing between me and anything I ever wanted was myself. The only goal in my life I have yet to accomplish is putting the stories of my life on paper.

Early on in chapter 1, I made a bold statement that I make no apologies for the life I've lived. I feel the need to clarify at this point. I very much want to apologize to those who are going to be hurt by what they read. To those who love me, I'm so sorry. If you don't want to know the truth, put this book down now. Everyone has a right to stand up in their own defense. Not that I'm offering a big defense on my part, I made a lot of mistakes. But I deserve to tell my story, if for no one else but myself.

I'm not writing this book to elicit pity or lament on how I've been wronged. It's not too place blame on anyone for the misfortunes of my life. Most especially, I don't blame my parents. In my heart of hearts, I really believe they did the best that they could given their circumstances.

Please be mindful that for every action we take in life; reactions will occur. Some good, some bad. It's just life, and how we respond will follow us all our days.

So, where was I…?

I believe I had just lost my *bug* after returning from the road trip with Renee. Daddy probably wouldn't have taken my *bug* if I hadn't worn out the clutch on the way home through the Arkansas mountains. After a couple of weeks, he replaced the clutch and gave me back my keys. Daddy never stayed mad at me long.

Bored, and not wanting to work at the donut shop, I applied at the 7-11 store up the street from where we lived. They must have been hard up for help because they called me the next morning to come in that day for an interview. The store manager asked me a handful of questions and said, "You're hired. You need to get a physical and a polygraph. Be here at six am tomorrow. "

Wow! I'd applied on a whim and hadn't even asked Daddy if I could work there yet. I never figured I'd get hired.

I didn't tell Daddy until after I went for my physical and the polygraph because I wasn't sure I could pass a polygraph. To be honest, I wasn't even sure what a polygraph was or how it worked.

Man, was I nervous? I took my physical and headed over to take the polygraph. I was visibly nervous. The examiner told me, of course, I knew when my birthday is when I failed that question. Luckily my altered driver's license stated I was 18 instead of 15.

Applying at 7-11 was easy; the hard part was going and talking to Daddy.

He made me promise I would not be selling beer or wine coolers to minors, and that I would give the lady a hard day's work for a good day's pay.

I was over the moon! I had an adult job and big plans. The problem was I was still a kid. I really wanted to make Daddy proud of me. All Daddy wanted was for his kids to be successful in life.

Sam was still coming around, playing with my emotions. I was growing weary with him and just knew this guy who'd been writing me was the one who'd help me forget Sam once and for all.

After two weeks of training, I was given my own shift at the store. I didn't really like working three to eleven cause I got scared sometimes thinking I was gonna get robbed. I eventually got used to the regulars and settled in.

It happened the first night I had the store to myself. It was storming like crazy, and there were tornado watches out in our area. 7-11 has huge plate glass windows, and my crazy imagination could see tornados coming right for me. Later that evening, Daddy and Bubba brought me up a plate of food for dinner. I begged Daddy to let Bubba stay with me cause I was so scared. Daddy said, "No." I was upset and hurt that Daddy couldn't see how worried I was. Not long after they left, the store got busy, and I forgot I was scared. But I was still mad at Daddy.

It finally stopped raining, and I never saw a tornado thank God. I was so busy that night; I never even had time to go to the bathroom. I had just finished stocking the coolers and was sweeping when Renee and our best friend Dee showed up. Dee had a driver's license, and I often let her and Renee ride around in my *bug* while I was working. They were there to pick me up. The minute they walked in, I began telling them what a night it had been and how mad I was at Daddy for not letting Bubba stay.

"If I had the money, I'd jump on an airplane right now, and I'd be outta here!"

Renee busted out laughing and said, "No, you wouldn't you big fat liar. You're chicken!"

Between Renee and me, them were fighting words!

"I'm not a chicken, and yes, I would!"

"Oh yeah, I bet you wouldn't," Renee said, looking at Dee and laughing at me.

"Take the money out of the register and go since you're such a bigshot," Renee said after several exchanges.

"I can't do that," I fired back.

"Oh, yes, you can. You could put a note in there with a paid out like we do at the donut shop. They will take it out of your check," Renee stated.

"For your information, I would do it, but there isn't enough money in the register. We have to make drops in the safe whenever there is one-hundred dollars in the register, so there. I would go if I could," I declared.

Renee finally let it go and went to look at the cheap rings on the display counter while I finished my chores.

I finished sweeping and mopping and started my paperwork for the night. I had been so busy that I had shoved receipts, trash, and everything else into the big pockets of my smock that night. When I went to emptying my pockets, money came flying out too.

Stepping up to the counter, Renee asked, "What's all that?"

Then it dawned on me; I had shoved the money and receipts in my pockets instead of making the drops into the safe throughout the night.

"There ya' go big shot. Let's see what ya' got to say now," Renee challenged. Then she came out with it, "I *double-dog* dare you! If you don't, then all you are is a big fat chicken!"

Renee and Dee exchanged glances that seemed to say, "We got her now!"

I was a lot of things back then, but I sure wasn't no chicken.

Daddy's way of keeping his employees from stealing from him was to allow them to borrow money from the register, leaving a paid out/IOU receipt in place of the money. At the end of the week, all paid-outs were deducted from the employee's salary. Renee's idea made perfect sense to me.

"I'm not a chicken! I'm gonna do it," I said, throwing their smugness right back in their faces.

My dreams of flying on a big airplane to Delaware were about to come true.

I'd been figuring Daddy's payroll at the donut shop for years, helping Momma add up the paid outs and the hours that each employee had. I could do this.

I got my timecard out and added up all the hours I had coming. I multiplied the hours times my hourly rate and then subtracted ten-percent for taxes. My net pay was close to six-hundred dollars, according to my figures.

I wrote my manager a notice of resignation and thanked her for hiring me. I explained an emergency had come up, and I had to leave right away. I made a nice little graph describing how I'd figured my payroll and gave her permission to sign my check so she could deposit it in place of the money I had taken. Once that was done, I made drops with the remaining cash I had into the safe.

I called the airline and found out that there was indeed a plane leaving for Pennsylvania in two and a half hours from Dallas-Fort Worth International airport. The biggest airport in the world. I would have to take the bus to Delaware once I landed in Pennsylvania.

I kinda felt sad as I slid the envelope which held my letter of resignation and the store keys under the crack in the door for the manager to see when she opened the next morning.

The regular cops who stopped by to ensure my safety as I locked up each night pulled in just as I turned from my task.

"Tonight was my last night. Thanks for looking out for me," I told the officers.

"No problem. Take care of yourself," said the officers as they pulled from the lot.

I got behind the wheel of my *bug*, and off we went.

When we got to the house, Renee sat in the car with Dee so we wouldn't wake anyone up. I grabbed a suitcase, threw some clothes in it and out the door I ran.

I had fantasized about flying off in a big airplane for so long that it never occurred to me to be scared or think what the heck am I doing? I mean, after all, Jay and my cousin had this little cottage by the ocean, which sounded so romantic. I figured I'd get a job and roommate with my cousin and Jay and see what happened next. I loved my parents deeply but was tired of being shipped back and forth between them. I just wanted to escape.

Dallas-Ft. Worth International airport was huge, and I'd never been there before. It took a while to find the right terminal, but once I'd made up my mind to do something, there was no stopping me.

To her credit, Renee tried. "I'm not sure you ought to do this, Wende," Renee said as I hugged her goodbye before running into the airport terminal.

I almost missed my flight because the agent questioned my age. She called her supervisor over to examine my license.

"She's of age. Sell her the ticket," the supervisor said.

I ran like a chicken with its neck cut off past gate after gate 'til I found mine. Several more questioning looks later; I was sitting on the plane. I will never, ever forget that poor man sitting next to me in a fancy suit and shiny shoes. I guess all the excitement had finally caught up with me as the plane lifted off the ground. Looking at me, the man reached for something in the pocket in the seat in front of him. Before he could retrieve it, I splattered his expensive suit and shiny shoes with the pork chops, and fried taters, Daddy, had brought me to eat earlier.

The look on that man's face scared me to death.

I started babbling I'd never flown before and how sorry I was.

As soon as the flight leveled off, the stewardess came and helped clean up my mess. That poor man did his best to keep me calm the whole flight. I'm guessing he didn't want me to throw up and start babbling again. That's really all I remember about my first airplane ride.

Except for the beautiful sunrise over the clouds, I saw looking out my window later in the flight.

Walking through the terminal in Pennsylvania after we landed was freaky to me cause I'd never heard Yankees talking.

From there, I was gonna have to catch a bus to go to Delaware. I figured this was as good a time as any to call my cousin and tell him I would be there soon. It had been months since the last letter I had received from Jay, but I was sure the offer for me to come was still open. When I tell you my cousin almost busted my eardrum when I told him I was at the airport in Pennsylvania, I'm not lying. I was confused since I had been invited to come. He was furious with me. He made me tell him exactly how I got there. It was so quiet on the other end of the phone for a minute after I finished my story that I thought he had hung up on me. He told me to call Daddy right away, and then to call him back. He said for Daddy to call him too.

I'd been up all night. I was tired and starting to get hungry cause that man had advised me not to eat the breakfast that was served during the flight. I didn't understand why my cousin was mad at me since I'd been invited to come up there to begin with. The last person on earth I really wanted to talk to was Daddy. I called the donut shop, and the phone barely rang before somebody snatched it up and said hello. It was Mom Nita.

"Hold on, please, let me get John," she said as if I were someone else.

It seemed like forever before Daddy got on the phone.

"The police are here. They're looking for my fifteen-year-old daughter.

They're saying she robbed a 7-11 store and took over five-thousand dollars in cash and merchandise," I heard my father saying.

I knew by the tone of my father's voice that he was pretending like he wasn't talking to me, and I heard something I had only heard a few times in my life.

I heard it the night we raced to Paw-Paw John's apartment after a neighbor called to say an ambulance was coming to get Paw-Paw. I heard it as Daddy told Paw-Paw everything was gonna be okay right before Paw-Paws' big ol' heart gave out on him at the hospital. I heard it when Daddy came out of Dr. Shoecraft's office and said Shelley was really sick, and he had to get us to Maw-Maw Lummus' house.

My Daddy was scared!

Chapter 12

Delaware and drug dealers

REMEMBERING THAT CONVERSATION SO LONG ago breaks my heart cause I can't call Daddy up and apologize for the heartache, I caused him. I'm not sure I ever realized how much it must have hurt Daddy until just now as I write these words. I don't believe a child can ever fully appreciate the depth of pain and fear of a parent until they become parents themselves. As I recalled that conversation just now, it felt like someone had sucker-punched me right below the ribs.

So much of what happened in my past has been locked away in little compartments in my mind. I often share bits and pieces of my stories in humor, or to help someone along their way, but recalling details is hard.

I could tell Daddy wanted the condensed version of my latest fiasco. I told him to talk to Renee cause she knew everything, but I swore to Daddy I hadn't robbed anyone. I told him where I was and that my cousin had asked for Daddy to call him.

"You go on without us. I'll let you know something once I talk to the rest of the family."

Just like that, Daddy hung up the phone.

I never felt so scared in all my life. I stood there shaking in my shoes, for I don't know how long. My imagination took flight, and everywhere I looked, I saw police officers. They were most likely airport security, but you couldn't have convinced me of that back then.

I finally called my cousin, who suspected I might be in trouble when I related my story earlier about how I got there. He helped me get a hold of myself, told me to get on the first bus I could and get out of that airport.

I can't remember how long the bus ride took, but I felt like a caged rabbit the whole way. I just knew any minute the police were gonna pull me off that bus, lock me up, and I'd never see my family again! I didn't understand what was happening or why. I didn't rob the store. I kept going over every detail piece by piece, and it just wasn't adding up.

My cousin met me at the bus station and took me straight to the barracks where he lived in. Some cottage! I remember feeling silly cause he made me put on his jacket and hat. He was more than upset with me, but he could tell I was scared out of my mind and went easy on me. He said his pal that had been writing to me got in big trouble after the last letter I mailed months ago. Apparently, the letter I had dumped talcum powder in to smell nice had been intercepted and sent off for testing.

"So, that's why he never wrote me back…"

Come to find out; he'd been admonished for writing a minor as well.

"Well, someone could have written and told me something."

My adopted cousin just shook his shoulders.

He said, "That is the least of your worries" and explained in detail why I was being accused of robbery. He had spoken to Daddy before I got there.

Whenever a store is robbed, there is always an immediate audit of that store. At least that's what had been going on all morning back in Ft. Worth. According to the latest figures, it was told to Daddy that several thousand dollars in cash and merchandise was missing from the store. I became light-headed before my knees gave way, and I hit the floor. I don't remember if I lost consciousness, but I recall my cousin saying we needed to leave there.

He took me to a motel on the outskirts of town and made sure I had a room for the next few days 'til Daddy could call me. There was an old diner there as well. He told me to stay out of sight as much as possible and he would be in touch.

I felt so alone that afternoon. I felt like the child I was, scared and wanting my Momma and Daddy. Daddy didn't call me that whole day. Momma called and cried the entire time she was on the phone with me. Man, had I screwed everything up this time? No one had to tell me to stay out of sight! I was so scared, I wanted to hide in the closet, but realized that wasn't necessary. Hunger finally forced me to the diner, right before they closed. I took the food to go. I just knew I had a huge neon sign above my head, telling everyone who

I was and what I'd done. This sure hadn't turned out like the romantic getaway my mind had envisioned all those many months. Crying myself to sleep that night, I sure didn't feel like that cocky girl who had said a mere 24 hours ago, "I'm not chicken!"

Daddy finally called the next morning. I remember bawling my eyes out during the whole conversation. The final tally was close to five-thousand-dollars worth of missing cash and merchandise.

"I swear, Daddy! I only took six hundred dollars and a few items when I left the store. I left a note with a paid out and everything," I cried.

I had expected Daddy to yell and scream at me, so I was surprised to hear the calmness in Daddy's voice. For once, Daddy wasn't telling me to come home. As a matter of fact, he told me I couldn't come home. He said it wasn't safe for me to be there. I hung up the phone, wondering if I would ever see Daddy again.

I finally felt secure enough to wander outside my hotel room a couple of days later and sat down to eat a meal. Unlike my usual chatty self, I buried my nose in a local newspaper. I always read the classifieds last because they were boring. I came across an ad that caught my attention, "*Nanny Wanted.*"

The ad stated the "Nanny" would live-in and be paid a small salary in addition to room and board. It sounded like the perfect solution to my problem. Daddy said it wasn't safe for me to go home, and I was out of money. I didn't want to ask Daddy for money cause I had got myself into this mess, and as a live-in babysitter, I could at least help myself out. I called Daddy, who said it was a good idea, but he and Momma needed to discuss it first. Momma called a little while later and told me it was okay if I responded to the ad. She said if the couple hired me that she wanted to speak with them before I left the motel.

The couple came to the diner and talked to me. I explained I had gotten stranded and needed somewhere to stay until I figured out if I was going home or not. The couple stepped outside of the diner and talked in private before coming in and telling me I was hired if I wanted the job. After they looked at my driver's license, they never mentioned my age again. They called and talked to Momma while I gathered my belongings from the motel room.

I was to have the lion's share of caring for the baby with a couple hours off each afternoon and all-day off on Sundays. They showed me around the apartment and laid out their rules. Unless the baby and I were eating, I was expected to stay in the room with the baby. I was surprised to see the baby's room cause it was actually the master bedroom. The baby bed and toy chest were against one wall. There was a couch and desk with a small TV on it against the back wall. Across from the baby bed was a full-size bed. Next to the closets on the far wall was the bathroom. It was just big enough for a toilet and bathtub. It didn't matter to me if I stayed in the big room all the time. I had a safe place to stay for the time being, and playing with a baby all the time might be fun.

Not!!!

It's one thing to play with a baby, but something totally different to have complete responsibility for one. I was still a kid myself but didn't know it at the time.

It didn't take long for me to figure out something was up with this couple. Mrs. Mommy went to work around six pm every evening and never got home before three in the morning. She was not to be disturbed until she woke up, which was usually two or three in the afternoon unless there was an emergency with the baby. Mr. Daddy didn't go to work at all but occasionally went out for a few hours in the evenings. He had more friends than I ever knew one person to have. The doorbell rang constantly. His friends never stayed more than a few minutes at a time best as I could tell.

When I commented on it one day, he told me that he had a little business he ran from his home and that a lot of his friends helped him out with it. It made sense to me even though he was vague about what he was selling.

Days turned into weeks. I settled into a routine and waited patiently to hear from my family. Long-distance calls were expensive, and Daddy said there weren't no reason to call all the time just to talk. Every time I asked what was going on with 7-11 and the police, Daddy just said he didn't know anything new. Momma called every few days, but she never knew what was happening with the police either. I was always looking over my shoulder when I went on afternoon walks around the neighborhood where I lived. It was a beautiful area with a public park at the end of the street. There was a little pond with ducks on it right in the middle. I would take bread with me to feed them every day. They always come a running when they saw me.

They were the closest things to friends I had. My so-called adopted cousin barely even talked to me. He claimed he was extra busy and couldn't leave the base when I asked him to come to see me. The couple I lived with was nice enough, but they preferred to stay to themselves. I felt more alone than I had ever felt in my whole life, and I just knew I was never gonna see my family again when the police caught up to me.

One evening after I put the baby down, I ventured out of our room. No one was home, but the baby and me when my curiosity got the best of me. I had been in every room but the couple's bedroom. The minute I opened the door, I smelled the faint smell of incense and marijuana.

I knew I shouldn't go *meddling* but couldn't seem to stop myself. On the bedside table, I saw an ashtray with several "*roaches*" in it. I thought about taking one but was afraid they might know how many they had and figure out I'd been in their room. The closet door was halfway open, and some sparkly material upfront caught my eye. I opened the door the rest of the way before walking inside the big, walk-in closet. I could only guess how many "*sparkly*" little outfits were hanging there. They were skimpy, sexy, and most were covered with fringe and sparkly looking sequins. Those bottoms, though! I'd never seen thongs in person and decided right then and there that I would never waste my money on underwear that wouldn't even cover my butt. I had never seen the lady wear these outfits and naively wondered if she wore them to bed. Running my fingers across the silky, shiny material stirred something in me that I didn't understand at all.

On the opposite wall, sitting on the floor underneath Mr. Daddy's clothes was a safe, and the door was open! Of course, I bent down and looked inside. I wish I hadn't afterward because it made me scared to think about what it meant. There were hundreds of neatly stacked, small bags filled with white powder and little chunks of white rocks. There were a couple of stacks of money sitting beside them. I didn't know much about guns, but the big ol' pistol lying just behind the pile of money looked like it could take an elephant down.

The light came on, and reality sunk in. I wasn't sure about Mrs. Mommy's filmy under clothes, but Mr. Daddy was a drug dealer! Oh boy, here is where my imagination took flight and made me hit my knees. "Dear Lord, please let me go home. I promise I will never get in trouble again."

I am forever grateful that God knows my heart. Looking back at my life, I can't tell you how many times I broke that promise. It's a wonder God loves me and forgives my faults. Laughing to myself, I wonder if that's why I'm not dead. Heaven's not ready for me yet. I mean, after all, they have Shelley… Sorry sister.

I closed everything up and left the room as I had found it. Luckily, I didn't wake anyone when I awoke from a nightmare that night. My imagination had crooks and cops busting the door to the apartment down any minute. The minute I got out of the house the next afternoon, I headed straight for the payphone at the store around the corner. I told Daddy everything. He said this one time he was glad I'd been nosy.

I waited to hear back from Daddy, but it was Mom who called the couple the next morning explaining that I was needed back home. Two days later her and my step-father picked me up at the couple's home. I was going home!

I was told very sternly by my Daddy and Momma that the police had me on their radar. If I got in any more trouble, I would not only have to answer for that crime, but they would add the 7-11 case to it as well. "No one has to worry 'bout me anymore. I am never getting in trouble again," I swore to myself!

Famous last words somehow never come true…

Chapter 13
CLARK

It would be years before I found out the truth regarding 7-11. Come to find out, the store manager was being watched for some time and was suspected of pilfering merchandise out the back door. When the investigators saw my resignation letter, they knew I was not trying to rob anyone. Not to mention the police that saw me the night before. I could not have loaded that much stuff into my little VW beetle if I'd wanted to.

My father was not about to let anyone lock up his daughter without a fight. As the story goes, my father made it known that if his fifteen-year-old daughter was charged with robbery, he was gonna sue the Southland corporation for hiring a minor. I failed the polygraph, but the examiner ignored the readings. The store manager didn't call any of my references before hiring me. Daddy said he believed she planned to set me up for her thieving from the start. In any event, I was never charged with any crime.

It seemed like so much had happened since I'd been in Delaware. Renee met this guy who was in the Army and was leaving with him for Georgia the day I got back to Daddy's. She claimed they were gonna get married.

I couldn't believe she was going to Georgia. She was just a baby. I no longer considered myself a child, but my little sister was another story. I am so proud of the woman she became; after all, she went through. Her story is another story that isn't mine to tell. Except for her involvement in mine, I'll leave that alone. When I tried to reason with her, she stood up for herself and reminded me folks used to get married at thirteen all the time back in the day. Even back to Jesus' day, she told me. She was determined to be on her own, so I guess no one could have stopped her anyway.

I was upset cause she wouldn't be around anymore. I have to admit with Renee gone it was kind of boring. Me and Dee still hung out, but it wasn't the same without Renee. I helped out at the donut shop but wasn't too interested in venturing out and getting another job.

Renee and I stayed in touch. She always went on and on about how much fun she was having. She was the big dog now… I couldn't hardly stand it that she had managed to get out on her own before me.

I can't help but laugh to myself, remembering the messes we got into. I guess it's worth remembering the hard times just so you can remember the good ones. My stories aren't just thought up and contrived. Remembering them to me are little lessons in life. If one doesn't learn from their mistakes, they'll reap what they sow. My stories, or memories of times past, keep me honest and moving forward. If I forget where I came from, I'll never get where I'm going.

Back in 1976… I reckon me, and just about every other female alive and of age was head over heels for Robert Redford back then. That blonde hair and sexy smile could melt the coldest of hearts. Renee knew of my obsession with Mr. Redford. One afternoon she couldn't wait to tell me about her husband's new best friend, Clark.

"He's a dead ringer for Robert Redford. And guess what? He can't wait to meet you!"

Another adventure in the making! You'd have thought I learned my lesson 'bout taking off, but as I said early on, I'd been bitten by wanderlust. Going out to Renee's in Georgia, which happened to be at the ocean, consumed every waking thought. I'm ashamed of how I got there, but I have no intention of sugar-coating anything.

I became so obsessed with going that I snuck in the living room late one night and took the money for the airplane flight to Georgia out of Daddy's money bag. I had a little coming and put an IOU in the bag for the rest. I called a taxi, and just like that, was headed to the airport for another flight.

No one questioned me at the airport ticket counter. Nor did I throw up on the plane. I felt like throwing up cause of what I'd done, but I couldn't help myself when I made my mind up to do something. Somehow or another, what Daddy had said was true. I could do anything I wanted if I put effort into making it happen. Problem is, not everything I wanted was good for me.

Arriving at the airport in Savanah, Georgia, a scary thought dawned on me. Renee didn't know I was coming. I called her number again and again, but never got an answer. I was also worried cause I wasn't sure if I had enough left for cab fare. The ride to Dallas-Ft. Worth International Airport had cost me three times what I thought it would. Sitting at the airport wasn't helping my situation. I got my bag and headed out to the taxi stand. I figured I'd take the taxi as far as what money I had lasted, and then walk the rest of the way.

Not long after leaving the airport, the taxi turned down a beautiful sprawling parkway. The houses that lined the streets were old Victorian-style but beautifully maintained. The landscape of the lawns made me want to get out and run barefooted. Renee had said she had a cute little apartment not far from the beach. I could see glimpses of the beach as we drove down the lane. Maybe this won't be too bad at all.

Those thoughts were soon tossed as we crossed some railroad tracks and headed for the other side of town. The farther the taxi went, the more run down the buildings and homes became. Speaking of the cab, I spoke up real quick asking how much further did we have to go, and how much the fare had increased too. I was starting to get scared when I saw two men walking down the street with their arms wrapped around each other. I'd never seen anything like that, and it scared me. Where in the world was I?

At long last, the taxi pulled up in front of a dilapidated, two-story house. Looking out the window, I almost had a heart attack. There on the front of the house was a huge white sign. Big, bright red letters spelled out one word, 'Condemned.'

I refused to get out of the taxi.

"You must be mistaken! This couldn't possibly be the right address." The poor taxi driver got out of the cab, asking my sister's name as he did. He stepped on the porch and looked at the mailboxes. Walking back and opening the cab door, he said, "I'm sorry, Miss, but your sister's name is on one of the boxes. I wouldn't worry much 'bout that sign. Lots of folks live in condemned buildings."

Standing there, watching the cab drive away, I knew I had to go inside that building.

Sure enough, there was a little paper taped on the mailbox with Renee's name on it. I noticed her writing off the bat. Pushing the screen door that was barely hanging onto its hinges, I stepped into a musky smelling hallway.

I could see several doors lining one wall. Stairs leading to the second floor lined the other. It was only mid-day, but with no light inside the entryway, it was creepy.

Walking down the narrow hallway, I noticed that not all the doors had numbers on them. I wasn't too sure I wanted to disturb anyone, but I had to find Renee. The last door was cracked, and I could hear the whir of a store-bought, fan. Peeking inside, I began screaming bloody murder.

"Renee!!!!!"

She bout near hit her head on the wall as she jumped up off the pallet, which was lying on the floor.

"Wende! Why you want to go and scare me like that?" As her surprise settled, she asked, "How'd you get here?"

"Me scare you. What in God's name have you gone and done now? This building has been condemned! Or can't you read?"

"Of course, I can read. And yes, I know it has been condemned. The landlord is giving us cheap rent until the court comes in and tears the place down. What are you doing here?"

"Ugh, excuse me. You invited me to come see your nice little apartment by the ocean and meet some guy who looks like Robert Redford. Remember? Where in the devil are we at? Why, I saw two men hugging and kissing each other, walking down the street just a few blocks away. All the buildings are run-down around here. Is this what they call a ghetto?"

"Oh Wende, stop being so dramatic. It'll be ok. My honey will be home before long, and we will take you to see the ocean."

She got up and got dressed while I looked around. There was old paint peeling from the walls and a rusty old radiator which had seen better days. And as if it couldn't get worse, Renee yelled out from the bathroom. "We have no hot water, so I hope you like cold showers."

"I could kill you, Renee. You were making out like a big dog, and all the time you were living in a dump. Now I'm stuck here too. I can't ever go back home this time. I took money from Daddy's money bag."

Here came the waterworks. Daddy would never forgive me. My conscience got the best of me, and across the street, I went to borrow Renee's neighbor's phone. Daddy was so mad he wouldn't even talk to me. I had broken his heart again. Renee's husband showed up not long before I went back to the apartment, or hole in the wall as I came to call it. Renee had filled him in on everything.

"More the merrier," he said when we met. "Besides, you need to meet my friend Clark. We'll head over to the beach. We might see him there."

We jumped in his car, and he took off like a bat out of hell. All of a sudden, he threw on his brakes, but it wasn't quick enough to avoid the Chevy turning the corner at breakneck speed.

Everything happened as if in slow motion. I flew out of my seat, hitting my head on the hump on the floorboard. Seatbelts do serve a purpose, but not back then. I heard the glass shattering before I raised myself off the floor.

Sitting up and looking out the window, I was ready to give the other driver a piece of my mind.

Getting out of the car, the driver came around like he wanted to punch Renee's husband in the jaw. Instead, they shook hands and shoulder bumped.

"What the hell? Who the hell is that Renee?"

Laughing, as though getting in a car wreck was a common occurrence, she said, "That's Clark!"

Turning back, I looked more closely at the man standing there in Army cook whites. He was blonde-headed and tanned like he lived on the beach. Just then, he turned and flashed a smile at me.

I knew right then, at that moment in time, that my life would never be the same again.

Chapter 14

Sex Skeletons.

EVERYONE HAS THEM, SOME MORE than others. You can bet anyone who says they have no skeletons hanging around probably have more than most. The problem I have is that every time I open the door, they fall out on top of each other.

It's not that I am deliberately trying to offend anyone by the telling of my stories, or how I feel about life. I'm trying my best to tell the truth as much as I can about my past. I say as much as I can because I have no desire to throw mud at others just to make myself look better. I made so many mistakes and sunk so low at times in my life that the only thing that could ever make me look better is my sweet Lord. His love tells me that he accepts me just as I am. He knows I am ever a work in progress. It doesn't matter what you think you know 'bout me cause God knows the truth.

And I sure don't care how folks feel when I mention God. Some folks don't believe he exists, and don't want to hear it, or tell me I can't publicly display manger scenes or other religious expressions on my property. News flash from a proud southern woman, I have rights too! If I'm not mistaken, America came to be, at least in part, so that folks were free to worship as they saw fit without fear of oppression.

Some would say, "How dare she mention God? Why, after all, she's done and the life she's lived, she's not good enough to utter the Lord's name!"

Here's another NEWS FLASH--- Jesus didn't hang out with perfect people much. I believe he hung out with folks a whole lot like me! Some of those horrible folks he hung out with sure turned out to be some righteous Saints if I'm not mistaken. As I carry on from here, please don't feel the need to judge me by your standards and what you think I ought to be; God knows exactly who I am. I was always taught that you oughtn't judge others 'til you've walked a mile in their shoes, or moccasins as Maw-Maw Lummus used to say.

SEX!

There, I said it. Might as well talk about it and stop skating 'round the edges. Sex has caused me more heartache and consequences than I care to admit. Yea, yea! I hear echoes and choruses of "Got what you deserved!" No doubt there's plenty of truth to that statement.

Anytime one goes against what the good book tells us, there's gonna be consequences. In that sense, I have gotten what I deserved. But let me be very clear on one thing; no one ever deserves to be raped or molested regardless of the circumstances. Regardless of who it is.

One mindless fool sits behind bars in the Texas Department of Corrections as we speak cause he didn't believe the "crazy old woman" as he called me. The first time I saw him, I had a gut-wrenching feeling. I knew, but what could I do?

"Look, dude, you don't know me from Adam, and you don't have to. All you need to know is that if you ever harm one of mine, I'm gonna nail your balls to the wall and help arrange for your new accommodations," I warned! I did reach out and try to make my uneasy feelings known to protect my loved one but was blown off as being a busy body.

Months later, within twelve hours of hearing how he ignored my warning, he was sitting in a cop car with cuffs around his wrists. He didn't even try to make bail. If not for a very understanding sheriff's officer, I'd have been in jail too. I begged for him to proceed with due haste fore I went over and killed that low-life POS/#pieceofshit! The kindly officer encouraged me never to say them words again 'lest I go to jail for Conspiracy/Terroristic Threat Charges or something such at that. He said he completely understood where I was coming from, but strongly encouraged me to allow them to do their job. Twelve hours is a very short time to have accomplished what that team of individuals did! I commend their efficiency, and for taking my complaint seriously. I'm also grateful to God that it's not me who's sitting behind prison bars…

He better be glad I didn't go with my first two ideas. It was all I could do to keep from taking my #10 iron skillet over there and beating him senseless!

That was my first thought. My second allowed that I might want back-up and needed to tell my 6'4 monster of a son. Who, in fact, had called earlier and heard the tone in my voice right after I had learned what had happened. I liked that idea cause I could sit back and watch him be torn limb from limb. My younger son was already on the way home, but I knew I'd have that *POS behind bars before he could get here.

Mr. POS's accommodations were set in stone at ten years flat, with ten years of probation to follow if he met the criteria. The second time the scum saw my face was the day of his sentencing. It was with great pleasure I had the opportunity of asking if he liked his new accommodations? Since it was only guaranteed he'd be put up for ten years all expenses paid, so to speak, I promised him that I'd be there for all future parole hearings to testify how his actions affected my loved one. His actions resulted in life-long scars to be sure, and it's not over yet. I trust God to keep his word. He is the great healer of hearts. In the meantime, I'm gonna make sure Mr. POS gets his duly deserved time. Unfortunately, he'll eventually hit the streets. You can bet this ol' gal will be hot on his heels. He must register his address for the rest of his life. I will be there every step of the way, making sure his accommodations fit his needs.

Where was I? I'm pretty sure a therapist might tell me that I got love confused with sex, lust, and desire somewhere along the way. There's no big secret there. The truth is, I love sex. I think it's the greatest pleasure God gave us to share with someone we love. Unfortunately, I didn't understand the difference between love and infatuation way back when. Sex, well, that's a whole 'nother story in itself.

I realize me and God's gonna have to talk about sex and its relevance in my life someday. Truth be known, my sex life would have been a whole lot raunchier if not for an understanding that I was gonna have to answer for myself someday. Who knows, maybe I'm wired all wrong. I suspect most folks feel the same but don't have the guts to admit it to themselves. I mean, look all around, sex is everywhere.

I mean, come on? Why do folks dress themselves up and head out to a bar? I'd seriously be interested in an exact percentage of those who would tell the truth? They wanna get laid tho' most will never admit it. It's on sale, on every corner. And I don't just mean hookers. I got a hilarious story to tell bout hookers on a street corner, but that's another story.

Sam had taught me, albeit erroneously, early on that sexual desire and love went hand in hand. By the time I actually had my first consensual intercourse, I was primed and ready. All those years of relieving Sam without being fulfilled myself had created a situation I can only equate to that of a pressure cooker waiting to blow.

When I met Clark, I was no virgin. I had a few experiences here and there but still claimed to be a virgin later that night when he started making out with me on the beach. Mind you, no one had ever made love to me, so I was a little overwhelmed the farther he went.

Savanah, Georgia August 17th, 1976

We'd all headed to the beach once they figured out the damages to their cars. A few scratches and a couple of busted headlights didn't slow those two down. I jumped in the car with Clark and off we went.

I was smitten from that first grin. I felt an immediate attraction, and somehow knew I would know this man forever. It makes me laugh to remember cause we were all just a bunch of kids trying to live in a grown-up world. I guess that could also make me cry if I flipped it around. I prefer to smile.

Renee and her man took off around six that evening, leaving me alone with Clark. Tell you what, he was indeed a dead ringer for Mr. Robert Redford. Sorry Clark, but the first time you took me all the way, in my mind, it was Mr. Redford himself assaulting my senses…

As Clark and I talked the evening away, we got to know one another. I was into horoscopes and got around to asking when his birthday was. I recall every fiber of my being going electric and standing on end as he answered.

"I don't believe you! Renee must have told you to say that!"

"What in the world are you talking about? I should know when my birthday is."

He had been born on the same exact day and same exact year as good ol' Sam. Thousands of miles apart. What were the odds that I could have done that on my own? It was a *sign*!

Do you believe in *signs*? 'Signs, signs, everywhere a sign…' I love that old song by Tesla. Wow, I went searching for the correct terminology of the *"sign"* I was speaking and was blown away. I never realized the complexity of the word sign. There's a whole study called Semiotics you ought to check out.

Pretty cool stuff. Well, if you're nerdy and into words and meanings.

The '*signs*' I'm referring to is like Annie in "*Sleepless in Seattle*," where she looks across and sees the Empire State Building with a heart on it and agrees with Walter, "*It's a sign.*"

Mind you; I haven't always interpreted "signs" correctly. I wonder if that's why I have accumulated more than my share of tickets throughout the years? Hmmm, I can just hear Daddy telling me to take care of his brand-new Ford 150 pick-up truck, metal-flake blue that sparkled in the sun. I wore the rubber off the first set of tires myself running errands for Daddy. Wonder if that's why he finally bought me a *bug*?

Chapter 15

Rats, Roaches, and Asthma

I MAY NOT HAVE BEEN a virgin when Clark and I began sleeping together, but I might as well have been for my lack of experience with intercourse. I became a quick study as Clark led the way. Those longings and yearnings, I'd felt so many times with Sam, was finally being fulfilled.

Clark rented us an apartment, upstairs from Renee, the day after we met. I thought it was crazy to pay one red cent for an apartment in a condemned building, but it wasn't my money. The third night we were there, I had a serious panic attack.

We were right in the middle of doing it when the slats broke on that old bed frame. The box springs and mattress went crashing to the floor. Suddenly, I felt something big, fat, furry, and with a long tail scurry across my naked body. I knew in an instant that it was a big, fat rat. I screamed so loud Renee came running up the rickety stairs and right into our apartment.

"Wende! Are you okay?"

"I will never be okay again. A big, fat rat just ran across my body!"

I don't remember the rest of that night or the nights that followed. A few days later, Clark gave me some money and told me to look for another place for us to live. I looked at several apartments, and finally found one that might work. The tiny apartment looked decent enough, and it was furnished. It only had three rooms, unless you counted the bathroom, then it had four. The living room was sparsely furnished with only a couch and a coffee table. The kitchen was painted a drab green color, which made it darker, even with the lights on. There was a small tabletop that was attached to the wall with two wobbly chairs to sit in. The stovetop was part of the counter, and it had an oven that was built into the wall. The musty smell that filled the room when I opened the icebox door nearly knocked me over, but I figured some Pine-Sol would take care of that. Down the tiny hallway was the bedroom. As I recall, it was the biggest room in the house. The bed was against the wall next to the window. The stained mattress had seen better days, and it looked lumpy. There was an old dresser and nightstand completing the group. I remember thinking it looked like a palace to me. I became upset when the landlord hesitated to rent to me.

"My husband is in the Army and is at work right now, but we could meet you back here when he gets off," I said in a rush.

I had seen several "dumps" already and did not want to lose my palace! Reluctantly, he took the money and handed me the keys. I was so excited. I was sixteen and had just rented my very first apartment! I found a payphone on the corner near the apartment and called Clark to give him our new address, so he could pick me up when he got off work. We had to get our meager belongings from the old place, and officially move into the new one.

I was so excited, in fact, that I went and applied for a job as a telephone operator right then and there. It wasn't for the telephone company, but a rather sizeable answering service.

The ad stated they were looking for someone with switchboard experience. I've never been one to turn down a challenge and applied even though I didn't have any experience. When I got there, the receptionist informed me they weren't taking any more applications, and that I had missed the deadline to apply.

"Are you sure because I really need a job," I asked pleadingly.

Just then, an older gentleman stepped up and told the lady to let me fill out an application. When I was finished, the lady ushered me into a larger office where that same man was sitting behind a huge desk. I felt intimidated by my surroundings as the man looked over my application. The euphoria of having rented my first apartment had worn off, and I felt like a kid with her hand caught in the cookie jar. The interviewer asked me why he should hire an inexperienced person when he had applicants that had years in the field. I was stumped for an answer when I remembered what Daddy always said.

"You should never say the first thing that comes to mind when you don't know the answer to a question. If you do, nine times out of ten, you'll sound stupid. Stop and think about it for a moment. If you can't think of nothing to say, be honest and say you don't know. Folks would much rather hear someone admit they don't know rather than pretending that they do. Always be yourself, and you can't go wrong."

I must admit, more often than not, Daddy reminded me that my mouth, and my inability to keep it shut, was my biggest problem. But thank the Lord above, when I really need to, I can reign my mouth in just enough to think about what I want to say, before I say it. Sometimes folks think I'm ignoring them when all I'm doing is trying not to sound stupid or say something I might regret later. Sitting there in front of this man who was about to dismiss me, I felt my cockiness returning. I thought about how Daddy might respond, and the light came on.

"Well, sir, I'm a fast learner. At my previous jobs, I used my father's advice and quickly advanced."

"I see. May I ask what advice your father gave you," looking up from my application, the man asked with a grin on his face.

"My father always said, 'Whenever you start a new job, look and see who's the hardest worker there. Don't stop until you're working as hard as that person is. In fact, you work harder than they do. If you always do that, you'll always have a job. If someone is gonna pay you an honest wage, then give them an honest days' work in exchange."

The crazy old man started laughing! I mean, deep belly laughs at that. I was both shocked and hurt! Especially since it took him a minute to stop. I almost got up and ran from the room.

He must have sensed what I felt because he got very serious.

"My dear girl, I apologize for my abrupt behavior. Listening to you brought back memories of my own youth. Your father is a very smart man, and I applaud his advice. I'm going to be very frank with you. I'd already decided who I was hiring for this position when you stopped by. Something about you caught my attention, and I wanted to hear what you had to say. I like your spunk, and your courage to learn something new. So, I'm going to hire you as well. I am going to have my 'hardest worker' train you. You have two weeks to convince me that I made the right choice."

"Thank you, sir. You won't regret it," I said as I got up to leave. Turning, I said smugly, "Unless I work so hard, I take your job."

"That might be kind of hard to do since I own the company," the man said, laughing once again.

Thinking back to that sunny afternoon, I remember skipping half-way back to our new apartment. I could hardly wait for Clark to get off, so I could tell him the good news!

Clark was so proud of me.

"This calls for a celebration," he said, telling me to grab my purse and come on.

We picked up some burgers and beer and headed for the beach. We sat on the beach eating, laughing, and enjoying ourselves 'til the light began to fade. On our way home, we stopped to pick up our belongings, and I told Renee about the days' events. By the time we got to our apartment, it was late. Clark suggested we take a shower together, but I wasn't so sure 'bout all that. He smiled that 'Redford' smile, and I couldn't say no. I hadn't bathed with another person since childhood, and certainly not with someone of the opposite sex. As worldly-wise, as I considered myself, I was still a naïve young woman in many ways. Whatever mistakes Clark made in our lives as time went on, I must give him credit for the gentleness he showed me as I learned to become a woman. He awakened feelings I had never known existed. Those hot summer nights in Georgia are forever burned into my memories. Lying on those damp, sheets with the window open and the breeze blowing across my naked skin still moves me as I drift back in time. I chuckle at the memories of Clark all dressed for work, leaning down to kiss me bye, and then suddenly his clothes flying off. Then afterward, his mad dash to get to Mess Hall before he missed muster, getting dressed as he ran out the door. Yes, sir, we might have got everything else all wrong, but when we touched… "*Fire*" by the Pointer Sister's says it all.

Daddy always jokingly said when me and Clark were separated, "Put 'em in the same house overnight, they'll be back together by the time the sun rises!" Built like a Greek god, and possessing a touch as I had never known, Clark had a hold on me Ajax couldn't wash off.

I was to start my job at the answering service the following Monday. With a few days to kill, I figured I could put some elbow grease into the apartment and spruce it up. Clark had given me the money to pick up a few things we needed, so off to the five and dime, I went the next morning after he went to work.

I thought I had seen a cockroach in the kitchen, so I picked up a can of

Raid along with my other purchases. Man, was it a good thing I did! I had scrubbed everything down, mopped, and swept before I started cooking that day. I was making beans, rice, and cornbread. I was gonna show off my talents in the kitchen. I turned on the oven and went to grab a quick shower while it was heating up.

When I walked into the kitchen after changing into fresh clothes, I almost lost it. Covering the walls and ceiling were cockroaches! The heat must have forced them out of hiding. That big, fat, rat was looking pretty good right about now. At least he had the decency to run off and hide after we nearly killed him that night. These boogers were staring me down with their little antennae's twitching away. I was so freaked out that it took everything I had to go in there and turn off the stove.

Quickly I grabbed the can of Raid and stepped out of the kitchen. Turning, I sprayed like a madwoman in every direction until the can was empty. Have I mentioned that I am an asthmatic? Well, respiratory problems and most aerosols do not fare well together. It wasn't long until I was hacking, coughing, and choking to death. By all rights, I should have gone straight to an emergency room, but somehow or another, I survived the afternoon.

Texas 1961

Asthma. I've had it for as long as I remember. I got double pneumonia when I was almost three and was hospitalized for two weeks. I have vague memories of sitting inside the hospital baby bed with the tent-like, plastic covering they used to envelop my bed. It was an oxygen tent. Momma said the doctors told her my lungs were scarred, and I might have asthma as a complication when I left the hospital. As I got older, I came to know all about asthma. I was never allowed to participate in strenuous activity at school cause Momma was afraid I would get an asthma attack. Dr. Shoecraft gave Momma a new letter each year, stating I was unable to participate due to health reasons.

Making late-night trips to Parkland Hospital Emergency Room was old hand for me. I could tell the nurses precisely what the doctor was gonna order: three shots of 0.25mg Epinepherine twenty minutes apart, two Bird treatments (breathing treatments) thirty minutes apart, a Chest x-ray, and if I looked dehydrated, I was to drink pint after pint of water. To this day, I cannot drink room temperature tap water without gagging and wanting to throw up. Momma would refill those big Styrofoam cups and keep me drinking until I either threw up or begged to stop drinking.

It's a wonder I didn't suffer from water intoxication and die. I learned decades later there is such a thing as dying from water intoxication. I didn't know it back then but clearly remember thanking God above the day I heard a young radio contestant had died from drinking too many water bottles at once to win a contest.

I didn't understand why Momma would sometimes tell me to breathe heavy, like when I was having an asthma attack, so me and her could sneak off for an adventure. She would tell Daddy I was sick, and she had to take me to the hospital. Most times she would take me all the way there, check me in, then a short time later tell the people at the desk I was over the attack, and that we were leaving.

Sometimes the nurse would look at Momma funny when Momma said we were leaving. Momma would look at me and claim she thought I pretended to be sick to get attention. One time I said, "But Momma, you told me to pretend I couldn't breathe so we could go on an adventure."

When we got to the car, Momma told me a story that broke my heart. She said that my Daddy was very mean to her, and sometimes she just needed to leave the house so that he would stop. She said she was terrified that Daddy was gonna hurt her sometimes. She explained that I must never say anything to anyone about this, and she said I should never correct her in front of anyone again. Besides, didn't she always take me to lots of different restaurants whenever we were out by ourselves? I thought about it and promised I would never tell anyone what she told me that night. Especially Daddy. I was hurt thinking 'bout how poor Momma must feel. At least when we went on our adventures, she would somehow meet up with good friends of hers who cheered her up, most every time it seemed. They were all men, but what did I care. They always gave me money to put in the candy machines. Sometimes we would be out so late; Momma would lay me down in the back seat on the blanket that Daddy kept in the car for emergencies, and I would fall asleep.

I got so used to hiding things from Daddy on Momma's behalf that when she said, "Whatever you do, don't tell your Daddy," I didn't question her. Momma always said how Daddy did this and that to her, and whatever she was hiding at that time was only right and fair because of Daddy's actions.

Lord knows I was used to hearing Daddy yelling and throwing things. I was afraid of Daddy at times like those myself, so I understood what Momma was talking about. I had seen the bruises where Daddy had hit her and slapped her around.

I never did tell Daddy about mine and Momma's adventures. By the time I was old enough to figure out what had actually been going on, Daddy was with Mom Nita, and it would have hurt him. I was crushed to learn that most of the things she told me about Daddy were not true. Sure, he did yell, but I only remember seeing Daddy strike her a few times. Not that Daddy was right for ever hitting Momma, but I found out that many of the bruises she showed me, and others were self-inflicted. I wanted to confront Momma, but she was already gone by the time I learned the truth. As I think back now, I guess I did confront Momma the only way I could at that time. Drugs were always my way of escape during those years. They helped me cover up how I felt about myself, my life, and my past. But that's another story to tell when I catch up to it.

Chapter 16
Reflection and leaving Georgia

I must be honest, sometimes as I share the stories of my life, I become frightened. Perhaps that's why it's taking me so long to put these stories on paper. I know just enough about the human psyche to know its complexity is limitless. I have never received psychiatric counseling for the many tragedies I've experienced. I have managed as best I could on my own, relying heavily on my faith and the twelve steps I learned when I stopped putting needles in my arm some twenty + years ago. I think I've done well all considered. Yet some of the memories I am dredging up are ones I haven't confronted since I experienced them way back when. The mind is a funny thing. It can store memory and hide it safely away for retrieval at a later time.

Traumatic experiences often force said memories to become hidden for the benefit of the one who experienced it. Many other things can trigger a memory to return. For instance, any one of our senses can induce memories. Think about it. Every time I eat a slice of watermelon, my mind immediately takes me back to family gatherings at Maw-Maw Lummus' house. Or, as I mentioned earlier, hearing an old song can take me back to the time when it was popular. Watching Rudolph takes me back to memories of how happy that time of year made Momma. Smelling fresh cut grass reminds me of Daddy mowing the yard in the summertime. Feeling the warmth of the sun on my face reminds me of lying on the beach in Galveston, wishing we could stay there forever.

As I revisit the memories of my past, deliberately calling them forth so I can put pen to paper, I feel a little overwhelmed and scared at times of what

I might remember next. It's not hard to remember events as a whole, but as I bring them out of their neat little compartments, one memory often leads to another. Some memories are painful for me to remember, let alone share with the world around me.

There have been a few times since I began writing this book where I became so depressed, I almost gave up the notion of ever finishing it. Especially since there is so much left to tell. Many times, I couldn't write for weeks or months as I dealt with the reality of specific memories.

I'm not only frightened that I won't be able to cope with a memory emotionally, but the fact that putting it on paper may somehow take away what I've accomplished thus far in my life. It's taken so long to achieve what I now have, and the thought of losing it all scares me. What if the telling of my life story destroys who I've become professionally? How will I, and those I'm responsible for, survive? These thoughts constantly plague me as I write.

Then again, I'm not sure how much longer I have to live, considering the damage I've done to my body. In any event, I refuse to let fear and shame stop me from sharing my story. I just can't. I know that when one door closes, another one opens. If my past destroys me professionally, then it will mean God has another adventure in store for me. So, I write on…

Savanah October 1976

At the end of my second week at the answering service, I was called into the boss's office. Smiling at me, he told me to have a seat.

"So, I hear you're quite talented and adept at learning new skills," he said. "For your efforts, I am giving you a twenty-five cent an hour raise. It would appear your father's advice is quite sound. Keep up the good work."

I was so proud of myself. I wanted to tell Daddy so bad but was ashamed of myself and afraid he wouldn't talk to me. I took a chance and called anyways. He listened as I bawled and begged him to forgive me. He said he forgave me, but my actions still hurt him. He said he was afraid I was gonna end up getting myself hurt or worse yet killed. I eventually got around to telling him about my new job and how I used what he had taught me.

"And guess what, Daddy? The bossman called me into his office today and gave me a twenty-five cent an hour raise for learning so fast!"

"You're really smart, Yvette, when you wanna be."

Yvette (pronounced with a long Y) was what Daddy called me most of my life, and hearing him say it made me homesick. I talked to Daddy a little while longer, and we said our goodbyes. It felt so good to hear my Daddy's voice and to know he had forgiven me. It took me a while, but I eventually paid Daddy back all the money I owed him from the money bag.

I was starting to get pretty attached to Clark, and I think the feeling was mutual. We spent a lot of time driving around, going to the beach, and visiting Renee and her husband. I can't remember having one single argument with Clark during our time in Georgia. What I do remember is being so lonely and homesick for my family. I had been gone this time for a couple of months, and every time I talked to Momma, she reminded me of all I was missing.

It finally got the best of me, and one afternoon Clark came home to find me crying my eyes out. I was crying partly because I released the squirrel I had rescued and was gonna miss him, but mostly cause I had decided I was going back home. I had talked to Momma earlier that morning and told her I wanted to come home. She was so happy that her and my step-father were on their way to come and get me.

I was okay with leaving until things were set in motion for me to do so. Once reality set in, and I knew I was gonna have to break up with Clark, I became distraught. We had shared a lot from our childhood and, in doing so, bonded. His childhood had been wrought with tragedy as well. I knew this was going to hurt him, and that was the last thing I wanted. As I suspected, it shook him up. He left the house with tears in his eyes, saying he'd be back later.

It was well after dark, and he still hadn't returned. I called Renee's husband and asked him to help me track him down. He called me back a short time later and said his friend had said Clark just left there and was on his way home. When he showed up, it was apparent he had been drinking. Clark was a mess for sure. He said there was a song he wanted me to hear. He kept trying to sing it to me but couldn't remember all the words. He just kept singing in a slurred voice, "Ooh baby, please don't go."

He made love to me later with such sweetness, I almost changed my mind and probably would have if Momma hadn't been on the way to get me. He finally fell asleep, lying close by my side. I couldn't sleep at all, wondering if I had made yet another mistake in my life. Right before I gave up on hearing the radio station play the song he'd been trying to sing to me, it came on.

"This song goes out to Wende from Clark, it's Chicago's '*If You Leave Me Now*,'" announced the radio disc jockey.

I felt so guilty knowing how much I had hurt him and hearing that he'd dedicated this song to me. Listening to the words of the song was my undoing. I cried myself to sleep.

Chapter 17
Sam, Special Deliveries, and Violence

FAR FROM HOME. SEEMS LIKE I've spent half my life far from home. I'm far from home right now and miss it so bad it's causing me to ache inside. I have so much on my plate that the pressure is about to be my undoing. I feel trapped by the obligations I have, but that's probably a good thing, or else I'd be on the go again. Over the years, I have learned to stop and think my irrational thoughts through to the end. In doing so, I have managed to save myself from creating even more drama to deal with. I have taught myself, to the best of my ability, to deal with the issues in my life. Looking back, I realize what a mess I made of it. But I refuse to quit now for someday I will find the answers I seek. Back to my story…

Momma arrived the next day to pick me up. I remember looking out the back window at Clark as he slowly faded out of sight. Momma did her best to cheer me up, but her attempts failed, and I cried all the way home.

I tried to go on with my life and forget I'd ever met Clark. I moped around for days. Then out of the blue, I got a letter from overseas. Sam! He said he'd been thinking about me and wondered how life was treating me. He'd also sent pictures. He said next time he was home; he'd give me a shout.

Wow! It suddenly dawned on me that I hadn't even had a single thought about Sam since the day I laid eyes on Clark. Wow!

My heart was in turmoil. How could thoughts of Sam make my heart flutter so when I was so heart-broken over Clark? Maybe I wasn't really in love with Clark after all. Sam missed me and said he had been thinking about me. He said he wanted to see me. I sat down and wrote Sam a long letter that very moment. Of course, I missed him and couldn't wait to see him. As soon as I finished the letter, I hurried to the mailbox and dropped my perfume-soaked letter inside.

I calculated how many days it took for Sam's letter to get to me, and decided it would take that many days for my letter to reach Sam. I counted the days as they went by, marking them off on the calendar with a red crayon. I had asked Sam to call me the moment he got my letter. I think Momma was happy to see me in such good spirits and was careful to never mention Clark's name around me. I was waiting patiently by the phone the very evening I had calculated that Sam would get my letter. When the phone rang, I jumped to pick it up. It was him!!!

"What letter," Sam asked.

"The one I sent you after I got yours," I laughed into the phone.

"Oh yea, what did you tell me?" He was acting like he didn't know.

"Silly, you know, or else you wouldn't be calling me. By the way, it doesn't sound like you're calling from overseas. There's no static on the line."

"There isn't? Hmm, probably because I'm not calling from overseas," Sam said as if revealing some hidden secret. "I'm in Ft. Worth about to leave to come and see you!"

It's a wonder I didn't bust his eardrums with my loud shriek. Momma came running from the living room, thinking something had happened to find me doing the happy dance. She picked up the phone and said, "Have you forgotten something?" In my excitement, I had dropped the phone to the floor.

I flew past Momma, saying, "I don't have time to waste. Sam is on the way from Fort Worth, and I want to look my best!"

"Go All the Way" by the Raspberries came on the radio as I started getting ready. It was a sign!

I took great care with my hair and make-up. I wanted Sam to see that I was a woman now. I wanted him to desire me the way I had desired him for so very long. I had just finished curling my bangs when I heard a knock at the door. I grabbed my purse and nearly knocked Sam over as I ran up to him. He looked a little embarrassedly at Momma and said, "I promise, I'm not kidnapping her. Good to see you again," Sam said over his shoulder. Always the gentleman, Sam opened the car door and waited for me to climb inside.

"But you gotta kiss me first," I pouted, puckering up my lips. Funny, it felt as if I was kissing my brother.

I climbed inside, and off we went. Sam asked if there was a park nearby and how to get there. I said sure and directed him to the Rec center near Momma's home. I wasn't sure what he was up to, but I didn't care as long as I could sit and take in the sight of him in. He had changed somehow too. It had been months since I had seen him last.

We sat on the swings for a while talking about our lives, and what had been going on since we'd seen each other last. We talked about his training and where he'd go next. He was so sure of himself and seemed to have his life all mapped out. I was so proud of his ambition and knew someday he would become an important, powerful man. In my heart of hearts, I kept waiting to hear where I'd fit into his scheme. He had written, and said he'd missed and wanted to see me. He'd only arrived back home this morning and drove over fifty miles just to see me. Surely that meant something.

Sam took my hand and led me back to the car, tired of swinging. I thought he was going to take me out to eat, or maybe to see a movie. He'd only taken me to a movie once that I recalled, and that was the night we got in a wreck, and his parents picked us up at the hospital.

We got inside his car, but instead of leaving, he just sat there.

"Well, don't you wanna see him," he blurted out in a rush. It took me a minute to catch on, but God only knows why. Sam began unzipping his pants, pulling his cock out and stroking it.

"But I thought you'd finally want to make love to me since I'm no longer a little girl," I said in a whisper.

"You're sixteen years old, and your Daddy could have me jailed if he wanted to," Sam retorted.

"Well, he didn't put Clark in jail, and I lived with him for two months."

"Probably cause he's in Georgia. Look, when I make love to you someday, I want it to be special. But right now, I only have a couple of days before I ship back out. I had to see you. See what being around you does to me?" He shook his hard cock at me to prove it.

Hadn't he just said he had plans of making love to me someday, and he wanted it to be special? I was so happy that I wanted to prove how much he meant to me. I leaned over the gear shifter and showed him just how much. I pulled all the tricks from the bag; he'd taught me to drive him crazy. I was gonna pleasure him so deeply this time that he would never forget me! I would make sure no other woman could ever take my place! My foolish heart believed that he would take me out once I'd finished but to no avail.

"Guess I better get you back home before your Momma sends out the search dogs," Sam said as soon as his jeans were zipped up. It was as if he'd slapped me square in the face.

"I thought you were coming to take me on a real date. I thought you might at least take me out to eat, so I skipped dinner at Momma's," I said on the verge of tears.

"You should have said something before we spent so much time on the swings. My parents are expecting me back soon. They planned a party for me at the Country Club," Sam said. "You want me to run through Dairy Queen before I drop you off?"

"I'm sure Momma would let me go with you," I pleaded.

"It'd be way too late to bring you back when the party was over," Sam said, driving out of the park.

"But you could drop me off at Daddy's. I'm sure it'd be alright with him," I said.

"I'm sorry, but I just can't," Sam said apologetically.

Sitting on my bed later that night, I felt like such a fool. I felt used. Try as I might, I could no longer buy the lies I had been telling myself about Sam. I finally accepted the cold, hard truth. Sam never loved me. He used me for his satisfaction. I was crushed at the realization. He didn't even bother calling to say goodbye before he drifted out of my life once again.

The next day Renee called to tell me Clark had gone on a drinking binge, gotten in a wreck, and was about to get kicked out of the Army. "He really misses you, Wende," she said as if I was the one to blame for all that Clark had done.

My conscience got the best of me, and I soon devised a plan to get him to Texas. I wanted to help him but had no desire to go back to Georgia. I was a few days late with my period; I might be pregnant. So, I wrote him a letter saying I was pregnant. Fearing what he might do next, I went on to say if he didn't come, I would kill myself.

I mailed the letter and waited for his response. I knew I shouldn't have lied about something so serious but felt desperate to help him. Little did I know, I was in fact, causing him more problems. After a week or so, I gave up on hearing from Clark and decided to go stay at Daddy's for a while.

I loved working at the shop and hanging out. I went to work with Daddy the next Saturday night and let Mom Nita sleep in. The next morning, she came and took me home before returning to the shop to help with Sunday morning business. I was about to fall asleep when Momma called and said I had gotten a Special Delivery package from Clark at her house.

"Oh, Momma, please bring it over to me," I begged. My *'bug'* was on the fritz, and Daddy was supposed to work on it when he came home from the shop that afternoon.

"I guess I can, but I gotta get up and get dressed. It might be a couple or three hours before I get there," Momma said.

"I wonder who delivers mail on Sunday," I thought, drifting off to sleep?

I woke to banging on the door. "Come in," I yelled, forgetting about my Special Delivery package until my bedroom door opened, and *IT* walked in. I almost fell out of bed when I looked up to see Clark standing there with a card in his hand.

I immediately felt guilty for lying and figured it was best to tell him the truth right then and there. I had gotten my period a couple of days after I wrote the letter but didn't bother sending him a message telling him so. He was a little upset but so happy to see me that he just blew it off.

He had gone AWOL, absent without leave, and was going to be in big trouble. His military career would be ruined if he didn't return. I was too young to understand the seriousness of the situation and only knew how happy I was to see him. Once Daddy and Clark got my *'bug'* running, me and Clark left Ft. Worth and went back to Momma's.

Momma sat us down as soon as we walked in the door and informed us that we would be sleeping in separate beds under her roof. I had younger stepsiblings there, and Momma said it wouldn't be proper for us to sleep together.

"But we've already lived together in Georgia," I exclaimed.

"I mean it! Unless you're married, you will sleep in separate beds. Is that understood?" Momma said sternly.

Clark and I walked outside to talk. I apologized profusely about the mess I had gotten him into. I never expected what he said next.

"So, it looks like we're getting married, huh?" Clark said with a grin across his face.

I couldn't help myself; I started crying my eyes out.

Clark frowned as he looked at me and said, "Hey, that was supposed to make you happy."

Momma pretended like she didn't know what would happen and acted surprised when we told her we were getting married and staying in Texas. It was too late to go to the 'Justice of the Peace' that day, but we made plans to go the next morning. Momma wasn't having none of my arguments, so we slept in separate beds that night.

My stepdad put Clark to work with him the day after we got married, and at the end of the week, him and Momma helped us rent an apartment. Momma took me to a discount store and bought several items I needed for the apartment to add to the things she had gathered from her house. Maw-Maw Lummus gave me two iron skillets as my wedding gift from her. She said, 'You need to fatten that boy up, he's too skinny!"

Those cherished iron skillets are under my cabinet to this day, and I wouldn't take no amount of money for them. Nor would I part with the antique Singer sewing machine that belonged to Maw-Maw Cruse. Someday they'll be passed down to my own granddaughters.

We soon settled into a routine. Clark worked, and I kept house. His dinner was waiting on him each evening, and his clothes laid out in the bathroom for his shower. I pretty much waited on him, hand and foot. As happens in most relationships, the new wore off. Sadly, it only took three months.

I was reading a book in bed one night when Clark decided he wanted the light off. As soon as he turned it off, I jumped up and turned it back on. Like a madman, he jumped up in bed and busted the light out with his fist. The look on his face terrified me. I got up and started getting dressed, telling him I was going to Momma's. He flew out of bed, slapping me across the face and yelling, "Get your fucking ass back in bed now! You're not going anywhere."

Chapter 18
Abilene and Methamphetamine

I AM LEARNING SO MUCH about myself as I go back and recall memories from my past. It's very therapeutic. Granted, not all my memories are happy ones. Sometimes I wish I could go back and keep myself from making the choices that caused so much heartache, but if I did, I wouldn't be the person I am today. Who knows, maybe I'd be worse off. I wouldn't take a gazillion dollars for the grandchildren I have, and I can see where it was the choices, I made that brought them to this earth. Funny how every decision we make, big and small, affects the world around us, like ripples across the water.

January 1977

The next morning as soon as Clark left for work, I packed up my '*bug*' and went straight to Daddy's. No way would he let Clark hurt me again. Imagine my surprise when Daddy said, "You can stay here, but I don't want to hear about what he did unless you're gonna stay away from him for good. I am not getting in the middle of your fights only to see you run back to him."

Clark didn't bother calling, and that was fine with me.

I went to work for Daddy and tried my best to forget about Clark. I started hanging out with a girl who was working at the shop. One day she told Daddy she was heading out to Abilene, where her new boyfriend was stationed in the Air Force. She asked me if I wanted to go with her. I thought about it and figured what the hell.

"Sure, I'll go with you," I said, looking forward to a new adventure.

We packed up the '*bug*' and headed to West Texas. We drove straight through to the Air Force base and met up with her new boyfriend. We walked into his barracks room, and I couldn't believe what I saw. There were three guys in there shooting up drugs! Candy looked at the shock on my face and said, "Oh come on, Wende, you've done drugs before."

"Not like this," I said emphatically.

"Have you ever taken speed," one of the guys asked. Thinking 'bout Momma's wake up pills, I nodded yes.

"Well, that's what this is, but it's a better high than swallowing it," the guy said.

I didn't say anything else as I watched my friend roll her sleeve up and stick her arm out.

When they were finished with her, the guy turned to me and said, "Come on, it won't hurt you, and I promise you will like it."

They were all staring at me, waiting for me to answer. I was scared to death, but no way was I gonna let them know it. I pushed up my sleeve and held my arm out. It was my first shot speed.

I watched as he pushed the plunger into the syringe. I felt immediate warmth travel through my body, making the hairs on my arm stand on end. I sat still, for I don't know how long, watching them watching me.

"What do you think? Pretty cool, huh," Candy asked excitedly.

"I need to pee," I said when I found my voice.

After I went to the bathroom, and the initial rush wore off, it felt pretty much like it did when I took Momma's wake up pills, except way more intense.

"The guys want us to follow them to the shopping mall," Candy said, dragging me out of the barracks.

"Okay. Let's go." I was in a hurry to go do something myself though I didn't understand why.

I was surprised to see Candy shove a bra down her pants at one of the stores, but I didn't say anything. Candy looked at me and said, "You outta try it. It's fun. The guys are looking for something of value to take so they can get some more speed." Not wanting to seem like a prude, I said nothing.

Looking around as if I wanted to buy something and not attract attention, I spotted a leather wallet that someone had lost. I picked it up and looked inside. I was astonished to see that I was identical to the girl on the driver's license. I pulled Candy to the side and said, "Look what I found."

Candy looked through it, and her eyes growing wide said, "Oh my God, you look just like this girl!"

She pulled my arm, saying, "We gotta leave here right away." She motioned for the others to follow as we went to the parking lot. She showed them the wallet, and they all said, "Score!"

Candy explained that I could use the girl's license to write checks and pay for stuff at other stores, but not here because the wallet had probably been reported lost at the mall.

"Can't we just take the eighty dollars and turn the wallet in," I asked. "I don't know if I can do it, Candy. I could get in big trouble for forging that girl's signature. You know I still have the 7-11 escapade hanging over my head. Daddy swore if I got in any more trouble, I'd have to answer for it as well."

"Look, we'll just pick up a few things today, and then throw the wallet in the trash," Candy's boyfriend said.

The first place we went to was a department store where everyone agreed I should try buying a new outfit. I tried on two outfits, and some shoes to match. Walking up to the register, I could feel the sweat gathering on my forehead. I just knew I was about to go to jail. How was I ever going to pass for a twenty-something-year-old when I was only seventeen?

Just as I went to step up when my turn came, Candy shouted, "Hey (whatever that lady's name was), we'll wait on you in the car."

I don't remember the poor girl's name, but I know now that Candy did that, so the cashier wouldn't doubt that's who I was when she looked at the driver's license. I was furious with Candy for deserting me, but it worked. The cashier just smiled and rang up my purchase.

"Why'd you leave me like that," I said to Candy when I got in the car.

"No sense in both of us going to jail if you got caught. Someone would need to bail you out, right?" Candy jokingly said.

Since it worked, the next place we went to was to a sporting store.

"Do this for us, and we'll get rid of the wallet, I promise?" Candy's boyfriend asked.

They picked out what they wanted and told me to tell the cashier it was for my father. I am haunted to this day by that mistake and regret it dearly. I pray to God above that it never resulted in loss of life. Not only that, but I feel guilty for the poor girl whose money and checks I stole. If I could remember her name, I would gladly pay her back for every cent I cost her.

True to his word, Candy's boyfriend tossed the wallet as soon as we left the sporting goods store. He told Candy for us to meet them back in his room in a couple of hours. We drove around looking for a cheap motel to stay in for the night. The one we found was connected to a restaurant. As luck would have it, there was a sign on the window, "Waitress Wanted."

We rented a room and got cleaned up. Candy didn't have an ID so that she couldn't apply for a job. My license showed me being twenty years old at that time, so I was hired on the spot.

"You be the breadwinner, and I'll keep everything cleaned up," Candy told me.

We went back to the barracks around eight that night, and again, they were shooting up speed. Candy took her turn and then turned to me.

"No, I'm good. I don't want anymore," I said thanking them anyways. I still felt like I could run a marathon and was afraid of what more speed would do to me.

For three days and nights, I couldn't sleep. I went to work and back to the room every day. I stopped going with Candy because her friends were creepy to me. In fact, Candy started acting weird too. When I finally woke up after being awake for three days, Candy had taken her stuff and split. I didn't care at this point and was glad she did. I lost my job since I slept so long and missed my shift at the restaurant. I was broke with no place to go. I wasn't about to call Daddy for fear of telling on myself, so I went to a Salvation Army. Some chick I met gave me a ticket for a concert which was taking place that night. It sounded cool to me even though KISS was not exactly my kind of music at the time.

I had only seen Bobby Sherman and Elvis with Momma. Was I ever shocked to see what happens at a rock concert? My ticket was for General Admission, which was on the concert floor with no seating. Everyone seemed to be standing around in no particular order. The smell of marijuana permeated the air in a thick fog. WOW! I had never cared much for pot up to this point in my life. It made me eat too much and be paranoid. Yet, when a joint was shoved into my hands, I thought, "What the hell! When in Rome."

I don't know what kind of weed it was, but pretty soon, I was high as a kite. I don't remember much else about that night, but hearing them sing "Beth." It made me think of Clark and wonder what he was doing. I thought about calling him but decided not to. I didn't want to be around anyone violent.

I don't remember going back to the shelter that night, but I must have because I remember waking up there the next morning. Everyone was told there would be a recruiter from the U.S. Navy coming who would be giving a speech. We were all encouraged to attend the meeting. I figured it wouldn't hurt to listen since I had nothing better to do.

Chapter 19

In the Navy…

I didn't enjoy the feeling I got from shooting up methamphetamine that first time. It scared me so bad I swore I'd never do it again. Hmm, I have learned to never say never since then. As soon as I say I'll never do it again, somehow it ends up biting me in the butt. I am eternally grateful to God above; they weren't shooting up heroin that day. I would probably be dead, and you wouldn't be reading the stories of my life.

Peer pressure is real! Sure, we all have the option to "Just Say No," but in certain situations, we are all just as capable of saying yes. I had already been introduced to drugs, so making the leap from swallowing speed to injecting it was easy with a little peer pressure. Marijuana in and of itself isn't so dangerous, not to mention the fact that it has tremendous medicinal uses. What makes it dangerous is that it is a leader drug. The average kid on the street would never start off injecting speed or heroin but could be swayed to try pot. Once said kid gets used to getting high, he becomes desensitized to its bad rep. Then someone comes along in the kids' group and says, "Hey, check this out; it's awesome!"

I know from experience.

Back in Abilene…

I was fascinated by what the Naval recruiter was sharing that morning. It all sounded so exciting! Gain a career. See the world for free. Adventure's galore. Adventures, that was right up my alley. I'd already tried getting in the military but chickened out because I wasn't old enough and knew they'd find out my license was fake.

I walked up and asked the recruiter, "Where do I sign?"

When he asked how old I was, I said 17.

"Would one of your parents' sign for you," the recruiter asked?

"My Daddy would for sure," I said knowingly.

"Why don't you call and ask him?"

I neglected to tell him that I was married, afraid that would stop me from joining. I called Daddy and told him Candy had split but neglected to tell him details. Daddy asked me what about Clark, and I said I could care less cause I wanted to make something of myself. That's all Daddy needed to hear. He agreed to sign the papers.

I went with the recruiter to his office to get the process started. I took the ASVAB and passed with flying colors. The recruiter had me fill out tons of paperwork but said I had to go to the MEPS building in Dallas to finish up with my physical and get Daddy to go with me and sign the papers. The recruiter gave me a voucher for gas, and out the door, I went.

Who knows, I might run across Sam in my travels. Not that I wanted to see him, I told myself, but he wasn't the only one who could travel the world and become successful.

It took me a few hours, but I finally reached Daddy's house. I went in that night and helped him knock out the donuts early so that he could go with me to Dallas. I avoided all talk about what had gone on in Abilene cause I knew if I did, I'd tell it all. I was so ashamed that I pushed it into the far reaches of my mind and never shared it until the writing of this book.

Daddy seemed to be so proud of me.

"I've always hoped you'd use the brains God gave you to better yourself. I know you can do anything you want if you try hard enough," Daddy said.

Daddy signed the paperwork and hung out with me while I waited to take my physical. Daddy seemed to be deep in thought, when he suddenly looked up and whispered, "They might not take you. You're flat-footed like me. They stopped taking flat-footed guys in my group when I went in the Army."

"That's alright, Daddy; I can squinch my feet up right before they check me," I laughed and said.

Sure enough, they did check my feet, but thanks to Daddy, I was ready for them. I finished up all the necessary documents, handing them my birth certificate, and telling them someone goofed up on my license. They told me I should clear that up, but it didn't seem necessary to my getting in the Navy.

They gave me my departure date and instructed me to be at the hotel they had for recruits the night before I was to be sworn in and leave. I had two weeks to enjoy my freedom, they said.

I was seventeen and about to embark on the adventure of a lifetime. I spent a few days with Momma before heading back to Daddy's house. I didn't see Clark. He had been arrested for going AWOL and was in jail. Momma said that he said he wouldn't cause me any grief about signing up for the Navy and wished me luck.

The day before I was to leave, I was sitting at the donut shop bullshitting with the guy who had helped me, doctor, my license when I pulled out the list of things I was allowed to carry with me.

"No brass knuckles, what is our military coming to," Ken joked.

"Oh no, I'm in trouble now," I said, jumping up.

I started pacing and said, "I can only take prescription medication with me. How am I gonna take my Primatene tablets with me? I lied when they asked if I had Asthma cause I thought it would keep me out of the Navy. I'll never make it without my medicine, what am I gonna do?"

I searched the list for ideas, for some way to sneak the medicine in.

"Kotex! It says I can bring my own feminine items if they are in the original box and sealed up. What I need is a magician," I pouted. "How can I get those tablets into a sealed box?"

I kept pacing until it came to me.

"I can pop the lid easily so that it won't tear. I can pull each pad out and gently pull the strip off, slit the pad up the middle with the razor blade, and put a few pills in each pad so they won't be bulky. I can replace the strips with a little bit of glue. When I'm done, I can use glue to reseal the box lid! It'll look like a brand-new box," I said smugly, proud of my idea.

"Hot glue would work best, but didn't you say boot camp was two months long?" Ken inquired.

"It's six weeks, so I'll just bring two boxes with me and tell them I have heavy periods. It'll work. Wanna help me do it?" I asked, rushing off to buy the stuff I needed.

When I returned, me and Ken worked on my little project all afternoon in between waiting on customers. It worked! The two boxes of Kotex looked like brand-new boxes. I got a few hours' sleep before going into work with Daddy that night. I wanted to spend as much time as I could with him before I left.

Daddy bragged to everyone who came in the shop that morning that his little girl had joined the Navy and was going off to serve her country. It meant a lot to me that I had finally made my Daddy proud. Daddy and Mom Nita took me to the MEPS building that evening. Momma and my stepdad met us there to see me off. Momma was bawling her eyes out, but Daddy just stood there as if he were ten feet tall. He was so proud.

I checked in with the staff and took my suitcase to my room before going down to the buffet for dinner. I wasn't sure what military food was gonna taste like, Daddy said it was awful, so I stuffed my gut knowing it might be the last real meal I'd eat in a while. I was so excited I barely slept that night. When the alarm went off, I was exhausted but jumped right out of bed. I had breakfast at the buffet before going to be officially sworn in. I remember feeling important as I repeated my pledge to honor and defend my country.

Then it was time to leave to go to the airport. The only Naval base that had basic training for women at that time was in Florida. This was my third time to fly, so I boarded the plane, like a seasoned flyer. I wasn't the least concerned cause this time; everyone knew what I was up to.

Ironically, *"I'm Leaving on a Jet Plane"* by Peter, Paul, and Mary was playing on my headset as the Delta jumbo jet backed out. Tears fell as I wondered about the path my life was now headed in. They were bittersweet tears, but my heart ached just the same.

"Yes, I'd love a beer," I said, pulling out my driver's license and handing it to the stewardess once the plane leveled off.

By the time we got to Orlando, and several beers later, I was smashed. I can't help but laugh as I recall that I wasn't the only one who had drank a bit much during the flight. None the less, our little group managed to stand in a straight line as we boarded the bus that would take us to the base.

It was late January 1977, long before the movie *"Private Benjamin"* came out that I arrived at basic training. To this day, I secretly believe someone used my boot camp experiences to write that movie!

As we filed through the first of many warehouse-type buildings, I became frantic. They took my suitcase and dumped it unceremoniously on a long table. Then a rather stout looking lady came up and began going through every item. One by one, she tossed item after item into a plastic bag stating they would be returned to me after basic, even my bras and underwear.

"I brought exactly what the list said I could bring, what am I supposed to wear?" I asked, confused.

"Military issues will be given out in the next building," she said as she continued looking through my things.

When she came to the boxes of Kotex, I held my breath. She opened the boxes, dumped them in front of me, then after searching the boxes, she told me to put the pads back in the box. Whew, what a close call! By the time the lady was through, all I was allowed to take with me were hygiene items.

All around me, I heard others complaining about their belongings being confiscated too. Wait 'til I told Ken that one girl actually had a pair of brass knuckles taken up. Man, I sure hoped she wouldn't be in my unit. She was over six feet tall and more buff than any man I'd ever seen. I was guessing she was a lesbian. Not that I had anything against lesbians, but she was scary looking. The next building we were filed through was where we were issued our uniforms, undies, shoes, and duffel bags.

"What do you mean we have to wear all blue all the time? You can't be serious. Can't I have white, or camouflage, or something such as that? You can't really expect me to wear these granny panties either," I argued.

"Wrong service. Move on; you're holding up the line," the burly woman behind the wire cage barked.

Farther down the line, I was fitted for my dress blues. Hmph, at least I knew I would get a white shirt to wear with it. By the time they were through loading us down, my bucket was quite heavy. They lined us all up in front of the last building and started calling out our names and directing us to the processing unit where we would spend the next few days. Finally, the day came where we were sectioned off into our separate companies.

"Seaman Recruit Beaird, 2nd Company," shouted the short, loud-mouth Company Commander, also known as CC.

Here we go, I thought to myself, moving toward the group standing behind her. Wouldn't you know it? Miss Brass Knuckles was standing there, grinning at me ear to ear. We were lined up and told to march behind the CC as we headed to our unit.

"Grab a rack, deposit your gear, and line up out front to go to chow, move it!" CC shouted at us as though we weren't standing right beside her. I assumed a rack was a bunk, so off I went.

By the time I got inside, there was only one 'rack' left, and it was on top. I set my stuff up top and headed outside. We marched, or tried to march, to chow as CC shouted what a lousy job we were doing.

"A few hours practice will whip you, greenhorns, into shape," she shouted.

The food was nothing to write home about, but at least it was edible.

Back at the unit, we were told to stow our stuff and then were allowed an hour of free time to smoke, shower, etc. I decided what I needed was a hot shower. Oh, my God! There were no shower curtains to be seen, no private stalls. I had never seen a room full of naked women showering in my life. I turned around and headed back to my rack as fast as my feet could take me. What had I gotten myself into?

Sitting on a rack across the way, staring at me and laughing her ass off, was none other than Miss Brass Knuckles. When she caught me looking over at her, she got up and came over to stand beside my rack. She was so tall her head was well over my rack. Leaning her arms against it, she leaned in and said, "Looks like we got us a shy little girl, don't worry honey, I will go in with you and protect you."

What I wanted right that minute was to go home! The last thing I wanted to do was insult Miss Brass Knuckles, so I just shrugged and said, "I appreciate it, but I'll just wait till the rush slows down."

"Well, if you change your mind, I'll be right over there," she smiled over her shoulder as she walked away.

I finally met my rack mate when she came out of the shower. She had the brightest red, almost orange hair I'd ever seen. She walked up and introduced herself before she plopped down on her rack.

"Come on down. I'm too tired to stand right now. Why'd you run out of the shower so fast," she asked as she towel-dried her hair.

"Your hair is so gorgeous! You ever been called Red," I asked, sitting down next to her?

She rolled her eyes and said her grandparents had called her that since she was a baby.

"I'm gonna call you Red too! I ran out of there because I never saw so many naked women in my life.

"How'd you take showers in high school gym then," my new friend Red asked.

"I never went to high school. My Momma took me out of school two months into the eighth grade and told them I was moving to California to live with relatives. I got my GED a couple of years later."

"Really? You must be a Miss Smarty Pants, huh?" Red laughed.

We talked a little while longer, becoming fast friends. Finally, she said, "Come on, I'll stand guard while you take your shower," somehow understanding my dilemma.

Before bed, we were lined up down both sides of the room at attention and given a brief explanation of how the next few days would go down, and basic rules for our unit.

"Once lights go out, you're not allowed out of your racks unless you have to go to the head. Understood?" CC shouted. I didn't understand why she always shouted, but hey, if she wanted a sore throat, that was her business.

Raising my hand, I blurted out, "Can you tell me what a head is?"

She came down the line toward me so fast that I knew it wasn't gonna be good. Standing in front of me, she looked me up and down before shouting full throttle.

"You will learn the proper form of speech when you open your mouth! Your correct response should have been: 'CC, permission to speak, CC.' When you are permitted to speak, you will reply: 'CC what is a head CC.' I can tell," pausing to look at my name she continued, "Seaman Recruit Beaird that you and I will get to know each other very well before our time here together ends. By this time tomorrow, you will memorize the terminology list you were given. Is that understood," she shouted up into my face.

"Company, tell Seaman Recruit Beaird what a head is!"

In unison, the whole room shouted, "CC, the bathroom, CC!"

Chapter 20
BOOT CAMP

I can't remember what it was about, but I was dreaming, when all of a sudden, I heard a shout in my ear. I opened my eyes to see CC's face inches from mine.

"Well, good morning, sleeping beauty. Did you rest well," CC asked in a sugary sweet voice.

"I did, thank you," I responded, genuinely believing the CC was being kind.

At that point, I looked around to see everyone but me lined up and standing at attention. The sugary sweet voice turned sour in a split second, shouting so loud I could barely understand what CC was saying to me.

"Get your sorry ass off that rack, get dressed, and get in line," CC shouted.

Walking up and down the line of recruits, CC began rattling off reasons we do not oversleep. I got dressed, spread the covers over my rack, and jumped in line in record speed. I worked really hard to stay under CC's radar for the rest of the day.

"Are you trying to get kicked out and sent home before you even get started," Red asked while we were eating at the Mess Hall.

"No, I just have a hard time waking up sometimes," I laughed.

The rest of the day passed uneventful, and soon it was time for lights out. I fell asleep determined to wake up early the next morning. No such luck.

I was falling. For a second, I thought I was dreaming until I landed with a thud on the deck. Instantly my eyes flew open. I was sitting on the deck with my mattress on top of me. I cautiously lifted the mattress off of me, knowing I was about to hear shouts of anger.

"Seaman Recruit Beaird! I knew you were trouble the moment I laid eyes on you!"

CC stepped out of my face and began pacing up and down the line as I scurried to get dressed and right my rack. She stopped at my rack and began eyeballing me as I hurried to finish. The light came on in her eyes, and I knew I was not gonna like what happened next.

Turning to face the other recruits who were standing at attention, CC shouted, "Company, drop and give me twenty!" No one had to be told what she meant as the company hit the deck. "Companies work together for the good of all. If you ladies want to see what it's like to drop and give me forty, let me come in here tomorrow morning and find Seaman Recruit Beaird snoozing away on her rack!" Raising her voice to higher decibel, CC shouted, "Do I make myself clear company?"

"CC, yes, CC," came the answer back.

Turning to look back at me, CC smiled sarcastically and said, "Seems to me Seaman Recruit Beaird, that you've just made yourself a whole lot of friends."

Standing in line, I could feel everyone's eyes on me, although no one looked my way. I knew I was in for it now.

"My God Red, why didn't you wake me up," I asked at chow an hour later?

"What are you talking about? I barely got myself together," Red said between bites. "But I can tell you this, you done went and got yourself some enemies this morning. I'll do my best to make sure you're up from now on."

Staggering back from chow, Miss Brass Knuckles fell in beside us and added her two cents.

"Tell you what sugar, I'll protect you if anyone tries to give you a hard time. Don't you worry 'bout a thing."

Red and I exchanged glances that said she couldn't wait to get me alone.

Back at our racks, Red leaned over and whispered, "Looks like you got yourself an admirer," blinking her eyes across the way toward Miss Brass Knuckles.

"Yea, but who's gonna protect me from her is what I wanna know," I replied nervously?

Remembering those days at boot camp fills my heart with joy. I had an amazing experience; I will never forget. Miss Brass Knuckles ended up being a real friend. I could feel her attraction toward me, but she never once crossed the line. I had immense respect for her by the time we parted ways.

I could tell from the glares I got from the rest of the company that day, that getting tossed off my rack would be the least of my worries if I overslept again.

Although I never overslept after that day, I continued to get myself in a pickle and in the *sites* of our bulldog CC. I was her whipping girl, and every time I did something wrong, CC would use it to make the company drop and give her twenty. I had no friends in the whole company besides Red and Miss Brass Knuckles. Truth be told, if not for Miss Brass Knuckles letting everyone know I was under her wing, I probably would have gotten the shit beat out of me on more than one occasion.

Red and I became inseparable. We had each other's back in everything. She even taught me how to go in and shower with everyone without feeling intimidated. My idea for my asthma pills worked out just fine. No one except Red knew that I was taking medication every day. Smiling to myself, I thought, this might work out after all. That is until images of CC squashed them flat. No matter how hard I tried, every other day, I had the bulldog breathing down my neck.

"Why don't you give it up and go on home, princess? You know you got better things to do than serve your country," she often sneered.

When she wasn't mocking me, she was making everyone drop and give her twenty for some minor infraction she caught me in. Man, all this because I asked a question the wrong way and overslept two mornings in a row. Whew, I had really pissed her off. Red dubbed us Gomer Pyle and Sarge wannabes. I just laughed at Red and told her, "You better be glad I'm taking all the heat, else her fury would be directed at you sister."

All my life, I have always been the first to come down with a contagious illness if it crossed my path. Wouldn't you know it? Two weeks into boot camp, a rash of German measles began spreading across the base. You guessed it; I was the first one to break out with them. I had to sit on my rack for days. One good thing about it, the bulldog steered clear of me for a few days.

No one else in the company seemed to be breaking out during those first few days after I did. Picture day for dress blues was a few short days away, and I didn't want to get blamed for everyone having sucky pictures. By the end of the week, my rash had started to disappear to the point that a little make-up would cover up anything that was left by picture day.

I got up extra early to do my make-up the morning of picture day. I came out of the head to a low, level rumble of voices as all eyes turned on me. I stopped dead in my tracks as I looked out among the company to see a sea of rash covered recruits. Miss Brass Knuckles came to stand by me, telling everyone that they couldn't blame this on me. Somehow, I don't think anyone believed her.

Everything runs on a strict schedule for the military. There's not much wiggle room when it comes to scheduling mass events. Such as picture day. As I recall, I was one of the very few in my company whose pictures didn't show a rash on their face. It was one more strike against me in the eyes of my company.

One area I excelled at, and actually had some of the recruits asking for my help, was in the classes we were taking. I've never had a problem scholastically. I've always approached studies with a vengeance. We were into our third week of training when Red came up to me, backing me into the wall behind our bunks, smiling the most mischievous grin I ever have seen.

"What do you want now," I asked, knowing I was gonna regret whatever she was asking, but also knowing I would do it anyways.

"Jr. and I have drawn the same dumpster detail this week. We were kinda hoping you would be so kind as to stand guard for us so we could catch a little quickie tomorrow night?"

Of all the things I had expected to hear, that was most certainly not on the list. Ours was a co-ed base, and the company's paired up females with males for classes and different events. Jr. was in our brother company. Him and Red had been instantly drawn to each other in their first class together. They sought out ways all the time to spend time together.

"You're kidding, right," I asked, praying that she was. She just continued to grin. "Do you know how much trouble we could get into for that?"

The look on her face told me there wasn't a snowball's chance in hell I was gonna talk her out of it. Oh my God, here I go. Flashes of 7-11 floating in my mind.

The next evening, standing not far from the dumpsters and trying to pretend I was busy, I just knew at any minute CC would walk up. My mission was to yell out if I saw anyone coming around the building. I was about as fidgety as a cat on a hot tin roof waiting on the love birds to finish their business. I was never so glad to see them jumping out of that dumpster. Jr. gave me a wink and thumbs up as he passed, leaving Red to float across the pavement toward me.

"Quickie my foot," I said, shooting a grin at my best bud.

"I think I'm in love," was about all Red got out all the way back to our unit.

I was rewarded with some of the homemade cookies her grandma sent her a few days later, and the knowledge that she'd do the same for me any day.

The following week, Red and I were staggering back from chow and had to stop as our brother company crossed in front of us. I thought I was being slick when I threw a short wave to a recruit I had been flirting with off and on. Maybe not so slick after all, I thought as the CC stopped his unit and walked up to where Red and I were standing.

"Skylarking is not allowed recruit." Admonishing me before the company, he handed me a chit, which I was to give to my CC as soon as I got back to my unit. I don't remember if I was more embarrassed or mad when he turned to walk back to his company. Before I could stop myself, out, it came.

"Sir, she stuck her tongue out at you, Sir," barked out his RCPO.

I'd done it now; I thought as he turned and walked back to me at break-neck speed. Over his shoulder, he instructed the rat fink RCPO to take the company back to their unit. Sending Red on her way, he turned me down the lane and told me to step it up as he led me directly to the Master at Arms building.

He marched me right into the head honchos office. I think he was a Master Chief Petty Officer if memory serves me correctly. Ordering me to stand at attention, the CC began to spit out the offenses I had commented. He not only said I stuck my tongue out at him but also said I responded to him disrespectfully. I never said a word at all to the man. I couldn't have stopped myself if I'd have wanted to, putting my hands on my hips and turning, I pointed my finger at him.

"You're a damn liar," I screamed out.

Instantly, I saw my naval career flash before my eyes as the CC's face turned from white to multiple shades of red like a cartoon character about to blow his lid. Looking at the Master Chief, I snapped back to attention, wishing I was anywhere but there. The CC was so disoriented he looked as though he was gonna foam at the mouth. He literally couldn't utter intelligible words for what seemed like forever.

"I think I get the picture here, CC. Leave the recruit with me, and I'll deal with her in an appropriate manner," Master Chief told the very upset CC.

I could only imagine what was coming next. The minute the door closed behind the flustered CC that Master Chief Petty Officer went to laughing like a madman. Taken by surprise, I didn't know what to think. I must gonna be in all manners of trouble if this man was so mad he was laughing.

"I'm sorry for losing it and displaying highly inappropriate behavior in this manner. At ease recruit," Master Chief said as his laughter subsided.

"I've been waiting a very long time to see him come undone. He has been known to stretch the truth at times, so how about you tell me your version of what happened," Master Chief suggested.

I told him the truth. Well, mostly the truth.

"I was only licking my lips out of nervousness. I hadn't meant to stick my tongue out at him. Master Chief," I replied, trying desperately to save myself from getting kicked out of the Navy. "I swear to you, sir, I never even spoke one word at all to him, Master Chief."

Master Chief was quiet for a while, studying my face as if to discern whether he could believe me or not. In the end, I knew that he knew I had stuck my tongue out at the CC.

"You understand I have to discipline you in some form because CC will follow up on this, and I have to do my job, or else I will get in trouble. But I believe you didn't speak to him disrespectfully. I'm going to go easy on you and order you to a one-hour PT session tomorrow evening during your free-time period. I hope you realize, coming from attention and calling a superior a liar, is grounds for a far more severe form of punishment than I am giving you, don't you?"

"Yes, Master Chief, and I promise I won't ever do that again, sir. Thank you," I said in the most grateful tone I could muster.

Grinning once more, he asked, "Am I correct in assuming everything that occurred in this office will remain here once you leave?"

"Sir, yes, sir," I promised.

"Don't let me see you back in this office, Seaman Recruit Beaird. Dismissed." Handing me the disciplinary slip to take back to the bulldog, he motioned for me to leave with a smile on his face.

By the time I got back to my company, Red was on pins and needles waiting to hear what had happened once she was sent back to the unit. I told her everything, sparing no details. Like me, she was surprised I wasn't packing to go home. We had a few good laughs over the whole mess and decided we'd best mind ourselves when we were out and about lest we encounter this situation again.

We had just completed the end of our fourth week when I made the sad mistake of going to the head in the middle of the night. From where my rack was, I had to pass by CC's office to get to the head. I heard a noise as I passed by the office. The lights were off, so I wondered what was going on. I should've minded my business, but no, not me. Curiosity getting the best of me, I turned around and walked back to the office, pushing the door, which was slightly ajar open. Too late, I realized what I had heard. I backed away as quickly and quietly as I could. I finished my business in the head and looked away as I passed the office to get back to my rack. Just maybe, they were too busy to notice me; I thought as I drifted back to sleep.

Two days later, after a very minor incident, CC referred me to the next incoming unit. She claimed I needed retraining. I guess I could have fought it, but I didn't.

"Better watch yourself there, Red. I'm not gonna be around to run interference for you. You already have one mark against you cause we were friends," I warned in a teasing manner.

Miss Brass Knuckles gave me a few stern reminders before giving me a huge bear hug lifting me off the deck, "Behave yourself!"

When I think back to my stint in the Navy, I always think of those two ladies and wonder where they are today. I hope they've had successful lives.

I was sent to the processing unit to wait on the next incoming unit, which arrived nearly two weeks later. I was beginning to panic, knowing I was about to run out of asthma medication. I don't remember anything at all about that unit. I'm guessing because I was only with them for two weeks before running out of medicine.

We were out running the day after I ran out of medication when I had an asthma attack. I was struggling to breathe to the point that I admitted that I had asthma. I was hospitalized for two weeks and then processed out of the Navy.

Looking out the window on my flight home, I wondered, what next?

Chapter 21
Pregnancy and Terror

MOMMA PICKED ME UP AT the airport and tried to cheer me up. She said I could live with her and my stepdad for a while till I figured out what I wanted to do next. She said she'd seen Clark a few times and he always asked about me.

Clark.

I'd thought about him too. I wanted to see him, but I wasn't sure it was a good idea. If he'd hit me once, what would stop him from hitting me again? Nonetheless, several days later, he called and asked to see me.

We went out riding around in his car that night and ended up at the lake. It was a beautiful night with the moon shining so bright it lit up the sky. Clark threw a blanket across the trunk of his car so we could sit on it and stare up at the sky. He said he'd met somebody new and it was getting serious. He said we should start thinking about getting a divorce. I don't know why, but it broke my heart to hear him say that. I couldn't blame him since I was the one who left. When the tears started running down my cheeks, he reached over to wipe them away. One thing led to another, and we were kissing. It should have stopped there, but it didn't. Taking me back to Momma's house, he apologized for what had happened. He said he couldn't help himself.

I'd heard those words before.

It couldn't have been more than three weeks later that I woke up one morning sick as a dog. Momma heard me throwing up all the way at the other end of the house.

"Are you okay," Momma asked, sticking her head through the bathroom door.

"No, Momma, I'm sick to my stomach," I managed to get out between violent bursts of vomiting.

Momma came in the bathroom and gave me a cold washcloth saying she was gonna get me some Pepto-Bismol.

I was lying on my bed when Momma brought the Pepto in. As soon as it hit my stomach, a wave of nausea swept over me, sending me straight back to the toilet. I'd thrown up so violently before that there wasn't anything left but nasty bile. I sat with dry heaves for a long time before I felt safe to leave the toilet. The nausea subsided, and I went to see where Momma was. She was in the kitchen frying bacon for my stepdad. One whiff sent me flying back to the toilet with dry heaves.

Sticking her head around the bathroom door, she laughed, "You're pregnant!"

She took me to the doctor later that afternoon, and the doctor said that it was too soon to tell, but given my symptoms, he ventured to say I was pregnant. He gave me a prescription for nausea medication and told Momma to bring me back in two weeks, and they'd run tests.

The nausea medication did not work. Nothing worked. I couldn't even smoke anymore. Every time I lit a cigarette, it would send me flying to the toilet. In fact, every time I smelled a cigarette, I got sick.

I didn't think I was pregnant; I felt I had some nasty bug because I wasn't just sick in the mornings; I was sick around the clock. I could barely get anything down other than 7-up and crackers. If this was pregnancy, I wanted no part of it. Besides, it was Clark's baby, and he wanted a divorce.

Two weeks later, when Momma took me to the doctor, he confirmed Momma's suspicions. I was pregnant. I bawled for days wondering how I was gonna raise a baby by myself. I was scared to death. Momma wasn't the least bit worried. She was excited by the fact she was about to be a grandmother. My stepdad knew how to get in touch with Clark, so he called and told him he was going to be a father. Clark came and saw me and agreed we'd wait 'til after the baby was born to get divorced. He promised to help me with whatever I needed. At least I had that, I thought to myself.

For two long months, I was barely able to eat. I lost fifteen pounds during that time. Momma kept looking for things to help ease the nausea, and finally run across something that worked. Someone had told her they knew someone who sipped on pure coke syrup throughout the day. I was so sick I would've tried anything, and sure enough, it worked.

Clark stopped by to check on me one afternoon and said he needed to talk to me. He said he'd broken up with his girlfriend and wanted to know if I was willing to give it another try for the baby's sake. Putting my fear aside, I agreed.

MawMaw Cruse had remarried her first husband, who she hadn't seen in over thirty-five years, and he was living with her. His house was empty, so he said we could live there. We moved out to Pleasant Grove, and things went well for a while. I don't remember the circumstances, but it wasn't long until I was back at Momma's once again separated from Clark. It went on like this back and forth during my whole pregnancy.

I had a tough pregnancy. Once I was able to eat, I began gaining weight. I didn't have any insurance and was forced to go to the county hospital. Each month I was weighed, measured, given a bottle of prenatal vitamins, and sent on my way. I never saw a doctor or had tests ran. The fact that I gained 90 pounds didn't seem to bother anyone, so I chalked it up to being pregnant.

I was coming up on my six-month of pregnancy when once again, I was going back to Clark. I had been staying with Momma in Lancaster for a few days when me and Clark decided to meet and talk. He had continued to live at Paw-Paw Roy's house during this split. I drove out and saw him on a Saturday afternoon when I got off work. For whatever reason, I can't recall, I had to go back and work the next day before I quit. They'd been expecting me to be leaving soon anyways. Momma worked there too and was friends with the manager. That next day is one I will never forget. Time has erased the terror I felt that day, and the days and weeks that followed, but it is still a memory I keep tucked away to remember when I choose to.

It was bustling at the Waffle House that Sunday morning. Luckily there were four waitresses on the floor because me and Momma weren't gonna be there long. I got a call around eight am from Shelley telling me that Clark had a sixteen-year-old minor girl at the house with him, and that her mother was about to have him arrested for statutory rape charges if her daughter wasn't returned home immediately. When she mentioned the girl's name, I said there had to be a mistake. The girl she was talking about was one of Bubba's old girlfriends.

"No, Wende. Clark picked her up in Ft. Worth and took her home with him. I'm sorry to have to tell you this. Bubba told us you were supposed to go back home to Clark today," Shelley said.

"Tell that lady I am leaving work right this minute, and I will personally deliver her little whore home to her," I said as I began taking off my apron and making a beeline for Momma.

"I have to go, Momma," I said, shaking so hard I thought I was gonna pass out.

"Give me a second, you can't drive in this condition," Mommas said as she headed toward the manager's office.

Within fifteen minutes of receiving the call, me and Momma were on our way to Pleasant Grove. I was torn in so many directions. Hurt and angry that Clark had cheated on me, knowing I was supposed to be coming home that day, and wondering what was to become of my marriage. I was also afraid that Clark could be arrested for rape whether or not we took the girl back. I was mostly feeling sorry for my unborn child and the mess he was being born into.

Momma flew down the road like a bat out of hell, and we were soon there. I told Momma to stay in the car cause this was mine to handle. I stepped inside the screen door and saw them standing at the door leading from the kitchen into the den area. They didn't hear me step in cause my brother-in-law had his music playing so loud. This was another, frozen in my tracks moments, as I took in the scene. She was standing nearest to me with Clark's arm draped over her shoulder. Both of their hair was wet, so I knew they'd just showered together. She was wearing my clothes I wore before I got so big and fat. I was crushed! As I started walking toward them, passing my bedroom with the bed sheets all in a tangle, the girl spotted me first.

"Clark, she's gonna hurt me," she cried out.

Clark looked my way and put the girl behind him.

"She'll have to go through me first," he had the nerve to say.

"Is that so Mr. Hotshot! Just so happens her mother called and is about to have you arrested for statutory rape charges if she isn't home in the next couple of hours. I came to drag the little slut by the hair of her head if she doesn't come willingly, but if you'd rather protect her and go to jail, that's fine by me. You'll never see me or your baby again," I spit out between clenched teeth.

Faster than you could shake a stick, Clark jerked the girl from behind him and shoved her in my direction. I grabbed her by my shirt and told her unless she wanted to get her butt kicked by a big fat pregnant woman, she best get her tail to my car. Turning to Clark, I told him, "I'll be back to get my things after

I take her to Ft. Worth."

Looking back, I kinda feel sorry for the poor girl. I screamed and cussed her all the way to her mother's house. Momma didn't say a word, letting me rid myself of the pain I was feeling. I vaguely remember Momma taking the girl up to her door and speaking with her mother, but I don't remember dropping Momma off at Waffle House, or the drive back to Pleasant Grove.

The house was silent as I stepped through the screen door. Walking into our bedroom, I sat down on the bed and saw it. The empty bottle that once contained a fifth of Jack Daniel's sent shivers down my spine.

"What the hell do you think you're doing?" Clark roared, coming into the bedroom. I was so heartbroken I forgot to be scared and threw back at him, "Maybe I'll just go pull a Clark!" Thinking if I wasn't pregnant, that's just what I'd do, pull a good drunk.

Before I could blink, Clark came up and shoved me onto the bed shouting, "Not with my baby in your belly!" He straddled me, pinning my arms beneath his knees as he leaned back on my belly.

I knew what was coming then, "Clark, Clark stop! I meant I was gonna pull a drunk. Clark, please, the baby," I begged for our child and me.

He never heard a word I said, landing the first fist to my face, sending my head flying to the other side. I was half senseless after the first couple of punches. It helped numb the pain. I have no idea how many times my head flew side to side. The last thing I remember before blackness overtook me was telling Clark something was wrong with the baby.

When I came to, I was very disoriented and didn't understand why I couldn't open my eyes. Through slits, I could make out Clark's shape at the end of the bed. He was crying as he threw a piece of paper at me, saying, "I'm sorry. I'm so sorry." I was so confused. I had no memory of what had just happened.

Making my way into the bathroom, I flipped the light switch on. Looking through the slits, I saw my face about the same time I heard the loud crash in the distance. In an instant, it all came back to me. Something in the way Clark had spoken, and the loud crash I just heard, sent me to look for the paper Clark had thrown at me. I could barely make it out but understood he had left to kill himself. Then it hit me. I couldn't feel my baby moving. I sat down in my rocker in a daze. I just kept rocking and rocking and begging God to spare my baby. I forgot about my face. I forgot about Clark. All I wanted was my baby to start moving again.

Sometime later, I saw Clark come up with a tow truck driver in front of the house. He'd hit a tree going over sixty miles an hour and put the motor in the front seat of the car. He walked away without a scratch on him.

He came in, and I stopped him dead in his tracks when I said, "I don't want to talk about this right now. The baby isn't moving. I should go to the hospital, but I can't. If I did, they'd put you in jail. If they didn't, Daddy would kill you. Then he'd be in prison. So, no, I can't go to the hospital. All I can do is sit here and pray to God for a miracle. Please, just go and let me be alone. Please."

I rocked back and forth all night long. I was pleading with God to spare my baby's life.

Just as the first rays of light broke the day, I felt my baby stir. I stopped rocking and waited for the next movement. When it came, I remember crying out and thanking God for his mercy.

I told Clark I had no choice but to stay there. I wasn't ready to be near him, and to his credit, he distanced himself from me. I couldn't bear the thought of what would happen to him and Daddy if I didn't at least hide out until my face wasn't black and blue; swoll so bad I couldn't see where my eyes were supposed to be. It was pretty hard to dodge Momma. I never stepped a foot out of that house for the next two weeks. Clark brought everything we needed to the house and continued to give me the space I needed.

Day by day, my little acrobat returned to its previous somersaulting antics. Those two weeks were the most peaceful of my pregnancy. I'm glad I didn't have a clue what was coming next.

Chapter 22

High-Risk pregnancy ward

SPEAKING OF MOMMA, I MUST tell y'all I have some family members that would just as soon I leave Momma out of my book. I was accused of slandering my Momma's name.

"You just want to blame your mother for your trashy life," I was told.

There's nothing farther from the truth.

My mother grew up with a very debilitating disease. She struggled her whole short life with mental illness, not to mention one serious physical illness after another. Even as a child, I somehow understood that. I didn't understand what was wrong with her, but I knew she couldn't help herself. As wrong as some of the stuff I did with Momma was, we sure had our moments to remember. Then there were the messes she'd get herself into. Some of them were pretty hilarious and memorable, as well.

Pleasant Grove, Texas 1977

Momma often came and took me shopping during my pregnancy. I remember Momma picking me up to take me somewhere I needed to go. She picked me up around three pm, and off we went. Momma was so excited 'bout whatever she was telling me that she didn't realize she was speeding in a school zone. Red lights and sirens got her attention, though, and she pulled to the side of the road.

"Yes sir, I realize I was in a school zone now. I'm so sorry. My daughter is having pains, and I'm trying to get her to the hospital," Momma said, using her most convincing tone while looking over at me as if to say, help.

"Are you okay ma'am," the officer asked me.

"I'm not hurting right this minute," I said, looking sideways at Momma, "but I was earlier," I lied.

"Ma'am, let me check your license, and if everything's okay, I will let you go this once," the officer smiled, walking away from the car. He wasn't gone a split second before Momma burst into tears.

"What's wrong, Momma," I asked before adding, "it's okay, Momma, I'll back you up."

"I got traffic warrants out for my arrest," Momma cried as though her world was about to end.

The look on that officer's face said it all as he walked back up to the car.

"I'm sorry, Ma'am, you have warrants out for your arrest. I'm gonna have to take you to jail. Does your daughter have a license? If so, you can release the car to her, and it will at least save a tow bill?"

Momma had come to her senses and had told me how to help get her out of jail.

"Yes sir, here it is," Momma said as she handed the officer my driver's license.

When he started walking off with my license, it was my turn to cry.

"I thought he was just gonna look at them; you never said he would run a check on mine too," I bawled out.

I remember the look on Momma's face when she realized that we were going to jail together. She started laughing so hard she had tears streaming down her face. I remember the ride to the police station. I was near hysterical cause I'd never been to jail before, let alone being pregnant at the same time. Momma was trying to cut up and get me to see the humor in all of it, but I wasn't having none of it. The poor officer was beside himself, trying to calm me down too, but I never did.

Momma called her boss, and he picked her up hours before Daddy came and bailed me out. Momma made friends with a rough-looking woman who came and sat by me when she left. She tried her best to keep me company while I waited, but all I wanted was to get out of there and go home. For all my worldly living, going to jail the first time scared me half to death. I saw things in those short few hours, which not only frightened me but also made me sad. I was never so glad to see my Daddy when he picked me up and took me home to Clark.

Parkland Hospital November 1977

It took a good two weeks for my face to heal up. I had faint brownish/yellow half-moons beneath my eyes on the day of my six-and-a-half-month checkup. I had forgotten all about my appointment until the last minute. I promised my cousin I would watch her little boy that day and had to take him with me to my appointment. They never did much, so I figured it wouldn't be a big deal. They put me in a room and did their usual routine. I had tried to cover the faint bruising under my eyes, but an astute nurse backed me in the corner and made me explain.

I told her I had raised my head up and hit the cabinets in the kitchen by accident. I knew she didn't believe me, but I wasn't 'bout to budge. Next thing I knew, an actual doctor came in and reviewed my chart. He gave me a physical exam before ordering all kinds of tests. Before he stepped from the room, he asked who was with me to care for my little boy. I explained he was my cousin's son, and we were there by ourselves.

"You need to call and have someone pick this child up because you're being admitted to the hospital," he paused before continuing, "I believe you have toxemia."

I don't remember who came and picked up my little cousin, but they were there and gone as the doctor came in to explain the serious illness I had. He was so serious it scared me. I was barely eighteen and had never been around anyone who was pregnant. I didn't understand half of what he was explaining but got the idea me and my baby were in danger. He was furious that no one had bothered to pay attention to the weight I had gained. I later learned that everyone who had initialed the chart beside my weight gain had been dealt with swiftly. I was admitted to the high-risk pregnancy ward on the spot.

I called Momma, then Clark. I was so big I had to use two hospital gowns to cover myself and wanted my own things. I asked Clark to gather some gowns and other stuff I needed from the house, but two weeks later, he had yet to get off in time to drop them off. I finally decided to call Clark's boss one afternoon and explain why I needed Clark to get off early one day.

"What do you mean, he gets off at four pm every day," he said, "but I'll let him off extra early today."

The pregnancy ward had six beds to each room and left no room for privacy. By nine pm, I was crying my heart out. Clark wasn't coming. Knowing him, he'd jump on me for calling his boss. It was apparent he'd been lying to me all along. At least my bed was next to the window, and I had a beautiful view of downtown Dallas I thought as the tears subsided. I was so frustrated I hadn't been able to eat dinner that evening and attributed the weakness I was feeling to that fact. I was close to falling asleep when I heard him.

"That's my g- damn wife back there, and you can't stop me from going in there if I want to," slurred my drunken husband.

Storming into the ward, he spotted me by the window and ran towards me. He threw the paper bag of stuff in my face before he said, "If you ever call my job again, I'll teach you a lesson you won't soon forget. Now, if you don't mind, me and Bubba have a couple of girls at the titty bar we're supposed to pick up," Clark shouted into my face.

Two big security guards came rushing into the ward as Clark was leaving. The ward I was in was full, so a room full of people heard everything Clark had said to me. I was so humiliated and hurt. All night long, I sat and looked at the tall, illuminated buildings of downtown Dallas with tears that wouldn't stop flowing. Imagining the father of my baby out with another woman once again, devastated me. By the time morning came, I was drained. When they brought the breakfast trays in, I refused mine. The aide must have sensed something was wrong because a nurse soon came in. I had gotten out of bed and took two steps toward the restroom when I looked up, and the room began spinning. I saw the nurse coming toward me before losing consciousness. When I awoke, I was in labor and delivery hooked up to all manners of machines. There was a curtain between another lady who was in labor and me.

When I said, "Hello," she pulled the curtain back and told me what she had heard when they brought me in. She said she heard something about me having convulsions, and that they had begun inducing my labor.

"Oh no, they can't do that, I'm barely seven months pregnant," I replied frantically.

I rang for a nurse and begged her to explain what was going on.

The nurse said I had passed out and went into convulsions on my way to the toilet. The nurse explained I was receiving Mag Sulfate every four hours to stop my convulsions. She went on to explain the seriousness of the situation, which could result in me and my baby dying. They had induced labor to save our lives. Just what I needed to hear. In 1977, preemies had a hard time surviving.

Momma showed up not long after the nurse left the room. She did her best to calm me down, but all I could think about was my poor baby, who the nurse said only weighed three pounds or so by their best judgment. I could hear my baby's heart beating loudly on the machine they had me hooked up to. I begged Momma to tell them I was willing to risk my life to keep him/her inside of me until it was safe for it to be born. Momma started crying then and telling me everything was gonna be okay.

A nurse came in with a syringe telling me it was time for my next Mag Sulfate shot, and I bought passed out looking at the length of the needle she had in her hands. She explained to Momma what had happened that morning and why they had started inducing my labor. I was so upset that it all went over my head. When the nurse left, Momma sat down and started crying. I looked up and asked Momma why she was crying; I was the one in a mess.

"You're fixing to be a mother. Your life will never be the same again," Momma said between tears. Those words would haunt me over the years, and it would be a long time before I understood what Momma had meant.

Over the next few hours, the doctor increased the medicine to induce my labor, but to no avail. Six hours in, a nurse came in and prepped me for delivery. A doctor came in just as she was finishing up and broke my water. They said it would help speed up the process. I was so scared but unable to stop what they were doing to me and my baby. I just wanted to stop everything and go home.

When I asked Momma if someone had talked to Clark, she said they couldn't find him. Daddy showed up, but he was so overcome with emotion, he could only stay in the room with me for a few minutes at a time. He promised me he was not leaving and would be right out in the waiting room if I needed him. Several hours passed with no labor pains felt. The nurses came in periodically to check on me and give me this or that medication. Daddy came in now and then, but never stayed long. Momma had stepped out to smoke when all hell broke loose with the lady in the bed next to me.

People were flying in the room by the dozens it seemed. They whisked her out of the room before I could understand what was going on. Not long after, two aides came in to clean everything up on her side of the curtain. They were talking amongst themselves, but I heard everything they were saying. Whoever had been monitoring her dropped the ball.

"I heard the doctor tell her husband they had lost the baby, and if they didn't hurry, they might lose her too," I heard one aide say.

That did it! As soon as they left the room, I began disconnecting myself from all the machinery. I wasn't about to let them kill my baby. I had just removed my I.V. and was about to stand up when Momma stepped in the door.

"What in God's name are you doing," Momma screamed at me.

"They let that ladies baby die, Momma," I said, pointing at the empty gurney next to me, "I'm not gonna let them kill my baby. I'm going home. I'll come back when my baby is stronger," I cried as Momma yelled for a nurse and kept me from getting out of bed.

The head labor and delivery nurse came in and hooked me back up to all those machines, and reinserted an I.V. She was tough as nails and made sure I understood the seriousness of my situation. She told me if I didn't get a hold of myself, I was gonna kill my baby myself. I could see Momma over her shoulder. The look on her face seemed to plead with me to listen to what I was being told.

It took everything I possessed, but I calmed down and decided I was going to start being a good Momma right then and do as I was told for my baby's sake.

Chapter 23
Welcome to the world Scuter!

A SHORT TIME LATER, I felt my first labor pain. Not knowing what was coming, I laughed and told Momma that wasn't so bad. Bless her heart; Momma started crying again. She wouldn't tell me why she had started crying, but soon stopped and started talking 'bout other things.

Ten hours into labor, Clark showed up drunker than a skunk, demanding to see me. Luckily Daddy was there and told him to get himself sobered up first. Clark wasn't about to buck Daddy, so he left saying he'd be back later. It's a good thing Daddy didn't know what had happened the night before cause they'd have both went to jail.

By this time, I was having hard labor pains every two minutes, but I wasn't dilating. They couldn't give me anything for pain because of my condition. I was on my own. My God, I thought I was gonna die from the pain that racked my body. I barely had time to catch my breath before another pain hit me.

Clark came in here and there to see me, but I wanted my Momma by my side. Only one person could come in at a time, and I begged Momma not to leave.

The pains started coming every minute, eighteen hours in. I had only dilated three or four cm, and the doctors were perplexed as to why. They were giving me the maximum dose to induce labor and said it was a waiting game at this point. I begged and pleaded for them to do a C-section, but they said they couldn't cause of my condition. Minutes seemed to drag by as pain after pain racked my body. Poor Momma did her best to be brave and not cry in front of me, but I could see this was taking a toll on her as well.

Twenty-three hours in, I was moved to a different room where this short red-headed doctor lady hooked me up yet to another machine. She said it was gonna monitor the strength of my contractions. Checking to see that I was still at four cm, she turned to leave the room, telling me to let them know when I felt the urge to push. She barely reached the door when I felt an enormous pain that almost made me pass out.

"Wait, wait somethings wrong," I screamed at the top of my lungs.

"I just checked you; you need to calm down and stop swearing," she said, turning to admonish me.

"Have you ever had a baby," I lashed back.

"Well, no, but that's neither here nor there," she said smugly.

"Don't you fucking tell me how I'm supposed to behave then," I got out before I felt something happening to my body.

Clark was in there with me and stepped up to the side of the bed. I grabbed his arm, begging him to do something quickly. He'd been watching the doctors and nurse scrub up when they entered my room, so he stepped over to the sink and began scrubbing up for what seemed an eternity. Walking back over to me with his hands in the air, he began pulling the sheet down to have a look himself. If I hadn't been in so much pain, it would have been funny. Thinking back now, I smile to myself, remembering the look on his face as he got a look at what was happening. The color drained from his face as he saw our baby's head crowning between my legs. The blood-curling scream that came from me seemed to break him out of the trance he was in, and he ran for the door.

"HELP, HELP I'M HAVING A BABY IN HERE," he screamed, which brought everyone running.

They didn't have time to move me from the bed I was in or perform an episiotomy as my baby decided he wanted out of there, now. The red-headed doctor came rushing in saying she'd just checked me five minutes ago, and I was only at four cm. She shut up real quick when she saw the baby's head crowning and began assisting others in getting me moved into the sterile birthing area. She was incredulous that I went from four cm to ten cm with one hard pain.

"Push, push," everyone kept saying. I was so worn out from twenty-three hours of labor with no pain medicine that I didn't have the strength to push. My baby's head ripped my skin as he began to emerge. I don't remember the intensity of the pains I had, but I'll never forget how it felt as my skin ripped apart. I mustered every ounce of energy I had and bared down as hard as I could clenching my teeth with determination.

"Don't stop, keeping pushing, the baby is coming now," yelled the doctor.

Grabbing a pair of forceps, the doctor clamped on to my baby's head and pulled. All the pain I'd been feeling disappeared as I saw the doctor hold my baby up in the air and exclaim, "You have a son!" He looked like an alien with his head misshapen, his long thin body, and dark eyes peering out at me. I barely got a glance at him before they grabbed him and ran to the side of the room. I heard them call codes over the system, asking for neonatal respiratory specialists in my room. No one would answer me when I begged to know what was going on. They just kept telling me I had to keep pushing.

"Why do I have to push now, my baby is out," I asked confusion clouding my head.

"You have to expel the afterbirth," I heard them say but not understanding what that meant.

They whisked my baby out of the room before I even had a chance to hold him. I didn't know what was going on, and not knowing was killing me. One nurse finally stepped up and explained my baby was experiencing respiratory problems, and they'd taken him to the neonatal ICU. That didn't make me feel better, but at least I knew something.

By the time they got me cleaned up, stitched up, and in my room, I got word that my son's condition had stabilized, and he was in an incubator. They wouldn't let me go see him because I had to stay flat on my back for three days as I continued to receive the Mag Sulfate injections. I vaguely remember Momma, Daddy, and Clark coming into my room before I went to sleep.

They said I slept off and on for those three days, exhausted from my experience. On the second morning, I awoke with my gown bunched up on my chest. I reached down to smooth it out and felt something firm. What the hell?

I jumped out of bed, running around it to the mirror. Just as I jerked my gown up to see the biggest, firmest breasts I'd ever seen, a large nurse walked into my room. I screamed out, looking at my breasts, and heard the nurse scream out before everything went black.

The nurse got me back in bed and explained the fluctuation in my blood pressure hadn't stabilized, so I had to remain in bed until it did. The nurse also explained that my breasts had swollen cause my milk had come down. I didn't know. I had managed to fill out a size B-cup bra before being admitted to the hospital, but I knew it wouldn't fit me now. I would have been in hog heaven with my new large breasts if they didn't hurt so bad.

I was released from the hospital on the fourth day after giving birth. It was also the first time I got to hold my son for a brief moment. They said he had to stay under the lights because he was jaundiced and couldn't leave the hospital. Every day for the next week, I went and stayed at the hospital all day just to be near my little boy.

He weighed five lb thirteen ounces at birth but had lost down below five pounds at this point. I was unable to breastfeed due to my breasts having fever and being so hard. They let me try to feed him a bottle, but he wouldn't stay awake. They showed me how to thump him on the bottom of his feet to wake him up, but it seemed so cruel. I had to get used to it though cause he continued that for another two months before staying awake for a whole feeding. When I changed his tiny diaper, I was horrified at the thick black tar looking poop he had in his diaper. They explained that it would go away with time.

Funny story about that… After we took him home, Mom Nita kept an Instamatic camera on top of the TV, which she used every time he sneezed it seemed. Well, a couple or three weeks after he was born, I went to change his diaper. I'd already found out you had to keep that little thing covered at all times during changing if you didn't want to get sprinkled. Looking into his diaper, I saw three perfectly formed balls. I jumped up and ran around the house until I found Mom Nita and said, "Where's the camera? Look, he pooped perfect little turds. Let's take a picture!" Nita laughed till she cried at me, but she didn't take a picture.

I'll never forget the day we took him home. Clark drove while I held the baby. Seat belt laws didn't exist back then, and as we drove, I took advantage of the fact that he was wide awake and fed him a bottle. Boy, did I have a lot to learn?

Just as I stepped into our bedroom holding the baby, he began projectile vomiting like a fire hose putting out a fire. Not knowing what to do, I panicked and screamed at Clark. He was standing by the bathroom door about three feet from me as he turned around to see what was wrong. Without thinking, I tossed the baby at him. He caught him, and then very calmly reached down and clutched him by the ankles before stepping over to the sink and turning him upside down. Once he stopped vomiting, Clark handed him back to me and said he wasn't cleaning up the mess.

My poor baby! He had to suffer through being my guinea pig, so to speak. I hadn't had much experience around babies up to this point and had neglected to take the parenting classes that had been offered. My first thought was that feeding him during the car ride had made him sick. But he would go through several formula changes by the pediatrician unable to tolerate any of them. He was about six weeks old and had tried half a dozen different formulas the day me and Mom Nita left him with Daddy to run to the grocery store. Mom Nita spoiled him rotten to the core. She couldn't go anywhere without buying him a new outfit, toy, or baby gadget. Her and Daddy went out and bought a complete nursery outfit, the day after he was born early, cause I hadn't gotten around to it yet. He was the first grandchild, after all.

The minute we walked in the front door, we looked at each other, knowing something was wrong since it was dead silent. Then all of a sudden, we heard Daddy yell for us to come quick! Running into their master bathroom, Mom Nita and I both busted out laughing, which made Daddy mad, but we couldn't help ourselves. Daddy was sprawled on the floor next to the garden tub with yellow, runny looking poop all over his pants legs while holding Scuter under his arms in the tub.

"John, how long you been sitting here this way," Mom Nita asked, trying hard not to laugh again.

"Long enough," Daddy huffed, waiting to be relieved of his duties.

I bent down and took over while Mom Nita went to help Daddy. I got Scuter all cleaned up and went into the living room. It was obvious Daddy had something important to tell me the way he and Mom Nita were talking when I entered the room. Daddy wasted no time before speaking up.

"I've had about all the nonsense with this *'I'm following the pediatrician's advice'* that I'm gonna take. This is my grandson, and y'all are about to starve the little guy to death. After y'all left, I gave him a bottle of cold of sweet milk (whole milk). He didn't throw up, spit-up, or nothing of the kind. From now on, you better feed that boy sweet milk and stop tearing his stomach up with all those different formulas. It wouldn't hurt to give him a little mashed potatoes and gravy either. I raised all y'all that way, and it hasn't killed none of you yet."

"It obviously gave him diarrhea, though," I spoke up, trying to defend the choices I'd made as a young mother.

"Well, hell yeah, it was pushing out all that nasty formula," Daddy half-jokingly said, "either you trust me enough to take my advice or don't bring that baby back around me."

"Okay, Daddy," I said, realizing how seriously Daddy had taken all of this.

Sure enough, Scuter took right to the cold sweet milk, as Daddy called it, without ever throwing up again. Daddy walked around like the head rooster with his head held high for some time after that proud of proving he knew what he'd been talking 'bout. It wasn't long before he had Scuter eating all manners of mashed up food as well. By the time he was six months old, he no longer resembled that wrinkled little baby I had brought home from the hospital, but a healthy, beautiful little boy.

Chapter 24

Floodgates, Bulimia, and things you can't take back...

I DON'T KNOW WHY, BUT I have a hard time staying mad at those who've hurt me. Perhaps it's because I have made so many mistakes in my own life and realize others are just as human as I am. It hurts me to share some of my stories cause I know how it's gonna look to others, and how it will humiliate some. But this is my life, and if I only shared parts of it, the rest wouldn't make sense.

Looking back on my life with Clark, it saddens me. We were a couple of kids with battle scars from our youth trying to live in a grown-up world. I had a big mouth, and he had a pair of fists. It took a very long time, but I eventually grew past the anger I had towards him. I genuinely hold no animosity toward him anymore. We've both grown up and realize that we have two sons, and a whole bunch of grandkids together. We talk ever so often, and if the conversation begins to go south, we both end it very quickly.

We've developed a mutual respect and work hard to maintain it. When I spoke to him about sharing my life's stories, he encouraged it. In fact, when I said I was giving him an alias, he disagreed. He said if you do that, it would be a work of fiction. If you're gonna tell it, tell the whole truth, and feel free to use my name.

Momma had nicknamed Clark Jr. the day it was confirmed I was pregnant. She told me she had always dreamed of having a grandchild named Scooter. I said ok, but I spelled it S-CUTE-R after he was born because I thought he was the cutest little thing I'd ever seen. I smile to myself, thinking about how I've always told my handsome son that he was the ugliest baby I'd ever seen, but that wasn't really true. He was two months premature and wrinkly like a little old man, but to me, he was beautiful. When I see babies with really long legs, and big feet, I always tell the baby momma's that their baby is gonna be a giant. Scuter stands six ft four inches in stocking feet and is one big, handsome man today, and I couldn't be prouder of the man he's become. I'm proud of both my sons. They had a hard way to grow up, but despite that, they are good-hearted men.

December 1977

I weighed around two-hundred pounds when I came home from the hospital with Scuter. To say I felt big and fat is an understatement. At first, Clark was sympathetic to me. He even did his best to help with my swollen breast situation. He said he'd heard that breast milk was an aphrodisiac. Not that I was the least interested in sex at the time, but he sure was. Thank God the doctor had explicitly told him we couldn't have sex for at least six weeks.

Every night before we went to bed, Clark would suck a glass of breast milk from my breasts. I was glad to let him do it because they hurt so badly. As I said, I was ignorant of all this new mommy stuff and had no clue what was coming.

I often went by Maw-Maw Lummus, and Aunt Windelyen's house with the baby while Clark was working. I realized my inexperience could potentially hurt my baby and felt safer with my elders near. I remember being asked if I took the little pill they gave you at the hospital to dry up your milk to which I replied, "Hell no, I didn't! Aunt Ida said it made her breasts smaller than they were to begin with. I'd sure hate to see how I look with no breasts at all."

One morning, I stopped by, and Maw-Maw was cooking breakfast. She was about to run out of milk and sent me to Skaggs-Albertson's to pick up a gallon. It was right up the street and wouldn't take a minute to get there. I left Scuter with MawMaw, and out the door, I ran.

Skaggs-Albertson's was a multi-dimensional store, kind of like a mini Walmart's. All types of people went in there to shop. I hurried to the back of the store and grabbed a gallon of milk. At the front of the store, I chose the ten items or less line stepping up behind an older gentleman. Another man fell in line behind me. I didn't think much of it as I sat the gallon of milk on the conveyor belt.

What happened next seemed to happen in slow motion. Just as the clerk rang up the last item for the man in front of me and my milk slid forward, the flood gates opened. I looked down in absolute horror to see that my grey sweatshirt was drenched in one fell swoop. We're not talking about a little leakage here, folks. We're talking about shirt soaking, dripping onto the floor kind of a mess. I looked up from my shirt to see both men and the clerk staring at me and trying hard not to laugh. When I get embarrassed today, I can easily joke my way out of it. But back then, I did the only thing I could do; I ran out of the store, leaving Maw-Maw's milk on the conveyor belt. I felt so bad; I cried all the way back to Maw-Maw's. I had forgotten all about her milk until I went inside, and she asked about it.

"I'm sorry, Maw-Maw, but just look at what happened to me?"

"Good Lord child, is that breast milk that done soaked your shirt?"

"Yes, ma'am," I cried, explaining what had happened at the store.

"I don't understand, your milk should've dried up by now even if you hadn't taken that little pill," Maw-Maw said looking at me closely, she asked, "is that boy messing with your breasts?"

"No Maw-Maw, not like that. But he's been sucking out a glass every night, so my titties don't feel so hard." I barely finished what I was saying before Maw-Maw went to hee-hawing and laughing herself silly.

"Well, it's no wonder you haven't dried up yet," she said between her laughter, "all he's been doing is making your breasts produce more milk."

Maw-Maw explained how all that worked as she went to her linen closet and pulled out an old sheet. Cutting it into strips, she wrapped them around my chest to bind my breasts, and then gave me one of Auntie's old bras to wear on top of the binding. She wouldn't let me take Scuter when I went to pick Clark up from work, saying we could come back there and eat dinner with them. She said she wanted to have a word with Clark.

The minute Clark stepped into the house that evening, Maw-Maw had her word all right. I felt sorry for him cause that little Cajun woman could be a force to be reckoned with when she wanted to.

"If I hear tell of you going near that child's breasts 'til she dries up, I'm gonna make you wish you hadn't," Maw-Maw said as if she was gonna burn him at the stake.

It's a good thing I never told anyone that Clark had threatened to go find another woman if I didn't have sex with him one night two weeks after Scuter was born. He ripped my stitches open, sending me to the emergency room to have them repaired. The ER doctor also warned Clark to stay away from me.

The ride home from MaMaw's house that night was so quiet you could have heard a pin drop. I just knew I was gonna get a beating; fortunately for me, I did not. Although looking back now, a beating would have been kinder than what was to come.

True to his word, Clark turned his back to me every night, going to sleep with not much more than a peck on the cheek. Sometimes I didn't even get that. It hurt my feelings, but I tried hard to understand when he said it was best this way.

What I didn't understand was the way he had begun to ridicule me at dinner each evening. I would barely start eating before he would start making snorting sounds like a pig, "Oink, oink. Oink, oink." His brother would hear it and shake his head before looking at me with sympathy in his eyes. I knew what Clark was implying and sunk deeper into depression over my weight, which still hovered around the one-hundred-ninety pound mark. I'd never felt so fat and ugly in my whole life.

The weeks rocked along, and before I knew it, Easter was here. I was excited about my baby's first Easter, even though he wasn't old enough to hunt eggs. I had bought him an adorable little outfit that I couldn't wait to show him off in. Everyone got together on holidays, and I knew my baby would be the center of attention this year. I had managed to lose down to one-hundred-seventy-five lbs and planned to enjoy Easter dinner knowing Clark wouldn't dare shame me in front of everyone.

Maw-Maw Lummus had me peeling tators the minute I stepped in the door. I didn't have to worry bout tending to the baby as he started his rounds from one person to the next even before I got in the door. Most of the menfolk were outside watching Daddy work on some car of his, so Clark went off to hang out with them. Before I knew it, I had taken so many *'tester bites'* of this and that dish, that I became sick to my stomach.

Maw-Maw gave me a heaping tablespoon of baking soda and a glass of warm water. She told me to take the baking soda then drink the water down all at once. I never questioned anything Maw-Maw told me to do as I followed her directions. I no sooner got the water down before my stomach swoll up even more. I was awful glad I made it to the bathroom before I threw up so hard it hit the wall behind the toilet. I didn't stop puking until I saw remnants of my breakfast there in the toilet. I rinsed my mouth out with mouth wash and cleaned up the mess I'd made before returning to the kitchen.

"Do you feel better now," Maw-Maw asked as I came into the kitchen.

"I feel much better," I said. And even though I had just puked my guts up, I did feel better.

It wasn't long before the familiar smells had my stomach rumbling again. To my great surprise, I was ready to start taste-testing all over again. I was careful to save room for the meal ahead, but I think in the back of my mind, a plan was already starting to form.

Eating disorders had yet to be discussed in mainstream media, and the term bulimia would be a long time coming before it reached my ears. But not before I had done extreme damage to my body both physically and mentally. I would eat whatever I wanted during the day, binging to my heart's content. As soon as I was full as a tick, I would use Maw-Maw's baking soda remedy to get rid of what I had just eaten.

For some reason, the baking soda wasn't as effective as it was the first time I took it. Each time I tried it, it seemed to work less and less. I finally stopped using it. It was a whole lot easier to stick my finger down my throat and make myself sick. I had no clue what I was doing to myself, but the secret behavior soon took on a life of its own. I seemed to have trained my body because, before long, all I had to do was bend at my waist to make the food come up.

I began losing weight not long after I started my secret behavior. Clark noticed and stopped ridiculing me at the supper table, but he still wouldn't have anything to do with me physically. He made a joke one night that his red-headed girlfriend wouldn't appreciate it, but later said he was only teasing. I began wondering if he had been teasing when he started getting home later than his brother from work. They were in construction type work, and I wondered how he could work outside after dark. He claimed they put up lights, but back then, I'd never heard of any such thing.

I was becoming desperate for Clark to pay attention to me, so one night, I suggested we go to an R-rated adult movie at the local drive-in theater. His brother went with us and sat in back with Scuter. I snuggled up to Clark after the movie started and began teasing him. It didn't take long before he shoved me away, saying, "Gonna take more than a fat cow to turn me on."

I moved as far away as I could from him and sat staring at the screen for the remainder of the movie. I couldn't have told you the first thing about the movie that played that night. I thought about how hard I'd been working to lose weight. I thought how I'd done my best to get all prettied up for him that evening. Then it all began to make sense to me. He hadn't been lying when he said he had a red-headed girlfriend. What a fool I was for ever believing him. Thoughts kept swirling through my head, but no way was I gonna open my mouth. Just wait 'til we got home; I was gonna show him!

The minute we walked in our bedroom door, I headed straight for the closet. Flipping through my clothes, I was looking for my sexiest outfit. Two could play this game.

"What do you think you're doing," Clark asked, walking up to me.

"I'm looking for something sexy to put on. I'm sure I can find someone who'd be glad to have a fat cow like me," I threw in his face.

Grabbing my hair and jerking me back around, Clark slapped me so hard I flew back into the closet door. Grabbing his jacket, he headed out the door, but not before confirming my greatest fears.

"Here's a quarter," he said, tossing the coin into my face, "call someone up who gives a fuck. As for me, I'm going to see my big tittied, red-headed girlfriend. She isn't a fat cow and knows how to treat a man."

I was near hysteria as I heard him peel out of the parking lot. My head felt like it was going to explode; it had begun to hurt so bad. Bless his heart, Clark's brother came in with a cold washcloth, two aspirin, and a glass of water. He sat down beside me on the bed after I'd taken the aspirin and held me as I bawled my eyes out. He'd been such a good friend to me these past few months. He'd always helped take care of Scuter, took out the trash, ran the vacuum, and anything else I needed help with. He even managed to keep Clark from beating me a time or two when my mouth got the best of me.

This wasn't the first time he'd put his arms around me as I cried, but something was different this time. Maybe it was just my overwhelmed state, but I felt a sudden rush of desire. As I looked up into his face, I knew we were about to cross a line that couldn't be uncrossed.

Try as I might, this time I couldn't find a reason to say no.

Chapter 25

Pregnant again...

WE ALL HAVE THOSE MOMENTS in life we'd take back if we could, but God only knows how it would've turned out. Crossing the line with Clark's brother was one of those times. The easy-going friendship we'd once shared became strained after that night. We avoided each other like the plague.

Clark was so caught up with whatever he had going on that he never even noticed what was happening under his roof. He came back from his outing that night in time to get dressed for work and head back out. I tried lying to myself, but by this time, I'd convinced myself he was cheating on me. My first instinct was to pack up the baby and leave, but I was a little intimidated at the thought of being a single parent, so I stayed.

Daddy and Mom Nita had invited us to join a new bowling league that was starting up in a couple of weeks. I thought that might be good for Clark and me. It was a fall/winter league and would last for months. Clark agreed, saying it might be fun.

A couple of weeks into the league, Clark started changing. I figured he'd stopped seeing his girlfriend because he was coming home earlier and had started to pay attention to me. After months of being ignored, we finally had sex one night when he'd had a little much to drink. After that, things seemed to go back to the way they had been before the baby was born.

My monthly came late for me and had been irregular from the start. I didn't think much of it when I started having light, spotty periods that fall. It never dawned on me that I could be pregnant. I came down with bronchitis around the first of December and had to be hospitalized. As always, I responded that I had unprotected sex and possibly be pregnant when the radiologist asked. Momma had stopped by to see me and just happened to be standing there when the nurse popped in the room.

"The doctor wants you to start prenatal vitamins..." she began saying as she entered.

The Dr. Pepper I had just taken a sip of came spewing out my nose as I started choking.

"What! I'm not pregnant; I just had my period last week."

"Didn't you say you'd been spotting for a few months," Momma asked, eyeballing me for some tell-tale sign of pregnancy, and grinning like a Cheshire cat.

"How many months have you been spotting Mrs. Stewart," the nurse asked, stepping up to my bedside.

"I don't know, maybe three or four, I guess. I haven't had any other signs like morning sickness or weight gain. I think someone made a mistake."

"I'll talk to the doctor and see if we can run a blood test. It would be the most accurate way to find out," the nurse said, trying to ease my mind.

"What in the world, Momma? Scuter isn't even a year old yet!"

Momma just smiled and said, "You're not the first to have babies close together, and you won't be the last. You will figure it out as you go. In the meantime, YIPPEE, I'm gonna have another grandchild!"

I was scared, but as I waited on the results of the blood test they'd run, I thought it would be nice for Scuter to have a sibling close to him in age. He'd always have someone to play with. Not to mention I'd be finished raising my children while I was still young. Yea well, what did I know?

Sure enough, the results came back positive. I was indeed pregnant for a second time. There was a lot of confusion as to my due date because of the irregular periods I'd had, but mid-June seemed to be the best the doctors could offer me. I finally stopped having my monthly in January, and thank God I never once experienced nausea the whole pregnancy. I figured God must have had pity on me since my first time out had been so rough.

My friends on the bowling league congratulated me on my news but kept asking where I'd hidden the baby since I wasn't showing yet and was said to be somewhere around five months pregnant. I'd gotten so big with Scuter that when this little basketball shape popped out from my belly over-night, I just knew it had to be a little girl. Everyone agreed, so I took it for granted. I was having a little girl.

This had been the longest stretch Clark and I had remained together without splitting up. I was beginning to believe everything might work out for us. When I thought back to the last time he'd hit me; I almost lost my breath. I'd had sex with Clark's brother around the time they said I must have gotten pregnant. I'd had sex with Clark too, and only a couple of weeks apart. Oh my God, I hadn't thought about that night for a long time. No matter how Clark had treated me, I felt terrible for letting that happen and was ashamed of myself. I knew Clark's brother felt just as bad cause he never mentioned it either.

I tried hard not to dwell on the what if's and soon became excited about my pregnancy. That is until the day we got the news that Clark's father had died. Clark and his brother were shocked to say the least. They were so upset that I drove our 1971 Camaro all the way to Florida by myself. We dropped Scuter off in Mississippi at a relative's cause; they said he was too young to go to a funeral. We planned to pick him up on the way back home. It was a rough drive for me at seven and a half months pregnant, but I made it. My feet were swollen like tree trunks, but other than that, I felt okay by the time we arrived there.

Walking into my father-in-law's home, I felt something wasn't quite right. I thought they'd said the family was all gathered with the body, yet I could see that everyone was here at his house. Rounding the corner, I caught glimpses of a casket set up in the front room.

"What is going on here Clark," I asked, panic rising in my throat as reality set in.

"They're having a wake for my father," Clark said before answering what he knew I would ask next, "he will stay here at the house until it is time for the funeral. Don't worry, that's only two days away."

I was not a happy camper. Come to find out, Clark and I would be sleeping in the bedroom nearest where the casket was positioned. I suggested we sleep in the car, but those words died on the wind as they were spoken.

The first night I was so exhausted from the long drive that I had no problems sleeping all night long. I wasn't so lucky the night before the funeral. I woke up in the middle of the night, needing to pee. I could hear one of Clark's brothers softly crying as he sat by the casket. I looked up as I passed by, but soon wish I hadn't. Just as I looked up, I saw Mr. Stewart's spirit sit up in the casket. Everything went blurry as I screamed out and slumped to the floor. The first pain came as Clark helped me to my feet.

"It's too soon to go into labor," I cried as Clark loaded me into our car.

"We'll let the doctors figure it out," Clark said, putting the car in drive and taking off.

The doctors at the hospital explained that I was experiencing Braxton-Hicks contractions. I was in false labor, but they kept us there several hours to monitor me.

We made it back to his father's home in time to get dressed and head to the funeral. He received military honors for his time in the Air Force. It was a somber event followed by lunch back at Mr. Stewart's house. I was grateful Clark wanted to get on the road as soon as possible. It meant he wouldn't hang out and get drunk. I felt terrible for him, but I knew if he drank, it would only make him feel worse than he already did. As we were getting ready to leave, I had the sudden urge to call Momma. I can't explain how or why, but I knew something was wrong. This wasn't the first time this had happened. Momma and I seemed to have this uncanny ability to sense when something was wrong with the other one. So far, every time I got this feeling, it was right.

"Why didn't you call and tell me you were in the hospital, Momma?"

"You had enough to deal with, and in your condition, I didn't want to add to it. How is everything going there? How's Clark and his family holding up?" Momma had clearly changed the subject, but I wasn't gonna let her slide that easy.

"Why did the doctor's put you in the hospital, and I want to know the truth, Momma! I know something is up; I can feel it."

The line was quiet for so long I thought I had lost connection to Momma. When she spoke up, I could hear the fear in her voice. Momma worried all her life that she was gonna die from cancer at a young age.

"They found a mass in my colon and want to run more tests. They're talking about doing exploratory surgery as a last result."

"We're about to leave here and head back to Mississippi to pick up Scuter; then we'll be coming home. I will come to the hospital as soon as I get there. One way or the other, everything is gonna be okay. Try not to worry yourself to death, Momma."

Chapter 26
Welcome to the world Patrick!

MOMMA WAS AT PARKLAND HOSPITAL, which was the county hospital for Dallas. I'd had Scuter there and planned to have the baby I was carrying there as well. Much had changed about the place since I'd come as a small girl with Momma.

Parkland is where they brought President Kennedy after he'd been shot. For the longest time after that sad day, whenever Momma brought me into the emergency room for an asthma attack, she'd cry and relive that day over and over. I'm sure she wasn't the only one who mourned the loss of President Kennedy's tragedy, but it certainly had a lasting effect on Momma.

Thinking 'bout those ugly green walls reminds me of another time I came through them, bawling my eyes out. We were living at the Piedmont apartments in Pleasant Grove, right up the street from John B. Hoode Middle School. Like many other memories, I remember that day crystal clear. Bubba had pitched a fit saying he was sick 'til Momma let him stay home from school. I begged Momma to stay home too, but she refused.

I caught Bubba grinning from behind Momma and told on him, but Momma just shook her head and told me to get out of there before I ended up late for school. I was fuming mad and yelled at Bubba, going out the door, "I hate you! I wish you was dead!"

It still makes me shudder when I recall saying those words.

I was walking home from school when the ambulance passed. I don't know how, but I got a sick feeling and just knew it had something to do with my family. I ran all the way to our apartment, but someone stopped me in the courtyard saying Momma just went up to Bubba's friend's house cause there had been an accident. I took off running as fast as I could for the house up the street. Momma was about to climb in the ambulance as I ran up. She stopped and explained that Bubba had jumped off the roof onto the trampoline and had broken his leg. She said Daddy was on his way to the hospital cause Bubba's leg bone had gone through the skin, and it was a serious injury. She told me to go to Maw-Maw Lummus' apartment, and they would call when they knew something. I stood there watching as the ambulance sped away, sirens blaring. All that kept screaming through my head were the last words I had yelled at my little brother, "I hate you. I wish you was dead."

Maw-Maw Lummus and Aunt Windelyen didn't seem to be too worried 'til they talked to Daddy a few hours later. The damage to Bubba's leg turned out to be worse than first expected. Daddy said the surgery that was only supposed to be a couple of hours long was still going on. The surgeons had run into complications, which, when all was said and done, almost took my little brother's life.

I was having such fits that Maw-Maw finally convinced Daddy to come and get me once the surgery was over. I had spent the night begging God to please spare my brother's life and for him to forgive me for the cruel things I had said to Bubba.

"Please, dear Lord, please don't take my little brother away. I swear I didn't mean what I said to him. I promise, dear Lord, I will never, ever tell another person I wish they were dead again! Just please let my brother be okay," I begged over and over.

Daddy let me get it out of my system on the ride to the hospital; I bawled and bawled. I could hardly wait to tell Bubba how sorry I was for what I'd said. He was still in recovery, and even though minors weren't allowed in there, Momma explained the situation to the nurses who let me see him, but just for a few minutes, they said.

Momma showed me where he was and said she'd be back in just a minute. I felt even worse seeing him lying there hooked up to IV lines and such as that. He looked to be sleeping, so I whispered how sorry I was and how I hoped he'd forgive me. Just then he opened his eyes. He told me if I really meant all that to get him some water cause he was thirsty. I looked around but didn't see any water pitchers. I saw an empty cup Momma had been drinking coffee out of and told Bubba I'd be right back. I found a faucet, and after rinsing the cup out, filled it with cool water. I took it back to Bubba, who drank it straight down.

Just about the time, Momma walked back around the curtain; Bubba started throwing up. Momma looked at me somehow, knowing this was my fault. Sure enough, he wasn't supposed to have anything by mouth. How was I supposed to know I asked? The nurse came to tend to Bubba while Momma took me back out to where Daddy was.

They moved Bubba into a semi-private room not long afterward, and we all went to spend time with him. He ended up staying in the hospital a few weeks before he could come home. Momma had to get his lessons from school and help him with them every day. It was pretty hectic without Momma around cause she stayed with Bubba at the hospital around the clock. Bubba said he hadn't even heard me say those ugly things to him that morning, but it was bad enough cause I had. I have kept my word to the good Lord and never told my siblings I hated them and wished them dead ever again. Whenever I hear my grandchildren say such as that, I tell them this story and how my wish almost came true.

April 1979

I don't remember much about the drive back home. All I could do was think about Momma. I couldn't imagine life without her. I told Momma to stay positive but found it impossible to do so myself. I had this sick feeling that it wasn't gonna turn out well at all. I was mad at Momma for jinxing herself all those years, saying she was going to end up with Cancer, but I knew it wasn't true. I needed someone to blame. I didn't know back then it was the beginning stages of grief I was feeling. I remember going straight to the hospital as soon as we got back home.

I had an appointment for my seven-and-a-half-month check-up the next day so I told Clark I was spending the night at the hospital with Momma. Clark dropped me off, saying he would take Scuter to Maw-Maw Lummus on his way to work the next morning. Momma was glad to see me but was worried after I told her about my trip to the E.R. in Florida.

"I'm not going home, Momma, and that is that. I have to come up here early in the morning for my check-up anyway," I explained.

I hadn't gotten toxemia with this pregnancy, but my blood pressure was higher than they wanted it to be. My weight had been monitored this pregnancy very carefully as well. When I saw the doctor the next morning, and he learned about the false labor episode and the fact that Momma was in the hospital downstairs, he let me have it.

"Given your history, and in light of all that is happening in your life, I am admitting you to the high-risk pregnancy ward for the duration of your pregnancy," the doctor stated matter of fact.

That was just fine with me. My Momma needed me, and this would make it easier to be near her. They were still running tests and waiting on results at the end of my first week in the hospital. Clark was much more attentive this time around and brought Scuter to see me every other day. I spent most days sitting down in Momma's room watching SOAPS with her and just hanging out. They finally scheduled the exploratory surgery for May 4th, which was a couple of days away. Momma started having severe pains on May 2nd and they were keeping her sedated. I had become frustrated with crowded elevators since one of them had broken down and had been walking up and down the stairs from the seventh floor to the second floor for the past several days. I had just made it back upstairs after telling Momma goodnight when I got a severe cramp in my lower abdomen. One of the nurses came and checked me to find that I was dilated to two cms.

"I'm only eight months pregnant. It's not time for me to deliver," I told the older nurse.

"I'll see what the doctor wants to do and get back to you," she said, asking if I was still hurting.

I told her that it wasn't hurting anymore, even though it was. Maybe if I go to sleep, I will feel better, I thought to myself. I most certainly wanted no part of having my labor induced again. I tossed and turned all night. I couldn't get comfortable to save my soul. Early the next morning, I was awakened to aides and orderlies, moving all the beds to the center of the room. All the women in the ward started freaking out and asking what was going on.

"Tornado warnings have been issued for Dallas County, and we are taking precautionary measures. Our televisions were turned off, and we were told that as soon as the watch expired, they would return things to normal. The date was May 3rd, 1979. When I refused my breakfast, my vital signs were taken. When they came to wheel me out to Labor ICU a little while later, I became frantic.

"Why, " I cried fearful of what was to come, "my momma is downstairs and having exploratory surgery tomorrow, she needs me!"

"Your baby needs you, even more, to calm down and behave yourself," the charge nurse said, "your blood pressure is dangerously high, and the doctor wants to induce your labor at this time."

Phone lines were down all over, but they finally managed to get a hold of Clark and my Daddy. It was decided not to tell Momma as she was in and out of sedation. It would have only worried her more. It was determined that I could not receive pain medication due to my condition, so once again, I had the whole experience au natural.

I spent the next twenty-one hours in labor before pushing out a beautiful baby boy early the morning of May 4th, 1979. He was six lb two ozs, nineteen inches long. His lungs were a little underdeveloped, and he was jaundiced, but other than that, he was pretty healthy. He, too, had to spend a whole week in an incubator under lights, but he was wide awake whenever it was time to eat. He wasn't about to miss any meal.

As soon as they got me to my room that morning after delivery, I begged for someone to wheel me down to Momma's room. I'd found out her surgery was over, and she'd just been brought back to her room. I couldn't wait to see her and ask her nurse what they'd found out. I was sitting by Momma's bed when she opened her eyes.

"Momma, Momma, wake-up! I have something to tell you!"

"What's wrong," she said, struggling to open her eyes.

"Nothing is wrong, Momma. I just want to tell you that "Patrick George Stewart" has arrived and can't wait to meet his namesake."

Boy, that got her attention, and her eyes popped wide open.

"I thought you were having a girl?"

"So did I Momma, but I guess the good Lord had other ideas. Patrick is a good strong name and just wait 'til you see him, he's beautiful."

Then it dawned on Momma.

"Y'all named him Patrick?" Her tears came in earnest. She became so choked up; she couldn't say a word. I sat down and held Momma while she cried.

I cried with her. I had spoken with her doctor before I came in to see her. I asked to be the one to give her the news. I cried because Momma had Stage IV Colon Cancer. I cried because I was gonna lose my Momma.

F-2 tornadoes had ripped across Dallas the day before. The mobile home park in Desoto where Momma's trailer sat had been ravaged, but Momma's trailer made it out unscathed. At least there was that.

Chapter 27
Just rewards and spirits

I DON'T KNOW ABOUT OTHERS, but for me, the hardest part of writing this book has been in the details. Major events are the ones we tell about over and over throughout our lives. You know the ones, where everyone rolls their eyes because they've heard them one too many times before. Those memories sit on the periphery of our consciousness.

For all that I consciously remember, there is so much I thought I had forgotten. I know that may not make sense to many, but as I sit here pen to paper, I remember why I'm writing the stories of my life to begin with. My life won't make any sense at all to most people. And you know what, I'm okay with that. I'm not writing this book for their benefit. I'm writing it for those who do get it. For everyone who ever dreamed, whoever believed that no matter how far you fall, that mountain is still attainable.

For everyone who was told you're not good enough, or you'll never make it.

Recalling the morning I gave birth to my second son and having to tell my precious Momma she was gonna die; was one of those times I had forgotten the details until I started putting it on paper. My first thought was to can the writing for a few days and let the pain subside, but I'm at a point in my life that I'm either gonna 'get 'er done' or give it up forever.

Momma took her news pretty well. I guess she'd been expecting it all her life. It's almost as if she welcomed it. Not really, but you know what I mean? The doctor's offered her experimental measures, which she refused after her first cobalt treatment. It had detrimental effects, which made her sick. She said it burned her, although at the time I didn't understand what she meant.

For the first time in my life, Momma shut me out of hers. Many times I was not allowed to go with Momma when she went to see her doctors. She became very secretive about the cancer she had shouted she would die from someday. She led me to believe that everything was going to be okay. She said they had burned her to the point the cancer was gone. I had limited medical knowledge back then and bought it, hook, line, and sinker. I wanted to buy it; it was much easier than accepting anything else. Momma didn't burden anyone with the knowledge she was dying. She carried on as if she had forever to live. Bless her heart, the hardest walk of her life, she did on her own.

Momma got the notion that she wanted to drive cross-country in a big-rig. She went out and got her CDL's with my stepfather, and off they went. I didn't understand what had gotten into her at the time, but now as I write these words, it makes perfect sense. She was dying and had things to do and see while she could. They went to work for Tandy-Radio Shack as team drivers.

It must have been in the water cause next thing I knew; Mom Nita and Daddy went out and got their CDL's and went to work for Tandy-Radio Shack as well. How I wish I could ask them all if they planned it that way? They probably did cause they went out on cross-country runs together. The younger kids got to take trips with them. I was envious but had two little boys to take care of.

Not that I didn't have my fair share of fun with my parents growing up. Daddy was just a big ol' kid at heart and never stopped having fun with his kids for that matter. Daddy always made sure us kids got to have fun. He took us camping and out to the lake all the time. He would go to work at night and come out and nap at the lake so that we could enjoy ourselves. I remember one summer when we went to Eagle Mountain Lake in Ft. Worth to camp for a week. Me and Bubba had been playing with this pretty snake he found right before dark. A lifeguard came up to tell us the beach area had closed, and we needed to make our way back to our campsite. He stepped up closer to Bubba to have a look at the snake.

"Throw that snake away from you. Now," the lifeguard yelled at Bubba.

Bubba, being Bubba, started to argue, but something in the life guard's stance caused him to toss the snake toward the grassy area.

"We found that snake on our own, and I'm telling my Daddy what you did," Bubba exclaimed.

"Go ahead, young man. While you're at it, explain to your father, it was a baby Coral snake and very venomous," the lifeguard said smugly.

We told Daddy all about the snake, and the lifeguard, whom Daddy thanked when he saw him next. We were lectured about messing with snakes, but Daddy didn't punish us for it. He tried hard to let us have fun during our vacation time and save grounding and whippings for more serious offenses.

Forum Bowling Alley May 1979

I only missed two bowling nights the entire season. A few women from the different teams had given me a small baby shower, and they couldn't wait to see my newborn son. I was so excited that first night to show off my baby boy.

Clark went to the restroom right after his turn when one of the ladies from the team we were playing that night asked to hold Patrick. I handed him to her, and she was oohing and awing when I saw Clark storming towards us. He snatched the baby out of the startled ladies' arms and backhanded me in one sweeping motion. I was stunned. The only person he ever hit me in front of was his brother. Not only had everyone around us witnessed the scene, but looking up, I saw Daddy standing there looking as if he was about to rip Clark into. Instead, he turned on his heels and walked away.

"Bitch, don't you let another person handle my son, you got it," Clark snarled. Shaking my head yes, I walked away to the bathroom, holding back the flood of tears that were sure to come. The rest of the night was very tense, and I knew everyone was glad when the last frame was bowled. I don't remember much else about that night other than I knew Clark had crossed a line with Daddy.

It wasn't but a couple of weeks later when it happened. At this time, we lived in Arlington in a complex with several family members. Mine and Clark's apartment was directly above Daddy's. Maw-Maw Lummus and Paw-Paw Ernest's was two doors down from Daddy's. Bubba and Clark's brother were sharing an apartment a few doors down from Clark and me. I don't remember where we were all going, but everyone came out of their apartment at the same time. Mom Nita and Daddy was standing in the vestibule area at the foot of the stairs that circled around from the second floor. Carrying Patrick in the baby carrier, I had started down the stairs when I saw Clark dangling Scuter over the rail as if he was gonna drop him down to his brother. It startled Scuter, and he began to cry. For whatever reason, Clark let go of him dropping him to his brother on the first floor. I had reached the bottom step when I looked over to see Daddy pulling off his watch and knew what was coming next.

It had been a long time since I saw Daddy lose his cool. After he married Mom Nita, she helped Daddy learn to control his temper, but I saw her step back this time as if she wanted Daddy to turn loose. Clark walked down the stairs, unaware of what was fixin' to happen. He was clearly in shock when Daddy stepped up and punched him square in the face sending him flying backward when he stepped off the stairway. Giving Clark time to gather his wits, Daddy unloaded on him.

"You have the nerve to slap my daughter for letting someone hold the baby, yet you toss my grandson over a second-story railing? Come on, fight someone your own size punk," Daddy roared at Clark before landing two more solid punches to Clark's face. Clark stepped forward, and Daddy knocked him off his feet with one last blow.

"Why you're nothing more than a coward. I thought you were supposed to be such a tough guy. You won't fight someone who can defend themself." Daddy said, clearly disgusted, "Don't you ever let me catch you putting my grandchildren in danger again. I better not find out you laid a finger on Yvette for this, or I'll finish what I started." Daddy stormed off with Mom Nita right behind him. Everyone else just stood there in shock. Except for me, I was scared to death.

I handed the baby to Bubba and went to look for Clark, who had walked off in the opposite direction from Daddy. I vaguely remember tending to Clark's wounds later when we returned to our apartment, but not much more than that comes to mind.

Come to think of it; I do have one more memory from that period and apartment complex. We were on our way home from bowling when Clark spotted a car on the side of the road with its hood up. He slowed down and pulled over in front of the car when he saw a man bent over, looking at the engine. Getting out of our car, he said, "I'm gonna see if he needs a jump or something." It wasn't long before I saw Clark shutting the man's hood and leading him back to our car.

"This man is in no shape to drive. I told him he could crash on our couch, and I'd bring him back to his car on my way to work in the morning," Clark said sympathetically. The strong odor of alcohol confirmed what Clark had said as the man practically fell into our back seat. I trusted Clark's judgment on this because the man was clearly no threat to anyone but himself. Arriving back at our apartment, I grabbed some sheets from the hall closet and made up the couch for our guest. Our little teacup chihuahua, Sassy, was snarling and barking her little head off at the stranger. How odd I thought cause Sassy liked everyone. Clark settled the man in the business suit down while I put Scuter to bed.

Clark was asleep before his head hit the pillow, and I wasn't far behind him.

It was springtime and warm in Texas, so when I awoke from a dead sleep to an almost wintry cold chill, it frightened me. I looked toward our bedroom window and saw a woman standing outside of it. She was dressed in a white terry cloth bathrobe and had long, wavy auburn hair. When she saw me sit up, she pointed toward our bedroom door, which led into our hallway. I was in a daze as I jumped up and ran around the bed. Looking down the hall, I saw Scuter's baby bed with a green, mist-like cloud above it.

As my eyes became accustomed to the darkness, I saw our guest bent over the crib about to snatch my little boy. My scream brought Clark straight up out of bed and sent the man running out of the apartment and down the stairs. Clark took off after him before I could turn around good. I ran to check on Scuter and make sure he was okay.

Then it dawned on me; I hadn't heard a peep out of Sassy. I went to look for her, afraid she'd got out in all the confusion. When I found her wrapped in the sheet with her neck broke, I realized that man had faked everything. Clark returned sometime later and said the man's car was gone. I showed him Sassy, and we both agreed that the man had meant to steal our baby. Then I remembered the lady at the window! When I described her to Clark, he got quiet before saying I had described his mother to a tee. His mother, who had died when he was seven years old. We lived on the second floor, but I knew what I had seen. To this day, I still wonder about the events of that night and thank God that Scuter was spared.

Chapter 28
Final goodbye, cabbie and rape

LIFE BECAME INCREASINGLY HARD BETWEEN Clark and me after Patrick was born. His dark complexion resembled that of Clark's brother, and my conscience wouldn't let it go. I ended up spilling the beans about the night we crossed the line. It was the beginning of the end for us. It hurt him deeply, and every argument after that found him throwing it in my face. I wanted to leave, but he had threatened to kill me or take the boys from me forever if I did. I believed him and stuck it out as long as I could. I put up with him slapping me around and terrorizing me, but the night he jerked Scuter up by one arm and started spanking him gave me the courage I needed to take action. With Patrick on one hip, I ran up behind Clark and hit him in the back of the head.

"You bully! Come hit someone your own size; why don't you," I screamed as I turned and ran as fast as I could for our bedroom. I dove across our bed and barely got Patrick into the crib before Clark caught up with me. Grabbing me by my hair, he pulled me back across the bed and gave me a beating to remember. The funny thing is, as I recall, it didn't hurt at all. I just kept telling myself it would be the last beating I ever took from him.

The next morning after he left for work, I packed our things and drove to Momma's. As many times as I had left in the past, I knew this time was different, and I'd never be back.

He tried to make good on his word a few weeks later. He had picked the boys up on Friday for the weekend, but come Sunday never showed up to bring them home. The later it got, the more worried I became. I became frantic when I couldn't reach him by phone. When he hadn't shown up by Monday morning, I called his sister in Mississippi. She said the boys and Clark were there with her and that everything was okay. She asked if I minded if the boys spent some time with her that summer and I agreed. She promised she'd see that Clark returned them to me. I trusted her like she was my own sister. I knew that my boys were in good hands and thought this would give me a chance to get on my feet.

I had previously worked for Winchell's donuts and contacted them once again for work. I was hired as a kind of *"roving assistant manager."* I was sent to different stores to fill in when there wasn't a manager in the store. My first assignment was to fly out to the Midland-Odessa area. There was a store in Odessa that the manager had walked out on. I received round-trip airfare, motel accommodations, transportation, and food allowances. In exchange, I was to go in, assess the situation, and help get the store back in order while the new managers were trained. It sounded exciting to me!

Momma dropped me off at the airport, and I was off on a new adventure.

After settling in at the motel, I showered and headed up to the donut shop. It was a mess and took me all afternoon to clean and organize. I contacted my supervisor and gave them the store supply list and made ready for the following day. Calling for a taxi, I puffed on a cigarette as I waited to be picked up.

The cab driver barely said two words to me as he drove me to the motel but kept staring at me in his rearview mirror. Something about him gave me the creeps, but I brushed it off. I didn't have the wisdom back then to know to trust my instincts above all else. I gave everyone the benefit of the doubt and trusted more than I should.

I fell into a daily routine by the end of the week. I'd go in around one am early each morning, make the donuts, assist the counter girls, clean the shop, and do paperwork. I usually left each afternoon at around one pm. I'd catch lunch at the restaurant by the motel before taking a nice long bath and falling into bed to watch tv 'til I fell asleep. Everything was going great for me; it seemed. The new managers would be arriving in a few days, and I could go home. I decided one afternoon that it wouldn't hurt to go and have a couple of drinks at a bar I'd seen on the way from the donut shop to the motel every day. I hurried and finished the days work and even set things up for that night's bake. I had brought one dress-up outfit with me cause a girl never knew when she might need one.

I can't remember his name, but after he picked me up the first time, the same cabbie started showing up each time I called for service. He had begun to talk a little more, which helped chase the creepy feeling I'd had away. He seemed kind enough, I guessed. Once he knew my routine, he started showing up early and waiting on me before I even had to call. I thought it was a sweet gesture and didn't bother discouraging him. It didn't matter to me who picked me up as long as I had a ride. I didn't mention to him that I was going out that evening and was surprised to see him when I called for a taxi.

"Don't you ever have time off," I asked as I slipped into the backseat of the taxi?

"Why didn't you tell me you were going out when I brought you home earlier today," the cabbie spit out between his teeth, anger oozing from the looks he was giving me.

"Excuse me, where is that any of your business. I can get out and ask for another taxi," I threw back half-way out of the cab by now.

"Wait, I'm so sorry. You're right; I was totally out of line there," he said, running around the taxi to block me from walking away. "I worry about you out here all by yourself. I don't want anyone driving you around but me."

His mood shifted so quickly from anger to concern that it caught me off-guard, yet it seemed vaguely familiar. I couldn't put my finger on it but decided to give him another chance. Climbing back inside, I was relieved he kept quiet all the way to the bar.

The uneasy feeling I'd gotten from the cabbie stayed with me as I sat listening to the music. The crowded bar only added to my unease. I kept feeling as though I was being watched. After a couple of drinks, I decided it was time to leave. Picking up my purse, I headed for the payphone by the door.

I went to pick it up but felt someone behind me.

"Boo," did I scare you the cabbie asked as I nearly jumped out of my skin.

"You sure did! How did you know I was ready to leave," I asked, growing impatient with my new shadow?

"Oh, I just had a feeling," he said as he led me out of the bar.

Lying in my bed later, I tried my best to figure out how to tell this cab driver I didn't want him to pick me up anymore. He was starting to make me feel uncomfortable. The pounding on the door woke me instantly. Looking at the bedside clock, I jumped up and ran to the door. It was the cabbie asking if I was okay.

"Yea, I'm just late. Give me a few to get dressed, and I'll be out," I yelled through the door, not wanting to open it in the nude.

He was all smiles as he dropped me off at the donut shop. I almost felt bad for wanting to get rid of him. I'll tell him later today; I thought to myself as I jumped from the taxi to hurry into work.

The donuts were late, the counter help was late, and I couldn't have been more frustrated if I'd wanted to by quitting time. The only thing that was right on time was the cabbie. That, too, made me upset because I needed to put a stop to this. He had begun acting like I was his property, and I didn't appreciate it at all. I finally decided to let it go since I was going home soon and didn't want any trouble.

I had stopped the chatty conversation with him and had started acting as though I was preoccupied with the paperwork I always carried around, but every now and then, I'd catch him staring at me in his rearview mirror. Pulling up to my motel room, I jumped out and was about to say, "See ya later," when he too got out of the taxi.

"Hey, could I borrow your restroom? I really need to go right now," he asked as though he were in pain?

As nice as he'd been, I didn't see in real harm in it. Opening the door, he rushed in past me, heading straight for the toilet. I sat my things down and turned to open the curtains, which ran the length of my room. Just as I reached for the lever, he came up behind me, wrapping a cord around my neck.

Oh, sweet Jesus! At once, the memories of Horseshoe Bend came rushing in, and I remembered why the cabbie's mood swing from the night before frightened me. He'd behaved just like that man had!

"You're gonna do as your told, slut! Do you understand? No screaming, no attracting attention!"

"Okay," I whispered, afraid to speak out.

Removing the cord from my neck, he sat me in the chair and made me watch as he jerked his clothes off. He laid back against the headboard of the bed, stroking himself as he told me in explicit detail how to remove my own clothing. Standing, he retrieved the cord and came up behind me. Sliding it around my neck, he shoved me face-first down onto the bed. He raped me as if I were no better than an animal. The filth that came out of his mouth disgusted me and made me feel almost as bad as what he was doing to me. Again, it was almost as if I were watching the whole thing from the outside. As if it were happening to someone else and not me.

I thought about my precious sons and wondered if I'd see them again. I was so afraid he was gonna strangle me when he finished with the cord he'd tossed beside the bed. I begged God not to let me die this way. I begged God to forgive me cause I knew it was my fault for letting him in my room. Please, Jesus, please let it end soon.

I was so lost in my thoughts; it took me a minute to realize he'd become still. Here it comes, I thought. He's gonna strangle me. I don't know where I got the courage from, but I was ready to fight him tooth and nail if I had to. I wasn't about to go down without a fight.

Next thing I knew, he was crying with his head in his hands.

"I'm so sorry; I never meant to hurt you. You're just so *dawgone* pretty; I had to have you. Please don't tell anyone what happened. I don't want to go to jail. Please," he kept begging in his sick pitiful voice.

The words he said were like a script I'd heard before, almost verbatim!

Relieved that he wasn't strangling me, I spoke up quickly, "Why would I tell on you? You have been very helpful to me. Momma will be calling soon, and it'd be better if you weren't here when she does," I said, praying he would leave and not hurt me anymore.

I gathered the sheet around me and acted like I didn't have a care in the world.

"I'll pick you up later; okay," he asked, quickly dressing to leave.

"Sure," I agreed. Anything, just please leave I silently begged.

As soon as I bolted the door, I fell on the floor and began shaking so hard my teeth chattered.

"How could I have been so stupid? Why God? Why did I let him in?"

I couldn't stop crying and finally fell asleep from the exhaustion and stress that had taken over my body. Sometime later, I was awakened by the shrilling of the phone. At first, I couldn't get my bearings. I was confused cause I was lying on the floor wrapped in a sheet. Then it came back to me. It hadn't been a nightmare at all!

"Where in the world have you been? I've been calling for the past three hours," Momma practically yelled into the phone. Hearing her voice was my undoing. I started crying all over again. It took a little while between sobs to get the whole story out, but when I was done, Momma finally spoke up.

"I'm calling the front desk and having the manager come sit with you until the police show up."

"No, Momma! I just want to come home," I pleaded.

The line was dead, and I knew she hadn't paid me any mind when I heard the knocking on the door a short time later. The police and motel manager were standing there when I opened the door. I remember thinking they must have been close by to get there so quickly.

It was two male officers who sneered at me as I told what had happened. They questioned almost everything I said. I was about ready to tell them to forget it when a female officer showed up and escorted me to the emergency room to be examined. What an ordeal that turned out to be. I never felt so degraded in all my life. The looks I got from the nurses and doctors made me feel as if I were the criminal. It felt as if I were an object devoid of feelings that was being processed like paperwork. Just as I was getting ready to call it all off, the female detective came rushing back into the room with good news for me.

"Looks like your story is panning out. A call just came in from a cab driver who said one of the other drivers had come in bragging that he had to leave town in a hurry cause he'd raped a girl from a donut shop. The driver had called the police station to see if it were true, and to let someone know if they didn't act fast, the guy would be long gone. Hurry and get dressed. I want you to come with me."

Sitting in the back seat of her car, on the side street of the police station, was nerve-wracking for me. I could hear the police chatter from her radio and knew everything that was happening. There was a squad car parked a short distance from his home, keeping him under surveillance while a warrant was being issued for his arrest. The minutes seemed to drag by with me wondering how this would all end. There was a flurry of excitement when he loaded the last bag into his car and looked as if he was gonna get away before the warrant was signed. It was decided that he would be pulled over and detained while his license was checked, but soon after he pulled away from his house, the word came that the warrant had been signed. The whooping and hollering I heard over the radio almost made me sick to my stomach, remembering how those very officers had treated me earlier. I saw the cabbie as the squad car turned the corner and pulled into the station, but he never saw me.

In fact, the cabbie confessed the minute they cuffed him. He ended up taking a plea bargain for a five-year sentence, and that was the last I ever heard about him. My conscience bothered me for years over that cause I still felt like it was my fault for letting him use my bathroom. If only I hadn't let him into my room…

I managed to go into work that night but was replaced and sent home the very next day. It would be my last employment with Winchell's Donuts.

Chapter 29
Divorce, loneliness, and one night stands...

"WHAT IS WRONG WITH ME? Ain't I got no better sense than to keep putting myself in bad situations." I scream out, to no one! How many times have I sat and asked myself the same thing over and over and over again? Even today, as I type these words into my computer, I am overcome with emotions thinking back across my life. What's it all about? Why? Am I so horrible of a person that I deserved all that I've been through? I need answers! Is this why I'm writing it all down? When I get to the end, will it make sense? Will it stop hurting then?

Irving 1981

Clark returned the boys to me at the end of the summer like he said he would. Not long after we talked about reconciling once more, but the plan he had in mind, shook me to my core.

He'd gotten a job with Bubba at Charlie's, a local Irving gas station. It had a garage and wrecker service. Clark said he'd met a guy who really liked him.

"What do you mean, he really likes you," I asked as a sick feeling came over me.

"He's straight-up queer," Clark said so matter of factly that it floored me.

I was in shock and at a loss for words. I'd seen Clark slug men he thought were homosexuals, so to hear him brag that one liked him thoroughly confused me.

"He's been tossing one-hundred-dollar bills at me like they were nothing," Clark grinned smugly, "let me drag him along for a little while, and we'll be all set-up."

"You're having sex with a man," I blurted out.

"No, are you crazy. Those are tips he's giving me for looking after his vehicles," Clark said a little too quickly for my liking.

Something in the way he was acting didn't make sense to me. Nothing was making sense to me anymore. I told Clark I had stuff to do and left the parking lot where we'd met to talk. I remember driving around aimlessly all evening, sick thoughts going through my mind. I stopped at a payphone and called Clark's sister. I told her I was worried about Clark, and I thought he'd fell off the deep end, but I don't think she believed me. I finally went home to my little apartment and my sons. The couple that lived with me and cared for the boys had been worried sick about me as I was supposed to have returned hours ago.

I filed for a divorce a couple of months later, thinking it was finally over. Clark's new girlfriend made me mad, so I dropped the divorce in order to stall her plans of becoming the next Mrs. Stewart. Too late for all that Clark said. His new best friend Steve picked up where I left off and finished the divorce.

Around this time, Clark had gone to work for another mechanic shop around the corner from Charlie's. He was having quite the time with his new financial freedom, and all his new friends. I didn't matter anymore other than having his boys ready for pick-up whenever he felt like playing Daddy. I was confused and scared about the future. I was own my own with two boys to raise. I thank God for my sons, for without them, God only knows where my life might have ended.

Speaking of my God.

Folks always want to question another's religious beliefs, or lack thereof, whether to enlighten them or put them down. After all these years, I finally figured out a sound argument for my Lord for those who don't understand or share my beliefs. I have plenty of personal, burning bush experiences to satisfy my faith in my Lord and Savior. I believe in God as deeply and passionately as the most devout, religious people I know. The difference between me and them is my disobedience to his word and often lack of dedication.

A more accurate message has never been given than the fact that we reap what we sow. Sometimes it feels like I got an extra heaping helping of the hard knocks, but it's probably to make up for either something I got away with in the past or else something I'm gonna be guilty of in the future.

I wish I could say I have all the answers.

I still have issues with choices at times and will 'til the day I die. I'm human. I'm gonna make mistakes. Heaven knows there are plenty of mental health issues in my lineage where I could search for excuses, or for somewhere to lay the blame. My lack of coping skills contributed to my becoming an addict.

I may not have found all the answers, but I have had something to hold onto. A belief in a personal savior who loves me despite myself. A belief that sustains me in the darkest hours of my life. Yes, even on my 'highest, drunkest days'!

I am closer to God in the midst of troubles than all other times in my life. Not that I'm proud to be screwing up, or in the middle of the next tragedy, but when I hit rock bottom, I know who's gonna show up. Folks can say I'm living in a fantasy world all they want and that my God doesn't exist, but it is that belief in God that sustains me! It offers me hope that goodness and mercy reign supreme over the evil in this world. It allows me to survive in an imperfect world with imperfect people.

For argument's sake, let's suppose I die, and was wrong about God. He never existed, and religion is only a tool used to control the masses after all. What did I lose by clinging to my beliefs? I can't think of one single thing; my beliefs cost me. Religious persecution comes to mind, but I have been fortunate not to have experienced that aspect of life. Although when I visited China, I saw first-hand what that picture might look like.

My belief that there is a loving father who will never forsake me is the rock I cling to. In the end, if those beliefs did nothing more than help me navigate my walk through this thing called life, then said beliefs served me well. I can't imagine waking up without knowing my God is on my side and with me always. I never have to face anything alone if I don't want to.

I was so lonely. I'd gotten used to a warm body sleeping next to me and had developed an even healthier desire for passion. There was a huge empty spot in my life that needed filling, but I didn't know how to fill it. I didn't know what was missing.

I remember the first time I saw "Urban Cowboy." In true Lucy fashion, my brain went to spinning. Here was my favorite movie hottie, two-stepping his heart out. Man, could he dance or what? All I needed to do was dust myself off, pick up some new outfits, and go honky-tonking! I was bound to meet a hunky cowboy to share my life with.

Not! "Lucy, what have you gotten yourself into now?"

Loneliness will tumble many a fine creature. It does not discriminate, not even across species. After a few one-night stands, I caught on real quick. Tired of being used, I thought to myself, two can play this game. I became the hunter. I decided who might be worthy of a good roll in the hay for the night.

I didn't always leave with someone, I was very selective, but when I did, it was my choice. Taking the path of least resistance was actually easier in some respects. Better to see the situation for what it is and keep it moving. I learned it hurt less when I was the one to jump up afterward, dress, and walk away as if having sex with someone I never planned to see again didn't hurt. God forgive the person who has no moral conscience. Funny thing, men don't like it when the shoe is on the other foot any more than women do. By the end of the summer, I'd had enough. The way I'd behaved sickened me and became the perfect backdrop for diving straight into the pits of hell.

If you'd ever chased a bump so hard you soaked a clean baggie down in hopes of the merest taste of dope, you'd understand what I mean. When you can get a rush by merely rigging up, you realize what hell feels like. The same can be said of feeling the burn down your throat from some good whiskey, I suppose. Been there, done that too. You may not know you're in hell 'til later, but you always know it's coming.

By summer's end, I knew I had to figure something out fast. I was barely into my twenties and didn't have a clue how I was gonna raise the boys by myself. I knew members of my family were talking amongst themselves and felt like it was only a matter of time before they started putting their two cents in.

I don't remember how I happened to be in touch with my ex-brother-in-law, but next thing I knew, he had come to Dallas for a visit. He'd joined the Army for a second time and was stationed down in Fort Hood near Waco. He seemed to empathize with my situation. We first talked about the boys and me moving down to Killeen and sharing a home as roommates, but by the end of our conversation, we'd decided getting married would be beneficial to all of us. He would get an additional stipend for housing if he married me, and me and the boys would get medical care. He'd always been a loner type guy who didn't date, but he wanted to help the boys and me.

Marriage was a means to an end for me.

Those words are so easy to type yet so hard to acknowledge. Back then, I was on a slippery slope; I was grabbing onto any idea I could to keep from falling off the edge. For someone who proclaimed to be so tough, I was a scared, hot mess. Bless his heart, my new husband did his best to provide for us, but our marriage was doomed from the start. After a few months, the boys and I moved back to Dallas.

Momma had to be flown in from her last trip on the road with Tandy-Radio Shack. She had collapsed and was seen in an E.R. out west. Mom Nita and Daddy had been on the same route, so Mom Nita flew home with Momma.

It was to be Momma's last road trip.

Chapter 30
August 1982

Sitting in Momma's room, waiting for them to return her from the X-ray department, I kept trying to remember what Momma had said about the cancer she'd had before. I was too young and self-absorbed to understand what was really going on with Momma and her cancer. We never discussed the lie she told about it being gone for good. When I asked her why she had collapsed and had to be flown home, she said, "What do the doctors know anyway? Now they want to run more tests."

Momma was good at deflecting questions she didn't want to answer.

By the time it was all said and done, the truth came out. Cancer from her colon had spread to her lungs. They'd never gotten rid of it. Momma had refused treatment a couple of years back, opting to go on the road with my stepfather instead.

For the next year or so, Momma was in and out of the hospital. She was dying, but It was easier to ignore the inevitable and pretend it was business as usual for Momma and me. I lived those months in complete denial and regret it to this day, so many regrets. I was unable to accept what was happening emotionally, so I just pretended it wasn't happening.

It was during this time that Bubba had been introduced to methamphetamine. I remember the night he called me to come by his apartment cause he had something he wanted to show me. God forgive me, but up until recently, he believed that he was the one who first introduced me to the needle and the spoon, and of course, the crystalline white, rocky powder otherwise known as methamphetamine.

It's hard for me to explain, but I learned at a very young age to stuff things I wanted to forget. It amazes me how, as I write stories I hadn't thought about in decades, other memories come back into focus crystal clear as if they happened yesterday.

I was discussing my book with Bubba a few weeks ago when I remembered Abilene and finally told him the truth. He wasn't mad at me, but I still feel like a heel for letting him carry that burden all these years. We talked about our lives and how blessed we are to be where we are today. Ha, lucky to be alive and not under the jailhouse, never mind with a few brain cells intact.

No one wakes up one day and decides to become a junkie. Folks usually start out snorting or eating methamphetamine. I'd become desensitized taking Momma's *wake up pills*, which I eventually found out were prescription speed, so in a way, sticking a needle in my arm was simply a progression from my earlier drug use.

The shot of dope I did at Bubba's that night scared me much as it had when I tried it in Abilene. I decided to snort it the next few times I did it, it would be some time before I became a full-blown junkie.

During the time I lived in Killeen, Shelley and Lynn had come down for a visit. Shelley met herself an Army guy and married him. He'd shipped off overseas not long after they found out Shelley was pregnant. Momma rented a house for her, Shelley, and the new baby (when it was born) to live in two doors down from Maw-Maw Cruse.

Momma had another flare up and was hospitalized around the middle of August 1982. The tests revealed the cancer had metastasized to her brain. Momma was in horrible pain, so they started '*amping*' up her IV pain meds. Momma agreed to a few treatments for the brain tumor, though, at the time, I didn't understand why.

Momma's doctor was such an amazing young man. I hope he has had an incredible life. I know that any patient of his was blessed for it. He took the time to stop by and see Momma before leaving for his honeymoon. I could tell he thought it would be his last time to see her.

I laugh to myself, thinking back to when he first started seeing Momma several years before. She was having so much trouble eating and keeping food down. He looked at Momma and told her he knew the perfect remedy for both anorexia and nausea.

"Well, do tell kind doctor, what might that be," Momma asked curiously.

"Now Pat, don't hit me because I'm being serious. Marijuana. It would take care of both for you," the young doctor said sheepishly.

"What?" Momma bout choked on her tongue, not expecting to hear that come out of his mouth. "Where am I supposed to get that from?"

The doctor peeped around Momma to grin at me before continuing. "I'm sure someone you know could help out with that."

I'd been trying forever to get Momma to smoke a joint with me so she would get the munchies, but nope, she wouldn't listen to me. Dr. Wonderful suggests it, and we're off to the races. He really was Dr. Wonderful with Momma. I won't mention his name out of respect for his privacy, but if he ever caught wind of this story, he'd know it was him. More about his awesomeness in a bit.

Shelley was due in a couple of weeks, so I said I would stay with Momma. I had just started working for a parts warehouse as a delivery driver, but as soon as I got off work, I would go to the hospital and stay until I had to go to work the next day. Mom Nita and Daddy kept Scuter; Aunt Windelyn took Patrick.

Momma had her days and nights mixed up. She would sleep all day, stay awake all night. I sat right by Momma's bed every night, holding her hands, and listening to her ramble. I say ramble because she went from one thing to the next in her drug-induced delusions. I never corrected her musings instead choosing to go along with her. It was kinder to let her forget, and 'bout the best I could do.

What I wouldn't give to go back and listen to Momma for one more night.

Writing has brought me close to memories of Momma. Man, do I miss her? She was a special person amid all the symptoms of her disease. What a shame that so many good people are devastated by forces beyond their control? If God ever blesses me big, I swear I'm gonna set up a trust fund to help educate impoverished people about mental illness. If I have a gripe with Big Brother, it's the fact that they don't tell our citizens enough that help is available.

Another thing, labels need to go in the trash!

How many people refuse to seek help for mental illness because of the stigma that's attached to it? I think it's time for people to come off their high horses and realize that just because some people's brain synapses are lacking doesn't make them less of a person! Balancing out chemicals in the brain can mean the difference between night and day for some folks. I can just imagine how Momma would have soared with the right help.

Momma.

Y'all must know that I have been dreading telling the story 'bout Momma dying. This is a biggie, and it hurts, but I can't go on 'til I tell it.

By the end of the second week, I was dragging my butt behind me. I knew the streets of Dallas/Ft. Worth like the back of my hand since I'd been driving by myself since age thirteen.

I was so tired and sleep-deprived that most days, I was driving by rote. Have you ever been driving and look up and wonder how you got where you were, having forgotten the drive you just made? Say that real fast three times. LOL

As you may have guessed by now, I had a wreck. As a matter of fact, I had two. The first was a minor fender bender, but if I had told the truth, I'd have been fired. I kept drifting off at a red light. When I came to, I thought the cars were moving and hit the gas, but they weren't moving, and I hit the car in front of me. It should have been a wake-up call for me, but I didn't have good sense back then. And really, what could I have done differently? There was only me to sit there with Momma. The only other person that had the time was Maw-Maw Cruse, and bless her heart; she couldn't deal with Momma dying before her eyes.

The things we have no choices over…

I guess there are always choices, but some things just go without saying. Standing by Momma was a no-brainer for me, but even so, I was a little upset with God for putting me by Momma's side. Looking back now, I'm glad he knows better than me.

I was sitting in the turn lane on a five-lane street in downtown Dallas about to pull into a huge, empty parking lot, well almost empty, when the second wreck occurred. Looking to the left of the lot, I saw several tractor-trailers that had been dropped there. I was hot, tired, and hungry. I remember thanking God this was my last pick up.

I was awakened by a crashing sound and being hit on the head. I recall coming too in a fog. I was dazed and confused for sure, but instinctively I applied the brakes stopping the nearly new El Camino I was driving. I was lying on my side across the seat but managed to put the car in park. I finally got my bearings and figured out what was going on. I heard the wailing of sirens and knew help was coming. I saw the blood covering my hands and felt it pouring down my nose, but for some reason, I wasn't scared at all. Not even when they used the jaws of life to peel the roof of the car back so they could get me out.

I was taken to a hospital where they run all kinds of tests and x-rays. The doctor who came in to give me the results was astonished.

"Are you the young woman who almost decapitated herself by driving her vehicle under an eighteen-wheeler?"

"Yes, sir, that would be me."

"I see they finally got all the pieces of glass off you and stitched your forehead. How are you feeling?"

"Pretty sore, but laying here for two hours having glass removed didn't help either," I said, asking how soon I could get out of there.

"I'll finish your discharge right away, but do us all a favor, huh, don't stay awake all night and drive all day anymore, okay?"

Momma had worried herself sick waiting for me to get to the hospital.

"No one wanted to tell me where you were for the longest. Momma finally told me what happened after they knew you were gonna be okay," Momma said sadly. "This is all my fault for keeping you up all the time."

"It's not your fault Momma. Everything is gonna be okay. Can you believe I drove that car under an eighteen-wheeler, and all it did was give me a tiny cut on my forehead? I barely needed two stitches to close it. The doctor said I was in the same mindset as if I'd been drunk when I came to. If I'd been wide awake, I would have been decapitated; instead, when the edge of the roof bumped my head, in my woozy state, I fell over sideways. I am so blessed. Besides, I needed to find another job anyways," I said, not wanting her to know I'd been fired.

"You need a break from this hospital and me. Tomorrow, I want you to bring my grandsons to see me, and then I want you to spend the day with them. Understand?"

"Yes, Momma."

It was a Saturday morning, bright and clear, as me and the boys pulled into the hospital parking lot. Patrick demanded to carry his Maw-Maw's flower himself. It was the cutest thing. The florist had fashioned a spider out of two mums and some black pipe cleaners. Scuter had her card and balloon as we hopped on the elevator. I even remembered to stop for the film for Momma's polaroid.

Walking into her room seemed to flip a switch for Momma, and she couldn't stop smiling. I can see the snapshots from that day in my mind's eye, and thank God the actual pictures are safe in an album. They are priceless to me. I don't know what came over Momma, but she let me snap picture after picture of her and the boys that morning. Wow. It just dawned on me why she let me take all those pictures when she would barely let anyone take her picture ever. Momma, let me take those pictures for the boys.

Momma reached for her purse and took out some money. She told the boys to come over to her.

"Here's a hundred-dollar bill for you and one for you," Momma said, handing both boys one-hundred-dollar bills. "Now, I want y'all to give them to your mother and tell her I said to take y'all to Six Flags today!"

It's too bad I didn't catch a picture of those boys faces. Their jaws hit the floor and then sprang up like pogo sticks in a flash. I know Momma hated to see us leave, but she knew the boys would drag me out of there once she gave them that money. As much as they wanted to go, Patrick was upset and didn't want to leave his Maw-Maw.

The elevator was situated diagonally from Momma's room. The boys kept blowing kisses and waving to Momma as we waited on the lift. It finally came, and we got on. Just as the doors were closing, Patrick jumped through them. It was perfect timing cause the doors continued to close, and the elevator began moving.

I lost it.

As soon as the elevator opened on the first floor, me and Scuter ran up the stairs 'til we got to Momma's floor. Patrick was sitting on the bed, clinging to his Maw-Maw with tears streaming down his fat chubby cheeks. We stayed a little longer, giving him time to calm down. He asked to take one more picture with his Maw-Maw before we left. It clearly shows a very unhappy camper; he loved his Maw-Maw Pat.

We had a blast even though it rained part of the day. Momma had me take her camera and get lots of pictures for her to see when I got back there later that night. Some had our heads cut off because the boys took turns taking pictures and couldn't get the hang of the viewfinder. The images of them in their sailor hats with their names embroidered on them are priceless.

One sure-fire way to put a smile on my son's faces is to ask about their first concert! Joan Jett and the Blackhearts played at Six Flags that night. My sons fell in love! I wish I had a dollar for every time I've heard them belt out, "I love rock and roll, put another dime in the jukebox baby…"

It was a day I treasured. It was the last, carefree day I was to have for a very, very long time.

Chapter 31

Visions, telethons, and burning bushes

Wednesday, September 1, 1982, began with much excitement.

Shelley gave birth to her first child, where Momma was hospitalized. How ironic, I thought. She had a real hard time of it and refused to let anyone but Daddy and Mom Nita in the labor room with her. Daddy spent most of the time pacing the waiting room cause he couldn't stand to see his baby girl in so much pain. Seems like I recall him feeling sorry for the nurses whom Shelley was cursing to the high heavens, but I could be wrong. Momma was too weak to come downstairs, but we kept her up to date throughout the day.

Momma's doctor had written a letter to Shelley's husband superior's so that he could get special permission to leave Germany and return to the states to help his wife, who was giving birth as her mother was in grave condition. Poor Shelley! I can't imagine how she must have felt at age seventeen, giving birth to her first child, and losing her mother at the same time. Then to find out your husband used his '*leave of absence*' to visit his mother instead of rushing to your side.

"Shelley and this baby are better off without that little punk in their lives," Daddy spit out many times throughout Shelley's labor. He also had plenty to say to me.

"You know your mother has been holding on to see this baby born, don't you? She'll probably go pretty fast after this," Daddy said.

I could tell by the look on Daddy's face that it hurt him to say that, and despite all Momma had done, he would always love her. Shelley had a healthy baby boy not long after the conversation with Daddy. Later that evening, after everyone left the hospital, I was able to get a quick nap in while Momma dozed. I was grateful when I heard Momma call out to me later, waking me from a dream.

I'd been walking in a maze when turning a corner; I saw a pearl-white casket with dainty pink flowers on the corners. It seemed to glow as if it contained energy/light from inside. I was drawn to it, and as I watched, Momma sat up and swung her legs around the side as if she were getting out of bed instead of moving herself in a *ghost-like* manner from a closed casket. The dream shook me up pretty bad, but I just figured I'd had it cause of what Daddy had said to me the day before.

Shelley was able to leave the hospital on Friday. Momma's social worker pulled some strings so she could see Shelley and the baby before they left that afternoon. Daddy wheeled Shelley upstairs, holding the baby. As luck would have it, there was one film left in Momma's camera. It's not very clear, but you can see Momma holding the baby.

"Would you mind stopping by my office, say in about an hour," Momma's social worker asked me.

"No problem. See you after they leave," I said, looking toward Daddy, Shelley, and the baby.

They couldn't stay long cause of the risk for the baby, but I'll never forget the bittersweet moments we all shared that afternoon.

"Your mother and I had a long talk this morning. She's reached the final step, which is acceptance. She told me that Jesus came to her last night in her sleep and told her she had less than a week left here on earth, and she needed to take care of a few things." The social worker paused, giving all that she had just said time to sink in before continuing, "Now, I don't know what your personal beliefs are regarding religion and spirituality, but I hope you'll accept that for your mother, this is all very real. I would encourage you to try, to the best of your ability, to help your mother accomplish whatever it is she needs to do over the weekend." Handing me her card, with tears beginning to slide down her cheeks, she said, "I personally believe that Pat spoke with her savior. Here's my number. If I can help in any way this weekend, please don't hesitate to call."

I left her office in a fog and wandered around the hospital corridors 'til suppertime. I couldn't face Momma. I didn't want to talk about it. I was relieved when she didn't bring anything up later when I got to her room. The elephant was large and looming in the room, but we left it there. Neither one of us able to go there.

Saturday, Momma asked me to write out her last will and testament as she dictated it to me. Mostly personal stuff, but she wanted to make sure her belongings went where she wanted them too. She spoke as if she weren't fixing to die, but merely stating her wishes. I called the social worker who had an administrator come in to notarize it for Momma when we were done.

Sunday afternoon, Momma waylaid me out of the blue when her cute respiratory therapist walked in to give her a breathing treatment. He was most certainly a hottie. He could have been Travolta's twin brother! I didn't have a clue that he and Momma had made plans for me the next day until the moment he began setting up her treatment.

"Pat told me you hadn't given her a minute to herself in days, and that I ought to drag you out of here tomorrow and give her a break. Why don't we pack a lunch and go out to Grapevine lake for the day?"

"But Momma, we have watched the telethon together for years," I said disappointedly. "I can't just go off and leave you alone."

"I'm not gonna be. Your Daddy and Nita are coming to spend the day with me." Momma grinned, knowing I had a crush on the young therapist and putting me on the spot to agree to the outing.

I admit, I was exhausted from the events of the past week and looking forward to a diversion. He picked me up in his, red sports car, and off we went. He put the top down even though it was a cloudy day. Stopping at a little deli not far from the lake, we picked up a few munchies before we got there.

I can't tell you what we talked about that Labor Day so long ago. I remember him being very attentive and understanding, though. He'd been teasing and joking with me ever since he'd been taking care of Momma. That day long ago, he was the friend I needed.

What I do remember is lying on the blanket and looking at the overcast sky as the clouds begin to multiply and become denser. There was a storm brewing. Just as sure as I saw the dark clouds gathering, I felt the storm within my soul and knew that my life was fixing to change forever.

The raindrops signaled it was time to go. Packing up to leave, I felt a wave of sadness, knowing I was powerless to stop what was happening all around me. I thanked God for giving me that afternoon for quiet reflection as we headed back to the hospital.

"Looks like we'll get to watch some of the telethon together after all," I smarted off to Momma after the therapist left. "I appreciate your efforts to hook me up, Momma, but I ain't in no hurry to get my heart broke again. I'm pretty busy with the boys, and you and Shelley are gonna need my help."

Plopping down in the recliner next to Momma's bed, I grabbed Momma's hand, and we watched the last couple of hours of Jerry Lewis's telethon in silence. Strange, but true story, somehow or the other, we had always ended up together every Labor Day for as long as either one of us could remember. We'd laugh together, cry together, and talk smack about this one or that one's outrageous attire. I had no idea as the credits rolled that night that it would be the last Lewis telethon I ever watched. I was making up the couch, getting ready to go to sleep when Momma asked me to get the legal pad out.

"I know this is hard for you, Yvette, but I have a couple more things I need you to write out for me," Momma asked apologetically.

I kept my head bowed best as I could, so Momma couldn't see the tears streaming down my cheeks as she dictated how she wanted her obituary to read. She told me what she wanted her funeral to be like and how she wanted to be put away.

"Whatever you want, Momma. Don't you worry, I'll make sure everything is like you want, but you ain't leaving us yet, Momma. Didn't you say the doctors are hopeful about the treatment you're gonna get tomorrow? Let's wait and see what happens fore you go talking 'bout leaving, okay," I said, changing the subject.

Remembering the look on Momma's face that night has forever haunted me. She was trying so hard to prepare me and talk to me about it, but I couldn't do it. God only knows how many times I used drugs, sex, alcohol, and/or all the above to numb the way those memories made me feel.

To this day, it breaks my heart to remember, but I have learned it's okay to feel those feelings. Crying is cathartic and a great release for tension when one doesn't overdo it.

"Ma'am, we really need to get going," the ambulance driver said.

I shook my head and opened my eyes to see two ambulance drivers standing by Momma's bed with their gurney.

"C'mon Momma; you're gonna be late for your appointment."

Momma just laid there as if she had all the time in the world to wake up.

"Momma! Wake up," I screamed out of frustration, but soon felt ashamed of myself.

"I'm sorry; I'm so tired. I couldn't sleep last night, but I didn't want to bother you cause you were sleeping so good," Momma said so quietly I barely heard her. She sounded like a child who'd just been scolded.

"Would y'all mind stepping out for a moment while my mother changes her clothes," I said before turning to Momma, "I'm sorry for yelling Momma, but you need to change your underwear, and you don't wanna be late."

Momma pushed herself up from the bed and let me help her dress for the appointment. I could tell something was bothering her, but I let it go.

The ambulance driver's loaded Momma up, and off we went to Wadley's Research center for her treatment. Momma hardly spoke a word all the way there; she just looked out the back window of the ambulance at the rain flooded streets.

"How long has it been raining like this," I asked the ambulance driver.

"All night long, and the forecaster's said the rain wouldn't let up all week."

"Man, I bet the rain is keeping y'all busy with accidents and such as that, huh," I said, trying to make conversation and fill the silence.

"It sure is," the driver answered without explanation.

I sat in a waiting area while they set Momma up for her treatment. I was getting into an article in a magazine when a nurse came and asked me to follow her. Walking into what looked like a control room, I was surprised. The room was semi-circular, with a huge plate-glass window above a desk with all types of monitors and instruments. The doctor stood upon my entrance and introduced himself.

"I thought you might like to know what's going on. I believe that once we give your mother this treatment, it will freeze the tumor in her brain and prohibit it from growing any more," the doctor said sure of himself. "I thought you might want to watch the procedure."

About that time, I heard the technicians say over the intercom that they were ready to begin. The doctor turned and sat down before issuing directives and asking Momma if she were comfortable and prepared to begin.

"I'm okay," Momma whispered into the microphone above her head.

I will never forget in a million years hearing Momma's whisper as they slowly guided the bed she was lying on through the circular, donut-shaped tube. I'm grateful I didn't understand what was happening at that moment, but I would before the day was out.

"Momma, Momma, didn't I tell you everything was gonna be okay?" I was so excited by what the doctor had said about the tumor in her brain. "He said you'd probably lose your hair, but oh Momma, we can buy you some wigs. It really is gonna be okay." I told Momma excitedly as we were leaving.

I didn't understand why Momma wasn't as excited as I was. Momma had been more alert and had been eating like a horse for the past few days. Surely this was the best news she'd had in a long time.

It was still raining when we returned to the hospital. Dark clouds and overcast skies made it seem like it was later in the day than it was. I was glad we were back without having gotten into a wreck myself. I wondered if rescue personnel took courses on how to drive like maniacs as the driver backed into the loading dock.

The ambulance crew took Momma to her room to get settled while I walked the paperwork to the nurse's station. The charge nurse asked how everything went and said she'd have Momma's lunch brought in right away. Her demeanor seemed a little off, but I shook it off, thinking it must be the weather cause everyone was acting strange that day.

"Your lunch will be here in a minute, Momma," turning on the television, I continued, "*All My Children* is just coming on. We didn't miss a thing."

The lunch trays were brought in, and it was Momma's favorite, beef tips with noodles. Momma ate like there was no tomorrow finishing off her entrée in nothing flat.

"Wow, Momma, you were starving. Do you want me to see if you can have some more?"

I walked out to the nurse's station and asked for them to have another plate of beef tips and noodles brought up for Momma.

"I'm so happy to see Momma eating better. That has to be a good sign." The nurses behind the desk smiled but said nothing other than they would call the kitchen right away.

Momma was staring at the television when I walked back into her room.

"They're ordering you another tray Momma," I said, walking up to her bed before seeing the look on her face, "Is something wrong?"

"Oh my God, Yvette, my head! Something's wrong with my head," Momma screamed as she grabbed my hand and sat bolt upright in the bed as though she'd been struck by lightning. Staring at the corner of the ceiling, Momma cried out in a child-like voice, "Help me, Jesus, please."

No sooner had the words left her mouth than she fell back onto the bed like a rag doll.

Momma had been staring so intently at the ceiling as she spoke that I turned to see what she'd been staring at. The brilliant light that shone down at the foot of Momma's bed was so piercing I had to look away. When I turned back to Momma, she was convulsing horrifically. Running to the door, I began screaming for help.

People came running from every direction. I tried to go back to Momma, but two nurses drug me from her room to the nurse's station. The social worker came and said she had contacted the family for me and that one of my aunts was on her way to the hospital. She said they'd taken Momma to ICU and was running tests to see what'd happened.

"You can go back to your mother's room now and start gathering your things," the social worker said in a way that alarmed me.

"Why aren't they bringing her back to this room? Is she gonna be okay?"

I knew by the tone of her voice that Momma was gone no matter what anyone else said.

"I'm not allowed to discuss the medical outcome for your mother. You'll have to speak to the doctor. For now, they asked me to have you gather up y'alls belongings."

When she said, I should send everything home with someone I was sure I would never speak to my precious mother again.

"I want to see my Momma now! And I want to talk to the doctor." I was frantic and demanding to know what was happening to Momma.

"Wende, they want you to calm down before you see anyone. Everyone knows how much stress you've been under, and seeing your mother like this won't help either one of you."

Seeing that it was getting me nowhere, I quieted down and said I wanted to be alone in Momma's room while I waited on Aunt Ida to get there. I had just finished packing up the last bag when she walked in.

"Your mother is gonna be okay. She choked on a meatball and had a convulsion. She's sleeping cause of the medicine they gave her, but they said you could see her if you're quiet." Aunt Ida said she'd spoke with the doctor and everything was fine.

"No, it's not fine, Aunt Ida! My Momma is gone, and she ain't ever gonna talk to me again. She's gone," I screamed out and must have been acting a fool cause Aunt Ida walked up and slapped me hard in the face.

'You gotta stop acting like this and pull yourself together. You're over-reacting, and it's gonna get you kicked outta here." Aunt Ida spoke so sternly it got my attention, but I ran from the room determined to see Momma for myself.

Momma was lying back against the pillows, hooked up to several machines, as I entered the cubicle that was her space in the ICU unit. The whooshing sound of the ventilator, which was forcing air into Momma's lungs, punctuated the silence as time seemed to stand still around me. Sitting down next to her bed, I picked up her hand and squeezed it as I spoke.

"Momma, Momma, please wake up and say something. Please, Momma. I'm not ready for you to die yet Momma please." I couldn't help it, I wanted so bad to be brave, but I couldn't be strong anymore. I needed my Momma.

Fifteen minutes didn't last long, and before I knew it, they said I had to leave. Standing, I gripped Momma's hand and said, "I love you, Momma. I'll be right outside if you need me." Raising up after kissing Momma on the cheek, I saw a single tear sliding down her cheek.

Chapter 32

Goodbye Momma...

THE SOCIAL WORKER WAS WAITING for me when I came out of ICU. She'd heard about the confrontation between my aunt and me.

"Would you like to come sit in my office while you gather yourself? I'll make sure no one disturbs you."

I sat in her office by myself most of the afternoon. When Daddy showed up with Shelley and Bubba later in the day, I came out and spoke with them. All the confusion seemed to stem from the fact that they'd performed heroic efforts to bring Momma back to '*life*.' Everyone knew that it was against Momma's wishes. Unfortunately, the only one who could take Momma off the machines was Momma's actual doctor, who was on his honeymoon in Colorado.

"Momma's doctor called and said he was on his way here. He said we'd have to meet and have a conference to decide how to help Momma now," Bubba explained.

"What about his honeymoon?"

"He's cutting it short for Momma's sake," Bubba said, walking from the room. I could tell this was hard on him too. Poor Shelley never even said a word, sitting close to Daddy and staring at the floor. All evening and into the next day, family and friends showed up to see Momma. I stayed hid out as much as possible since I wasn't 'bout to leave the hospital as long as Momma was breathing.

Dr. Wonderful was true to his word showing up early the next day. Me, Bubba, Shelley, Maw-Maw Cruse, Daddy, and Mom Nita were there so we could discuss Momma's options with the doctor.

"I guess you all can see how much Pat meant to me since I cut my honeymoon short to come back. Pat made me promise to never let her be kept alive by machines. I'm sure she made that known to all of you too. Unfortunately, the paperwork was never completed to protect her wishes. There is no way I can live with myself if I don't try to keep my promise to her. I'm not family, and can't force y'all to honor her wishes, but as someone who loved her and knew what she wanted, I ask you to search your own hearts," the kind-hearted doctor said as tears gathered in his eyes.

"Is there any way Pat could ever come back and have any life at all," Maw-Maw Cruse asked, fear in her voice apparent.

"I'm so sorry, Belle, but no, I don't believe so. You see, the tumor which was in her brain was growing so rapidly that within a short time, she wouldn't have been able to sustain life without interventions. Pat didn't want to be kept alive by artificial means, so she chose to try the radiation treatment to freeze it. Unfortunately, Pat had an aneurysm in her brain. She knew there was a risk of it rupturing as a result of the radiation, but she chose to keep that to herself and not worry any of you. She was afraid y'all would try to stop her. As her doctor, my hands were tied. I'm so sorry."

"Will she die the minute you take her off the machines," I said, asking the obvious question on everyone's mind.

"That will be up to Pat and her maker," the young doctor said. "y'all can take some time if you'd like to discuss this and let me know how y'all want to proceed."

"I know y'all don't want to let your mother go, but we all know what her wishes were," Daddy spoke up, signaling for the doctor to hold on before continuing, "Belle, I know you don't want her to suffer no more right?"

"No, I don't want my girl to suffer no more," Maw-Maw Cruse cried out before putting her head in her hands.

Us kids looked at each other knowingly before I spoke up and said, "Please do what needs to be done doctor, just make sure she doesn't have to suffer."

Once he got started, it was no time 'til the compassionate young doctor had Momma back in a private room where she could be surrounded by family and friends. She was still hooked up to a ventilator, but that too would be turned off once everyone had a chance to pay their last respects the nurse said.

Momma spiked a fever around eight that evening of 105 f. The nurse said it was normal, given Momma's condition. Everyone but Bubba and his wife had left the hospital by eleven pm when one of the nurses asked to talk to me.

"I want you to know I never meant to upset you the night I didn't give your mother's pain med right away. I wanted to give her a chance to become alert and see if she needed to talk about anything. A lot of times, patients need an outlet, someone they can talk about their fears with. Many times, it's easier for them to talk to total strangers, so they don't have to feel that they are burdening their loved ones. I always felt like I was helping Pat by giving her that chance to share how she felt. I'm sorry for not explaining that to you back then." Taking my arm, the wise nurse turned me toward the end of the hall, "It might be a long night, why don't you go down to the last room on the left and try to get some sleep? I promise I'll personally come and get you if anything changes."

If it had been any other nurse, I'm not sure if I'd have gone. But I'd had a run-in with this little red-headed Irish sounding nurse a few weeks back when she didn't bring Momma's pain medicine in right away one night; I recalled it clearly.

"What do you mean, Momma needs to wait a little while before she can have it? Don't you think I know how often Momma can get her pain medications?" I was furious with this nurse, who thought she knew better than me!

"Why don't you go and get yourself something to eat, and I'll bring your mother's medications in shortly."

It all made sense now.

"I'm sorry for being so short with you since then. I didn't know," feeling like a heel, I heeded her advice and did as she suggested.

The nurse awakened me a couple of hours later to say Momma probably wouldn't last the night through. Not long after she left the room, as I was getting ready to go back down to Momma's room, I felt the temperature of the room drop dramatically. I knew that was Momma come to say goodbye. Rushing out the door and down the hall toward Momma's room, I heard my sister-in-law scream as she was pulled from Momma's room. I almost made it into Momma's room before someone saw me and kept me from it.

"Let us clean her up, and we'll let y'all back in, okay," the nurses pleaded.

She looked more peaceful without the vent down her throat, but the battle she'd just fought had been hard on her physically. Me, Bubba, and his wife went in together and said our goodbyes. Bubba told me he was gonna wait on the funeral home to pick up Momma, and he'd see me at his house. We'd have

199

to go to the funeral home the next morning to make Momma's arrangements.

There ought to be some kind of law to protect deceased individual's families from the goons who take advantage of them in their times of need. Who knows, maybe there is, but it didn't protect none of us way back when. One day, before I die, I will fix what was done wrong on Momma's behalf.

Me and Bubba went down to see Momma's corpse. She'd been embalmed and bathed. I remember feeling her long hair that hung off the cold table where she was laying and wishing I could close my eyes and pretend this was only a dream. Addressing the mortician, I handed him Momma's make-up, lipstick, fingernail polish, and driver's license.

"My Momma was very particular bout how she looked when she left the house every day. Please try your best to make her look as natural as you can."

"Don't you worry, I'll do my best," the mortician replied apologetically.

I'd been worried to death all morning that me, Bubba, Shelley, and Maw-Maw wouldn't agree on how to bury Momma, but surprisingly, everything came together peacefully. I gave the administrator the obituary Momma had dictated to me, and we were asked to choose what songs we wanted. Bubba and Maw-Maw each had a song they wanted, Shelley didn't know what song she wanted but agreed the instant she heard what I had in mind. Momma had said she wanted "Bridge Over Troubled Waters" by Simon and Garfunkel to be played I told everyone. The administrator said they wouldn't play the original song, but if I could find sheet music for it, they would have their people sing it.

Moving right along, the administrator directed us toward the casket rooms. He turned us toward a hall we had to walk through to get to their display rooms, but seeing the tiny caskets situated in the alcove, I chose to go the other direction. No way did I want to see any coffins my young boys could fill.

Walking through what seemed like a maze, I turned a corner to see a beautiful, pearl-white casket adorned with tiny pink flowers sitting by itself in the corner of an empty room. I was standing there, unable to move when everyone else came to stand behind me.

"We'll take that casket," I heard my brother say.

As we made our way back to the administrator's office, we passed a row of burial gowns and such as that. We'd already decided we were going to go and find the type of gown Momma had asked for, but something inside caused me to reach out and grab one of the gowns.

The gown with the high ruffled collar and sheer puffy sleeves looked just like the one Momma had been wearing that night in my dreams. The gown was exactly what Momma had asked for. I handed the gown to the administrator and said we'll take this one.

Of course, the administrator gave us whatever we wanted, and even encouraged all kinds of other extras. The concrete vault, flowers, and everything else brought the total of Momma's funeral into the thousands of dollars by the time we were through. I had no idea what we were doing back then; I just wanted to make sure Momma had a beautiful funeral. The respiratory therapist stayed close by my side those few days and even drove me all over Dallas to find sheet music for "Bridge Over Troubled Waters."

None of us could believe how Momma looked the evening we went to view her body. She looked like she was lying there sleeping. Everyone remarked how beautiful she looked. The mortician had pulled off a miracle. One of Daddy's biggest complaints over the years with Momma had been how she was never satisfied with how the hairdresser fixed her bangs. She would always, every single time, re-comb them herself after she came home. Momma also had a nervous twitch in her hands. It caused her eyebrows, which she always drew on, to have a little crook in them. Staring down at Momma's corpse, it looked as if Momma herself had fixed her bangs and eyebrows. It was downright spooky to everyone who knew Momma. I found the mortician and gave him a hundred-dollar tip for taking such meticulous care of Momma. Handing me back her personal items, he thanked me and said he was just doing his job.

The morning of Momma's funeral was beautiful. The sun was shining brightly, not a cloud in the sky. I had decided not to take the boys to Momma's funeral, thinking I couldn't handle it, and that they were too young to understand. One more regret for something that can't be undone. They never had a chance to say goodbye. I didn't realize, even at their age, they needed closure.

Chapter 33

Reflections and acid trips!

THE THERAPEUTIC VALUE I'VE RECEIVED through my writing is priceless. It's been hard to wade back across decades of failures and poor choices. It was a lot harder, pretending it never happened. It was pretending that kept me using at times.

When I first began this journey of self-exploration, I didn't realize how involved it would become. It's impossible to tell just one story from your life. It's all the stories put together that speak of a person's character. The stories explain how they came to be themselves. I'm not proud of all the choices I made in my life, but I can't change what's happened. So many times, I made choices that could have ended my life.

Like the time, not long before Momma died, when I went to a Texxas Jam concert in Dallas. Bubba and his wife were supposed to go with me but backed out at the last minute. I ended up going by myself. I drank a couple of tall boys while I was waiting in line to go in. It was pretty much festival seating cause everyone moved around and sat wherever they felt like sitting far as I could tell.

I meandered around until I got to the very front of the stage. I found the perfect area in the bleachers just to the right of the left front stage. It wasn't crowded, and I didn't see many security personnel. The sun was beginning to set over the back of the Cotton Bowl when I lit one of the big fat joints I'd smuggled into the concert. I remember the strong, musty skunk smell that filled the air after I fired up.

I knew someone would be saying something, but I didn't expect to hear laughter. Just behind me and a couple of rows up was a group of Hispanic guys, and I understood when I heard "Molta" what they were laughing 'bout.

"Y'all want some," I asked, passing the joint in their direction.

"Sure, sure. Thank you very much," the one who spoke broken English said.

The joint was smoked after a couple of rounds, so I pulled out the second joint and passed it around too.

"You wanna do some acid, man?" The young guy asked, holding out a thin strip of paper with 5 Mickey Mouse heads stamped on it.

"Remind me how to do this," I asked as I took the strip from his hand?

"You know, you pop it in your mouth and chew and suck on it before you swallow it," the guy said as if to jog my memory.

I popped the strip of paper in my mouth and began to chew when all five of the guys started speaking.

"Wait a minute, what you doin'? Haven't you ever done no acid before," the young guy yelled out while leaning down to look at me closer.

I was so startled that I swallowed the strip of paper about the same time he yelled for me to spit it out. As soon as I swallowed it, he began cursing and smacking his head like I'd committed some grievous sin.

"Man, you just took five hits of acid! You shoulda only took half of one of those Mickey Mouse heads. Who you here with? You gonna need someone to look after you. Man."

Oh no, I thought, what am I gonna do now. God only knew where a payphone was, and right at the moment, I was feeling pretty good. I'll figure it out later; I thought to myself as I listened to Lover Boy crooning out a favorite love song.

Turning toward the other end of the stadium, to look at the last of the sunrays creeping over the back of the stadium, my vision was distorted. Everything was fat in the middle and thin on the sides. It was like I was trapped in a bubble. It was funny for a minute until it made me feel kind of sick. I laid back on the bleacher seat and closed my eyes for a second to collect my bearings.

I lost track of time cause when I opened my eyes; it was dark out.

The Hispanic guys had moved down and were sitting in a circle, all staring at me. I could hear the music blaring and vaguely recalled that I was at a concert. Looking up at the night sky, I saw my first '*tracer*.' The stars put on a show for me. Zoom, zoom, zoom. It was awesome to behold, but scary at the same time.

I passed out at some point and was awakened by a security guard telling me it was time to go. Sitting up and looking around, I soon realized I was still *'tripping.'* The stadium was mostly empty, with only a handful of concert-goers making their way toward the exits. After what seemed like forever, I made it to the parking areas. I was pretty freaked out when I couldn't find my car right away. I walked around the entire area twice before spotting it. Paranoid, I climbed behind the wheel and sat for I don't know how long before I started the car. I found my way out to the freeway, and for a moment thought I had everything under control. Cars were flying past me, leaving *tracers* in their wake.

"I don't have to worry bout policemen pulling me over cause they're gonna be chasing all these speeders flying down the road," I laughed to myself. It looked like I was driving inside a long tube, I guess I had tunnel vision. The image I saw in my mind was funny, and I started laughing so hard I almost peed my pants! One of the *'flying cars'* slowed down and pulled alongside me, and the driver motioned for me to roll down my window.

"Hey, I don't know what's wrong with you, but you better speed up before you get pulled over by a cop," the driver shouted before pulling away from me to continue his journey.

Looking down at the speedometer, I was shocked to see I was only driving twenty-five mph! Since I felt like I was already going fast, I decided to pull off the freeway and call Bubba. I needed help; now. Luckily for me, there was a payphone at the store right off the highway. The place looked familiar yet frightening to me, but I didn't understand why. After half a dozen tries, I finally punched Bubba's number in correctly. The minute I heard his voice, I started crying and couldn't stop.

"Wende, stop it now! You gotta tell me what's wrong and where you're at if you want me to help you," Bubba screamed into the phone to get my attention.

Bubba said it was after two in the morning, and when he finally figured out where I was from my descriptions, he became very alarmed.

"Listen to me carefully. You're gonna have to drive yourself away from there as fast as you can. You're in South Dallas, and that ain't no place for a woman to be by herself. It would take me too long to get to you, and I don't want you there any longer than you have to be."

Bubba's stern words sobered me enough to listen to the directions he was giving me before I hung up the payphone and got the hell out of there. I got lost a few times but found my way to Bubba's house. What should have only taken twenty-minutes became an hour and a half drive. Man, was he mad at me? I remember the stern lecture he gave me to this day. He said I scared the living daylights outta him! I pinky-promised my little brother I would never experiment with any drug by myself again.

Two days after the concert I finally went to sleep. I *tripped* so hard during those two days that I vowed I would never touch acid again. Thirty-something years later, I'm happy to say; I've kept that promise to myself.

Chapter 34

Revelations, college, and prison penpals

I HELD MYSELF TOGETHER UNTIL we buried Momma. Then I took to the bed and slept and slept. Bubba's wife bent down to help me sit up on the third day when she looked at me and said, "You're burning up with fever. I'm taking you to the emergency room."

"Your temperature is 103, and the x-rays show you have pneumonia. I'm admitting you," the emergency room doctor said as he spouted off a list of orders to the nurse.

My room was on the third floor, not far from where Momma had spent the last weeks of her life. I couldn't bear looking down the hallway cause it hurt too bad. I was in and out of it for the next few days wanting nothing more than to sleep.

"Okay, you've had enough time to lay around and cry; it's time to join the land of the living," Momma's social worker and friend said, jerking open the curtains and letting the sunshine stream through. "The nurses tell me you've refused to eat, shower, or get out of this bed for any reason. Your mother wouldn't have wanted you to fall apart this way. Think about those precious boys of yours. What good are you to them this way?" She got through to me when she mentioned the boys.

"I know, it just hurts so bad," I cried, dropping my head into my hands.

"I'm going to help you get through this, but you have to trust me, okay," the social worker said empathetically, "I want you to get up and take a long, hot shower. When you're done, call me, I'll come up, and we'll talk."

As the water poured over me, I began to cry, really cry. I leaned against the cold tiles of the shower wall and let it all out. Deep racking sobs convulsed through me. Spent at last, I began recalling the details of my final morning with Momma. Replaying our final conversation one more time, the realization of what had transpired, hit me like a ton of bricks.

It had stormed like crazy the morning the ambulance drivers picked us up to go to Wadley's and continued the rest of that day and several days that followed. There wasn't a ray of sunshine to be seen until the morning we buried Momma. Momma's final words rang out loud and clear, "Help me, Jesus, please."

The bright, piercing light I saw at the foot of Momma's bed that day was Jesus come to take her home, and out of her misery. He answered her plea and allowed me to witness his presence. I felt a peace I hadn't felt since I was a child at that moment, knowing God was still by my side.

The social worker came back as she promised and helped me formulate a plan for moving on. It took some time and a lot of leg work, but by January 1983, I was enrolled in Eastfield Junior College. I had to take a few developmental courses starting out, but I didn't care. I was working toward becoming a nurse. I was the first person from either side of my family who'd went to college, and bless his heart; Daddy was beside himself with pride and joy.

The boys and I moved into a small, one-bedroom house up the street from Maw-Maw Cruse. It was cramped, but we managed just fine. Everything was great; unless you count the night when we were getting ready for bed and saw a man's arm come through the window. The would-be burglar had pushed the accordion folds to the side and was fixing to pull the ac unit from the window when Scuter saw his arm and screamed. Thankfully it ran the man off.

We soon had our daily routine down pat. We'd all get up, get dressed and head off to school together. They went to nursery school, and I went off to college. Every afternoon we'd have a snack when we got home before they sat down to watch cartoons, and I sat down with my homework. Life seemed full of possibilities.

One afternoon when we stopped by NaNe's and Maw-Maw's, Aunt Ida was there. She was saying how hard it was for her to drive to the prison and see my cousin by herself. The person who'd been taking her wasn't available anymore.

"Would you go with me, Yvette? You can drive my car. You'd have to sit outside and wait on me until the visit was over, but once you're on the visiting

What's Wrong With Wende?

list, you can go in with me," Aunt Ida asked.

"Y'all can drop the boys off here while y'all are gone," Aunt Windelyen offered.

"Sure, Aunt Ida, I'll go with you."

I enjoyed the ride through the East Texas countryside. It was in stark contrast to the hustle and bustle of city life. Aunt Ida was fun to hang out with and always had me laughing my butt off. One Saturday, just as we were getting ready to leave, my cousin had a question for me.

"Hey, one of the guys I met here was wondering if you'd like to be pen pals with him, and maybe visit him when you come down here with Momma," my cousin asked.

"Why not? Give him my address and tell him to write to me," I said.

I was so busy with school that I didn't have time for dating, but being a pen pal might be fun, I thought to myself. What could it possibly hurt to befriend a lonely soul?

I received my first letter from Jerry Claude Ferguson a few days later. It wasn't much, but I could tell he was lonely. He said he had no one to write him, and his only acquaintances were the guys he knew in prison. He wanted to know if I'd come to see him if he put me on his visiting list? Jerry said he was in prison over drug charges. He seemed harmless enough, and I agreed to let him put me on his visiting list.

I was taken by surprise when I met Jerry for the first time. He looked just like Nick Nolte and was charming to boot. Time flew during that first visit, and neither one of us wanted to say goodbye. Letters flew back and forth between us like we were long lost, lovers. I was thrilled to learn he and I shared so much in common.

I was twenty-three years old and walking on clouds.

Going to college was everything I'd dreamed of. I excelled in my studies, acing everything that came my way. I'd done so well in fact, that I was offered an assistant position in the English department as a tutor. I was accepted into the LVN nursing program that was to begin in the fall the first time I applied.

Jerry and I had big plans for our future together. Our visits and letters continued throughout the spring and summer months. Jerry assured me he would be released from prison in September, and I could hardly wait. Each night I marked the days off the calendar before I went to sleep. I thought it couldn't get much better than this.

"What do you mean you're being released to the State of Arkansas and will be transferred there at the end of the week," I asked nervously, unable to believe what I was hearing.

"Baby, I'm sorry. I had a couple of drug cases in Arkansas that I thought were being served consecutively with these cases in Texas. I promise I only have a few months left to serve up there. Please don't give up on us," Jerry pleaded as he placed his hand flat against the glass. It was our way of reaching out to each other since we weren't allowed to touch.

"I start nursing classes this week, Jerry. How are we gonna see each other if you're in Arkansas," I pouted?

"Silly, you'll drive up there once a month until I get out," he said, grinning. "Besides, we can get contact visits in Arkansas, and I can't wait to kiss those sweet lips of yours."

"Well, I guess when you put it that way," I agreed, not realizing I'd just turned my whole life upside down. The fateful choices that followed affected not only my life but the lives of most of my family as well for years to come.

I started nursing school, but my heart was no longer in it. I missed Jerry so much. It was going to be a few weeks before we could visit, and his letters had slowed down as well. I didn't understand what was happening. It felt like my life was falling apart.

It was nearing the end of September by the time I got the letter that said I could drive up for a visit the following week if I wanted to. The tone of his letter sounded different, and it alarmed me. He'd included a telephone number for his cellmate's girlfriend. He asked me to give her a call and do what she asked, saying he'd explain everything when he saw me next week.

I was shocked after I got off the phone with this woman. Her fiancé had a drug business in prison and had recruited Jerry to help him get drugs in through me.

"You can't be serious? You want me to shove a couple of balloons filled with heroin and cocaine up my twat? Go to the bathroom once I am in the visiting area and put them in my mouth, and then transfer them to Jerry while we're kissing. He then swallows them and vomits them back up once he's back on his unit. Are y'all out of your minds, or what? Not only is this highly illegal and could send me to prison where I'd lose my boys, but what if the bags bust and Jerry overdoses?"

"I am a pharmacist hun; I know how to package products for transport."

I agreed to meet this woman at a station near the prison the following week, but I wasn't sure I could go through with this crazy plan. I loved Jerry to death, but this was definitely over the top. All week long, I struggled with my conscience. I finally decided I couldn't go through with it. Jerry would just have to understand when I spoke with him in person. Pulling into the parking area that Saturday afternoon, I was shocked to find a smart-dressed woman waiting on me to exit the car.

"Jerry was afraid you'd bail on us. Follow me down the road so we can talk in private," the lady more or less ordered, instead of asking.

I couldn't believe I let her talk me into this as I stood in line to be searched before entering the prison. I was scared half to death, knowing everyone could see right through me. Man, oh man, was I gonna get in big trouble if they caught me. All the excitement I felt on the drive from Texas was gone.

"I can't believe I can finally touch you," Jerry whispered, looking down into my eyes.

"I can't believe you'd jeopardize my freedom," I said, pulling away from his embrace and sitting down at the table in front of us. "Why would you do that?"

"To help you with some extra cash. It's gonna be hard on you to make this trip every month."

"I'm not ever doing this again. As a matter of fact, I wasn't gonna do it today, but that lady was waiting for me when I got here. She said you told her I would back out. Don't ever put me on the spot again, okay?"

"I won't ask you to do anything you don't want to, I promise. Now is a good time to go potty. The guards seem distracted," Jerry said as he watched the guards move to the corner of the room to break apart a romantic couple.

Warning bells were ringing loudly inside my head as I drove home later that afternoon. Jerry's behavior had changed once he was transferred to Arkansas. If I had been mature enough to heed those warnings, God only knows how many lives might have been spared.

Chapter 35

Smuggling drugs into prison

Getting involved with Jerry Ferguson was one of the biggest mistakes I ever made. God only knows what my life might have been if I'd have stayed in nursing school way back then. Unfortunately, the choices I made affected everyone around me, as well.

Jerry's transfer to Arkansas took the wind out of my sails. I no longer looked forward to school. All I could think about was Jerry. Daddy was furious with me for driving the long distance to visit Jerry, and the last visit I made from Texas, my car broke down in Arkansas. Daddy refused to help me get home. I was still making visits with the pharmacist, so she let me, and the boys stay with her. A friend of hers drove me down to get our clothes, and I withdraw from school. I moved what little furniture we had down the street to Maw-Maw Cruse's house, and boy was she upset that I was leaving.

"You promised your Momma; you wouldn't leave my side, Yvette. How could you," Maw-Maw cried out as I left her house that morning?

"I'll be back, Maw-Maw. It's not that far away, and I'll get a phone as soon as I get settled," I promised.

Jerry had come to expect me to bring drugs in every time I visited. It began to wear on my nerves that he'd jeopardize my freedom for money and the privileges it afforded him. After one emotional visit, I'd had enough. I made him choose. His hesitation in answering me told me all I needed to know.

"I can't do this anymore, Jerry. I'm serious. Isn't my coming to see you enough?"

"You know how I feel about you, but … this is important for me too," Jerry answered way too slowly.

I'd met a young man, and he let me, and the boys move in with him to get away from the pharmacist lady whom I was sure was going to be arrested anytime for the drugs she was taking into the prison. A short time after the boys and I began staying in his trailer, I came down with a severe upper respiratory infection, and the emergency room physician wanted to admit me to the hospital. The boys were sitting there with me, and I didn't know what to do. I was still mad at Daddy and refused to call and ask for help. The pastor who came to visit me offered to let the boys come and stay with him and his wife so that I could be hospitalized. He seemed genuinely concerned and assured me child protective services wouldn't be called. Every day he or his wife came and visited me. They didn't bring the boys cause they weren't old enough to visit. Toward the middle of the second week, I was there; the kind pastor asked what my plans were. I was confused and didn't know which way to turn.

The pastor offered me a solution. He had spoken with others at his church, and they wanted to help me. They wanted to fix my car and help me and the boys get into an apartment. I was overwhelmed by the kindness that was being shown and accepted with a grateful heart. I could feel God's love reaching out to me once again.

When I was released from the hospital, I was driven to the apartment complex, and after filling out the paperwork, was given the keys to my new studio apartment. Next, I was taken to pick my car up. Later that evening, folks came out of the woodwork to help fill the apartment up with furniture, dishes, linen, and everything we needed. It felt like God was blessing me for stepping away from Jerry, and the activity I'd known all along was wrong.

The boys and I settled into a routine, and again, I felt like our lives were gonna be okay. We became involved with the church as I set out to enroll in the local college to pick up where I'd left off. There are a couple of stories I remember about that apartment I must share.

Not long after me and the boys moved in, it came heavy snow. The boys had never seen that much snow and were dying to build a snowman. The only area big enough was a patch of ground in front of the nursing home across the way from us. I walked over and got permission for us to build our snowman there. I came up with the idea to make it a *"senior"* snowman and gathered the items we needed. Bundled and ready for our adventure, we set up the area we were working. It wasn't long before we had an audience. The staff sat the seniors in front of the plate-glass windows to watch as me and the boys worked. Those confined to their rooms watched from their windows as well. The light snow that fell added to the magical feeling of the morning as our *senior snowman* came to life. When we were done, everyone commented on our ingenuity. Everyone said the spectacles made from a coat hanger was the best article our snow senior had on. We were invited in for hot chocolate once we were done and asked to come back and visit any time we wanted.

The other story is funny now, but it sure wasn't the day it happened.

Patrick hero-worshipped his older brother and did whatever Scuter told him to, always. I warned him frequently that one day it was gonna get him in big trouble.

One Saturday morning, I grounded them both to their bedroom upstairs for some outrageous, little boys' act they'd committed. They were always driving me up the wall with hair-raising stunts, and I figured I could get some cleaning done with them upstairs and out of the way. An hour or so later, I was listening to my favorite music as I worked and barely heard the knock at the door. Opening the door, I almost had a heart attack. Looking down, I saw Patrick wide-eyed and being pushed forward by Scuter.

"What the, how the hell…" I stammered, unable to get my mind wrapped around what I was seeing.

"Patrick wanted to see what it would feel like to jump off the edge, and I had to jump down and protect him," Scuter said, all the while continuing to push Patrick toward me and pointing to the door awning which jutted down from their window over our front door.

"Is that what happened," I asked, looking from Scuter to Patrick.

Poor Patrick, he was so scared he couldn't say a word.

I grabbed the hammer and nails, and up the stairs, we went. It would take an act of congress to get that window open again once I nailed it shut. I was beyond furious and knew I didn't dare spank them in this frame of mind. Later that afternoon, I gave them a paddling they didn't soon forget. I was raised to believe a good paddling never hurt any child as long as it was done appropriately. I admit that there were a few times I might have been a bit harsh, but it was usually over a life-threatening offense they'd committed. Being a single mother, raising two boys, wasn't easy. I'd like to believe I did the best I could, but trying to raise children when you're barely past being a kid yourself is near 'bout impossible, pretty much like the blind leading the blind. My boys and I grew up together, so to speak. We called ourselves the three musketeers. It was us against the world.

I finally made peace with Daddy, and the boys and I drove down and saw him and the family every few weeks. One drive home is one I'll never forget.

Driving along Highway 175, we were coming into the city of Seagoville. I saw a cow meandering down a hillside toward the service road which ran beside the highway. I just knew if I didn't stop that cow, he was gonna get killed when he made it to the busy road. I pulled off on to the service road, and jumping the curb, drove my Mustang within a few feet of the big brute.

"Momma, this isn't a good idea. You might get hurt," the boys warned as I climbed out of the car.

"I'm going to the police station up the road and tell them about this situation," the lady who'd stopped on the service road below us said, "be careful!" I assured her I would as she sped off.

"Shoo, shoo. You'd better go back in that fence," I said, waving my jean purse toward the cow as if the dumb animal understood what I meant as I pointed in the direction of the torn fence he'd gotten out of.

The big cow and I stood our ground and stared each other down for what seemed an eternity. What happened next replays in my mind slow-motion, but I know it happened within seconds.

I saw a police car driving toward us, throwing dirt and grass in its wake from the corner of my eye at the same time I saw the cow snorting as he began to paw the ground. I heard the boys first, then the officer.

"Momma get away from him, he's gonna hurt you," the boys screamed.

I heard the message over the loud speaker from the cruiser, "Walk backwards from the animal, get in your car, and back up as fast as you can!" The authoritative command from the officer threw me into action.

I no sooner jumped in my car, threw it into reverse, and gunned it backward 'til the sheriff drove his car between the cow and me. Sure enough, the cow charged the police cruiser, hitting it in the door and almost flipping it over. By this time, a rancher with a trailer and a couple of riders came up to corral the big animal.

"What in the love of God's name do you think you were doing," the sheriff shouted at me as he rushed over to where I was sitting in my car, "you almost got yourself, and those boys, killed!"

"The cow was headed toward the road, and I was afraid he'd get hit and killed. I was trying to save his life."

"Cow, what cow," the sheriff asked incredulously. "When is the last time you saw a cow with a hump on his neck and skin hanging beneath his chin, oh, and with horns on his head? Please tell me you didn't think this Brahma bull was a cow?"

"Ugh, yeah, I really did think it was a cow. I don't know much about farm animals, I guess."

"In that case," the sheriff said in a low voice as he came within inches of my face snarling, "don't you ever let me catch you within arm's reach of another animal in my city. Do you understand," he shouted, before sending me on my way!

I managed to enroll in the university and was back on track to become a nurse. I'd long since stopped communicating with Jerry but missed the companionship of a man. I began dating a guy from church right after I started taking classes. A couple of months into our relationship, I thought I was pregnant because I'd missed my period. I didn't want to be pregnant and had decided I was going to have an abortion. The young man wanted to marry me and have the baby, but I didn't love him that way and didn't want to get married. He gave me the money I needed for the abortion, and I made an appointment. The morning I woke to go to the appointment, I had horrible cramps and started my period. I've lived my life haunted that I naturally aborted. I'll never know because I didn't keep the appointment. I kept the money and pretended that I'd had the abortion as planned. Ashamed of myself, I stopped dating that young man. I began smoking pot with a nearby neighbor after that and started skipping classes. It wasn't long before me, and the boys packed up and moved back to Texas. Once again, I withdrew from college, unable to finish what I'd started. One more failure I had to own.

Chapter 36

It's time to meet the man you married!!!

WE MOVED IN WITH MAW-MAW Cruse and had been there about a month when I heard from Jerry. He'd been paroled to a halfway house in Ft. Worth. We talked a few times before I picked him up to go riding around. He apologized and begged for another chance with me. He wanted to move near his family in West Texas so that he could go to work in the oil field. I told him I needed time to think about it.

Daddy didn't like the idea of me being pen pals with a convict, to begin with. He said that was a strike against us from the start. He said, "You don't know this man, what he's done, or anything else about him for that matter. He's gonna tell you exactly what you want to hear. Do you really think he's gonna be honest with you?" We'd been over this time and again. Daddy was hurt when I told him me and the boys were moving to Midland with Jerry. Bless his heart (and shame on me); he tried so hard to talk me out of going. Bull-headed and determined to prove Daddy wrong, I left with Jerry as soon as he had permission from his parole officer to go.

Between us, Jerry and I had enough money to rent a two-bedroom house when we got there. Jerry was hired on an oil rig outside of town the day he applied. We set up house and began our lives together. He was pretty good with the boys and left their care in my hands. It was understood from the start that their father and me were the only ones who whipped them if the need arose.

I was unpacking a few days after we got there when I run across something that made the hairs stand up all over my body. I had picked up one of

Jerry's boxes to set up on the shelf in the closet. It was a little heavy, and I lost control of it. It fell backward over my head, dumping its contents all over the floor. I was stacking everything back in the box when curiosity got the best of me. The worn-out, spiral notebook I picked up begged to be open. The pages had long since yellowed, the ink fading but still legible.

At first glance, it looked like a logbook where someone had recorded their activity over a period of time. All entries were numbered with vague dates beside each one, i.e., Fall 1975. My surprise came when I looked closer and read the entries.

1. Blonde girl, cut-off blue jeans, shorts, laundry mat…. Winter 1972
2. Skinny prostitute in front of movie theater…. Spring 1974
3. Black girl with afro at mall…. Fall 1975

On and on were descriptions of random women.

Reading through the pages gave me an eerie feeling, so I stopped after the first dozen. There were almost two-dozen pages with hundreds of entries. I finally shook it off, telling myself these were girls Jerry had dated all his life, and he'd kept a record of them. Later that evening, when he got in from work, I asked him about it.

"How dare you go through my belongings," Jerry screamed as he went to retrieve the precious spiral, "you had no right to invade my privacy! Don't you ever touch my things again!"

He never answered or explained what those entries were all about. I never saw his box of things again and have no clue what became of them. Something in his tone of voice and manner frightened me so that I never brought it up again.

We smoked weed and drank a little recreationally, but other than that, we never did hard drugs together. I was adamant that my sons be shielded from the drugs I did throughout the years. Ask either one of them; they never even knew I smoked marijuana until they were in their teens.

Jerry was determined that we get married. He said it would look good for his parole, and it might help him see his daughter. He believed if he could prove to his daughter's mother, he was stable, she might trust him to become a part of his daughter's life. It was a means to an end. We were married at the county courthouse.

I finally got a job at a gas station not far from where we lived. I bugged the man for a job until he finally relented. "I need a State Inspector. They have a class about to start down at the DMV. If you can pass that test and bring me a license, I'll hire you," the owner said.

I was the only female in a group of thirty who took the class, and one of five who passed. I felt proud of myself for a change. Jerry worked hard and brought his paycheck to me every two-weeks. He bought the boys BB guns and taught them how to shoot them, and also managed to speak to his daughter for the first time in their lives. Our lives couldn't have been better, and for a while, I believed everything was going to work out just fine.

We'd only been there a couple of months when I began to suspect Jerry was messing with hard drugs. He was coming home later than usual after work, sometimes going straight to bed. Our sex life, which had been hot and heavy, started cooling off. He was having erectile problems, which led me to believe he was doing cocaine. When I asked what was going on and if he was doing hard drugs, he laughed it off, saying he was just tired from working so hard. One week later, it all came to a head.

"You brought a hitch-hiker home to stay with us? Are you crazy? We know nothing about this man. He may be some deranged killer for all we know," I questioned as we stood in our kitchen?

"Keep your voice down, he'll hear you. He's just a guy down on his luck, and I told him he could stay a few days. You have nothing to worry about," Jerry stated in a tone that let me know there would be no more discussion on the subject.

I barely slept that night worrying about our safety, especially my boys. The next day I told my boss what was going on, and how frightened I was. He offered the boys and me a place to stay 'til I figured out what I was doing. He and his wife were a loving, spiritual couple and had a houseful of kids, but they made room for us. His wife followed me home after work, so I could drop the car off for Jerry and leave a note for him. I grabbed a couple of outfits for the three of us and hurried from the house. The hitch-hiker was sleeping on the couch, and I didn't want to wake him.

I wanted to go back to Dallas, but we'd sold my car for extra cash. Daddy was mad at me and said I had to get myself out of the mess I'd made. I had no choice but to work and save the money to get me and the boys home.

Jerry called my job several times each day, but I refused to talk to him. One time I picked up the phone when it rang, and sure enough, it was Jerry. He begged me not to hang up, saying how sorry he was.

"Look, I know you need more clothes, why don't you come by after work and pick some up?"

I agreed and told him I'd see him later.

I pulled up in front of the house in my boss' car not long after work that evening. The door was locked, and I heard music blaring. Knocking on the door, I had an eerie feeling and turned to walk away.

Not fast enough.

"There you are, come on in," Jerry said with a sick grin covering his face. I knew I was in trouble and started backing away, but he reached out and grabbed me by my shoulder.

"I can come back another time when you're not busy," I replied shakily, trying to break loose of the grip he had on my shoulder. The more I resisted, the more he pulled. He soon had me inside the house and slammed the door.

Over the roar of the music, he shouted at the hitch-hiker, "If someone comes looking for my little wife here, tell them we went for a walk up the street. And no matter what you hear, don't disturb us, is that clear," Jerry spoke to the hitch-hiker in a voice I didn't recognize. Dragging me, by the shoulder he had yet to let go of, he pulled me into our bedroom.

The room was completely destroyed as he had rifled through all my belongings and left them thrown about. Turning to look at Jerry, his appearance appalled me. He was very unkept and smelled like he hadn't bathed since I left. His breath stank of booze and cigarettes, but it was the look on his face that had me terrified. It was a twisted, maniacal looking monster face that I'll never forget.

"Aww, did her get her little feelings hurt seeing her stuff gone through? Don't like someone going through your stuff, do you," raising his voice a few decibels, he screamed, "well neither did I! I think it's time you met the man you married!"

Slamming me down on the bed with one arm, he began undoing his pants with the other. My eyes were even with the bedside table, and I saw the blade of the oversized pocket knife lying inches from where I was. Jerry saw me staring at the knife and began to laugh.

"Oh yes, princess, that beauty is just for you," he snarled through gritted teeth.

Stepping over to the bed, he bent down and wrapped my hair around his fist before jerking me up to a half-sitting position. Grabbing the knife with his other hand, he pushed the blade against my neck so hard I thought he was gonna cut my throat.

"You don't want me to cut your throat, do ya'? Tell ya what, you're gonna suck my cock like your life depends on it, cause guess what bitch, it does!"

"Please don't," was all I got out before he shoved his dick in my mouth and began slamming it against the back of my throat. The violent movement made me nauseous, and I felt vomit rushing forward.

The monster was insane and seemed to be turned on by the fact that I was choking on my own vomit; it seemed to push him harder. I prayed for it to end quickly.

"Keep sucking cunt. Suck harder, suck harder, I'm coming," he gasped with the last shove into my mouth.

I don't know how I swallowed the mouthful of sperm and vomit, but I did. Must have been the fear of having my throat slit any second, or better yet, the fact that I needed to breathe. Either way, this part was over.

Jerry pulled his pants up before stumbling from the room. I laid there terrified to move for fear of what he might do to me. He came back and threw a washcloth in my face saying, "Clean yourself up, you look like hell."

I couldn't believe how quickly his demeanor changed. He still wasn't the man I knew, but the monster seemed to have disappeared. He allowed me to get whatever I wanted and even helped me load the car. He didn't beg forgiveness or threaten to kill me if I told on him. He could have cared less. He said very little to me as I got in the car and drove away.

I pretended everything went well when I got to my boss's home. I didn't see any sense in calling the police. All I wanted to do was save enough money to get my sons and me home. I vowed to myself that I'd never be alone with Jerry again.

Chapter 37
SERIAL-RAPIST-MURDERER

Famous last words never come true.

Ten days after I was alone with Jerry, I saw him pulling into the service station. It was early Sunday morning, and I had the place to myself. Surely, he wouldn't attack me; at work, I thought to myself. I finished pumping the customer's gas and walked over to where he'd parked. When he asked me to sit in the car and talk to him, I did. I was too afraid to do otherwise.

"What in the world happened to you, Jerry?" He was shirtless and had big, gaping claw marks across his chest, sides, and face. "What happened here," I asked, pointing to the huge area in the front seat that was burned through the cushion.

"This is what you're being gone is doing to me. I miss you so damn much that I started hanging out at the bars and getting drunk. I got in a fight last night and fell in a rose bush. The bouncer threw me in the car, and I passed out with a cigarette in my hand. 'Bout near burned myself and the car up," he answered my questions before adding, "baby, I'm so sorry for hurting you the way I did. You were right, I've been doing '*coke*,' and when I'm on it, I can't control myself. Please, baby, please forgive me and come back to me. If you don't, I'll end up back in prison."

"I don't know Jerry. The boys are pretty freaked out by everything, and I don't think I could ever go back to that house after what happened there. I still feel uneasy 'bout that hitchhiker dude around my sons."

"I figured you'd say something like that, so I went and talked to my parents. They really believe in you. They opened this checking account in your name so that we could start over," Jerry pleaded as he handed me a starter checkbook with my name written in. The balance had fifteen-hundred dollars written in the check register as well. I'd never had a checking account before and felt honored they trusted me that much.

"As far as the hitchhiker, he planned to leave this coming Friday, but I'll make him go today if you'll just come back to me, baby, please," Jerry begged with tears sliding down his cheeks.

As repentant as he seemed, there was something else I couldn't put my finger on. The hairs standing up on the back of my neck seemed to scream, *'don't say no.'*

"Okay, Jerry, I guess if your parents believe in me that much, we should give it one more try. I get off at two pm this afternoon, pick me up, and we'll go find another house."

I called my boss and explained what was going on. He said the boys could hang out with them, so Jerry and I could have some time alone. I wasn't sure I wanted to be alone with Jerry, but the thought I'd had earlier was still nagging at the back of my mind. Crazy as it seemed, I had the feeling I'd better not push him too far.

The hitchhiker was with Jerry when he picked me up later that afternoon. To be honest, I was glad he was in the car. Then it came to me.

"You know, I may have been too hasty in my judgment of you. Motherly instincts can be pretty strong, ya' know?" Looking at Jerry, I continued, "I don't care if he stays a while longer."

"Ma'am, I appreciate it. I plan on leaving in a few days anyway, but I promise to be on my best behavior 'round your boys," the soft-spoken man said.

We rented the first house we looked at. I assured the owner I would have the utilities transferred first thing in the morning if we could move in that evening. Handing me the keys, the landlord said that'd be fine.

"I knew you'd sweet talk that old feller," Jerry said as we got back in the car. "I'll call one of my boys with a truck, and we'll be moved in before nightfall."

Several of the guys Jerry worked with came over, and true to his word, we were sleeping in our new home that night. Scuter and Patrick saw it all as another adventure. They became fast friends with the hitchhiker and wanted to hear all about his travels on the road.

I took the next day off and tended to the utility transfers and unpacked our things. Jerry helped me since his rig was being moved, and he had the next week or so off. Jerry said we were going out to eat in celebration of our new home but wouldn't say where. He said it was a surprise for his wonderful wife. Pulling into the Chinese restaurant later, all feelings of trepidation I had been feeling went out the window. Jerry was being the kindest, sweetest man I'd ever known. He continued to spoil me and treat me like a princess all week long.

I awoke to breakfast in bed that following Sunday morning. I couldn't believe only a week had passed since he pulled into the station and begged me to take him back.

"Good morning, beautiful," he said, laying the makeshift tray across my lap. "What would her highness like to do today?"

"Stop… I appreciate all the flattery, but you're spoiling me too much. Pretty soon, you won't be able to stand me," I gushed, taking the napkin and displaying it across my chest in an extravagant manner.

"Nothing is too good for my baby. Besides, I'll be getting ready for my next rig tomorrow, and I want to make today extra special for you."

It was a lazy Sunday. We watched some movies, went to the park and played tag football, and drove around for a while before going back to the Chinese restaurant for dinner.

"I appreciate y'alls hospitality, but I'll be leaving first thing in the morning," the hitchhiker said as we pulled into the driveway that night after dinner.

"No problem, man! Been nice having you," Jerry said before turning to me, "I know the boys start school tomorrow as well. How 'bout I drop you at work, drop the boys off at school and then give this guy a ride outta town. He'll have better luck if I drop him out by the truck stop?"

"Sure, no problem. Y'all don't mind if Jerry drops y'all off for your first day of school, do y'all," I asked the boys?

"Can we go with Jerry to drop him off and get to school a little later," the boys chimed in together?

"Sorry dudes, gotta set a good impression right off the bat," Jerry said, laughing. "You boys get ready for bed while I take your mother on a stroll around the block, capiche?"

"Aww, how sweet Jerry," I said as he took my arm and began walking me down the block.

"Look up at this beautiful sky. The moon is shining brighter than I've seen in a very long time. The stars are twinkling like lights on a Christmas tree.

Why wouldn't I want to share this with you? You've given me so much, and all I've given you is pain."

"That's not true. I forgave you; now it's time for you to forgive yourself."

"If only it were that easy," Jerry said, his voice trailing off.

I leaned into him, and he held me close as we walked back home, neither one of us feeling the need to speak. Returning home, he made a bubble bath for me. He bathed me as though I were a porcelain doll, fragile and precious. Carrying me to our bed, he took his sweet time and made love to me as if it was the last chance; he'd ever have. Listening to him snore later, feelings of trepidation returned.

The next morning started off bad.

I overslept and rushed around, trying to make sure the boys had everything they needed for their first day of school. I grabbed some breakfast while I packed my lunch. Jerry seemed pre-occupied and didn't hear a word I was saying to him. I said goodbye to the hitch-hiker dude and finally got Jerry's attention when I said I was ready to go.

"C'mon Jerry; I'm late," I said.

"You boys enjoy your first day of school and try to behave yourselves," I said with a raised eyebrow, hugging them I ran out the door.

"I'll pick you up at three; then we can pick the boys up together, okay?" Jerry said, giving me a quick peck on the cheek as I scrambled out of the car.

With a quick apology to my boss, I jumped right into work. Monday mornings were always busy, and I soon got lost in my work. The rush passed, and business had slowed when the huge Cadillac pulled onto the lot. All the car's occupants were staring at me as it passed me on the bay. Feeling uneasy, I looked away. They were all wearing the biggest hats I'd ever seen, and somehow, I knew they were there to see me. Glancing up from the gas, I was pumping; I saw the four men get out of their car and walk inside. My boss spoke to them before coming out to me.

"I'll take over. Those men want to speak with you," my boss said, reaching for the gas pump.

"Who are they," I asked, my voice breaking.

"They're Texas Ranger's Wende, and I'd suggest you cooperate with them, whatever they want."

Far as I knew, I'd never seen a Texas Ranger before and wasn't at all sure what they did other than they had something to do with law enforcement. I couldn't begin to imagine what they wanted with me.

"Wende, where is Jerry," I heard the moment I stepped in the lobby of the station.

"Ugh," I stuttered, trying to register what I'd heard.

"Don't try protecting him, we know he's with you," one of the men admonished.

I didn't respond, out of fear and confusion, not because I was protecting someone. The look on my face must have said it all because the gentleman who'd spoken first spoke again.

"You are aware that Jerry is on parole, aren't you," he asked.

"Yes sir, he said he went to prison over drugs," I said, finding my voice.

"There's no time to explain right now, but we need you to help us pick up Jerry as soon as possible. Your life is in grave danger," the big man cautioned.

They had my attention now fearing for my sons' lives.

"My sons are with him," I gasped. "He kept the car today to take them to school."

"Call him and tell him you're sick and need to come home right away," the Ranger said, handing me the phone.

"Hello," Jerry yelled into the phone when he finally answered.

"Jerry, I'm sick and need you to come and get me."

"I'm kinda busy, but it is what it is. I'll be up there in a minute," Jerry said, angrily.

The Rangers had been eavesdropping on the other line, and as soon as Jerry hung up, they rushed out of the building without another word to me, jumped in their big ol' car, and peeled out of the lot. I was in complete shock. A million questions were swirling through my head as I went to stand outside and wait for Jerry. Why was I in grave danger? What had Jerry done? What about my sons, were they okay? What was I gonna tell Jerry when he got there? I thought my heart was gonna beat out of my chest as I stood there waiting. If not for my sons, I would've hidden in my boss's office and never came out. Just when I thought I couldn't stand any more suspense, Jerry turned the corner and pulled up to where I was standing.

Before Jerry could put the car in park and climb out of the vehicle, every law enforcement agency in the county and state swarmed in behind him. There must have been a couple dozen or so vehicles, lights blazing, in that lot. A huge man in combat gear jerked Jerry from the car and slammed him down onto the pavement cracking one of the lenses in Jerry's glasses.

"What the hell is going on here," Jerry screamed.

I was in such shock I don't remember what the man said other than Jerry was under arrest.

"Can I please release my car to my wife, and say goodbye to her," Jerry asked, the bravado in his voice fading as they drew him to his feet.

"What's happening Jerry," I cried out as he stepped forward and kissed me on the cheek.

"I'm so sorry Wende, I'm so sorry," Jerry said as they led him away.

The many officers stood talking amongst themselves as the original four Rangers led me into my boss' office. I was shaking like a leaf and about ready to puke my guts up. I needed answers but was afraid to hear them. Once I called and found out the boys were indeed at school, they began their questioning.

"We know you have questions for us, and we'll answer all of them. First, we must move fast on this, so we need some answers from you. Okay," the same big man asked. I sensed the urgency in his tone and agreed to do my best.

"Has Jerry been looking to buy another car recently?"

"Yes, he has as a matter of fact," I answered chills going up my spine. You could have heard a pin drop. The men seemed to lean in closer, staring at me as the next question was asked.

"How was he looking to buy one? From a car lot, a friend?"

"He always looked at the boards whenever he saw notes posted at the grocery store or on laundromat walls, but mostly, he always looked in those Thrifty Nickel newspapers."

I barely got the words out of my mouth before they were all speaking at once.

"Will you testify to that on record?"

"We got him!"

"Don't you watch the news?"

The big 'ol man who'd been the kindest to me spoke up.

"Saturday before last, a young woman called her neighbor to say she was going for a ride around the block with a man who wanted to buy the car she and her husband had for sale in the Thrifty Nickel newspaper. The neighbor caught a glimpse of the man as he climbed in the driver's seat. The neighbor became distracted and lost track of time. Later, when the husband called the neighbor, asking if she knew where his wife had gone, it was then the neighbor remembered. By this time, several hours had passed. The young woman's body was found the next morning, beaten and viciously raped. The young woman was six months pregnant. The description the neighbor gave fit Jerry to a tee, and the poor woman's body was found near the site where Jerry's rig had just moved from."

Ding, ding, ding, ding, ding the bells began going off in my head left and right. I became physically ill and threw up in my boss' trash can, remembering the huge claw marks on Jerry's face and chest. When I recovered myself, the man continued.

"In addition, we have a half dozen reports of rapes that have been committed here in town recently. They all fit the same M.O., Jerry's M.O. You see, Jerry wasn't truthful with you. Jerry is on parole for deviant, sexual assaults, both here and in Arkansas. He is a serial rapist. He broke in one home and beat the man nearly to death before viscously attacking his wife in front of him. Jerry is a very dangerous man, and you're lucky to be alive."

I was in such shock and disbelief, but it all made sense. I told the men how Jerry had been clawed up the morning he came to the station and how he claimed he had fallen in a rose bush. I told them how he'd raped me the evening I came to get our clothes. Then I remembered the old, worn-out spiral I had found. When I mentioned it, they asked if I knew where it was. I told them I didn't have a clue and hadn't seen it since the day Jerry warned me to never touch his stuff again.

"We are going to search your car and your home. It will be a lot easier if you sign consent forms, but we can get a search warrant if we need to," the kind man explained.

"No, there's no need for that, I'll sign whatever forms you need me to. Will Jerry be able to get out anytime soon? Will I have enough time to pack our things and get my boys and me back home before he can get out," I asked praying they'd say Jerry couldn't get out at all. "There was a hitch-hiker guy staying at our house, but I don't know if he's still around."

"No. We have enough on him to revoke his parole, and that's where we plan to start. Why don't you drive to your home, and we'll follow you?"

I wasn't allowed to go in our home when we arrived there and was asked to sit in a patrol car while they searched our vehicle.

I thought about Daddy while I sat there. If only I'd listened to him. He was right about Jerry from the start. Everything Jerry had ever said to me were lies. I had wasted so much of my life on this man. Not to mention risking my freedom. I was so ashamed of myself. If only I'd listened to Daddy, I'd be a nurse by now, I thought. As soon as these folks were done with me, I was gonna pick up my boys and our stuff and leave. I would close out my bank account, pick up what little I had coming from my job, and we'd be out of here.

It was shortly after noon when they released my home and car to me.

Chapter 38
I'm going to kill you!

I CALLED DADDY AND TOLD him all that had happened that morning. Daddy was upset, but he didn't rub it in my face. I told him I was going to the bank before I withdrew the boys from school. Then we'd pack up the car and head home.

I walked up to the bank teller and handed her my bank book. I explained to her that I wanted to close my account and get the cash I was owed. The teller looked at my checkbook and typed information into her monitor. I didn't know why she looked at me so strangely but felt the hair on my neck rising once again. She whispered something to the guard who escorted me into an office where I spoke with a bank official.

"Ma'am, are you aware this checkbook you handed the teller is stolen, and hundreds of dollars have been forged on this account?"

I passed smooth out. When I came to, I began crying hysterically. It took the bank official a few minutes to calm me enough to understand what I was saying, but once I did, he became very sympathetic. He knew that I was telling the truth because I had voluntarily walked into the bank to close the account.

The bank official had an offer for me. Under the circumstances, he didn't feel he could bring charges against me, but he had to recoup the money the bank had lost. He said if I could talk to the landlord and explain the situation, perhaps the landlord would refund the lion's share of the money I had given him, and vice versa with the utility companies, etc. If I could recoup 80% of the money back to the bank, he would write the rest off. I promised to get all the money back to the bank if he gave me a couple of days. The kind man shook my hand and asked me to do the best I could.

Driving to pick up the boys, I became scared. What if that man changed his mind? What if the landlord wouldn't work with me? All I could think about was protecting my boys. I refused to let anyone take them to child protective services. I called Clark, and after telling him all that had happened, I asked him to please come get the boys away from there. He said he would be on his way as soon as he could.

The boys were pretty upset they were leaving without me but excited their Daddy was coming to get them. I withdrew them from school and gathered their records to give to Clark when he got there.

When we got to the house, I couldn't believe how torn up it was. The kind Ranger who'd spoken softly had told me it was torn up when they went in and looked as if Jerry had been getting ready to leave town. I was guessing the officer's searching had made it worse. Gathering the boy's clothes and toys together, all I could do was cry.

Clark and his girlfriend got there around midnight to pick up the boys. I handed Clark the paperwork and told him that I trusted him to protect our boys while I took care of the mess I was in.

"Don't worry, Wende; I'll take care of our boys. You just take care of yourself and get back home."

The next morning, I got busy and talked to the landlord, utility companies, and local stores I had written checks to. Everyone was very empathetic to my situation and agreed to work with me. I had a garage sale that afternoon and sold everything I couldn't fit in my car. For a last-minute event, I did well, selling everything. I cleaned the house up spotless, and the landlord refunded almost all the money I had paid to him. I paid the bank back all the money I had fraudulently spent the first thing the following morning. I stopped off at the police station, and they arranged for me to see Jerry so that he could sign our car title. I told him it was to sell the car, but I didn't tell him what my plans were. He must have seen it in my eyes.

"What's wrong with you, look at me. Oh, I get it. You're leaving me, aren't you? Wait a minute; you helped set me up, didn't you? Well, guess what, princess, I'm gonna get out of here, and I will find you. I know you wouldn't miss your grandmother's funeral for the world, would you?" Once again, I caught a glimpse of the monster as he threatened to kill me someday. It was an image that would haunt me for many years to come. Standing to leave, as they led him away, I knew I hadn't heard the last of Jerry Claude Ferguson.

Years later, Maw-Maw Cruse let it slip that Jerry had continued writing me for the next year and a half after that, but Daddy had told her to throw the letters away, and not to say anything about them to me. Looking back now, I'm sure glad they made that decision.

Chapter 39
Dealing drugs...

It's been over six months since I last sat at my computer. I hadn't thought about that period of my life in years. Going back and recalling those events in detail brought back all the terror I'd felt when it first happened. It was as though remembering it had opened the door and let the evilness out to engulf me all over again. It crippled me into believing I'd never be able to walk through the aftermath of all that happened afterward; the years of wasted life...

Waking this morning to the sun shining brightly through my windows and the birds chirping merrily outside my window, I realized that if I didn't finish what I'd started, I'd never be free.

September 1984

I vaguely remember driving back to Dallas after I saw Jerry that day. My mind was totally blown. How could I have been so blind as to believe what Jerry had fed me? My mind kept racing from one thought to the next. It felt like my thoughts were all scattered and jumbled at the same time. Like in a Fun House where you're in a mirror maze, and you keep running into the same corner you've seen before, my thoughts kept scattering and running back into one another. Not just recent memories, but all the way back to my childhood. I wondered if I was going crazy. One memory kept vying for the top spot. I wondered if all my other memories had come back to push that one away to protect me. For the longest time afterward, every time I remembered Jerry's clawed up face and chest, I became physically ill and puked my guts up. In my mind's eye, I imagined that poor woman fighting for hers and her child's life. I really should have sought professional help, but just as I did with everything else, I sucked it up and moved on. Those memories that threatened to destroy me packed away once again in neat little compartments and stowed in the far reaches of my mind.

I moved back in with Maw-Maw and tried to pick up the pieces of my life. Bubba had long since divorced his wife and was on his own. We hung out here and there, and occasionally snorted methamphetamine together, neither one of us quite ready to become dedicated needle freaks just yet. He introduced me to a guy he worked with who I dated now and then.

Clark said I should leave the boys with him until I got on my feet. His girlfriend, Sally, agreed with him and said she wanted to help in any way she could. One weekend when I was bringing the boys back after a visit, Sally pulled me to the side. She told me to stop by one afternoon while Clark was at work and visit with her.

"We both know how Clark can be about things; just keep this between us, okay," she asked with a wink?

I got a delivery job not long after I moved back in with Maw-Maw Cruse. I was delivering for a printing/graphics company and had a regular route from downtown Dallas all the way out to the other side of Plano. Long before cell phones arrived on the scene, I had my very own pager. With my pager, I added stops throughout my route as needed. This delivery job was much more fun than the auto parts delivery I'd had before. I had to use my brain to coordinate all of my stops, which was very stimulating. I was always up for a challenge.

I finished my route early one afternoon and decided to swing by and see what Sally had in mind. I figured if she wanted to help me so much, it was cause she didn't want to be tied down with my sons all the time. I wanted my boys home, so I decided to go along with whatever she had up her sleeve. What a win/win situation I thought smugly to myself. Of all the times I felt I had control of a situation; unfortunately, I did not. The single decision I made to go along with Sally would be my downfall.

"I know you can't wait to take the boys home with you. I see you struggling financially, and I want to help you," Sally said, sympathetically, as she handed me a glass of tea and motioned for me to sit down.

"That's very kind of you," I responded, thinking to myself how thoughtful she was being.

Methamphetamine had become the next big "*IT*" in social circles, and most everyone I knew was involved with it. It was shared right along with the weed. Passing me a lit joint, Sally asked if I wanted to do a line.

"Sure," I grinned, my nose already watering.

"Do you know many people who like this stuff," Sally asked nonchalantly.

"Duh, you know I do, what's up," I asked, taking a long pull off the joint.

"I thought maybe we could do a little business together." Pulling out a handful of triangle-shaped bags filled with tiny white rocks and powder, she tossed them to me. "Those are quarter baggies, and they're twenty-five dollars each. Every one of them is a quarter gram of methamphetamine. I'll give you fourteen of them which equals three and a half grams, or an eight ball however you want to call it, for three-hundred dollars. You'd make a fifty-dollars profit if you didn't use the free quarters."

"Hmm, sounds good. At that rate, I might save up the money for an apartment in six months," I replied facetiously.

"Well, let's try that and see how it goes," Sally said, eye-balling me carefully, "there's always room for negotiations later."

Just like that, I became a drug dealer.

Little did I know that by the time I stepped away from the craziness, I would become involved in one of the largest organized crime syndicates in North America. Always on the fringes mind you, but involved nonetheless. Like evil does, it permeated my entire family, destroying lives in its wake.

Sally's product was top shelf, and everyone wanted more. My job soon became a front for my daily deliveries. It got to where I had customers scattered all along my delivery route. At first, I was selling all the quarters and saving the money. As time went on, I began taking advantage of the '*free*' speed and started dipping into my profits. It was one such morning at work that I lost my job. I was sitting in a toilet stall, trying to snort a line before I left out on my deliveries. I lost my balance and sent the baggie flying under the stall right into the stall where one of the bosses just happened to be. They didn't call the police; they just asked me to leave the premises right away.

It was my day to re-up with Sally, so I called and told her what had happened. She told me not to worry about it, and to come on over cause she had good news for me. I drove the short distance to Clark, and Sally's wondering what she was up to now.

"What's good about today," I asked, "I'm pretty bummed out myself."

"Oh, nothing much. You remember I told you I have a business partner, and he's been monitoring your sales?" Sally asked, passing me a big fat joint, she continued, "He's impressed with your sales ability. He's decided it is time to set you up on your own. You won't be selling my quarters anymore; instead, he will be fronting you solid rocks of pure meth."

If I didn't know better, I'd say Sally was jealous, but I didn't know why at the time. I would be boiling ass mad at her one day down the road when I realized her real motivation in 'helping me,' but it wasn't long before I knew what had her in this current tizzy.

"This is a quarter ounce of pure meth. It hasn't been cut, so be careful with it," Sally said, handing me the small Tupperware container. I could see what looked like a ping pong ball inside the container.

"Whew, is that strong or what," I asked after popping the lid and taking a whiff of the contents. "I don't know how to cut anything or make the quarters as you do. What do you mean by cut anyways?"

"Do you want me to sell it for you too," Sally said, sarcastically, as she got up and left the room, returning with a larger box. She pulled out a scale, a small jar of white powder, a small spoon/scoop, and a stack of sandwich baggies. "I'm not going to do it for you, but I will explain." Holding up the jar of white powder, she continued, "This is mannitol. It is a baby laxative which won't do anything to anyone but make them shit if they take too much. Chopping up the meth and mixing it with mannitol not only doubles your money but, more importantly, keeps people from overdosing on the drug. This method is called 'cutting.' If you add too much mannitol, it weakens the meth, and no one will like your product. You have to figure out how much you want to use each new batch of meth you get. I usually put one to one and a half grams of mannitol to every eight ball. An eight ball is three and a half grams, remember. The fourteen quarters I fronted you are three and a half grams. Do you understand now," Sally asked in an irritable, annoyed tone?

"Sure, I think I can figure it out from here," I replied, anger building by the moment. I pasted a smile on my face, determined to let her think I hadn't realized how much she had made off my hard work, and pleased that she was losing her cash cow. "So one-quarter ounce is seven grams, huh? If I add 3 grams of mannitol, I'll have 10 grams to sell. How much do I have to pay your partner then?"

"Five hundred dollars," Sally said, barely able to contain her frustration.

"Wow, I can actually double my money," squealing, I jumped up and did the happy dance.

"Were you able to pick up the weed? My customers keep asking when I'm gonna share my primo weed? I usually fire up when I have time. It looks like I'm gonna have plenty of time now that I am no longer employed."

Sally shook her head since she was holding her breath for max absorption of the THC.

"Let me get it." Handing me a gallon-sized storage bag filled with bright green buds, she explained, "This is different than what you've been getting, but I promise you're gonna love it. They're calling it Christmas tree pine. All I could get was a quarter-pound for now, and it's two-hundred-twenty-five dollars your cost."

"Cool, cool. Well, I better be splitting since I have to pick up some accessories for my little business venture. Thanks, chickie!"

As usual, Sally reminded me that this was all top-secret business, and Clark must never find out she was helping me.

Stopping at the head shop, I found they had most of what I needed. One more stop to pick up the baby laxative and sandwich baggies, and soon I was headed home. I was excited thinking about my new business venture. I was no longer worried about losing my job and couldn't help but think of all the money I was gonna make!

Somewhere along the way, I'd lost sight of the morals I knew existed. Good at justifying, I told myself that these were all people my age who would be buying it whether I sold it to them or not. I promised myself that I would never sell to minors, and if I knew someone was using bill money, I'd give them a bump free of charge. I wasn't hurting anybody, so why shouldn't I make the money myself. How naïve I was in those early days.

Chapter 40

Lethal bumps, and kind-hearted cop from New York!

I HAVE VERY MIXED EMOTIONS as I write about this era in my life. I can't help but wonder how folks' perception of me will change when they read about my sordid past. But more than that, it is messing with me by setting off triggers in my mind.

Even though I have almost twenty years of sobriety, the thought crosses my mind to turn to the quick financial fix I know exists in the drug world. The lure of easy money has been the downfall of many before me and will continue to destroy millions upon millions until this earth shall pass away.

The high, I hear romanticized about the newer version of meth called Ice, beckons to me, "What harm could one little bump do? You're older and much wiser now. You could walk away knowing what it was like instead of always wondering?"

I must admit, the pull is strong, but I have plenty of weapons to fight back with and waste no time shutting those thoughts down. I could never go back to that world. Shivers run up my spine, recalling the evilness that hangs in the air just out of sight, waiting to engulf one who has no will left to fight.

Then there is the whole matter of who I've become today. I am a professional, and as such, I'm required to maintain a certain amount of dignity and character. I'm not sure if sharing the stories of my life is going to destroy all I worked to achieve or not. I truly believe God wants me to share my experiences with others to glorify his name. Everything works to the glory of God when we turn it over to him.

The mere mention that someone is a drug dealer evokes images of seedy characters hiding in darkened stoops, or back alleyways. Stereotypical images can be accurate, but more often than not, very misleading. I think I escaped notice because I carried on as I always had, except for the fact that I became so busy delivering drugs that I didn't have time to work. It wasn't long before my whole family knew what I was up to. Not all of them approved, I might add.

My clientele began growing, and I soon crossed paths with individuals who wanted more than the quarter bags I was peddling. Speaking of quarter bags, I found out the first time I made my own quarters just how much dear Ms. Sally had been ripping my customers and me off. Her quarters were actually dime bags (ten-dollar bags) when weighed. I refused to cheat anyone in that manner and simply told my people that I was getting a better deal and wanted to pass it on to them when they remarked that the amount I was selling them, was double what I had in the past. Despite how low I sunk back in those days, I never dealt my product underhandedly. It might be hard to understand, but there is a code of honor in the criminal world to a certain extent.

I caught on to the idea that buying in bulk meant lower prices and began asking Sally when I could move up to an ounce. Finally, she said her partner wanted to meet me. Imagine my shock when her partner turned out to be Steve, Clark's homosexual friend. He was just as adamant as Sally that we keep our dealings under wraps. I was beginning to smell a rat but left it be since I was starting to make big bucks. The boys were doing fine, and I saw them often. I didn't want to rock the boat.

It was hard to believe that it'd only been a few short months since I'd left Midland. I rarely allowed myself to linger on thoughts of Jerry when they surfaced. I was unable to process it all. It was much easier to live in the day. I dove straight off into the drug world, and all that entailed. I hit the ground running and never looked back.

Steve dismissed Sally right away, which really pissed her off, but Steve was a businessman. I was soon to find out more about organized crime than I wanted too. As time went on, Steve shared more and more info with me. I couldn't believe it the day he explained that he was involved with a well-known crime syndicate, which included members of law enforcement and officials who held high offices in local governments. By this time, I was well on my way to becoming a full-fledged junkie. I kept searching for that first-time feeling with each shot of dope I did.

I had a couple of people I sold to who bought in bulk. They bought ounces at a time and always rewarded me with big fat shots upon arrival. Steve paid me a flat fee for delivering to my bulk customers at cost, so they would keep buying more. It was a win/win situation for me.

I knew if I complained about the shot they gave me, they'd up the ante. One time I learned a near-fatal lesson when I woke in a tub of ice water with my customer frantically begging his wife not to call an ambulance. I remember teasing that his shots had been getting weak when I arrived earlier that night.

"Oh yea, well, I'm gonna fix you up a shot that will shut your mouth," my customer replied in a joking manner. How prophetic would those words soon become?

I still remember the anticipation I felt as I watched him dump a solid rock into the spoon. I don't know what in God's name I was thinking 'bout knowing that the dope was straight from the cook's, pure and uncut. I could hear Sally in the back of my mind telling me that I had to make sure the dope was cut before anyone used it. I ignored every warning that teased the back of my mind, intent on experiencing the ultimate rush that evening.

He hit my vein with the first try and slowly began pushing the plunger forward. He'd only injected half of the syringe when I felt the rush with such intensity that I became paralyzed and couldn't tell him to stop. I remember my body feeling like jelly as I began sliding off the chair and onto the floor.

The next thing I remember was waking up in a tub ice water, and my customer's wife was sobbing profusely. They said I had collapsed into unconsciousness and had voided both urine and feces. They thought I was dying and put me in a tub of ice water to revive me. It had taken nearly an hour for me to open my eyes.

It scared the man and his wife so badly that they wouldn't deal with me anymore. I sold my connection with them to Steve for one-thousand dollars. He sent one of his runners to take care of them after that, and I never saw them again.

I nearly died that night, but it didn't slow me down at all.

I had gotten pretty hung up on the guy Bubba introduced me to, but he wasn't interested in a ready-made family. I was getting ready to get my boys back when he broke up with me. Or at least I thought I was getting them back.

Unbeknownst to me, little Ms. Sally had let it slip I had been buying dope from Steve for quite some time. They told Clark I was the one who had begged her and Steve to sell me dope so I could support my habit and earn enough money to get the boys back. They pointed out I wasn't fit to raise my sons. Sally convinced Clark that his only choice was to take me to court. He readily accepted Sally's father's offer to use his lawyer for the task.

The weekend after Bubba's friend dumped me; I got the shock of my life. I had gone to pick the boys up and discuss them coming home with me permanently. Clark was there waiting on me.

"Where are the boys," I asked when I sat down in Clark's living room?

"They're with Sally," Clark said, staring at me intently before continuing, "Wende, are you strung out on dope?"

"No, why would you ask that," I countered, beginning to get very nervous?

"You must think I'm stupid! You've been going behind my back for months now to my girl and friends begging for dope," Clark spat out, unable to control his temper.

"It's not what you think Clark, let me explain," I begged, knowing where this was going.

"No, I want you out of my house now! I have hired a lawyer and will see you in court. You are not to come near my boys until then. Do I make myself clear," Clark threatened in a tone that sent me tearing out the house before he decided to show me just what he meant?

I was so confused. How had this happened? Now not only had I been dumped, but I had just been denied access to my precious sons. I was devastated, to say the least. I wanted to fight back, but I was in no position to do so. I wasn't strung out at the time but would be in the very near future.

The home I had rented to bring the boys to was in Grand Prairie. Bubba and his new girlfriend came to live with me not long after Clark refused to let me have the boys back. I was depressed and unsure of what to do. I think Bubba, in his own way, was trying to look out for me.

Strange enough, Steve continued to sell to me even though Clark and I weren't talking. Steve said he didn't want to be in the middle and suggested I keep our business between us.

I don't remember why, but one night right after I left Steve's house with an ounce of meth and a pound of weed, my car broke down. Bubba came and pulled my car back to the house on NE 22nd St. in Grand Prairie.

"What am I gonna do now? I am supposed to be out and about selling my product tonight?"

"I guess you can use the Monte Carlo if you put gas in it," Bubba said though he didn't sound happy about it.

I did a bump with Bubba, his girlfriend, and a friend of mine that was staying at the house temporarily before heading out for my first sale. I weighed out a quarter-ounce of meth and sealed it in an airtight tea canister and rolled the gallon-sized bag containing a quarter-pound of weed tightly in a newspaper before shoving them both in the bottom of my big, blue-jean, hippie purse that I always carried.

Promising Bubba I'd be back before he had to leave for work, I headed out the door.

Three hours later, and on the other side of Lake Dallas (now Lake Lewisville), my customer failed to show up. I had waited and waited because he was supposed to have bought the quarter-ounce of meth, and quarter-pound of weed. I was gonna profit enough to pay our rent for the month. Man was I pissed!

I barely had enough gas to get home, let alone worrying about buying Bubba's gas to get to work. I was so upset I missed the turn for I-30, the old Turnpike, and ended up on Commerce St. The car started making a grinding, horrible noise right before it stopped dead still right in front of Lew Sterrett Jail otherwise known as Dallas County Jail. Oh my God, what in the world was I gonna do now? I didn't even have a quarter to make a phone call.

I managed to guide the car off the road. It was sitting right at the bottom of the hill from the jail, so I figured it would be okay for a minute. There were no other businesses open at four in the morning near where I'd broken down, so I saw no other choice but to try to borrow a phone at Lew Sterrett. No way I was gonna carry my hippie purse containing drugs into the jailhouse, so I locked it in the trunk of the car before heading up the hill.

"No, ma'am, we don't have phones for the public's personal use," the rude lady behind the window stated.

It was at that moment that the situation got the best of me, and I began crying. I never could help myself. When I become frustrated, mad, sad, and can't think of what to say, the tears come. Even when I'm overwhelmed with joy, they come. It makes me mad that I have no control over my internal waterworks; I could just spit sometimes!

A big burly jailer on his way out the door saw me and came to my rescue. He gave me a couple of quarters and even offered to look at the car.

"You sure you don't want me to take a look at the car for you," the kind officer asked?

"No, I appreciate it, but my brother is particular about who touches his car," I said, hoping he wouldn't insist.

"Well then, I'll let you get to your phone calls," he said, walking away.

I was shaking in my shoes, thinking about the officer getting a whiff of the inside of the car, not to mention looking in the trunk where the drugs were stashed in my purse.

I called Bubba, who was madder than a wet hen, because he had to find a way to work. He suggested I call the wrecker service Clark worked for and have them tow the car to his job. The wrecker service finally arrived and pulled into Bubba's job at the same time Bubba showed up. Bubba's boss paid the tow driver, and I thought all would be well until I stepped over to talk to Bubba.

"I'll talk to you when I get home," Bubba snapped at me before turning and walking off.

Standing there, my purse on my shoulder, I didn't know what to do. I was in the middle of downtown Dallas with no money or way to get home.

"I'm gonna hitch-hike," I hollered at Bubba, not caring who heard my threat.

I walked the half-block out to Woodall Rogers Freeway and crossed the lanes to walk on the inside shoulder in the middle of the freeway cause I thought it was the best way to catch a ride. Imagine my surprise when a police car pulled up right ahead of me.

"Ma'am, are you aware it's against the law to hitch-hike," the young officer asked as he exited his car and walked toward me?

"I wasn't a hitch-hiking officer, but I thought it would be the quickest way to walk down to where I could get to I-30 the safest way," crying in earnest as the tears began to flow, "I just got in a fight with my brother cause his car broke down on me. I have no money, and he refused to help me get home. Walking down I-30 is the shortest way for me to get there. I'm sorry, officer; I promise I'm not trying to cause any trouble." I babble when I get nervous, and man was I a basket case right that minute.

Looking at his watch, he shook his head before saying, "I got a few minutes before my shift begins, hop in, and I will give you a ride to the end of the freeway."

"I don't want to trouble you, I'll just walk back over to my brother's job, he'll probably help me now," I said trying to walk away.

"No, I insist. It's the least I can do to help you," the officer said, taking me by my elbow and leading me to his car and sitting me up front next to him. As fascinated as I was, I was also terrified that the pot would reek in his nice sanitized patrol car. He reminded me to put on the seat belt as he pulled away. I noticed he had a Yankee accent and asked him where he was from trying to distract him any way I could think of.

"I'm from New York, and as a matter of fact, my family and I just got back from there yesterday. We've been on vacation visiting our family."

"What brought y'all all the way down here to Texas?"

"One of my buddies lived here and said it was pretty easy to get on with the Dallas PD, so we moved here last year."

"Do you like it? Is it very different from New York," I asked, trying to keep the conversation rolling?

We'd reached Industrial Blvd (now called Riverfront Blvd) when he looked at his watch again.

"I can't just leave you stranded. I'll drive to your house in Grand Prairie. It shouldn't take me long to go and get back, but it's just between us, okay," the young officer winked as he turned left on Industrial to make the short trek over to the I-30 entrance. I pushed my purse further under my legs, trying to roll the top closed as much as I could knowing that any minute, he was gonna smell the weed at the bottom of my purse. Please, dear God, help me, I begged from my heart.

I continued talking my butt off, mostly thanking his mother for raising such a fine man to rescue ladies in distress while risking his life as a police officer. I admit I was laying it on thick as I could. In my mind, I was wondering how much time I could get locked up with the amount of drugs I had on me.

I couldn't believe that he had driven me all the way home as he pulled into my driveway. I saw the curtains open before shutting just as fast as he walked around to open the door for me.

"I can't thank you enough officer for all your help. God will bless you for this," I said as I reached out to shake his hand.

"I'm glad I had the time, ma'am. I hope you work things out with your brother. Take care and don't be walking on freeways, okay," he winked before getting in his patrol car.

I barely got in the house before my friend, and Bubba's girlfriend bombarded me with questions. When I told them what happened, and that I had ridden all the way from downtown Dallas in a squad car carrying drugs, they thought I was lying.

"Oh yea," I said, dumping my purse upside down, causing the drugs to fall out. I fell out on the floor right then and thanked God above for protecting my sorry ass. I vowed I'd never forget how blessed and lucky I'd been that morning, and I never have.

Chapter 41

Buried fortunes, Ted, and boys come home!

Daddy began having financial troubles around the time I started making money hand over fist in the meth world. Not to mention his health had started declining. I'd turned Dad and Mom Nita on to my white, fluffy 'candy,' which produced instant alertness no matter how it was ingested, the first time Sally fronted me. Meth was the perfect eye-opener for those on the graveyard shift, and it didn't take long for my parents to want more and more. At first, no one knew I was getting it for them, but ever the businessman, Daddy asked to see Steve himself eventually. To this day, I feel responsible for dragging Daddy and the others down with me.

Daddy never did anything small. He always aimed high, and it wasn't long before he was playing with the big boys. It wasn't long before I was buying my product from Daddy, as was Bubba and Shelley. It would take a few more years, but eventually, Daddy retired from the donut business and became a full-time drug dealer. He became involved with the same organized crime group Steve was involved with. He had to pay his dues like everyone else, and it cost him thousands of dollars a month to play the game. He would spend the next fifteen years or so in the racket before being arrested when he tried to bow out.

He'd flown out to California with one of the big boys in a small plane and was on the way back when he had a moment of clarity. Me and Mom Nita had sensed he was getting in too deep and had been begging him for months to get out of the business before it was too late. Daddy would humor us for so long before he would tell us to stop nagging and shut us out. Finally, flying through the mountains in a thunderstorm woke him up. Daddy said they'd had engine problems, and the plane took a nosedive and began losing altitude. Daddy said he'd never been so scared in all his life. He said he promised God he would walk away from the business if he could just make it back home to his family. The pilot was able to recover after some harrowing moments, but not before Daddy saw the light.

I picked Daddy up at the airport when he arrived home. Daddy was shaken up for sure. I was too as we loaded my car down with PVC pipes filled with pounds of meth, over a hundred-pounds as I recall. I remember that day well.

We'd just pulled up to a stoplight after exiting the small airfield when I saw a police car facing us on the opposite side of the street. I started to panic when Daddy told me to look at him. He made the silliest face I'd ever seen, causing me to laugh. Then he became serious and said, keep your cool and imagine we just picked up groceries from the store. Turning to face forward, I took Daddy's advice. The light turned green, and I drove past the cop car with ease. Daddy had always calmed me when I was nervous about anything. The day I rode my bike without training wheels, the day I drove a motorcycle the first time, and the first time a tire blew out on me. Daddy always talked me through it.

Daddy had been asked to prove his loyalty to the group before the trip out West. Returning in one piece, Daddy, said he was afraid to tempt God, and decided to keep his word. It was the beginning of the end, and soon Daddy would lose more than he'd ever gained. Several of Daddy's runners were arrested, including Bubba. It cost Daddy thousands of dollars in lawyer's fees to defend his associates and family. The next bit of bad luck would have been hilarious if it hadn't been so devastating to Daddy and Mom Nita.

Daddy and Mom Nita lived in the house cater-cornered across the street from Grandma Georgia Belle and had for many years. They rented the little shop on the corner next to Grandma's and ran a beauty shop/thrift store there once Daddy retired from the donut shop. I'm guessing it was used as a front as well.

Daddy had amassed quite a fortune in profits over the years and knew better than to deposit the money in the bank with no way to account for where it came from. He wasn't about to hide it in the house and take a chance on someone stealing him blind either. He finally came up with a foolproof plan to protect his fortune. He decided to bury it in Grandma Georgia Belle's back yard in the middle of the pet cemetery, where her favorite pets were buried. Over time, he had buried close to a million dollars in Grandma's back yard.

One day he decided to dig up one of the huge coffee cans to see how it had weathered a storm that had blown through, flooding everything. His worst fears were realized as he pulled the lid from the can. The can was filled with mud and water. Terrified that his money would be ruined, Daddy dug up all the cans and pulled the money from the muck each can held. Daddy filled the bathtub with water and filled the tub with all the soiled cash. Daddy left the money soaking to run an errand. While he was gone, Mom Nita came up with the idea to put all the wet money in the dryer to dry it and surprise Daddy. Over seven-hundred-thousand dollars worth of wet, waterlogged money tumbled in the dryer for over an hour until Daddy got back.

He was surprised, alright, when he walked into the bathroom and saw the tub empty.

"Nita," Daddy yelled in horror.

"What is it, John," Mom Nita cried as she ran to the bathroom. "Oh, the money," smiling, Mom Nita told Daddy she'd put it in the dryer.

"Oh no! You didn't," Daddy said, making a dead run for the utility room.

Opening the dryer, Daddy fell to his knees, screaming out unintelligible words. The first thing Daddy noticed when he opened the dryer door was the smell of burnt paper. Balls of dried money stuck together flew from the dryer onto the floor. Mom Nita had followed Daddy and stood behind him, watching in horror as Daddy gathered the balls of partially burnt money from the floor and tossed them in a clothes basket. He scooped the rest of the money from the dryer into the basket and carried it to their bedroom.

"Hey y'all," I said, walking into their bedroom hours later, "I came to pick up…," my words were forgotten as I looked from Daddy to Mom Nita and the bed covered with what appeared to be money. "What in the world is going on?"

Mom Nita took one look at me and left the room. I could tell she'd been crying and didn't want to talk. Daddy looked up at me with such a pitiful look; it hurt my heart. When Daddy finally spoke, he could barely get the words out. He explained what had happened earlier in the afternoon in a voice; I almost didn't recognize. My Daddy was devastated. He'd never planned to sell drugs forever and had been saving the money so that he could support himself and

Mom Nita for the rest of their lives. He'd been planning to walk away from the business since he got back from California.

We worked on the money for the next couple of months, unfolding the wads of dried cash, being careful not to lose the serial numbers in the process. It was very tedious work. As long as the hundred-dollar bills had one viable set of serial numbers on one end and one or two showing on the ruined side, the banks would exchange them for us. Shelley and I took the bills we were able to salvage to banks all over north Texas and fed the bankers stories about accidentally burning our money up in the dryer. We also used the money to pay our bills. It took months, but we eventually recovered three-hundred-thousand dollars of the money Daddy lost.

Daddy came up with the idea to manufacture his own product after he met a guy who claimed to know the ins and outs of cooking methamphetamine. Daddy invested thousands of dollars in the special laboratory equipment and ingredients based on the man's word, but that's another story. More on that later.

I met a cool guy while I was dating Bubba's friend; his name was Ted. He and his girlfriend loved my product, and he got in touch with me not long after Bubba's friend broke up with me. I was glad he did because I was having a hard time 'cutting' and packaging the product I was getting from Steve.

Ted was more than happy to help me out. I was very generous with anyone who went out of their way for me, and he knew it. He was a good friend who always got on to me for shooting up and convinced me to switch to snorting for a while. He was very worried about me because he knew I was living on the edge and distraught over my sons. It wasn't long before we became more than friends.

His girlfriend was a rough old gal from the Northside of Ft. Worth, and he'd stayed with her there at the end more because he was afraid of what she would do if he left her. When he approached her to say he was leaving, she bit him in the cheek, leaving a huge bite mark for all to see. Then, grabbing a tire tool, she ran into the garage and beat the hood of his 1969 Hurst Olds before he could stop her. He'd had enough. He rented a home for us in Mansfield and began the process of leaving her. I felt so bad that I sold my car and gave Ted the money, so he could buy her a car to drive so she wouldn't be afoot. I tried hard to be understanding, and for two weeks, I said nothing as Ted spent hours after work each evening helping her move to her own home.

During this time, some of my family had more or less turned their back on me once Clark convinced them that I was unfit to be a mother. It was also during this time that I finally caught on to what Sally and Steve had done. They had deliberately set me up to become a junkie, so Clark could waltz into court and take the boys from me without a fight.

I began to devise my own plan. I started sending Clark money for child support every week on my own. I asked him to meet with me one night to discuss this court business. I explained I wouldn't fight him as long as he gave me ample visitation. Clark was listening very patiently, so I decided to toss out the white elephant.

"I need for you to understand how this all happened, Clark. I never meant to get fucked up on meth. The truth is, Sally and Steve, set me up. Now before you say a word, please understand, I think their intentions on your part were good, but the way they went about this was rotten. I'm not trying to cause trouble, but I deserve to see my boys. Please. I haven't stuck a needle in my arm for almost a month. Ted is a good man, and he is helping me stay strong. He doesn't want a ready-made family, but he believes I deserve to see my boys just the same. I miss them so much it's killing me inside. It's been so long since I've held them in my arms, please give me a chance," I begged.

Clark stood there under the streetlamp listening to me intently before speaking and asking me exactly how I'd been set up. As I explained in detail, tears began sliding down his cheeks.

"Oh my God Wende, I had no idea. I'm so sorry, I swear I had nothing to do with this," Clark cried as he grabbed me up in his arms, holding me tightly. "You can pick the boys up after school tomorrow," Clark promised letting me go and staring into my eyes. "I will never deny you your sons again. I will deal with Sally and Steve, trust me, they will answer for what they've done."

I drove home happier than I'd been in a very long time. I wasn't worried about Sally and Steve anymore. They were gonna have to answer to Clark for what they'd done, and I didn't envy them the storm headed their way.

I didn't sleep at all that night, anticipating seeing my precious sons. The next day remains one of the longest days I've ever known in my life, the minutes dragged by like molasses. I'd begun to believe I would never see them again until they were grown, and now it was a mere few hours 'til I could hold them tight. Pulling up to Clark's, I could see the boys standing at the window watching for me. They were as excited as I was.

I remember Patrick running as fast as his chubby little legs would let him, arms stretched out for me, screaming Mommy at the top of his lungs. I dropped to my knees and waited for him to fly into my embrace, Scuter right behind him, shouting, "Where have you been, Mommy?"

Sally stood at the screen door staring with such hatred that if looks could kill, I'd be dead. I couldn't have cared less. I had my boys back.

Chapter 42

Cottonwood Park and Skating Rinks...

WE WERE STARTING TO SETTLE in as a family when Ted's ex found out about Ted and me, and somehow got our home phone number. She began calling at all hours of the day and night. Back then, there was no way of knowing who was calling on the phone when it rang. I'd have never answered the phone when she called if I'd known it was her. In the beginning, I tried reasoning with her to no avail. She cursed me and threatened me every time she called, so I just started hanging up on her as soon as I knew it was her. One Sunday morning, about six am, the phone rang, waking me from a dead sleep. It was her.

"You need to hear what I have to say, don't hang up," she said in a very serious tone.

I sat there and listened quietly as she spoke the words that no mother ever wants to hear.

"I know where y'all live now. In fact, I know which room your two boys sleep in. If you don't agree to come to Grand Prairie and face me like a woman, I'm gonna drive my car straight into the room with your sons one night when you least expect it," she spat out venomously.

"I tell you what, that did it! You just went too damn far! You might be a badass bitch and whip my ass, but you better pack a lunch cause you're gonna have it to do," I screamed into the phone, "where do you wanna meet cause I'm on my way?"

She gave me the address to her house, and I hung up. Preparing for the fight of my life, I put on a flannel shirt with no bra, put my long hair in a tight ponytail, threw on some jeans, and tennis shoes. When I turned to see Ted looking at me, I was fuming. He refused to give me the keys to the car, so I took off down the road, walking. I hitch-hiked all the way to her front door. I banged on it loudly, not caring what kind of scene I was causing.

"Well, well, well… The little whore actually showed up," she said, laughing at me, "C'mon, hop in the car and we'll drive down to Cottonwood Park. I don't want a scene in front of my house. I have to live here."

I don't know why, but I jumped in her car and went with her. As crazy as she was, she could have taken me off somewhere and killed me, but sure enough, she drove straight to the park. I jumped out and ran around her car to meet her head-on as she was getting out of the driver's side.

"Ok, let's have it," I said, stepping up to her, "you might threaten me and whip my ass, but you're damn well gonna stay the fuck away from my home and my boys," I yelled in her face.

"Hold on sugar; I want to let you know how much fun Ted's been having with me. We've fucked more since he left than we have in the past year we were together," she said, laughing in my face, "you're only with him cause of Bill."

Ted's employee's words were roaring through my head, and I suddenly knew Ted had lied after all. Unable to contain my anger, I reached out and slapped her as hard as I could.

"Is that all you got, sugar," she laughed, never missing a beat.

I remember my head roaring before I blacked out.

"Ma'am, ma'am, you're gonna need to get up now. Don't hit her again," the police officer standing over me ordered.

"Please, please help me. Get this crazy woman off me please," she cried as if she were terrified.

Looking down, I saw her face. It was swollen and red with bruises already appearing. Her eyes were almost swollen shut. I had her arms pinned beneath my legs, and my fist was held high fixing to nail her again. My flannel shirt was hanging off my arms, my chest, bare for all to see. I looked from the officer and back at her before getting up. The officer handed me his jacket to put on, and it was then I realized the crowd that had gathered, gawking at the scene before them. Judging by their clothing, they had just left the church on the other side of the park.

A second officer helped her off the ground and over to his patrol car, where she sat down in his front seat. On the walk over to his car, she spat out several teeth.

"She knocked my teeth out," she cried to the officer helping her.

"Ma'am, can you tell me what happened, and who started this," the officer standing with me asked?

"I hit her first, I sure did," I spoke up, still madder than a wet hen. Both officers were doing their best to hide their mirth, but it only added to my chagrin.

"She attacked me," Ted's ex cried out, playing the part of the pitiful victim as the officer patted her shoulder.

"Do you want to press charges against this woman ma'am," the officer nearest her asked?

"I sure do," she cried with a hint of satisfaction in her voice.

The officer with me didn't seem satisfied with the answer I gave him, sensing there was more to our little soiree than met the eye.

"So why did you hit her," he asked me with a questioning look?

"Her ex-boyfriend left her for me, and we share a home now. She's been calling at all hours of the day and night, threatening me. Two weeks ago, she called my step-mother and told her she was gonna put a bullet between my eyes if I didn't leave Ted," I blurted out. "When she called this morning and threatened to run her car into my son's bedroom if I didn't come over here and face her in person, that did it. I told her she was gonna have to beat my ass cause she crossed the line when she threatened to hurt my sons! I hitch-hiked over here cause Ted wouldn't let me have the keys to the car. She knew damn good and well I was afraid of her cause of the chunk she bit out of Ted's cheek, but I didn't care anymore, she wasn't 'bout to hurt my sons."

"Looks to me, she's the one that got hurt, but how about it ma'am, have you been threatening this woman and her son's," the officer standing by me asked?

"Yes," she said so quietly that the officer asked her to speak up. "Yes, I have."

Both officers stared at her in disbelief, unable to believe she'd spoken the truth. They looked at each other for a moment before the officer next to me spoke again.

"Are you aware that the threats you've made toward this woman and her family are considered terroristic threats and can result in two to ten-year felony sentences for each separate threat?"

"No, I wasn't," she spoke without a hint of tears in her voice.

"In light of these developments, do you wish to file charges of your own ma'am," the officer next to me asked?

"If she promises to stop calling me and my family, and threatening me, no, I don't. I just want her to leave us alone," I said, ready for all the drama with her to end once and for all.

"So, do you still want to press charges against this woman," the officer next to her asked. When she replied no, the officer next to me left her with something to think about.

"Just so you understand, if you make one more phone call to this woman now that we are aware of the situation, all of the previous threats you have made will be added to the new charges," he stated.

"I understand," she muttered, glaring at me with looks that could kill.

Unfortunately, the officer's asked for our driver's license to fill out their reports.

I knew I was going to jail before the officer ever returned with my license. I actually felt sorry for the officer as he was walking back over to the picnic table I was sitting on.

I was taken to jail for an outstanding traffic ticket, and she left in her car. I'm not sure if it was cause she could go to prison, or the unexpected beating I gave her, but I never heard from her again. I found out later that she ended up going to the hospital that day with some broken ribs, a dislocated collar bone, two black eyes, and five teeth knocked out.

As for me, I had to sit in jail all day cause Ted refused to let anyone get me out to teach me a lesson. Pa finally came and got me around eleven pm that night. I thought about how scared I'd been of that woman all day sitting in jail; she was the only woman I've ever been afraid of. By the time Pa picked me up, I had decided that no one would ever terrorize me that way again.

Famous last words…

Clark broke up with Sally shortly after he gave me the boys back. He moved to the little house behind Steve with his older brother. It was December 1985 when I invited them to a skating rink in Grand Prairie to celebrate Scuter's eighth birthday. Ted didn't skate, so he said sure when Clark asked his permission to 'couple' skate with me.

I could tell something was weighing heavily on Clark's mind but let it go knowing some things are better left unsaid as we skated together throughout the night. The boys were in hog heaven with all of us hanging out together, and for a moment, I believed we'd turned a corner and could share the responsibility of raising the boys this way in the future.

"Sure, the boys can go with you, and I'll pick them up Sunday evening," I told Clark when he asked if the boys could go with him after the party.

I forget why Ted didn't go with me to pick up the boys on Sunday, but he didn't. I got there about six that evening, and no one was there. There was a note on the door that said they'd run up the street, and I was welcome to wait inside. Walking in the front door, a chill run up my spine when I spotted an empty half-gallon Jack Daniel's bottle. It didn't register in my mind right away why I should be worried.

Something in Clark's demeanor as he walked through the door a half-hour later scared me, and I tried walking out the door with the boys immediately. He blocked my way and grabbed me by the arm, dragging me to the bedroom.

"You boys sit down and watch TV with your uncle while I talk to y'all's momma. Don't let the boys or anyone come in here," he nodded to his brother before slamming the bedroom door behind us.

"You want to tease me at the skating rink in front of your new man and think you can get by with it? I'm gonna show you why you should never play games with me," Clark slurred as he grabbed me and began jerking my clothes from my body.

"Please Clark, I swear I wasn't trying to tease you, I just thought we were learning to be friends, so we could raise the boys together. Please don't do this, Clark, please don't hurt me," I cried over and over knowing, or thinking I knew what was coming.

"Stop screaming, you better not raise your voice, or I'll shut your mouth for you," he threatened. Shoving my naked body back across his bed, he stripped his clothes off. He seemed as though he had taken some sort of enhancement, and it scared me to the core of my being.

"Please, please, Clark, I'm begging you, the boys are sitting in the next room," I continued begging, grasping at straws.

There was something sinister about the way he lit his cigarette and then lifted the single-sided razor blade off the mirror on the desk with his empty hand. Straddling me, he bent over and held the lit cigarette and razor blade close to my eyes. An ashy, ember fell in one of my eyes, causing me to flinch, and Clark to laugh.

"If you yell out one more time, you're gonna find out what I can do with these little items," Clark threatened while he waved the cigarette and razor blade closely in front of my face.

I just thought I knew what Clark was capable of doing to me. What I felt at that moment was pure, unadulterated terror! I wanted to scream for Clark's brother, but something in Clark's manner had paralyzed me in fear. He tossed the cigarette and razor blade into the ashtray with a sick, twisted grin on his face.

Flipping me over, I knew what was coming next. I had never let anyone engage in anal sex with me, especially Clark, because of his size. He'd begged me in the past to allow it, always promising to be gentle, but I knew before he slammed into me in the next moment that nothing about this night was gonna be gentle.

I felt the first half-dozen thrusts, felt my skin ripping, with a blinding pain as I'd never felt before. My eyes closed tight with each slam; I saw light exploding in the back of my eyelids. Shoving my face into the pillow, I issued silent screams, praying they could only be heard in my mind. I thought I was gonna pass out from the horrific pain, when all of a sudden, I became numb. I knew what was happening, but I didn't feel anything anymore. It was such a surreal feeling to me. It took me a while to figure out I had escaped to a place in my mind where he couldn't hurt me anymore. It was as though I was a spectator and not a participant. When my body went limp, it seemed to excite him more, but I lost track of time and feelings where I had gone. I remember, at some point, thinking to myself, "He's gone mad! He's gonna kill me now for sure like he'd threatened so many times in the past." I didn't care what he did anymore; death seemed a welcome option. I finally floated off into oblivion at some point during the ordeal. I never passed out but felt as though I were in a dream sleep, waiting on the periphery of my mind for the torture to end. Finally spent, he fell on top of me. I pretended to be asleep, praying he'd pass out himself so that I could escape. I was shocked to learn he'd held me, hostage, for over six hours when I left his home.

Once I was sure he had passed out, I crawled from beneath him. It was then I saw the sheets with bloody smears on them. I didn't have to look; I knew where it had come from. I threw my clothes on as fast as I could, grabbed my shoes, and slipped from the bedroom. The boys were sleeping on the couch, still dressed from the night before. I gently shook them awake and told them to be extra quiet and not wake up their uncle or father.

It was after two am when we got back to Mansfield. I remember walking into mine and Ted's bedroom. When I collapsed on the bed crying, and blurting out what Clark had done to me, Ted just sat there and stared at me in disbelief.

"Are you sure y'all didn't plan all this the other night when y'all were skating together," Ted asked sarcastically.

"Are you fucking kidding me? You think I made this shit up," I cried. "You wanna see where he ripped me open?"

"No, I'm going to bed. I've heard enough," Ted mumbled as he turned his back to me and crawled under the covers.

I couldn't believe Ted accused me of lying, and making all of this up.

I felt like I was living a nightmare over and over, and over again. A part of me wanted to call the police and bury Clark under a prison where he belonged, but I thought about the boys and how much they loved their Daddy. I couldn't do it. No matter how much he'd hurt me, I couldn't do it. Besides, who'd believe me? Clark would say it had been consensual.

I went and soaked in a tub of hot water for so long my skin shriveled up, and the water turned cold. I promised myself I would never be alone with Clark again, and that one way or the other, I was gonna put distance between him and our boys. I didn't want him to have any influence on my precious sons, and I swore to myself that I would never let him hurt me again.

Chapter 43

College, Sam, and rehab...

March 1985

WE LIVED IN THAT LITTLE house in Mansfield for several months. We backed off from using meth for a while after the boys came to live with us and did pretty well. I even re-enrolled in college for another go at a nursing license. I was about mid-semester into college when I stopped by the donut shop one day before school.

I was standing at the donut showcases talking to one of Daddy's employees when someone stepped up behind me and covered my eyes with their hands.

"Guess who" came the deep, familiar voice from my past. All the familiar feelings overtook me at once, heart racing, butterflies in my stomach, the instant dry mouth making it difficult for me to speak.

"Sam…" was all I could get past my lips. Turning around to look into his eyes, '*I felt the blood go to my feet*' as Lobo once sang in, "*I'd love you to want me.*" It never mattered how long the time was since I'd seen him last, the mere sound of his voice took me back to the early years.

"Hmm, how long has it been this time, seven-eight years? Every time I think I've seen the last of you, you pop up outta nowhere," I say once I finally found my voice.

"Hey, what kind of welcome is that? I thought you'd be happy to see me," Sam said in a mockful tone.

"Who says I'm not? You just caught me by surprise," I said casually, trying to sound coy as if seeing him wasn't making my stomach do somersaults.

"You wanna get out of here and go riding around," Sam asked, hesitantly, as if he wondered what I'd say.

So much for school that day.

He stuck around the area for a while, and it seems like we met up a few times, but I can't recall any specifics. He was married and had a couple of kids by now, and I was pretty into Ted. I remember the day he came and told me he was leaving the area once again. This time he was traveling out of the country. I wondered if I'd ever see him again as he drove off that day. My heart said I would, but a decade would come and go first.

Towards the middle of the summer of eighty-six, Ted and I were back into meth pretty heavy. College for me, long-forgotten once again, we moved to Pleasant Grove up the street from Maw-Maw Cruse. I struggled to maintain any semblance of normalcy for my boys, but I was in too deep. I was down to one-hundred-ten pounds soaking wet, the skinniest I had been since I was a child. My cheeks were sunken in as were my eyes. My family had plenty to say about what I was doing, but their idea of helping me came in the form of threats. They threatened to call Child Protective Services on me. No one offered to help me with the boys, or suggest I go into rehab. Ted wasn't helping matters either. By this time, he was shooting up with me. He was cheating on me too, but he thought I didn't know it. I was at my wit's end and had no clue how I was ever going to stop shooting up dope. I was sick of the life I was living and knew in my heart I wasn't fit to be a mother; my boys deserved better.

I decided enough was enough and packed the Hurst Olds with mine and the boy's clothes and headed down south. If I was gonna lose my sons again, I was gonna make sure they were raised in a Christian home. I knew the couple I was taking them to would raise them to know the Lord, and at that moment in time, that was all that mattered.

I remember that Saturday drive, east on I-20, and then heading south out of Jackson, Mississippi. It was a bright sunny morning when I crossed that Texas state line into Louisiana. I told the boys we were going on an adventure, so they were excited, but inside my heart was breaking apart. I had a hard time staying upbeat, so I put on Chicago's *Saturday In the Park* and kept hitting replay. To this day, my sons love this song and always think of the three of us together when they hear it.

Arriving at the couple's home, I broke down and poured my heart out. When I was done, I had one final request of them.

"All I ask is that I be allowed to stay in touch with my sons," I begged with a heavy heart.

The couple excused themselves to discuss what I'd dropped in their laps while I sat at their kitchen table, looking out across the wooded acreage that I was so familiar with. As they returned to the kitchen after some time, I held my breath, waiting to hear our fate.

"Don't you love your boys and want to raise them," the woman asked, looking into my eyes, searching for the truth.

"Of course, I do, but I know I'm not fit to right now. I don't know how I will ever be again," speaking honestly, tears flowing freely; I stared back into her eyes, willing her to see into my soul.

"Are you willing to go into rehab and get help," the man questioned?

"I'd give anything to be free of this life I've been living, yes, I'd gladly go into rehab," hoping against hope that the conversation was going where I thought it was, I spoke from my heart.

"We want to help you get your life straightened out cause these boys need their momma," the woman spoke up, "you've got a lot of work to do, but as long as you're trying, we won't take your boys from you."

We spent the rest of the afternoon working out the details and finding a rehab I could get into right away. I slept like a baby that night curled up next to my sons and thanking God for once again giving me refuge from the storm. Tomorrow would come soon enough bearing the mountain I was to climb, but I drifted off to sleep, knowing I wouldn't have to climb it alone.

Chapter 44

Last rape and Cancer

September 1986

ONCE AGAIN, I FOUND MYSELF saying goodbye to my sons and explaining it would be a while before I saw them. They looked confused but tried their best to put on their big boy smiles. I felt lower than dirt to have to put them through this and prayed it would be our last separation. The kind couple loaded me up, and off to Gulf Port, we went. The rehab was a state-run facility that didn't require tons of money before being accepted into their program. I was grateful since I had no money at all.

I took Primatene tablets for my asthma when I ran out of my prescription medication. Being strung out on methamphetamine made it hard to see the doctor for refills. Unfortunately, the rehab facility couldn't allow me to take over the counter medications. I would have to wait to see a doctor and have my asthma medication prescribed the next day. I felt panicked but hoped for the best since I couldn't ask this couple to bring me back the next day.

Later that night, around eleven pm, it started. I got too hot and started coughing, and before I knew it, I was having a full-blown asthma attack. The facility called an ambulance to transport me to the E.R. but told me I'd have to wait until the following morning to be picked up. I didn't care as long as I could get some relief. I was panicking and out of breath.

Arriving at the E.R. that night, I got my first taste of prejudice toward junkies. As strung out as I was that night, I still remember the feelings of hatred directed toward me. As I recall, they gave me a couple of breathing treatments before kicking me to the curb, so to speak. I knew I received less than normal care because they knew I came from a treatment facility.

They discharged me and said I could wait in the waiting room until morning. It was around one am, and I'd only been there a couple of hours. The worker at the facility said it would be eight am before someone came to pick me up, and that meant I'd have to sit in those cold, hard chairs for another seven hours or so. I tried to get comfortable but felt like everyone was staring at me and whispering. I remember being very paranoid sitting there. It got to be too much for me to cope with, and off I went out the door. I was gonna walk back to the facility. Anything beat sitting there, and besides, it didn't seem like it took no time before the ambulance got me there, how far away could it be?

When I got out to the street, I knew I'd made a mistake.

The biggest car I'd ever seen drove past me slowly. The inside light was on, and I could see the big man behind the wheel, staring at me as he drove past. As he got to the stop sign at the end of the street, he made a huge, sweeping u-turn, heading back toward me.

Just then, an old '57 Chevy stopped in front of me, out of nowhere's, with two young males in the car. I could smell marijuana the minute the window was rolled down.

"Hey, you in some kind of trouble with the man in that car comin' up the street," the driver asked, sticking his head out the window?

"I don't know, but he sure scares me," I admitted.

"Hop in, we'll give you a ride," the driver smiled and said.

Looking back at the E.R., I knew I couldn't get there before the man in the big car could get to me. In my strung-out mind, I figured these two guys were smoking a joint, so they had to be cool. Weighing my odds against these two, and the man creeping slowly up the street, I decided to take my chances with the two stoners. I jumped in, and they passed the joint back to me.

"I'm in rehab and not supposed to do this, but what the hell," I said, taking a long pull off the joint in my hand.

"I gotta drop my buddy off, and I'll take you where you need to go," the driver said over his shoulder.

'What up, man," the passenger asked as if he didn't agree with the plan?

The two men stared at each other as though they were communicating silently, causing me concern for the first time since I got in the car. The driver made several turns before going across a set of railroad tracks. Next thing

I knew, he's pulling up in front of a house/bar with so many people milling around in the gravel lot that I could only imagine how many were standing there. I heard the driver and passenger speaking outside the car, and it didn't sound good as they stepped away toward the crowd of people.

"Man, let me in on the action," the passenger said in a pleading manner.

"Naw man, this one's all mine," the driver spoke authoritatively.

Knowing I was in trouble deep, I quietly slipped out the back of the car, careful not to make any noise. I made it half-way across the yard adjacent to the bar when someone pointed out to the driver his chick was getting away.

"The only place you're goin' is wit' me," the driver said, catching up to me and dragging me behind him back to his car.

"Hey, I'm cool; I can walk, no problem," I blurted out, trying to sound nonchalant.

"Naw, you shorely don't want to take off walkin' from here," he laughed, closing the front passenger door behind me, "your chances are a lot better off with me than some of that crowd."

I wondered exactly what he meant by "my chances" as he jumped behind the wheel of the car and flipped a U-turn. Crossing back over the tracks, he turned the opposite direction from the way we'd come in. When he pulled up to a stop sign that looked like the last safe place I could jump out, I reached for the door handle, and to my great horror, there wasn't one! The driver looked over at me, trying to figure out how to open the door, and he went postal on me.

"Don't start trippin' on me, girl," he exploded in a rage, "I ain't playin' wit' you, I'll hurt ya!"

I knew then I was gonna be raped, and based on what he'd just said, beat up if I resisted. For all I knew, he might kill me. At that moment, I decided to go along with whatever he wanted. I'd had one night stands before, far as I was concerned this was gonna be another one, albeit one where I had no choice.

"I'm sorry, I'm just on edge cause I'm coming down off meth," I said as calmly as I could. "Where we going?"

"I know a nice little spot where we ain't gonna be disturbed," he said, pre-absorbed in his thoughts.

I was scared half to death when he drove down a long, desolate road that seemed to go on forever. He could murder me, and no one would know it. I went into survival mode and decided my virtue had been destroyed long ago. I'd seen a glimpse of this man's anger and didn't want to evoke it again.

"You know, you ain't gotta hurt me to get what you want," I said, nausea creeping up the back of my throat as he slid the car off the road.

"Now that's what I'm talkin' 'bout, a girl that wants to have a little fun," he said, throwing the car in park and pulling me out of the vehicle.

He had me strip down to what God gave me, then pulled his clothes off and tossed them on top of mine. He leaned back against his car and had me on my knees in front of him, to begin with, followed by a couple of hours of twisting me into every position he could think of.

Little did he know I wasn't really there. I had escaped to space in my mind, where I was a spectator again. I kept thinking of my boys and my family. I wondered if I would ever see them again. I prayed to God to forgive me for leaving the hospital the way I did and promised I wouldn't pull another stupid stunt like that if he'd just let me survive this night.

Just as the first rays of light peeked through the darkened sky, the man finished his deed. He tossed an old t-shirt from his trunk at me and told me to clean myself up, asking for the shirt back when I'd finished. He told me I needed to hurry and get dressed so he could drop me in town. His words were music to my ears!

"Dear sweet Jesus, thank you, thank you, thank you," I screamed silently to the heavens above.

"We good now, right," the driver asked as he let me out of his car in the service station parking lot.

"Oh yea, it was fun," I replied, lying to him for the last time.

I barely made it to the back of the station before I began throwing up everything inside of me. My nerves had been stretched to their limits, and now they had their way. The man running the station happened to see me running behind the station and came out to investigate. He walked up just as I began dry heaving.

"Are you okay Miss," the older gentleman asked?

"No, I'm sick, and I need to get back to the rehab I'm staying at," I cried softly.

The man helped me find the number and call the facility. I sat on the station curb for almost an hour before someone finally picked me up. I don't know why I didn't tell the worker what had happened right away; instead, I rode back in silence.

Safely back in my dorm, I sat down on my bunk and began crying my eyes out. When the girl in the bed next to me asked what was wrong, I blurted out the whole story to her. Naturally, she went and told the director, who promptly brought me down to the office.

I refused to file a police report because I didn't have it in me, besides as far as I could tell, it was all my fault. I felt guilty now that it was all over because I hadn't resisted. There was a big question mark in my mind about my willing participation, so no, I didn't want to go through the whole ordeal having been there before and told the director so. Funny, thinking back now, that director didn't try to change my mind either. I'm guessing the facility didn't want to be connected to any bad publicity. However, the facility director insisted I be taken to a clinic they used and be checked out right then and there. He said they could give me some medicine to help me ward off any sexually transmitted disease the man may have given me. Not to mention, I needed the prescription medication for my asthma.

I remember being put through the hoops that morning at the clinic. Even though I didn't want to file charges, a policeman came out to the clinic and made a report. I had to tell my story to the nurse, then the doctor, and finally, a policeman. They ran blood and urine tests and had me wait in a room for the test results. The nurse came back to the room on two separate occasions to ask me if I was on my period. I remember she looked at me funny the second time I told her, "No, I'm not on my period."

I was beginning to grow weary after sitting in that room for so long when a doctor came in and explained I had blood in my urine.

"Could it be from that man having rough sex with me," I asked the doctor?

"I suppose it could, but there is a possibility that its cancer," he said matter of factly.

"Cancer," I yelled out, "how in the world could I have cancer? What kind of cancer?"

"We need to draw some more blood and take some x-rays, then you'll need to be seen by the urologist tomorrow."

The rest of the afternoon passed in a daze for me. It hadn't been that long ago that I'd lost my Momma to cancer, now I was being told I might have it. I felt so lost and all alone in the world. Suddenly, being raped again didn't seem like the worst tragedy in the world. What next dear Lord?

Chapter 45

MIRACLES REALLY DO COME TRUE

God's timing is always right as I was reminded in rehab in the Fall of 1986. If ever there was a good time for me to be diagnosed with cancer, then I suppose while I was in rehab was it. I had plenty of support all around me. Ironically, had I not been raped, God only knows how long I would have gone before finding out.

I went to see the urologist the very next day. He was no-nonsense and very knowledgeable. In fact, he was a teaching professor at the local university. He was very frank with me from the start. Wasting no time, he told me right up front that he suspected my bladder cancer was a rare form he hadn't seen but in one other person under age fifty, and that was a 35-year-old man. He explained that he wanted to do several tests before doing a biopsy. I agreed to do whatever he thought best as he was the expert. Truth be told, I felt intimidated by him and would have never thought to question him.

He had me in his office a few times leading up to my biopsy. He seemed intrigued by my case and asked if he might use me as a case study. I signed the paperwork allowing him to discuss and research my case using all my medical information, but calling me Study Pt A.

I graduated rehab a few weeks later and went straight to the hospital from the facility to prep for my biopsy the next morning. While I was waiting to be picked up for the surgical/biopsy procedure the following day, one of the nurses turned on the TV. and told me that Dr. J was on the local education channel talking about my case. How cool was that I thought to myself as I listened to the doctor talking about my situation. Later that day, I was released to go home with the kind couple who was helping my boys and me. I was to return to Dr. J's office the next morning for the results and how my treatment was to proceed.

"It's as I suspected; the mass is malignant. It has gone into the organ wall, which means it's most likely spread to other parts of your body. I'm scheduling you for surgery next week, where I will take the cancer from the inside lining of your bladder. Next, I want to send you to the University of Mississippi in Jackson to undergo aggressive treatment. You will receive radiation before your bladder is removed, and you're given a urostomy," pausing to let that sink, he then continued, "if we're lucky, this might buy you an additional six months to a year."

"What do you mean, buy me six months to a year," I asked, praying he didn't mean what I thought he said?

"Six months to a year longer to live," he stated benignly.

I sat there quietly, taking in what he'd just said. My first thoughts were 'help me, God, help me to accept this news as only you can.' I felt immediate peace from my head to my toes. It was a supernatural feeling that could have only come from God. I felt him speak to me, "Trust in me, my child, I've got this." Lost in quiet reflection, I didn't hear Dr. J the first time he spoke up.

"Do you understand what I'm saying, you don't have much longer to live, this is going to kill you," he said as though I hadn't heard him the first time.

"I understand," I answered quietly.

"Aren't you scared? You have a lot to consider here. You're going to need to make arrangements for your sons' future, do you understand," he asked again?

"I know I have a lot of decisions to make Dr. J, but I know that my God is going to help me get through this and let me know what to do. I can't do anything without his help and guidance. He has never let me down in the past, and he won't this time either...."

Dr. J interrupted my dialogue about how wonderful my God was by reaching out to pat my hands that were folded and resting on his desk before speaking again.

"I'm sorry to interrupt you. I don't want to hurt your feelings, but I don't believe in God, and all this talk about him offends me. I appreciate your right to believe, but I'd rather not hear about it."

Regardless of his words, my feelings were immediately hurt.

"Yes, sir. I understand. I will tend to my business and make sure I set my affairs in order. Thank you for being straight with me."

I didn't dare tell the kind couple what had been said about God when they picked me up. They might have said I needed to change doctors. Despite what Dr. J had said, I don't know why, but I trusted him to take care of me. I didn't understand why I wasn't scared half to death by what Dr. J had said, but I really wasn't. I felt peace as never before and knew no matter what, God was in control.

I contacted Daddy and told him what was going on, but I don't think he actually believed me. He was still angry at me for running off to Mississippi to give my sons away, to begin with, and didn't want to talk to me. I hung up with an empty feeling and prayed to God that Daddy would forgive me someday.

I remember the week leading up to my surgery like it was yesterday. I was standing in the middle of the local grocery store when I lost complete control of my bladder and peed all over myself. I was so embarrassed that I ran out of the store before anyone could see what I'd done. Crying my heart out, I told my friend what had happened when I got back to her house. She comforted me as best she could, then went and bought adult diapers for me to wear so that wouldn't happen again. I was so humiliated I didn't leave the house until it was time to go to the hospital for my surgery on Thursday.

Seeing my boys playing in the sunshine that Wednesday afternoon, I prayed that God would watch over them when I was gone. I wondered to myself what they would turn out to be. Would they grow to be strong men who loved the Lord? I knew if the kind couple had anything to say about that, that they would most certainly love the Lord. I reckoned that was 'bout the most I could hope for, and all that really mattered.

Saying goodbye to my boys Thursday afternoon was especially hard since I didn't know when I'd see them again, but I kept my cool and didn't cry 'til we'd pulled away from the house. Then the tears came in earnest. All the pent-up emotions poured from my heart by way of tears. My friends said nothing, letting me cry and release the tension I had built up inside of me. I was glad when we reached the hospital, and I could be alone with my thoughts. They offered to stay, but I shooed them out of my room as soon as I was settled in.

Later that evening, I wished I had someone there to keep me company. I turned on the T.V. and began flipping through the channels looking for something to take my mind off everything. I paused when I got to the 700 Club, hoping to hear divine inspiration. They were having a prayer-thon where folks were encouraged to call in.

"Are you, or someone you know, experiencing hardships that you need prayer for? Pick up your phone right now and call our prayer line at the number on the bottom of your screen. Let one of our mighty prayer warriors pray with you. God is waiting to hear from you," the pretty blonde-haired woman urged.

I felt a stirring inside about the same time I grabbed the phone. I figured an extra prayer or two couldn't hurt. I was connected to a woman I imagined to be Hispanic from her thick accent. I explained my situation to the sweet woman on the other end of the line and listened as she began to pray fervently in a language I didn't understand. It was in an unintelligible dialect, which I guessed might be what I'd heard called speaking in tongues. Daddy used to talk about his granny that was crippled except for Sunday mornings. She'd get to speaking in tongues at church and leap from her wheel church to dance around in the name of Jesus. The lady kept right on praying long after I thought she'd have stopped. I would be surprised when we hung up to find she'd prayed for well over a half-hour.

"Thank you, sweet Jesus, praise be to your holy name! Oh, Wende, I have amazing news to tell you," the woman cried, "Jesus told me to tell you he's heard your prayers and knows your heart. Jesus said to tell you that you are healed by his stripes! Wende, Jesus said to tell you that you've been cured. The cancer is gone."

I didn't know what to say to that, but I thanked the woman for her prayers and for giving me the word from God before I hung up the phone. I wasn't sure I'd been cured since I was still in pain, but I felt more peaceful than I had in a while as I fell asleep that night.

The next morning, I awoke to a nurse telling me she had a shot that would make me woozy while I waited to be picked up for surgery. I was happy to hear that knowing my nerves would get the best of me without it. Sure enough, it wasn't no time until I felt downright giddy. Before I knew it, I was being wheeled out of my room and down the hallway to the operating room. I was surprised when Dr. J showed up to walk with me.

"Are you ready to get this over with," he asked in a better mood than he was usually in?

"I hate to burst your bubble, Dr. J, but the cancer is gone," I said in a light, carefree manner, smiling up at him.

"Oh yea, and who gave you that information," Dr. J asked quizzically?

"The lady that prayed for me on the phone last night said Jesus told her to tell me I was cured and that the cancer was gone," I blurted out, forgetting that Dr. J had said I couldn't mention Jesus around him.

I might've been woozy from the shot I'd been given, but as long as I live, I will never forget the way Dr. J looked at me when I'd finished telling him 'bout my miracle. His expression went from confusion, to comical in nothing flat. It was apparent he didn't believe a word I'd said.

"Okay, well, I'll see you this afternoon in recovery," he snickered as he walked away from my gurney.

I vaguely remembered the good doctor waking me in recovery to tell me he'd see me Monday morning before they transported me to the hospital in Jackson, so I was surprised to see him Sunday morning. I was watching a television evangelist program when I looked up to see him standing in my doorway. He was dressed in street clothes and holding huge manila envelopes, one in each hand. When he saw me look up at him, he came to stand at the foot of my bed. He stood there staring at me for so long that it frightened me.

"What's wrong, Dr. J? Am I gonna die today," I begged for an answer?

"I, ugh, let me show you," he stammered in what sounded like a tearful voice. The envelopes contained x-rays, which he removed at once. "What do you see in this one," he asked?

"Isn't that where you said cancer had gone into my bladder wall," I asked?

"Yes. What do you see in this one," he asked, holding the second x-ray in front of me?

"I'm not sure what I'm supposed to see, but I don't see anything at all," I answered, unsure where this was leading, but beginning to get worried at the look on Dr. J's face.

Dr. J turned his back to me as he placed the x-rays back inside the envelopes, taking his time before he turned to face me.

"There is no medical explanation for what I'm about to tell you," he began saying as a single tear slid down his cheek, "but it's gone, Wende. I got a call this morning with the findings and had them repeat everything before coming to see you. The cancer no longer shows inside your bladder wall; it's gone."

Somehow that didn't surprise me near as much as what happened next.

"Would you tell me more about your Jesus," Dr. J asked as he sat down to listen.

I don't remember how long he spent listening to me explain all that God had done for me, but I remember the absolute joy I felt inside. It was an afternoon I will always treasure.

Dr. J canceled the plans for me to go to Jackson but kept me in the hospital a few more days running test after test to make sure there had been no mistakes made. By mid-week, I got to leave the hospital. Dr. J had me come to see him every two weeks for the next couple of months to keep an eye on everything, and every time I saw him, he asked me to tell him more about my Jesus.

I'd stayed in touch with Ted and had begun missing him. I was lonely without his company, so I decided that me and the boys were moving back to Texas to be with him. My friends were disappointed but said they understood. I called Dr. J's office to pick up any paperwork I might need to stay on top of things with my bladder and was told I could stop in anytime for copies of what I needed. I told them I'd be stopping by later that afternoon.

"Dr. J asked to see you when you got here if you have a moment," the receptionist said.

"Sure, I'd like to say goodbye to him," I said happily.

I didn't have to wait long before being ushered into his office. Jumping up from his desk when he saw me, he ran around his desk and grabbed me up off the floor in a bear hug.

"Sister Wende, I'm gonna miss you," he said as he put me down.

"Dr. J, have you lost your mind," I asked as I looked up at the once, cold and clinical doctor, who was now a dear friend of mine.

"Nope, I'm just never gonna forget you," he said, smiling down at me.

Thinking back on my last conversation with Dr. J, I smile to myself. I know he never forgot me because I called to get more records not long after Katrina hit the Gulf coast. The secretary said she wasn't sure if they had lost my documents in the storm or not. I assured her that Dr. J would have kept my records somewhere safe and suggested she might ask him. She acted as if I'd lost my mind but put me on hold. When she came back on the line, she was almost breathless as she spoke.

"You were absolutely right, Dr. J remembered you as soon as I spoke your name. He knew right where your records are and said to tell you we'll send copies right away. He said to tell you, hello, and he hopes you're doing well," the young woman said excitedly.

I've thought of Dr. J many times throughout the years and wondered why he called me 'Sister Wende" the last time I saw him. I'd like to believe his meeting me and studying my case led him to the Lord. I have no doubts that was the only reason I got cancer to begin with. God knew my faith was strong enough to go through all that was set before me so I could witness to Dr. J. Through me, God certainly planted the seed; maybe someday I'll get to see how it was sown.

Chapter 46

Momma Beatrice and Covington, Louisiana

TED AND I WORKED HARD to put our lives back together, but he couldn't leave meth alone. I was doing my best to remain strong and not be tempted by Ted's weakness, but I wasn't sure I could defeat Satan on my own. I called my friend's in Mississippi and asked them to pray for us for good measure. A few days later, they called me back with a proposition. They suggested we all come back to Mississippi. They agreed to sit down with us and help us figure it all out if we'd just come back. I thought about it and talked to Ted. I couldn't believe it, but he agreed.

True to their word, they sat down and offered to help us in a big way if we'd just get married. They agreed to help Ted get his own place to live for the time being since they didn't believe in 'shacking up,' then co-sign for us to buy our own mobile home once we were married. It was going to take a couple of months for me to get divorced, so they let me, and the boys live in the little travel trailer they had provided for me when we were there last.

Ted and I had never discussed marriage before, and I was pretty sure the only reason he agreed to this was their generous offer to help us. I don't guess it mattered to me one way or the other, as marriage was nothing more than a means to end for me anyways.

March 7, 1987, we married in a small service with a few friends from church, and Pa, Ted's father, who'd driven over from Texas. We spent our honeymoon in a motel before settling into our two-bedroom mobile home the next day. Less than two months later, we were moving the mobile home to

Louisiana on Ted's boss' property.

Moving to Covington, Louisiana, changed me in ways I'll never forget. I just thought I understood racism before I moved there, but thanks to one extraordinary woman, I left there with my eyes wide open.

Whenever I think of Beatrice Prioleau, who I'd come to know as Momma Beatrice, I think of God, and of love. Momma Beatrice's' love of God oozed from her pores the way some folks expel sweat. She had the purest soul of anyone I'd ever met, and I don't believe I ever witnessed one time when she was angry with anyone. The closest I ever came to seeing her upset was the day I whipped my oldest son with a switch.

Ted's boss lived down, toward the end of Josephine Ln in Covington, and his property line ran all the way up to where he put our trailer. I'd soon learn that we were smack dab in the middle of an African American community, and at first, I must admit, I felt intimidated by that fact. I don't know why because I'd never been prejudiced, but I think the fear of the unknown is always unsettling. I remember our very first night there and how strong bonds began forming from the start.

Ted's boss had come down with a bush hog and cleared our living area earlier that morning before the movers showed up with our mobile home. Ted was tightening down the trailer and making minor adjustments when I heard him scream and saw him jump back a foot. When I ran up to him, I saw the biggest snake I'd ever seen at the time, slithering near one of the trailer straps a few feet away from us.

"Oh my God, help, help," I screamed bloody murder to no one in particular as I ran toward the street.

"Lord child, what's wrong," the kind African American woman hollered as she made her way from across the street to me?

"There's a huge snake bout to attack my husband by our trailer," I cried, pointing toward Ted, who was frozen in the same spot I'd left him.

"Calvin, grab the hoe and bring it out here. Hurry now," she yelled. "Don't you worry; my Calvin will make everything right as rain in no time. My name is Beatrice Prioleau. Nice to meet ya'" she smiled as she stuck her hand out to me.

"Oh my goodness, gracious, thanks so much for the help! My name is Wende Theodore, nice to meet you too," I said, watching Mr. Prioleau rare back and swing that hoe with expert precision.

I saw Ted shake hands with Mr. Calvin and exchange words. Walking to the street, Ted held the long snake out, causing me to jump again.

"Don't worry, it lost its head," Ted laughed, tossing the snake carcass in the ditch where the boys promptly retrieved it for their inspection.

"I got a big pot of red beans and rice and a pan of cornbread on the stove. Y'all come and eat with us when y'all get ready," Momma Beatrice said. She and Calvin said their goodbyes before walking back home.

Ted was an extremely picky eater, so he stayed behind as me, and the boys took our neighbor up on her offer. A pleasant aroma assaulted my nose the minute we walked in the door. I remember thinking to myself that it didn't smell like my red beans; it smelled better. The home was nicely furnished and more spacious than it appeared from the outside. We made it to the kitchen, where my boys started making introductions to the children sitting around the table.

"This is Lakeysia, Tasha, and Barry," Scuter said, "these are the kids I told you we were playing with."

"This is our Momma, Wende," Patrick beamed.

"This little guy here," Momma Beatrice said as she pulled a little boy of about three years old from behind her skirts forward, "is Rara. He's a might bashful 'till he gets to know ya.'"

"Well, hello there, Rara. It's so nice to meet you," I said, bending down to squeeze the little boys' hand.

"Do y'all like red beans and rice? I didn't think to ask, but we got plenty of lunch meat for sandwiches if ya' don't," Momma Beatrice asked worriedly.

"Are you kidding me? I grew up on beans and rice, and so did these boys. I tell ya' what though, that husband of mine would starve before he'd eat a bean. I'd be grateful to take him back a couple of sandwiches when we go. He stayed behind to finish what he was doing earlier. What can I do to help," I asked, stepping up to take the plates and silverware she had in her hand?

"Go ahead and try a bite or two," Momma Beatrice encouraged the boys, "I bet y'all are gonna like 'em. Those are the real red beans, not pintos. I put smoke sausage, ham hocks, bell pepper, and onion in my kidney beans and cook them slow all day, so they have a deep, rich flavor and a thick juice to spoon over your rice. Go ahead, try them."

I didn't need no coaxing; I was shoving spoonful after spoonful in my mouth. Momma Beatrice's cornbread made my mouth water, and I ate a second slice as if it were dessert. Just as we were getting ready to leave, a young woman, my age came bustling through the door.

"Momma, did you know we're getting neighbor's," a female voice asked from the living room before stepping into the kitchen and seeing the boys and me.

"I sure did, and here they are to prove it," Momma Beatrice exclaimed, "this is Wende Theodore and her boys Scuter and Patrick. Her husband, Ted, is working on their house across the street."

"Wow! Nice to meet ya', and ya'll too," speaking first to me, then the boys, the young woman continued, "my name is Calvinette, and we're sure glad to have y'all as our new neighbor's. Anything we can do to help y'all out, just let us know." Calvinette went on to explain that Lakeysia and Rara were her's and her husband Ralph's children and that Tasha and Barry were her brother and sister. Another young woman Emily was also a sister, but she wasn't home at the time. We visited and made small talk as I fixed Ted a couple of ham sandwiches before me, and the boys headed home.

It didn't take long to settle into the community thanks to Momma Beatrice and her daughter Calvinette. I soon found out I had nothing to worry about regarding being the only white folk around. Folks in Lonesome Pines looked right past skin color and straight into a person's heart. Momma Beatrice cornered me 'bout visiting with them at church the very next morning after we met. I promised I would visit once we settled in. I needed to go to work as soon as possible, and Momma Beatrice suggested I talk to Calvinette that evening to see if they needed help where she worked.

"Sure, we're always needing help. Come on down tomorrow morning around ten am, I'll tell my manager about you," Calvinette said when I mentioned it to her later.

I went to work at Shoney's right beside Calvinette. We became quick friends and confidants. Calvinette was a hard worker and taught me everything she knew about the restaurant. I loved her personality, and her genuine love for God was infectious.

Momma Beatrice's family adopted us as their own. We shared many meals and holidays around that dining room table over the years. When I finally gathered my family to visit Rosehill Missionary Baptist Church, I was hooked. You couldn't walk through those doors without feeling the Lord's presence. When the music began, folks were on their feet, proclaiming the love of God and rejoicing in the power of the Holy Spirit. As indifferent as he was, Ted was moved to stand and clap his hands alongside the boys and me. I can honestly say that of all the churches I've ever attended, I've never felt the power of the Holy Spirit more than I did whenever I stepped through the doors of Rosehill! Nor will you find a more loving group of Christians who embody the love of Christ. If you're ever in the area, stop in and see for yourself, ask for Calvinette.

I remember when Hurricane Florence came through, September 1988. I was doing okay until Maw-Maw Cruse and Aunt Windelyen kept calling, worried we were gonna get blown away. Momma Beatrice told us we were all welcome to come batten down with them at her house, but Ted refused to leave our animals alone. I sent the boys across the street while I stayed at the trailer with Ted. We sat on the couch watching the news until we lost signal. I happened to look out the window in time to see the wind bending those tall pine trees 'til their tips touched the ground. I was just about ready to head for Momma Beatrice's when I heard a loud roar that caused the trailer to shake so hard our fake fireplace went falling over. Ted barely caught it before it hit the ground. I was too scared to leave the trailer and too scared to stay. Ted put his arms around me and held me tight, promising we were gonna be okay.

It finally settled down, and before long, Mr. Calvin came over to check on us. He said the boys were gonna spend the night and to holler if we needed anything. We lit some candles and settled in. The next morning, we found out that neighboring towns in Mississippi had been hit pretty hard by the wind damage. It took a few days for everything to get back to normal, but I'd never forget my first hurricane.

I spent many a day sitting on Momma Beatrice's porch, or in her front yard passing time, and soaking up her wisdom. She was a great, spiritual woman whom I am honored to have been loved by. The most meaningful conversation we ever had about racism occurred one afternoon when she stepped between Scuter and me and pulled the switch I was whipping him with from my hands. It all started when Lakeysia knocked on my front door.

"Ms. Wende, Scuter made Tasha cry," the poor child said, almost crying herself.

"What did he do," I asked as I stepped down onto our patio?

"He called her the "N" word," Lakeysia whispered as if the word was evil personified.

"Scuter, get your ass over here, right now," I screamed, making for the bush that had the strong limbs on it, knowing he was across the street with the other kids and would hear my command.

"What in the world has gotten into you," I yelled as he came dragging up the driveway, "you know that word is off-limits and not in your vocabulary. I'm fixin' to make sure you understand how I feel about that ugly, ugly word!"

The look on Scuter's face held pure terror, but I couldn't stop myself. My blood was boiling, and I felt so bad for poor little Tasha. She was such a sweet, shy young woman. I grabbed Scuter by the arm and went to wailing that switch up and down his legs. He was dancing 'round and 'round and trying to pull away from me.

"Stop child, stop," Momma Beatrice hollered out as she ran up to me, taking the switch from my hands, and wrapping her arms around a very grief-stricken Scuter.

It took me a few seconds to catch my breath and realize I had blacked-out, losing track of what I was doing. Poor Scuter had blood oozing from the wounds on his legs.

"Go on in the house and wash your face. Come across the street once you've settled down," she said as she led Scuter out of the yard toward her house, "I'll tend to this boy's legs."

A half-hour later, I walked into Momma Beatrice's yard to find her with a glass of lemonade waiting on me.

"Have a seat child," she ordered as she handed me the cold beverage. "You know he didn't really understand what he was saying. He's just repeating what he heard someone else say. These children all love each other, but they are children, and they gonna be ugly to one another from time to time, but they don't mean no real harm."

Momma Beatrice spent the afternoon explaining what racism meant to her, and her views on the subject. She explained her outlook for her children going forward and the promise of better futures for them than what history had bestowed on her ancestors. There wasn't a bitter bone in her body for her fellow human beings, only the love of God poured from her soul. Closing my eyes, I can just smell the sweet honeysuckle that floated on the warm, south Louisiana breeze as Momma Beatrice taught me about unconditional love that transcends the color of one's skin. What I wouldn't give to go back and talk to her now.

I stayed in touch with Momma Beatrice for quite some time after I left Louisiana, and I thank God for the last time I saw her. I was passing through on a last-minute trip down to Gulfport when I decided to stop by and see her and the family.

"What do you mean she had a stroke," I asked Calvinette as I made my way back to Momma Beatrice's room.

"Yea, girl, she's had a time of it," Calvinette said as she led the way, "She may, or may not recognize you."

"Momma Beatrice," I cried out as I bent down to hug her. "It's Wende, Momma!"

Opening her eyes, she looked up at me and smiled that beautiful smile I remembered in my heart. The smile was kind of lopsided, but I didn't care, I knew she remembered me, her long-lost wannabe daughter! She tried so hard to talk, and I could see it upset her cause she couldn't.

"Don't worry 'bout it, Momma. I know you're glad to see me, and most of all, I know how much you love me," I said, placing her hand across my heart. Tears were streaming down her cheeks, and mine too at that point.

"We gotta stop this, Momma," I said, pasting a smile across my face and wiping away our tears.

I spent a while sitting by her side and made small talk 'til I saw her struggling to stay awake.

"I want you to know how much you mean to me, Momma Beatrice. I will always remember you in my heart, you hear. I will never forget all that you taught me, either. I love you, sweet mother of my heart," I cried freely, as I bent to kiss her goodbye. I slipped from the room right before my tears came in earnest. Calvinette and I stood for the longest, hugging each other tightly, comforting each other in our time of need.

"Be sure and let me know how Momma's doing, okay? I'll stay in touch too," I promised.

My heart was broken, and I knew I'd never see my dear, sweet friend alive again as I drove off that night.

The next time I got down that way was after Hurricane Katrina. Patrick and I took the seats out of the back of my van and filled it with can goods, water, and other necessities to take to family and friends devastated in Katrina's wake. We dropped some off with family in Mississippi before taking the rest to Calvinette, her family, and friends. I hadn't made it to Momma Beatrice's funeral, but before we left to head back home, me and Patrick went and located her gravesite.

Thanks to the advent of Facebook, we all stay in touch now regularly. Calvinette, me, and our children are family that neither time nor distance will ever change. I had an occasion to drive down to Slidell just last weekend and see my sister from another mister in a small stage production of "The Color Purple." Seeing the play was a *sign* from God, for just like Celie, "*I AM HERE!*"

Chapter 47

Poor choices, and the Undercover Narc!

I HAD A FALLING OUT with Shoney's manager and quit working there to work for a local convenience store during the last year we lived in Louisiana. Ted and I had been having problems for quite some time when I began working at the store, and it only got worse from there.

I suspected he was doing drugs behind my back as well as cheating on me again. It wasn't the first time I'd caught him, and I was growing weary of the heartache. We'd been together for nearly five years, and I wasn't sure how much longer I could put up with his deceptions.

Our last hurrah came in the form of a concert to see the Rolling Stones. I was coming up on my thirtieth birthday and decided to take Ted to see his favorite rock group of all time for my birthday. I wanted to show him how much he meant to me. We took turns standing in the pouring rain all night to get the best seats for the concert. It only cost me a week in the hospital with near pneumonia, but the night of the show was magical. I treasure the pictures that captured the memories of that night. It was one of the happiest times we ever spent together.

One week after the concert, I found a crack pipe under the couch. I was furious when I left for work that afternoon and couldn't wait to confront Ted later that night when I got home. I didn't have to guess anymore.

Later that evening, one of the regulars came into the store, and as usual, was flirting with me. I had never considered cheating on Ted (I had with Sam, but for some reason, I'd never considered my dalliances with him as cheating), but that night I was so mad at him I no longer cared. I flirted back for all I was worth. Next thing I knew, I was backed up against the wall being kissed with reckless abandon.

It had been a very long time since I'd been kissed so thoroughly, and I'll say this, the man had gotten my attention. He'd also started something neither one of us were able to walk away from. When I got home later that night, I confronted Ted with his crack pipe and informed him that me and the boys were moving out the next day. I felt terrible cause he begged me to stay, but I wasn't gonna have drugs under the roof with my sons anymore. I'd almost lost them once and refused to go there again.

The following day I rented a trailer in a trailer park between where Ted lived and the convenience store where I worked. The boys were so mad at me for leaving Ted. They considered him as much their father as they did Clark. I told Ted he'd better keep his shit away from the trailer if he wanted to see the boys, and he promised he would. Every evening they walked the two blocks down the railroad tracks to see him. As for me, I was smitten with the long, tall drink of water, who was determined to have me to himself.

Bubba had moved to Oklahoma with his love and their children. I had visited him there many times, and he always encouraged me to move up there. When I told my new love that I was thinking 'bout moving up there, he was all in. My brother promised to help him get on where he was working. It was for a seismic company that was traveling out to California for two weeks at a time. Ted and the boys weren't too happy 'bout the move, but I felt the need for a change.

We rented a small house in Oklahoma and soon settled in. My love got a job with my brother and was soon out of town for weeks at a time. In the meantime, Ted and I were missing each other. Thus, began a very troubling time for me that lasted most of the following year. I'd been living with my boyfriend for about three months when I decided I'd made a mistake. My brother had recently broke-up from his children's mother and rented an apartment in Elk City. I talked him into to letting my boyfriend move in with him cause I was fixin' to kick my boyfriend to the curb and go back after Ted. And oh, by the way, Ted was gonna need a job too.

Crazy as it sounds, that's exactly how it went down. My boyfriend moved in with my brother, and I went back and convinced Ted to move to Sayre with me, and yes, he got a job with my brother and ex-boyfriend, but he was on the alternate two-week schedule. Life got pretty crazy after that, and I'm not even sure how it all happened.

My ex-boyfriend wasn't taking rejection very well and kept finding reasons to come and see me when Ted was gone. Neither one of the men in my life was backing down, so I decided I needed a break and asked Ted to move out. I had become a yo-yo between these two men, and I couldn't choose who to be with. This lasted for several months.

I decided to go back to college, but set my sites too high and failed, withdrawing from school yet again.

In the meantime, Bubba had gone off the deep end and was on the verge of being suicidal over the loss of his love. I didn't have much to offer him as my car had broken down, and I'd lost my job. It was in the middle of winter, and the nearest town for viable work was 15 miles or so away. Me and the boys were living on welfare when I let Bubba stay at my house.

I was sick and tired of being a part of a love triangle. What I really wanted was to take my boys and go back home to Texas. When I called Daddy, he told me in no uncertain terms, "Nope. I'm not bailing you out. You got yourself into this mess; you can get yourself out of it." I already figured that was what he would say, but I had to ask anyway. Feeling like a failure, I turned to pot to self-medicate, and blot out the pain and confusion in my life.

I was sitting with an acquaintance of mine one morning, smoking a joint and laughing myself silly about my latest predicament, but it wasn't really funny. Someone had turned me into the welfare office, saying my brother was living with me. Since I hadn't reported it, I lost all my assistance. Soon all my food would run out, and I wouldn't be able to feed my sons. I was desperate.

"Where'd you get this weed, it's pretty good," my friend asked.

"It's the last of the stuff I bought from my Daddy's friend when I was in Ft. Worth," I replied.

"Hey, if you could get a quarter pound of this, you could make enough money to move home on. I'd help you for a little kick-back myself," she said.

We tossed that idea around 'til I agreed to do it. When I called Daddy later, he said he'd see what he could do. It was coming up on Thanksgiving, 1990, and Ted had agreed to drive the boys and me down to Daddy's for the big meal.

Daddy's friend had a new batch of weed that had been sealed in pesticide, which he was selling at rock bottom prices cause it tasted funny. I never considered the potential danger it might cause since it smoked okay, and left a hell of a buzz behind, so I took it anyways. All I could see was triple profits, which would allow me to move back to Texas on my own. Once we got back to Oklahoma, I put the word out that I had weed for sale to my acquaintances. I'd be going home soon, I just knew it.

Bubba's new girlfriend, Cassie, was young and clueless, but I liked her spunk. When she found out I had weed for sale, she decided to help me out. I quartered up a couple of baggies and met this friend of hers at the laundry mat next to her job. I'd only been back with the weed one day from Texas and already had a sell. I was on cloud nine! The bearded man paid me and grinned ear to ear, saying he'd probably be back for more. Cool, this was going easier than I'd hoped it would.

The very next day, Cassie called me up saying that man had liked the weed so much that he wanted another quarter of it. I was busy, so I told her to tell him where I lived so he could stop by the house and pick it up. The boys were at school, so I figured it'd be okay. A thought came to me that it was kind of strange that he'd liked the tainted weed, but I blew it off as paranoia.

"Yeah, man, that was some good shit," he said, looking around like he was searching for something, "I'll take another quarter now, but what I'd really like is to buy a large quantity, say like a pound of it."

"Wow, really? I'd have to check it out with my dude," I said, dollar signs adding up in my head, "are you serious, or are ya' pulling my leg?"

"Oh yea, I'm definitely serious," he said, paying me for the quarter I'd just pulled out of my gallon-sized bag which held all the quarter-ounce bags I'd weighed out. He seemed to be eyeballing everything I was doing, but I didn't think nothing of it as I thought about what he'd ask for.

"Let me call my Daddy and see what he says," I blurted out before I thought about it.

"Your father," he asked incredulously?

"Yep," I said reluctantly, "I'll get back to you in a couple of days and let you know what he says."

The dude left, and I immediately called Daddy.

"Hey, I got away to unload a pound of that messed up weed. Yea, there's a guy up here that likes it so much he's bought two quarters in two days. Yea, he's cool. He's a friend of Cassie's. Okay, I'll tell him. I love you, Daddy. Bye"

If everything went okay, I would make as much selling a pound to one person as I would have to sell all these quarters. I was so excited that I went looking for the dude that evening after I got the boys settled into bed. Sure enough, I found him sitting in his truck up on the drag in town.

"I was wondering if you'd be interested in trading me an ounce of pot for a gram of some cocaine I'm getting in tomorrow," the bearded man asked when I hopped in his truck?

"Yea, but I'm not really into coke. I can probably find someone who'll want it, though. So, let me know when you want that pound, and I can have it delivered up here to ya'" I said, trying not to sound like a hotshot.

"Really, that's awesome," smiling, he continued, "we're gonna be great business partners, you and I."

The man said he'd stop by the house and see me tomorrow afternoon with the coke before I got out of his truck. I went home and crawled in bed about as excited as I'd ever been. The boys and I would be home by Christmas!

"Anyone home," the man asked, walking in my house without knocking the next afternoon?

Almost immediately, I felt the hairs stand on the back of my neck. I took a deep breath and suggested he might be careful sneaking up on me like that.

"Oh, my bad, sorry for scaring you. Hey, ya'wanna see the coke," he smiled as he pulled the baggie from his pocket and shook it in front of my face.

Reaching out to take it, he snatched it out of my grasp.

"Ugh, I gotta go make sure it weighs out properly before we trade," he said nervously.

Something in his manner sent the hairs back to attention on my neck. My gut came alive at the same time, and I began to get a sick feeling.

"Hey, I was just about to roll a joint. Let me get you something to drink, and we'll smoke it," I tossed out, hoping he'd agree.

"No, actually, I gotta run and weigh this right quick," he stammered, "hold that thought, and I'll be right back."

By the time he walked out the front door, I knew I'd been had. This man was an undercover narc!!!

I called my neighbor and asked him to hold the bags of weed for me 'til I could see what was going on. I was scared half out of my mind as I waited for the bearded man to return. If he was, in fact, a cop, then I was in big trouble. I was pacing the floor when I saw him pull up in my driveway.

"C'mon, hop in the truck, and I'll take you down to the payphone to call your Dad. I got the money for that pound," the bearded man said and continued when I hesitated, "don't worry, I plan to make it well worth your while."

For a brief moment, on the ride to the payphone, I was hopeful that I'd just been paranoid; but I couldn't shake the hinky feeling I felt inside. I was glad he waited in the truck when I called Daddy.

"Daddy, I'm pretty sure I'm fixin' to get busted. Don't bring anything up here. I'm gonna tell this guy that Dad is what everyone calls my weed dealer, and that I wasn't actually talking about my father. He's looking straight at me, yea, he's a cop. I feel it in my gut. If I don't call you back within the next couple of hours, then you can bet I was arrested. I love you, Daddy."

"When can he have it here," the man asked as soon as I closed his truck door?

"Maybe tomorrow, I have to call him back in the morning," I lied.

"Here's the coke," holding the baggie out to me, he asked, "did you bring the ounce of weed?"

I pulled the weed from my purse and handed it over as I took the baggie he was offering. My hand had barely closed around the cocaine when he flashed his badge.

"You're busted," grinning; he said, "I'll take that back if you don't mind. Possession of cocaine is against the law. So is selling marijuana. We're going to handle this a little differently. I am taking you back to your house where we are being met by other local law enforcement officials to decide how this is going to go down." He read the Miranda Warning and ask me if I understood, and I shook my head yes.

I was afraid to open my mouth at this point and agreed to accompany him back to my house to find out what he meant. When we got there, he let several police officer's in my back door. One of the female officers gathered the boys and went directly to their room. They called me into my kitchen and informed me that if I cooperated, they wouldn't call child protective services out to take my sons away, nor would they arrest me that night. Looking out my windows, I wondered where all their cop cars were. Something very strange was going on, but I had no clue what was happening.

"Where's the rest of the weed," the bearded man asked?

"It's gone," I said.

"This is not what I consider cooperating," one of the other officers stated, "maybe you should tell her how it *could* go down," he said to a bearded man.

"I'm not going to waste my time with you, if you don't cooperate fully, your sons will be taken, and you will be arrested and charged with narcotics sales, as well as having possession of a controlled substance. Now, I'm going to ask you again, where is the rest of the weed?"

"I asked my next-door neighbor to hold it for me," I answered without hesitation, never realizing the trouble it would cause him.

Next, they informed me that an officer would be picking up burgers for my sons and that she would remain in my sons' room with them for the duration of what they had planned to carry out. Just then, someone knocked on the back door. The officer nearest the door opened it to allow another officer in the kitchen who had Cassie with him. They sat me and her down in the living room while they talked amongst themselves in my kitchen.

"They just picked me up at my job. I'm probably gonna get fired," crying, she went on, "I'm sorry for getting you into this. I didn't know he was a cop."

"Oh my God, look, they are putting handcuffs on my neighbor. He's gonna kill me," I gasped as I looked out one of my side windows.

They coerced Cassie to contact three different people to come to my house that night and buy weed. Each time they arrested the individuals as they got up to leave my home. The looks on their faces could have killed me and her both. I wanted to kill her myself cause she didn't know the bearded guy at all. How could she possibly have known he was cool if she didn't know him to begin with?

It was well after midnight when the officer's left my home. I was still confused as to what they were doing, all they told us was that we would be contacted regarding when to show up at the courthouse for our formal charges. We were told not to leave the county.

"Do you think we're gonna be safe after setting those people up," Cassie cried, her eyes wide with fright?

"I have no idea what to think at this point," I said as I grabbed a piece of paper and wrote 'Be careful what you say, they may have *bugged* the house' showing it to her I continued, "but I need to check on the boys."

Walking into their room, I could tell they were fast asleep, thank God! Cassie was afraid to leave the house, so I gave her a blanket and pillow and told her to crash on the couch. I went into my room and laid awake most of the night, berating myself for my latest fiasco. What in the world was I gonna do now?

Chapter 48

Incarceration and Intimidation

No matter where we were, every now and then, Clark Sr. would show up out the blue. Sometimes to terrorize me, other times cause he said he wanted to check up on us and make sure we were okay. The morning after I was busted was one such time that he claimed he'd had a premonition that something was wrong.

"I got to thinking 'bout you and the boys and had this eerie feeling that something was wrong," Clark said when he stepped inside the house.

"Yep, something's wrong," I barely said before two police officers walked in the house through the back and stood behind Clark.

"Well, hello Dad," the first one said, thinking he'd just made the nab of a lifetime.

What I wouldn't give, for a snapshot of the look on Clark's face, at that moment in time. He near 'bout jumped through the small ceiling in my tiny living room he'd been so startled by the officer's remark.

"Yes sir, what can I do for you," Clark Sr. asked, unaware that the officer wasn't referring to him when he said, *Dad*.

"No, y'all have it all wrong. This is Clark Stewart Sr., my sons' father. He just happened to show up at the wrong time to see his sons," I said, fighting hard not to laugh at the expressions flitting across Clark's face. I knew this wasn't a laughing matter, but somehow, I couldn't help but feel joy to see Clark tormented if only for a moment. I'd already smelled alcohol on Clark and knew he was in the hot seat wondering how he could escape in his condition.

"Yea, what she said," Clark murmured, "I can see y'all have something else going on here, and as soon as I see my boys for a bit, I'll be on my way back to Texas."

The policemen didn't care much for jumping the gun and having egg on their faces and hurriedly excused themselves from the situation. I explained what had happened to Clark after they left, and he commented he'd felt something was up. He told me to let him know if he needed to come back, get the boys, and after spending a half-hour with them, made a hasty exit out of there.

Later that day, I checked to see how much my neighbor's bond amount was. I knew the moment I saw him being handcuffed; I was responsible for getting him out of this mess. I didn't have enough for his bond, so I asked a friend to loan me the money on the title to my motorcycle. By late that evening, I had bonded him out of jail. He wanted nothing to do with me and told me to stay away from him. I told his sister that I would find a way to hire an attorney for him as well. By the time it was all said and done, I spent close to twenty-five-hundred dollars to help him avoid jail time. He was charged with sales and distribution because I had the pot all weighed out and in separate baggies.

I finally called Daddy and told him what happened. He was upset, to say the least, but he said he would wire me the money to hire an attorney to represent Cassie and me. When I hadn't heard from the policemen by Monday morning, I asked around for the best criminal defense lawyer. We went and spoke with him that very afternoon. Daddy wired me the money to pay him, and he took on our cases. He promised us we would never spend a day in jail since we'd never been in trouble before. It sounded good to me, so I never questioned his abilities or motives as he set out to defend us.

The day came for me to testify at my neighbor's hearing. I remember the conversation that morning between the District Attorney and me. It happened in the hallway outside the courtroom, where my neighbor's trial was taking place.

"You do plan to plead the Fifth when you testify, don't you," the DA asked?

"What do you mean," I asked though I knew where he was going with his questioning.

"You are going to refuse to admit the drugs were yours, aren't you? I mean otherwise, it can be used against you at your own trial," he asked in a nervous voice.

"I can't lie. They were mine, and truth of the matter is that he thought he was stashing Christmas presents for me," I admitted though it was in part a lie.

In a million years, I never expected what came next.

The poor man turned beet red in the face before taking his sheath of papers and tossing them straight up in the air, causing them to flutter down in a paper waterfall, scattering across the floor. My statement to the D.A. changed the whole course of my neighbor's trial and led to my neighbor receiving a deal he didn't turn down. I felt terrible that he received anything at all since he was only helping me out.

Just as the D.A. stated, my refusal to plead the Fifth affected my own sentencing. In hindsight, I know my lawyer sold me out and never provided me with a proper defense. I was young and didn't know any better. The arrest, coercion by the police officer's, and even the possession of cocaine charge I received were bogus at best. A reasonable attorney would have turned them upside down in a courtroom. Nonetheless, in the end, it would save my life, but that's another story I'll get to later.

Standing before the judge, I expected to receive probation as Cassie had. I was shocked beyond belief when I heard the judge sentence me to five years' probation with the first six months to be served in the county jail. When he remanded me to the bailiff, for immediate transport, I lost it.

"Wait, this isn't the way you said it would go. You said I'd get probation and never go to jail," I choked out between sobs. "I wasn't prepared for this. My boys will be coming in from school in a couple of hours to an empty house. Please, can't I go home and make arrangements for my sons and turn myself in to the jail tomorrow," I begged the judge.

Shaking his head, no, he called for his next case as the bailiff came and began handcuffing me.

"I honestly never saw this coming," my lawyer said, looking away as he spoke, "I'm sure they will let you call someone when you get to the jail."

It took me hours to get a hold of Ted to get the boys. They were completely freaked out by the time he got there, not knowing where I was. He took them back to his apartment in Elk City for the night and packed up all his belongings. The next morning, he moved into my house with the boys.

Spending the next four months in the county jail was a nightmare for me. The cells at Beckham County Jail were no joke when I was there. Paint peeling off the walls in an ugly faded-green hue. There was a stand-up shower that was barely big enough to turn around in. Two sets of bunk beds that were so close together if someone threw their arm out in their sleep, they'd hit you.

Forget about the food; whatever it was, you had to eat it or starve. Four women smoking in such a small, non-ventilated area meant that everything reeked of tobacco. The biggest bummer was when someone decided to go poop in the middle of mealtimes. The toilet set a mere 3 feet away from the small dining table without a door or covering to separate it. Unfortunately, it happened all the time.

I got to visit the boys once a week in the sheriff's office upstairs from my cell. They always brought me a Dr. Pepper and a Snicker's. They'd tell me all about their week and ask me all about mine. I tried to keep my cool and be brave for them, but the minute they'd leave, I'd cry the rest of the day. They seemed to take it in stride, which made me happy.

After I got out, me and Ted gave it another shot, but he couldn't leave the drugs alone, and I asked him to move out again. Tim, my ex-boyfriend, came to see me a few weeks later and asked me to marry him. I said yes., and he moved back in with the boys and me to await my divorce from Ted.

Once we married, we moved to Texas across the street from Daddy and next door to Grandma, Georgia Bell. I had my probation transferred to Texas and got a job waitressing to help pay the bills. Tim was working at a small airport while he continued to work on getting his pilot license. We settled into a routine, and for a couple of weeks, I was happy as I could be. Then it happened.

I got a call from Clark's wife that he was on the way to Ft. Worth to see me, he was drunk, and he was carrying a gun. I should have called the police right then and there, but I didn't. He was still my sons' father. I knew if I went with Tim and the boys over to my Daddy's house, he would come over there for me. Mom Nita was there by herself, and if Clark terrorized her, Daddy would kill him and go to jail. So, I did the only thing that made sense to me at the time. I sent Tim and the boys over to Daddy's house and sat and waited on Clark. I didn't have to wait long.

"Open this damn door," he yelled, banging loud enough to wake the neighborhood.

"What is wrong, Clark, why are you here?"

"I came to see you. I wanted to find out if that new man of yours has any balls," he said as he walked throughout the house.

"He and the boys are gone off with Daddy. Why don't you go back home to your wife, and stop this nonsense?"

Reaching behind his back, he withdrew the gun from the back of his pants and pointed it straight at me.

"Nonsense. I'll show you some nonsense," grabbing me, by my hair, Clark drug me to sit by him on the couch.

"What do you think of my new toy," he asked as he slid the barrel down the side of my cheek, then tracing it across my forehead. Cocking and uncocking it so I could hear it click.

I was wary of him, always terrorizing me. If he was gonna kill me, I wish he'd just get it over with, I thought to myself. He continued tormenting me with the gun for a couple of hours before going into the kitchen and coming back with a beer for himself and a glass of tea for me. I thought it odd, but I was thirsty and drank it straight down.

"Good, that's just what I wanted you to do," Clark said with a sinister grin.

"What did I do," I asked, becoming frightened.

"I put poison in that drink. In a little while, you're going to get very sleepy. I won't have to deal with you ever again," he sneered. "I wanted to shoot you, but it would have been too messy.

It wasn't long before my heart began beating rapidly, and I felt like I was gonna pass out. I laid down on the couch and started crying my heart out, begging Clark to let my boys know I loved them.

"Why do you hate me so much," I cried, begging for him to answer me. "Whatever it was, I'm sorry, Clark. Please do something, don't let me die."

Clark went back into the kitchen and brought me some baking soda and a glass of warm water.

"Drink this quick, and go throw up," he said as if he was scared himself.

I did as I was told, puking my guts up until there was nothing left to puke up. Returning to the living room, I found Clark sitting on the couch, crying his heart out.

"I'm so sorry, Wende. I didn't mean to hurt you. I don't know what's wrong with me," he said as his tears subsided. "Can you ever forgive me?"

I knew whatever had been on his mind; it had passed for now. He'd had episodes like this in the past where he'd terrorize me, then cry and beg my forgiveness. I was just glad it hadn't escalated any further than it had. I promised him I wasn't mad and then convinced him he needed to go home so he'd make it to work. Once I knew he wasn't coming back, I called and told Tim and the boys they could come home.

The episode with Clark caused a lot of arguments between Tim and me. He thought I should have put Clark in jail, and though I knew he was right, I just couldn't do it. My boys loved their father, and I was afraid they would never forgive me if I had him put in jail. We'd been married just over six weeks when it came to a head in our front yard. Daddy and Tim were looking under the hood of a car when Tim snapped at me.

"Yea, you and whose Army," I smarted off, daring him to say something else.

"I'm gonna lay her out, John," he snarled, drawing his arm back, clenching his fist, and pointing it toward me.

Something inside of me snapped, and before I could stop myself, I bent down and grabbed the baseball bat lying in the yard. Grabbing the base of the bat with both hands, I drew the bat back and started swinging it toward Tim's head. Luckily, I came to my senses before I swung through my whole swing. Right before I got to his head, I pulled back. It was too late to keep from hitting him, but it kept me from potentially killing him. I connected with his head right across his temple, dropping his six ft four-inch frame to his knees. Throwing the bat to the ground, I let him have it.

"There you son-of-a-bitch, now you got a reason to 'lay me out'! When you're through, you can get your shit and get out of my life," I yelled.

"Yvette, calm down. Do you know you could've killed him," Daddy asked?

"He better be glad I didn't," I spat out, heading for my front door.

I was furious! I had warned him more than once that I would never tolerate any form of physical violence or threats of physical abuse. I started grabbing his personal belongings and threw them out the front door a fast as I could.

"Wende, I'm sorry. I would never lay a hand on you. Please stop this. I don't want to leave. I love you," Tim begged as he dodged his belongings that were flying through the air at him.

I'd never been more serious in my life. His threat of violence toward me ended it all. Marriage number six was over, barely lasting six weeks. I stuck around Texas a few more weeks before I headed back to Oklahoma, and Ted for the last time.

Chapter 49

Donut shop and the old GEEZER!

I KNEW BEFORE I MOVED back to Oklahoma with Ted that it was wasted effort, but at the time, I felt lost and didn't know what to do. The boys were fast becoming teenagers, and I needed help with them. I tried to believe the lies he told me, but no matter how hard I tried, I couldn't.

I ended up moving to a small Oklahoma town, forty miles up the road from Ted. He said the boys could stay with him while I found my footing. I became very close with the family of a cowboy I met, and through that connection, I came up with a way to turn an old gas station there into a donut shop. Daddy delivered his equipment to me personally, helping me set everything up. He was proud to help me try to better myself.

My business took off with a bang. I had the breakfast business tied up from the start. In addition to the usual donut fare, I served homemade biscuits and gravy, and short-order items. Cars pulled in three deep for hours every morning. I became the talk of the town. It wasn't long before I started serving lunch. I bought some picnic tables and set them up behind my shop for the teen crowd that began hanging out during lunch. My lunch specials geared toward teens took all the lunch revenue from the Love's convenience store across from my shop. I was shocked when a couple of corporate executives from Love's showed up for lunch at my business one afternoon. They didn't hide their reason from coming at all. They informed me that they planned to redesign their store based on what I was doing. I wasn't worried; I had plenty of business.

My problem was not having enough capital to keep my business afloat 'til it generated enough cash flow for the boys and me to live on. The friend of the woman who'd put up cash for the start-up of the business came and offered me a foolproof way to keep things rolling. He said he would loan me two-thousand dollars to pay my bills a month in advance and throw more cash in the kitty as I needed it. He said he trusted me and knew I'd pay him back, but he required collateral to show his wife so she wouldn't get mad at him.

"What would you need exactly," I asked, knowing I owned nothing of value.

"You could use this equipment," he said, waving his hand around Daddy's donut equipment.

"Oh no, Daddy would kill me if I hocked his stuff," I said emphatically.

"I'm not saying I'd really want your Daddy's stuff. I'm suggesting drawing up a contract that you and I would know is phony; but would satisfy my wife."

I turned him down the first time he offered. I couldn't do that to Daddy as much trust as he'd put in me. The old geezer wouldn't let it rest and finally convinced me to trust him. He drew up a contract which we both signed in front of a notary. Each time he'd throw more money in the pot, he'd have me sign a separate paper. I stopped when it reached twenty-five hundred dollars and told him I couldn't accept it anymore.

I got to a point where I was starting to make some headway and began trying to pay him a little on my loan. Each time I offered, he assured me he was in no hurry. I didn't see the writing on the wall until it was too late. The buzzard was marking time, and I don't know how he knew, but right when I couldn't have been struggling more, he came in for the kill. He stopped by and asked me to go for a ride with him so we could talk uninterrupted.

"I've been patient with you and done my best to give you plenty of time, but I'm afraid time is up. My wife is coming down on me and expecting this loan to be paid in full by the first of the month," he said, watching me closely.

"You mean next week? Are you freaking kidding me," I asked in shocked surprise?

"I'm quite serious," he continued in a calm voice, "but if you were to convince me how much it meant to spare your Daddy's equipment, I might be persuaded to take out a private loan and pay the whole thing off for you."

"And just how am I supposed to convince you," I asked.

"Come on, Wende, I'm sure I don't have to spell it out for you. You're not some naive kid. I need a woman to give me what my wife no longer can," he said as he trailed his fingers up my arm.

"What happens if I say no," I questioned yet knowing what his answer would be?

"It's simple; I'll be taking possession of your Daddy's equipment next week."

I wanted to wring his ever-loving neck right then and there, but I knew I needed to buy myself some time.

"Can I at least have a couple of days to think about this? Surely you didn't expect me to jump in bed with you this minute?"

"No, you can have a couple of days to consider your options," starting the car and pulling out of the vacant lot he continued, "but I promise you, I will bring the sheriff with me to pick up my collateral if we can't come to some kind of agreement."

I was in total shock by this man's revelation. He was considered a very prominent citizen of the community, a government employee, and a deacon at his church. He had backed me into a corner, and he knew it. My first inclination was to go to his wife, but I knew if I did, he'd deny it. No way would she believe me since they'd been married over fifty years. How in the world had I let myself get in this position? It was because I trusted him and believed he was everything I'd heard he was, I told myself.

I spent the next couple of days trying my best to rob Peter to pay Paul and scrape up the money, but my best efforts only netted eight-hundred dollars. When the old man showed up, we went for another ride in the country.

"Please take the eight-hundred dollars and give me a couple more weeks," I begged, "if you take Daddy's equipment, he'll never forgive me."

"I'm sorry Wende, I thought I made myself clear."

"Ok, well, I guess we'll have to plan to go out somewhere next weekend while the boys are with their step-dad," I lied, but knew I needed a few more days to come up with a plan.

"I thought you'd come around and see it my way," he leaned over and puckered his wrinkled lips, "how about a kiss for your new sugar-daddy?"

I almost gagged in disgust, but I kissed the old fool and smiled afterward. I would find a way to protect Daddy's equipment one way or the other. Others came in the form of a commercial later that evening as I watched T.V. with the boys. Bright and early the next morning, I got out the yellow pages. Under attorney's, I searched for Bankruptcy specialists.

It cost me seven-hundred dollars and irreparable damage to my credit, but by the time he showed up for his coffee and donuts a few days later, I was ready for him. Luckily, we were the only ones in there.

"Well, hello, lover. How about laying another juicy kiss on me," he asked, sliding into the booth and patting the bench for me to sit down next to him?

"Not so fast, cowboy," I said as I pulled the papers out of the folder I was holding. Slamming a copy of my bankruptcy filings on the table before him, I said in no uncertain terms, "get your ass up out of my booth and get the hell out of my shop. If you ever come near me again with your threatening ass self, I promise you I am going to smear your name all over this town." Pulling the pocket recorder out of my pocket, I held it up and rewound it before pushing play. The old pervert turned beet red when he heard himself calling me lover and asking for a kiss. "Yes sir, I will take this straight over to your wife if you look at me sideways ever again. Do I make myself crystal clear, you old bastard?"

He never said a word as he got up and left my shop. I don't know what happened between him and his wife, and frankly, I didn't care. The whole mess caused me so much stress; I ended up closing the shop down.

Me and the manager of Love's had become friends while my shop was open. Over time, I met one of her son's and began dating him. We continued dating after my shop closed and spent quite a bit of time together. He got along with my boys, which was always a plus for me. His mother had never gotten over me, closing the donut shop. I ended up confiding in her about the old pervert, which made her even madder. One day she sat her son and me down after the dinner she'd cooked for us saying she wanted to talk to us. I nearly fell out of my chair when I heard her proposition.

"You'll do what," I asked as if I couldn't believe my ears?

"If you and my son get married, I'll give y'all the money to open the donut shop as a wedding present," she said, grinning from ear to ear.

Marriage was once again a means to an end. Six months after I'd closed my shop, I was back in business.

Two weeks after we married, my husband came in drunk and picked a fight with me. Slapping me twice across the face, he drew back to hit me again. I blacked out, and the next thing I knew, he was stumbling backward off the porch. Scuter and Patrick just happened to be walking up at that precise moment, but I was so mad. I turned and walked into the house, slamming the door behind me.

Marriage number seven bit the dust. His Momma was so ashamed for the way he'd treated me; she told me not to worry about the money she'd given me to open the shop. I found out later he'd picked the fight so he could leave and go back to his old girlfriend.

I wondered for a very long time what I had done to hubby number seven that day when I blacked out, cause every time I saw him around town, he wouldn't come near me. Many years later, the mystery was solved at Scuter's wedding. He and Patrick had been sharing a laugh. When I walked up to them and asked what was so funny, Scuter answered.

"Did you ever wonder how come your 'two-week' husband always stayed away from you after that day you shoved him backward off the porch?"

"As a matter of fact, I've always wondered about that," I said, a sneaking suspicion forming in my mind.

"Me and Patrick followed him away from the house and threatened to tie him up and beat the living daylights out of him if he ever came near you again," Scuter said between big, belly laughs.

"Yea, we told him he better cross the street and go in the opposite direction when he saw you coming," Patrick added, laughing himself silly.

Hmph… Mystery solved.

Chapter 50

End it all and Rescues!

TED AND I TRIED ONE last time before calling it quits forever.

He moved in with me and the boys and helped run the shop. He had said he wasn't messing with methamphetamine, but I should have known better. It wasn't long before I had jumped back on the bandwagon with him. Once again, off to the races, it led to our demise. One morning as the boys were getting ready for school, it all came to a head.

"What's this Mom," Patrick asked, walking into the kitchen and holding a syringe out to me?

"Where'd you get that," I questioned while grabbing the syringe out of his hand and trying to keep my anger at bay.

"I was looking for my key chain in between the cushions of the couch and found this instead," Patrick wasn't gonna let it slide, "what is it?"

Thinking fast on my feet, I answered, "Ted gave Montana her vaccinations last weekend. He must have sat it down on the couch, and it fell between the cushions."

"Oh, okay. See ya later, Mom," Patrick said, running to catch up with his brother.

"Get out," I yelled at Ted as he came out of the restroom, "NOW!"

"What," he asked in obvious confusion?

"I said, get the hell out of my house! I want you out of mine, and my boys lives forever," I screamed out in frustration.

He just stood there looking at me as if he didn't have a clue. When I held up the syringe, the look on his face said it all.

"I'm sorry, Wende," looking toward the couch, he bowed his head, "I meant to go back and get it, but I forgot. It won't happen again," he promised as his tears began to fall. He took a step forward and reached for me, but it was too late. Pushing past him, I walked into our bedroom, he followed.

"Wende," he began, but I stopped him in his tracks.

"It's over, Ted. I want you to go before the boys come home for lunch. I'll tell them you had to go back to Texas to help Pa. I'm sorry, I just can't do this anymore. Please, just go."

I knew it was over between us, once and for all, as I watched him drive away. It broke my heart, but I knew if I didn't end it here and now, I'd never be able to get away from methamphetamine. Little did I know the struggle that awaited me.

Barely a week later, my probation officer came to see me.

"What I have to tell you is off the record, but I think you have a right to know," he said. "Your ex-boyfriend's girlfriend is in the hospital with hepatitis C. She's very sick. You might want to keep him away from your business if he happens to come around."

"I haven't seen him in quite some time, but I appreciate the heads up. Don't worry; I'll keep this between us."

I tried to stay clean, but the financial pull was too strong for me. I knew if I made a few trips down to Ft. Worth, I could keep my business afloat. The lies we tell ourselves when we're using is what keeps us in the middle of chaos, and I was no exception to the rule.

A friend of mine came to me and let me know there was talk around town regarding my extracurricular activities. No one knew for sure, but the rumor mill had begun. She said folks were voicing concerns about my boys and suggested I give some serious thought to getting help before it was too late. She named a Christian boy's home in a small town thirty miles away that helped women such as me. I thanked her and made up some errand I needed to run to cut our visit short. My greatest fears were being realized yet again, and I had only myself to blame. I knew I had to act fast if I wanted a say in where my boys would land.

I called the home and made an appointment to bring the boys to them the very next day.

I tried so hard to explain things to the boys, but they were furious with me. They blamed me for everything saying it was my fault; I ran Ted off. They said he'd never let me put them in a boy's home. Nonetheless, the next morning saw us headed for the small Oklahoma town. I tried to make it seem like a new adventure, but they weren't buying it. They barely spoke to me on the ride over, nor did they have much to say when the paperwork was completed, and it was time for me to leave. I'd never seen them so depressed. I'd never felt so disgusted with myself as I did on the ride back home. I went out to the drug rehab outside of town and signed up for out-patient counseling to begin the following week. I was still running the donut shop and couldn't go into rehab.

I tried to talk to the boys a few days after I dropped them off, but they said they didn't want to talk to me. Hanging up the phone, I was so ashamed of myself I wanted to die. No matter how hard I tried, I couldn't shake that thought. The more the afternoon wore on, the crazier my thoughts became. I worked myself into a frenzy of no return.

"What kind of mother sinks low enough to put their sons in a boy's home? They would be better off without me," I said to myself, "they'd be better off if I was dead."

I had not stopped shooting meth yet since I told myself I would quit when I started counseling. I was no longer thinking coherently as I took out my stash and fixed myself up a lethal shot of uncut meth. My precious labrador, Montana, looked at me as if to say, "What about me," but I was beyond all reasoning.

I grabbed the keys to my motorcycle and fled my home in tears. Driving ninety to nothing, I tore up those back roads, heading out to my quiet spot to end it all.

I hit my knees in the soft grass and felt the summer breeze blowing across my face. I knew when I shoved the syringe full of dope into my veins; I would surely die. I was both conflicted and tormented inside, but pulling the tourniquet from my jeans, I tied my arm off. Inserting the syringe into my vein, I slowly advanced the plunger forward. From somewhere inside, I heard myself screaming, "Help me, Jesus, please," or was it Momma screaming?

I don't know if it was my inner turmoil or the strong taste of meth that hit the back of my throat, but my hand jerked, and the needle came out of my vein. I knew there was a short window for me to do the shot of dope before my blood coagulated inside the syringe. The rush I felt from the taste I had gotten told me that the rest of the needle would kill me dead in my tracks when I shot it in my veins. Tying off my arm again, I tried to find a vein. Over and over,

I stuck the needle into my arm, but no matter what I tried, it didn't work. I switched arms, but that didn't work either.

"Help me, Jesus, help me," I cried. The funny thing is that after I started begging for Jesus to help me, I became confused as to what I wanted him to help me with. Was I asking him to help me do the shot of dope, or not do the shot of dope? In the pinnacle of my utter confusion, a vision came to me.

In my mind's eye, I saw the brilliant light which had been at the foot of Momma's bed the day her aneurysm ruptured. Then I heard Jesus speaking to me as clear as if he were standing next to me.

"I allowed you to see me the day I rescued your mother from her suffering so that you would know I am who I claim to be. I didn't forget her, and I'll never forget you. All you ever need to do is call out to me, and I'll be there."

Running to the concrete street, I slammed the syringe needle into the pavement until it broke. Then turning, I threw the blood-filled syringe as far as I could away from me into the gulley below. Walking back to the soft grassy meadow, I threw myself down and cried out for forgiveness. Deep, gut-wrenching sobs tore from my soul as I begged God for deliverance from the evil that wouldn't let me go. As the sun began to set, I felt peace wrap around me like a warm blanket. I sat watching the last rays of sun disappear from the sky before climbing on my bike and riding home. A plan began to form in my head as I made my way back into town. Come morning; I was gonna face my fears and get help.

I called my probation officer and asked him to stop by my shop cause I had an urgent matter I needed to discuss in private. He said he would when he got a chance but wasn't too happy about it. When he got there, I asked him to step in the prep area and closed the door.

"What is so urgent that I had to leave my office and come down here," he asked in an authoritative manner?

"I need your help," pushing up both of my sleeves; I held my arms out for him to see. The many puncture wounds and needle tracks resembled hamburger meat. I was ashamed but determined to find a way to stop the madness.

"What the hell," he stammered, "you want help? Help hell; I could send you to prison right now. What were you thinking?"

"If I can't find a way to stop, I need to go to prison," I cried as I broke down.

"And just what do you think I can do besides lock you up that will help you?"

"Make me pee in a up every week and roll up my sleeves every time you see me."

The understanding probation officer did just that and had every officer in town asking to see my arms too. I didn't care as long as I was held accountable for my actions. I started counseling, and by the end of the second week, I was feeling more confident than I had in years.

When I went to see the boys on the third weekend, they were at the boy's home; they let me have it.

"Either you take us home with you today, or else we're gonna run off to Texas," Scuter threatened.

Shaking his head affirmatively, Patrick backed his brother up. What else could I do? I took them home with me.

Chapter 51

Hep C, SWAT, and Grandma Georgia Bell

I DISCHARGED MY PROBATION, AND the boys and I moved home to Texas in the fall of '96. I rented a small two-bedroom house not far from Daddy. I got a job working as a waitress at an I-Hop in Arlington off I-20. It was good to be back home where I belonged.

Daddy had returned from his harrowing flight from California and had decided when his last batch of meth was gone; he was gonna get out of the biz and out from under the organized crime affiliate he had gotten hung up with. Unfortunately, that's easier said than done. Folks don't like it when you stop paying those high dollar dues.

A few weeks after I moved home from Oklahoma, I went to John Peter Smith hospital for some routine tests to follow up on my previous bladder cancer and was waiting to be released to go home. Expecting to see the med-tech who had been in previously, I was surprised when a female doctor came in to talk to me.

"Are you aware you have a liver disease," the doctor asked bluntly?

"Liver disease," I was thrown for a loop, "no, I can't say that's anything I've ever heard. How do you know I do?"

"You have hepatitis C. It showed up in your lab work. You'll need to make an appointment to follow-up on this as it is a very serious and contagious disease."

I was supposed to go to Daddy's house later but decided to go as soon as I left the hospital. I knew the minute the doctor said hepatitis C where I'd gotten it from. The problem now was how to get rid of it.

"Hey y'all," I said, coming through the front door. "What are y'all doing? Was that Shelley I saw going down the street?"

"Yea, you just missed Shelley," Mom Nita said, "how did your doctor appointment go?"

"They found hepatitis C in my blood and said that means I have a liver disease."

Daddy, who'd been fiddling with his Zippo lighter, looked up.

"How'd you get that," Daddy asked.

"I suspect that it was that cowboy in Oklahoma. His girlfriend was really sick in the hospital with it. It's contagious, so he probably got it from her and gave it to me. I'm fixin' to get the phone book out and see if I can find an organization to send me out some information about it."

Daddy showed me the latest gadget he'd found while Mom Nita messed around in the kitchen. I picked up the yellow pages from the hallway, went to the living room, and sat down on the couch next to the front door. I began thumbing through the book when I found what I was looking for. I had the phone in my hand and was just about to dial the number when I heard a loud explosion type sound, and the front door flew open with a violent force.

"POLICE," one of the men in SWAT combat gear yelled as he stormed through the door, followed by several others dressed the same as he was. The couch, though it was by the front door, sat back against the wall, so it was partially hidden. The fourth officer that ran into the house happened to look to his right and notice me. He stopped and ordered me to stand. Taking the phone and phone book from me, he told me to turn around so he could handcuff me. Calling out to a female officer, he asked her to come and search me. When they were done, they had me sit back down on the couch where I'd been sitting.

All the while they were messing with me, I could hear the other SWAT officer's yelling at Daddy and Mom Nita to put their hands up where they could be seen. All total, I counted a dozen officer's running around Daddy's house searching one room, then the next, before yelling out, "Clear."

I could hear Daddy saying they didn't have to handle him so rough from the bedroom, and that all they had to do was ask and he would do what they wanted. From the kitchen, I heard Mom Nita yell out.

"You just planted that in my pocket, that's not mine! John, they just planted dope on me," Mom Nita yelled out loudly.

When the Swat team was satisfied that they had contained all the people in the house, they led Daddy and Mom Nita into the living room and sat them on the couch next to me.

"What in the world is going on, Daddy?"

"I bet Shelley got set up and busted," Daddy whispered. "I told her I didn't trust that girl she brought over here earlier. Shelley came in and bought a half-gram for her."

"Were you able to hide the rest before they came in," Mom Nita asked Daddy in a whisper?

"Hell yeah, I did," Daddy craned his neck toward the kitchen, then turned back to Mom Nita, "as soon as Shelley left. I had a funny feeling, and I was right."

We sat there quiet for a little while, listening to the officers that had climbed into the attic via the drop-down staircase in the hallway. They thought they'd hit the jackpot when they came down with a box filled with paperwork.

"Look what we have here," the officer bragged, "it's a recipe for manufacturing methamphetamine." Walking into the living room where we were, the officer asked Daddy where his stash was.

"Your other daughter just picked up some dope for her friend from here, so we know you have a stash somewhere," the officer said.

"How about you pull that ski mask off and face me like a man," Daddy challenged, "I don't know what you're talking about, and I'm not saying a word until I talk to a lawyer," Daddy exclaimed.

They continued to tear Daddy's house apart for over an hour. It's a good thing they weren't paying much attention to us cause Daddy had a lot to say to me.

"Here, take these," Daddy managed to push a small keyring with three keys on it over to me. "They've already searched you, right? Shove them in the back of your pants, hurry. They unlock the locker over at the beauty shop, the money bag, and my storage unit. They aren't going to arrest you cause you're just here visiting me. You're my daughter and have a right to visit me without being charged with a crime. You need to go to the beauty shop and get that money bag as quick as you can. There's two-hundred-fifty thousand dollars in that bag, guard it with your life. Behind the shop, sitting against the wall and covered with plastic, is a gallon jar of P2P, the oil used to make meth, get it away from there. Go to my storage unit and get the guns and laboratory equipment. There are three boxes of pistols, and several rifles wrapped in moving

319

blankets. There are two big plastic bags with glass laboratory equipment in them. Be careful with that stuff; it's expensive."

Daddy hushed when the SWAT officers walked into the hall. When they walked away, he continued.

"Get on the phone and find a bail bondsman and bond us out as soon as they post our bonds. It probably won't be until tomorrow morning." After a few more minor instructions, Daddy clammed up. Mom Nita wasn't saying much of nothing at all. Though she did mention, she wondered if Grandma Georgia Bell was flipping out.

The SWAT team finally finished their searching and decided there was nothing there for them to find. They arrested Daddy and Mom Nita, but just like Daddy said, they didn't arrest me. As they got Daddy up, he asked if he could leave his house keys with me so I could feed their animals, and they said it was okay. I stood on the front porch and watched as they loaded them into two separate police cars.

Mom Nita had been right. Standing in the front yard, with her arms folded across her chest, and her right foot tapping the ground, stood Grandma Georgia Bell. The police no sooner pulled away from the curb until she pointed her finger at me in a motion that clearly said, "Get your ass over here right now!"

As soon as the door was closed, Grandma cornered me.

"I want to know what's goin' on, and don't leave anything out, do you understand?"

"Yes, ma'am," I answered without hesitation. I gave her a brief history of the drugs and then caught her up on what had just occurred. "I need to go over to the beauty shop and do what Daddy asked me to." When she asked what that was, I explained in detail.

"Well, come on, let's go," she said, hurrying me out the door.

I opened the locker door and took the large money bag out. I took the smaller key and unlocked the money bag next. It was stuffed full of banded hundred-dollar bills.

"Daddy said there was over two-hundred-fifty-thousand-dollars in here," I told Grandma.

"Oh my," Grandma said with an incredulous look across her face, reaching out for the bag she said, "I believe I'll take that."

"Thank goodness; I really didn't want to be responsible for it anyways. I'll need to come get the money in the morning to pay the bail bondsman, though."

Grandma took the bag and went in her house while I stepped out back to look for the jar of P2P. It was right where Daddy said it was. I didn't know what to do with it. I got to wondering how much jail time it would cost Daddy if anyone ever lifted his prints off the jar, and it scared me to death. They'd bury Daddy under the prison, and we'd never see him again. Without considering the consequences, I put my foot on the edge of the gallon jar and shoved it as hard as I could. It went crashing over and shattered across the concrete walkway, the oily substance spreading out in a huge circle.

"Oops, I'm sorry Daddy, I don't know how it happened," I thought to myself, wondering if Daddy was gonna kill me. In the meantime, I went to get the trash can and a garden hose. I cleaned up the mess looking over my shoulder in the process. I just knew those SWAT officers were hiding in the bushes to see what I was doing. My paranoia building, I got in my car and headed to Daddy's storage unit.

Daddy neglected to tell me where to look for the boxes of pistols, but I finally found them, and the rifles buried under some boxes of junk trinkets. The large plastic bags of lab equipment were out in the open. I loaded everything up and headed to my house. I stashed the pistols and rifles in my attic but figured the lab equipment should be stashed at Maw-Maw Cruse's.

I was so paranoid on the drive to Dallas. I figured those SWAT officers were smart enough to know that all they had to do to get evidence on Daddy was to follow the daughter they didn't arrest. It's what I would've done. I couldn't help but wonder how much Daddy had handled all that glass lab equipment leaving behind his prints. I'd already destroyed a gallon of P2P, and God only knew what that had cost him. He'd said himself that the lab equipment was expensive, but keeping Daddy out of prison meant more to me than any amount of money.

I was about to turn on Pemberton Hill off Loop 12 in Pleasant Grove when I finally made up my mind. Instead of turning, I continued straight until I got to the long bridge that spanned a barren, brushy area that flooded when it rained. Pulling close to the railing, I jumped out and ran around the car. I knew Daddy was gonna be furious with me, but I was more afraid of DEA getting their hands-on lab equipment with Daddy's fingerprints on it. I sent both bags flying, one at a time, to the rocky area below. Jumping back in my car, I headed over to Maw-Maw Cruse's house. I figured I'd stop and see her before I headed back to Ft. Worth. I knew Daddy wasn't gonna believe my stories, but anything was better than him going to prison forever.

The next morning, I met with a bail bondsman who got Daddy, Mom Nita, and Shelley out of jail. Daddy's luck went from bad to worse as he sought to extricate himself from the affiliations, he'd gotten involved with. He was set up and took a hard hit about a month after DEA and SWAT ran in on him. He spent thousands of dollars over the next couple of years to evade prison. In the end, all the cases against Daddy and Mom Nita were thrown out.

Daddy was never afraid of anything or anyone. He stood his ground and was eventually left alone.

He did venture out and attempt to 'cook' his own product once. It didn't end well, to say the least. He and another individual blew up a barn, barely escaping themselves. Needing to hide out and heal, Daddy went and stayed at Aunt Windelyen's. Man, oh man, did she read him the riot act on a daily basis.

"Poonie, (Daddy's childhood nickname), you're gonna give me a heart attack with some of these crazy stunts you're pulling," Aunt Windelyen cried!

Regardless, she fussed over Daddy and took care of him for several weeks. Daddy burned all the hair off his head, burned part of his face, and burnt a layer of skin off his forearms and hands. He had to have burn cream applied twice a day. Na-Ne loved her little brother no matter what he did, but she still gave him the business every day 'til he got well.

Thinking back on those times makes me feel ashamed for ever getting Daddy caught up in that world. I know he was a grown man and made his own decisions, but I know he only did it to survive. He'd been the one everyone turned to all his life for help. It wasn't until an unfortunate set of circumstances caused him to lose his business that he chose the only out he saw. With no education, his age, and ailing health, Daddy sold out.

It is the world we live in.

Poor, uneducated people don't stand a chance. I have seen many, many cases where other folks like Daddy made similar choices. It's sad, but God never promised life would be easy.

Chapter 52

Maw-Maw's Promise and Paw-Paw's Demise

January 30, 2018.

I'm not sure bout other writers, but for me, how to end my book has burdened me from the start. Forget about the fear of facing your demons, if you don't have an end in sight, kinda hard to tell the tale. Here lately, I've been struggling with my life. Trying to weave the ends together in meaning, which makes sense. Like the end to my book, I need closure.

We all have those ah-ha moments when the light comes on… Epiphanies lighting the way through the darkness. I had the granddaddy of all enlightenment this morning watching the sunrise over my beautiful Texas sky. Of course, I am in the middle of another fine mess I got myself into. Images of Lucy flutter across my mind. Unlike fiction, real-life lays your story out for you. It's just a matter of slowing down enough to tell your story where it makes some sense.

Yesterday I felt like Lizzy crossing the field as the fog lifts to reveal Mr. Darcy striding toward her. The fog begins to lift, and the ends are falling into place. Looking out across the morning sky, I understand.

For now, it's "*Full speed ahead, Rudolph!*" We have some unfinished business… Leaving the motel in my rear-view mirror, I set out for the drive back north. It's colder than a well-diggers butt out as Maw-Maw Lummus's used to say.

Driving along, I recall the last serious conversation I had with my little Cajun grandmother… Maw-Maw had taken to the bed after Paw-Paw Ernest did what he did. She told me she wanted to share something important with me as I pulled a chair next to the hospital bed in her living room. I have a video from her that day. It was the last video of her talking to me. We were talking 'bout life and the future.

"You know what? Come tomorrow, I'll have twelve years without a beer," Maw-Maw said as if it was a big secret.

"I'm so proud of you Maw-Maw, I know it must have been hard at times, but I also know how much it meant to you," I said, my heart swelling with love.

"I did it for you kids. I had a talk with the Lord and made a deal with him. I told him I'd quit drinking if he'd help my kids get off dope. I wanted to show y'all if I could do it, y'all could too," she said, with such conviction, I could feel it in my bones.

"I told God I wasn't proud of myself and that I know I'd done wrong drinking all my life, and not being a better mother and grandmother. I told him I was sorry and asked him to please forgive me. He said he did, and now I'm going to heaven," she said with tears swelling in her eyes.

"Oh Maw-Maw," I said, grabbing her in a deep hug. "You're wrong 'bout saying you wasn't a good mother and grandmother. I wouldn't trade you for the world! You're the only one who let me be a child. As I grew older, you taught me how to take care of my family. How to cook, and clean, and care for my babies. You taught me 'bout family get-togethers and how important it was to circle the wagons when one of us was hurting. You taught me so much 'bout being strong cause there was no other way to be. I've been trying to put the dope down, and I promise you one way or the other it's gonna happen soon. You're right, if you could give up your beer, then I can stop sticking needles in my arms," I promised with tears streaming down my cheeks.

Neither of us knew what a tremendous impact that conversation would have on my life. Must have been a year before that conversation that Paw-Paw Ernest ended his life.

I always hate calls in the middle of the night cause they almost always result in bad news. Picking up the phone that night, I braced myself. It was Daddy telling me Paw-Paw Ernest had killed cousin Elbert and had shot Aunt Windelyen in the head before turning the gun on himself.

Time stopped. I couldn't catch my breath. Daddy must have sensed it and spoke up, "There are news people here filming everything, so the police said we needed to notify the family. They're loading Windelyen and Momma in the ambulance. I'm following them to Parkland. I will call you when we get there."

I don't know if he heard me scream, "I'm coming, Daddy!" before he hung up the phone.

I'd stopped smoking cigarettes for a whole month, but that didn't stop me from picking up a pack as I raced to the hospital. "Lord, please let me see Auntie before she dies," I plead. Every memory of my "NaNe," aka Aunt Windelyen, fought to be remembered at the same time.

How many times in my life had I raced to a hospital in the middle of the night, I wondered, trying to take my mind off the nightmare I was smack dab in the middle of.

Coming round the corner of the lot that held Parkland's emergency room, relief overcame me as I pulled up to see my precious NaNe standing there holding an IV pole still with one hand and a cigarette in the other. Her head was wrapped in gauze covering half her face. NaNe had demanded to step outside and smoke. Daddy and Nita were standing there by her side.

NaNe told me the story between tears and drags off her cigarette.

Paw-Paw had bought several pistols over the years, which NaNe had always gotten rid of cause Paw-Paw always threatened to shoot somebody. This time he'd made good on his threats. We found out later that Paw-Paw had managed to buy the antique pistol at the flea market across the freeway from the mobile home park where they lived.

NaNe said Paw-Paw had gotten upset over what he'd seen on television that night. I believe it had been some political debate. Paw-Paw often got mad and yelled at the TV, and NaNe said she told him to shut his damn mouth and go on to bed.

NaNe had her hands full and was fed up with Paw-Paw's constant ranting and raving. Maw-Maw's health had been declining as well as Paw-Paw's. Maw-Maw had recently had surgery on her jaw for cancer, and Paw-Paw's cataract surgery had failed. They both depended on NaNe for everything now, which irked Paw-Paw to no end. All those years he had terrorized, NaNe was coming back to haunt him.

Paw-Paw left the living room at the same time Elbert and Aunt Ida did. Elbert, whom Paw-Paw despised, was Maw-Maw's nephew. Throughout the years, Elbert had come to stay with Maw-Maw '*for as spell*' as he always used to say. He went out to the screened-in porch where he slept while Aunt Ida went to the spare bedroom to get ready for bed. At that time, Maw-Maw had been sleeping in the recliner in the living room with NaNe on the couch beside her.

Everyone had settled in when NaNe heard Paw-Paw in the kitchen. The living room and kitchen/dining area was one big open area separated only by a little wooden rail.

Paw-Paw was standing at the stove banging around. NaNe said she had just started to sit up when all of a sudden, Paw-Paw was standing behind Maw-Maw in the recliner, pointing a gun at her.

"I'm tired of you bossing me 'round like child!" Paw-Paw was screaming.

Just as NaNe sat up, Paw-Paw fired the gun. It grazed the side of NaNe's ear as she jumped up.

Maw-Maw began screaming, "Get outta here" to NaNe and Aunt Ida, who'd stumbled into the hallway. NaNe said she cried and begged Paw-Paw, "Please don't hurt my momma" as her and Aunt Ida ran out the door and down the ramp that led off the porch. Aunt Windelyen was in front of Aunt Ida, who stumbled and fell on the ramp. Elbert stopped and helped Aunt Ida get up. Just as Aunt Ida left the ramp, she heard gunfire followed by Elbert's dying screams. Paw-Paw had fired two rounds into Elbert's back as he ran down the ramp. Poor Elbert! When his autopsy report came out, it stated he was eaten up with cancer and hadn't had much time left to live anyways. But still… NaNe said they ran to a neighbor's and called the police who showed up not long after, news vans in tow.

It was months later before Maw-Maw told what had happened when Paw-Paw came back in the house. Maw-Maw had managed to get up and roll her walker down the hall to the bathroom. Just as she turned to go in the bathroom, she looked back down the hall. Paw-Paw had sat down in his chair, took one last look at her, then raised the gun to his head. Maw-Maw said she saw Paw-Paw's head explode and barely made it to the commode before she collapsed.

My heart was so heavy. Everyone was cussing Paw-Paw, but I didn't know what to feel. To everyone else, he was just Maw-Maw's husband, but to me, he had always been my Paw-Paw, and I loved him dearly.

Aunt Ida had taken Maw-Maw home with her once the police released them from the crime scene, and NaNe had to stay overnight at the hospital for observation. The cops told Daddy the family was free to have the crime scene cleaned up, but Daddy said it would cost too much money to have professionals do it.

I can't explain all the thoughts that were going through my mind at the time. I was upset that Elbert had been murdered. I was upset 'bout the terror Paw-Paw had put everyone through. I was devastated because Paw-Paw had committed suicide, and I would never see him again.

"I'll do it, Daddy! I can rent a steam cleaner myself!"

They all tried to talk me out of it, but I said it was the last thing I could do for Paw-Paw. Daddy ended up going with me. It was barely breaking day when we started. We ended up having to pull up the carpet and use sponges to soak up Paw-Paw's blood from the padding before we could get it out of the rug. He'd bled out sitting there before the police came in and found him dead.

I'll never forget the sweet, stickiness of Paw--Paw's blood as I soaked up sponge after sponge from the carpet padding. In between tears, I prayed for PawPaw's soul. It took years before numerous steam cleanings finally erased the faint stains from that carpet. It was a lot easier washing Elbert's blood from the ramp.

Elbert's family had him shipped back to Louisiana, but getting Paw-Paw buried was a whole 'nother story. He had donated his body to the Health and Sciences organization in Dallas, but for whatever reason, they wouldn't take him. Come to find out; Paw-Paw had been ate up with cancer as well all over his body. I told myself that's why Paw-Paw did what he did. It hurt too much to consider the alternatives.

Three weeks later, we finally raised enough money for a cheap funeral and pauper's grave for Paw-Paw. I fixed Paw-Paw's hair, so he'd look like himself, and put his glasses on his face. They hid the bruises which scarred his face where the bullet exited his head. I did it for me, and Maw-Maw cause we were the only ones left who didn't hate Paw-Paw. That's when Maw-Maw took to the bed and never got out of it again.

I recently found out why everyone hated Paw-Paw Ernest. I just always thought it was because he was so *ornery*. I was told that he molested and attempted rape on two of my cousins. I was saddened and confused to hear the stories. I will always wonder why Aunt Windelyen let him stay around after those things occurred unless it was because of Maw-Maw. I can't imagine Maw-Maw wanting him around afterward, either. These are questions I'll never have the answers to since they're all long gone now.

Not long after we talked that last time, Maw-Maw died. How she died is another story I can't tell right now. I'll get back to it later.

Chapter 53

James, Andy, and Negotiations

LATE 1996, BUBBA WAS ARRESTED for probation violation and was setting in the county jail waiting to go to prison. When I went to see him, he said he was worried about his wife and son. He and Cassie had gotten married and had a year-old son, James. He asked me to go check on them and make sure they were alright.

I see no need to explain how but suffice it to say; I ended up getting custody of my nephew when his mother was locked up for probation violation just like my brother. James and I moved in with Na-Ne to help her take care of Maw-Maw Lummus, who had taken to the bed after we buried Paw-Paw Ernest. I took my nephew to see his mother on Daddy's birthday on January 11, 1997, before she was sent to prison.

Holding my nephew up to get a drink of water at the Parker County Jail in Weatherford, Texas, I was startled by the man who'd walked up behind me and said, "I bet your name is James."

"Excuse me, do I know you," I asked?

"I don't think so, but I bet you're his aunt," the man with the long ponytail laughingly said.

"Okay, what's going on here? How do you know so much about us?"

"My girlfriend is cellmates with this boy's mother," the man said. "The girl asked my girlfriend if I would go hunt you up to see if you would bring her son to see her. You live on Sharondale St., don't you?"

"No, you're talking about my sister, Shelley."

Taking a closer look at this man, I saw that he was wearing a maintenance-type uniform. I had heard that my sister-in-law was seeing a maintenance man behind my brother's back, an older man at that.

"So, your girlfriend is my sister-in-law's cellmate, huh," I repeated back to him as if to say, *I just bet*.

"Yes, she is," the man with the smiling eyes said.

"My name is Wende Beaird, and you are," I asked?

"Andy. Andy Nabors," he grinned, "we're always next door."

"Huh," I asked, puzzled.

"Nabors, you know, the next-door neighbor?"

"Oh, I get it. Well, nice to meet you, neighbor."

We talked a bit about James, the cold weather, and what brought us to the jailhouse that day. When they called me to visit Cassie, the maintenance man followed. How odd, I thought, when he sat down next to us as we waited for her to be brought in. Stranger still was the fact that he stayed and visited with us the whole time. When the visit was over, he followed us to my car.

"Thanks for holding the door, he can get a little heavy," I said, carrying a sleepy James in my arms.

"No problem, I'm one of the last of the good guys," he said, bragging.

"Oh yea, well, I'm not from Missouri, but you'd have to show me," I challenged.

The man had some kind of nerve. He was blatantly flirting with me! His supposed girlfriend, I was willing to bet, was actually my sister-in-law. In two seconds flat, I decided to fix both of their wagons.

"Here's my number, call me some time," I said, handing him a scrap of paper I had quickly scribbled my pager and Na-Ne's number on. I was gonna string him along until I broke them up, then I was gonna dump him on his butt. I'd show this philandering Casanova a thing or two. Not to mention, teach my sister-in-law a lesson for cheating on my brother!

"Na-Ne, you're not gonna believe this, but I met Cassie's boyfriend at the jailhouse. He was there to see her," I said as soon as I walked in the door. "I'm gonna steal him away from her, then dump him on his butt once they're good and broke up. You just wait and see."

"Did you give him this number," Na-Ne asked, looking at me like I was crazy?

"Oh my gosh, you mean he's already called here," I said, laughing my butt off, "he is quite a player, ain't he?"

I barely got James settled into bed, and changed into my pajamas when the phone rang.

"You don't waste no time do ya," I asked. "I wasn't expecting you to call before I even made it home."

"I wanted to make sure you and that boy made it home safe," he said as if we'd known each other forever.

"Well, thank you, that's awful, sweet," I replied.

We talked on the phone for so long that Na-Ne asked me if I'd went back to my teenage years. I told Andy I had to get off the phone, but we could talk again the next day. He claimed that he and his girlfriend had been on the verge of breaking up when she was arrested. I still believed that his girlfriend was Cassie, but I pretended to go along with his story.

So began a texting, talking frenzy that continued every day for a week. Finally, he asked if he could take me out for coffee that next weekend. I kept telling myself that I was only gonna steal him away from Cassie and then dump him, but I was really enjoying getting to know him.

He took me to Denny's on Buckner Blvd for coffee that Friday night. The waitress brought our coffee, and we'd talked for a while when a thought occurred to me.

"You've met James. I have custody of him. At any given time, I might have a houseful of kids to raise. If you're afraid of kids, this is gonna be our first and last date," I threw out just to see how he would react.

"Kids? I'm not afraid of kids. I got one of my own, and I don't see him often enough," he answered nonchalantly. He was the most laid-back man I believe I'd ever met. No matter what I tossed at him, he remained relaxed and confident. He had an excellent sense of humor and made me laugh frequently.

When he took me back to Na-Ne's, I invited him in. He had Na-Ne and Maw-Maw Lummus, eating out of his hands from "How do you do, Ma'am?" I guess that was a good thing since we decided to live together by the end of the second week. Clinton Ray, my cousin, was fit to be tied cause Na-Ne wouldn't let him have a girlfriend spend the night, let alone move in with him. Nonetheless, move into Na-Ne's house Andy did. Come to find out, I did steal Andy from his girlfriend, and it wasn't Cassie after all.

A couple of months after Andy moved into Na-Ne's house, we moved to Ft. Worth. Six months later, we had to leave there and move in with Maw-Maw Cruse. She'd been robbed again, and I knew it was time for me to take care of her.

"The young girl said she got locked out of her house and needed to call her boyfriend. She asked me for a glass of water, but when I came back from the kitchen, she was gone, and so was my purse," Maw-Maw said, worry etched across her face. "All my bill money was in my coin purse. I don't know what I'm gonna do now."

"Did you call the police," I asked.

"No, they'll put that poor girl in jail," Maw-Maw said, wringing her hands.

"I'm calling them, and I hope they do catch her and put her in jail!"

I called 911 and made a report with the officer who came out. Maw-Maw's vague description left the police with little to go on, but hopefully, the next person she robbed would give a better account. I gave Maw-Maw a stern lecture about letting strangers in the house and hoped I'd put the fear of God in her. I hated to be so harsh, but Maw-Maw was much too trusting, and I was afraid she'd let someone in that would hurt her, or worse yet kill her.

Andy and I moved into the large back bedroom and put James in the smaller one next to us. Maw-Maw was on cloud nine. Her favorite person in the whole world was right under her roof. She got the biggest kick out of James running around with his little bad self. What that boy didn't get into would be easier to tell than what he did. He could be quite the little character. I remember waking up one morning to the largest spider-web made of yarn that I'd ever seen. He had wound the yarn through the dresser handles back and forth to the doorknobs until I had to use Andy's pocketknife to get through James' room to the front of the house. Another morning, I woke up to Louisiana hot sauce splattered across the wall in the shape of a rainbow. Yes, sir, that little boy was a *hot* mess.

Everything was going fine until an old friend stopped by with some ether-based meth. I hadn't seen any of that 'pink' tinted speed in a while. It produced a different kind of high which I really liked.

"What's a little taste gonna hurt," I asked myself?

I was off to the races again. I'd managed to get a handful of months clean time under my belt so I could get custody of James this time, but I couldn't seem to find the footing I'd had in Louisiana. Andy liked it too, and soon we were both caught up in a mess. He worked odd jobs; I took care of James and kept an eye on Maw-Maw. I'd sell enough meth here and there, so we got ours free.

Christmas came and went, and soon, it was January 1998. Andy and I often took turns going to Na-Ne's and helping with Maw-Maw Lummus. Her health had been going downhill for the past couple of months, and we all knew our time with her was growing shorter.

Monday, January 19, 1998, I went to Na-Ne's to stay up with Maw-Maw Lummus so everyone else could get some sleep. Poor Maw-Maw, she had all but stopped eating around Thanksgiving, and had survived on Ensure ever since. She'd been sleeping more and more and had started becoming non-responsive.

I'd been sitting on the couch next to her bed reading ever since the others had gone to bed. It was around four am when I started nodding off and couldn't hold my eyes open no matter how hard I tried. I knew if I fell asleep and Na-Ne got up and caught me, she'd have a cow. It was then I remembered that I had some speed in the car. Slipping out of the house, I retrieved the drug and syringe from my glove box.

If Na-Ne caught me shooting up drugs in her house, she'd never let me hear the end of it, but she would have my hide if she found me sleeping on the job too. I was in a no-win situation, or so I told myself. Sitting on the side of the tub, I injected the drug into my vein and felt the rush creep over the back of my head. I was instantly awake, no longer fearing I'd fall asleep. Just the same, I admonished the reflection I saw in the mirror over the sink as I walked past. "Shame on you! How could you do this in Na-Ne's house?" I'd sunk to a new all-time low.

I grabbed Maw-Maw's Bible and sat down by her bed. Looking at her pained expression, I felt guilt wash over me, remembering the conversation we'd had a few months before where she said she'd prayed to Jesus for her grandkids to stop messing with those drugs. I sat there with my head hung in shame, asking God to forgive me as well.

There was a marker for Ecclesiastes 3. I opened it up to that chapter and began reading aloud to Maw-Maw. The more I read, the more I felt as though God was speaking to me. When I finished reading, I looked down at my Maw-Maw, and she was frowning and moaning in pain. It tore my heart out.

I'd always heard that the spoken word was powerful. Right, that minute, I was feeling very powerful emotions, and I meant to give God a piece of my mind. I went to the back of the trailer, next to the back door and hit my knees. Raising my hands to the heavens, I let her rip!

"God, you said you would never suffer your children, well you better get your ass down here and take my Maw-Maw out of her pain!" I screamed out. The minute the challenge left my lips, I felt fear as I'd never felt before course through my body. Oh my gosh, what had I just done?

"Oh God, I'm so sorry, sweet Jesus! Oh, Lord, please forgive. I'm just so hurt for my Maw-Maw. If you're that entity I've believed in all my life, give me a sign. Lord God, I know you're not in to deal-making, but if you'll take my Maw-Maw out of her pain, I swear I will never do speed again," I pleadingly yelled out to God.

I sat there for a minute on my knees, praying fervently for God to hear my pleas before I went back to sit by Maw-Maw's bed. I picked up her Bible, turned to Psalm's 23, and began to read. I'd barely started on the third line when something caught my attention out the corner of my eye.

Looking down at Maw-Maw, I saw her smile the biggest, most joyous, and beautiful smile I'd seen on her face since way before Paw-Paw pulled his stunt. Almost immediately, her lips began moving as though she were talking to someone, yet no sound could be heard. Then she smiled again. This exchange of lips moving and smiling went back and forth for several moments. I was mesmerized. To this day, I swear, I believe she was talking to Jesus.

Needless to say, my urgent prayers woke Na-Ne and Clinton up. Na-Ne came rushing into the living room with a scowl on her face.

"My God Yvette are you trying to wake up the neighborhood," Na-Ne asked as Clinton came out of his room.

"Now you went and upset Liz," Clinton said.

"I'm sorry, Na-Ne, but Maw-Maw was in so much pain. After I screamed out to God, he answered my prayers, and Maw-Maw even smiled. Na-Ne, she was moving her lips like she was talking to someone. I think she was talking to God," I swore.

"I can't see any smile on her face," Na-Ne said, exasperated. "You better go on down to your Maw-Maw Cruse's and let me calm Clinton and Liz down. You can come back later."

I felt so bad as I bent to kiss Maw-Maw Lummus goodbye. I had no way of knowing it was the last time I'd see her alive.

I went by and checked on Andy, James, and Maw-Maw Cruse before getting in the car and driving out to Laurel Land, where Momma was buried. I sat on top of Momma's grave, pulling the weeds that had grown up there. Daddy used to do that whenever we visited family gravesites back in the day. I guess I picked up that habit from him. I spent the day in reflection of memories with Maw-Maw Lummus, and how I'd cursed God earlier in the morning. In my drug-induced state, my thoughts raced between the past and present in my mind.

"Oh, Momma, I wish you were here. I wish you could help me unravel this mess I've made of my life." I laughed to myself realizing Momma never figured out her own life, how could she have helped me figure out mine.

"God, please forgive me for cursing you. Please, sweet Jesus, help me escape my madness!" It was at that moment that the flood gates opened up, and I cried deep, gut-wrenching sobs. Falling over onto the ground, I cried myself to sleep. I'm sure the cemetery workers paid me no heed that day as they were used to my presence by then. Momma's gravesite was my go-to spot when I needed to be alone.

It was late afternoon when I awoke cold and shivering. Stumbling to the car, I drove back to Maw-Maw Cruse's and sorted out dinner. I never made it back over to Na-Ne's, but she left word with Andy that she didn't need my help with Maw-Maw that night. We all went to bed after dinner, and it wasn't long before I fell fast asleep. I remember I was dreaming, and in my dream, a phone was ringing.

"Yvette, come talk to Windelyen, she's on the phone," I heard Maw-Maw Cruse screaming from the front of the house.

"Guess I wasn't dreaming I heard the phone ringing," I said to Andy as I crawled from the bed. Looking at the bedside clock as my eyes focused, I saw it was just past five am. Then it hit me, Maw-Maw Lummus is gone! I knew in my heart that must be why Na-Ne was calling that time of the morning.

"I'll be right there, Na-Ne," I cried into the phone.

Driving to Na-Ne's trailer, a cold chill settled in my bones. I recalled the words I'd screamed at God twenty-four hours earlier. I'd cursed and challenged God in a manner that frightened me to my core. Then I'd thrown down the gauntlet, "If you'll just take Maw-Maw out of her misery, I'll never do another shot of dope as long as I live."

Maw-Maw's doctor couldn't fathom how or why she'd kept hanging on to life, but pulling in front of Na-Ne's trailer that morning to watch them wheel Maw-Maw out of her home one last time, I had a pretty good idea. The date was January 21, 1998. It was a date I'd never forget.

Chapter 54

Twelve steps, and another death...

Getting through the days leading up to Maw-Maw Lummus' funeral was so hectic and heart-wrenching that it was easy to stick by the promise I'd made to God about never doing speed again. Not to mention how spooked I was feeling that he'd done, exactly as I'd asked, by taking her out of her misery so soon after I'd demanded him to. No way in hell was I gonna go near a shot of dope after making a bold declaration such as that.

As I recall, my resolve lasted just long enough to see her buried. It wasn't long before the natural adrenaline from the past few days wore off, and I began to detox. Still feeling spooked, and wanting to keep my word to God, I searched out the nearest Narcotics Anonymous meeting. I told Andy it was something I had to do as I drove off like a madwoman hell-bent for leather.

I don't know that I was looking to clean-up forever, but at that moment in time, I had to get help right away, and in a hurry. I dove into those N.A. meetings headlong, soaking up every morsel of information I could find. I remember those early meetings to this day. I kept hearing that if I wanted to seriously get clean, I needed to make ninety meetings in ninrty days. Being the overachiever that I was, I made over two-hundred meetings those first ninety days. My fanny was in a seat every time the doors opened at my homegroup. I kept going several times a day for the next ninety days after that too. Before I knew it, I was receiving my six-month chip! I was free at last.

At six months clean, I knew I was free. My oldest son, Scuter, grasped my shoulders one afternoon as I was walking from my bedroom to the front of Maw-Maw Cruse's house, and looking down at me uttered words that blazed onto my heart.

"You've really given up meth, haven't you? I finally have my Mom back," my son cried from his heart of hearts.

At that moment, I realized how deeply my drug use had hurt my sons and my family. I vowed to God that I would indeed keep my word to him as long as he was there to help me.

Narcotics Anonymous paved my way back to sanity, but I knew my higher power personally. He was my Lord and Savior, Jesus Christ.

Twenty-two years (as of this writing) later, I can say without a doubt that God still has my back! I'm not gonna lie, it's been hard, but nothing worth having ever comes easy, does it?

"I can do all things through Christ who strengthens me… Philippians 4:13" When times are hard, and I feel I can't go any further, I remember this verse above all others. I have clung to it for dear life.

I can't always quote scripture and verse, but another one I stand on in times of trouble is:

"And we know that all things work together for good to them that love God, to them who are the called according to his purpose… Romans 8:28"

Around the same time, Scuter remarked how relieved he was to have his mother back; I was sitting in my bedroom looking at James sleeping so peacefully, his angelic features tugging at my heartstrings. I got to wondering what 'P.J.' was gonna look like. My grandchild was due in a couple of months, and I feared for his future. My son and his soon to be wife struggled to stay together, which didn't bode well for my precious grandchild, nor did the fact of his heritage.

"It's not fair," I complained aloud to God, "my grandchildren will be born into vicious cycles of poverty, illiteracy, alcoholism, and addiction from all sides of their families. How can they ever hope to have rewarding and successful lives?" I was sitting on a poor me, pity pot, bemoaning not only my grandchildren's bleak futures but mine as well.

"If you don't like your lot in life, change it," I heard the voice loud and clear, and immediately knew it was God speaking to me. My God has an amazing sense of humor.

"Oh yeah, and just how am I supposed to do that," I shot back at my Savior.

"Continue to put as much time between your last shot of dope and the time that you'll need to be held accountable for your actions. Just keep trusting me and doing the next right thing before you. You will have to fight for your grandchildren someday," I heard God say as sure as he'd been standing in front of me.

The conversation I had with God that afternoon still moves me as it did that day. It was real and powerful! So, I began putting one foot in front of the other, and when I felt weak, I would recall the message God had given me. I wish I could tell you the road got easier after that, but I can't. In fact, it got a whole lot harder before it became easier. Ha, who am I kidding? Life isn't for the faint of heart, and if it seems easy, you're doing something wrong...

Thinking back to those early days of attending N.A. when I finally got clean, I can say it has gotten easier from that aspect. The more you practice anything, the easier it becomes. Come to find out; drugs weren't the reason for my downfall; it was life I hadn't learned to deal with. I was receiving information that would help me build a firm foundation from which to grow. I hadn't arrived yet, but at last, I was on my way.

It took time to distance myself from the constant obsession of searching for my next shot of dope. I learned techniques for distracting myself or finding new, healthy past times. I learned to redirect my thoughts when they snuck up on me. Most importantly, I learned not to dwell on the glamorous aspects of speed, such as the euphoric rush after a shot of it, the increased energy, easy weight loss, etc. etc. Those surface attributes are the outside packaging of profound, destructive, and life-changing chemicals for folks like me.

I don't view drugs the way I did twenty-plus years ago. I accept them for what they are and what they can do for me; or to me. I must always respect their boundaries as well as mine. As crazy as it sounds, I respect the fact that if I allowed them to, drugs could once again rule my life. I prefer to face life head on these days. It is what it is, and no amount of drugs, sex, food, or alcohol will change it. Might as well face it, fix it, or move on if you can't. In the end, it's all about acceptance.

Fall 1998 was hectic for me. October 5, 1998, Patrick George Stewart Jr. came into this world. 'P.J.' was born not long before Patrick graduated from boot camp. Me, him, and his Momma flew out to San Diego for the big day. I was in complete shock when my baby boy came walking up to me thirty-five pounds lighter than I'd last seen him. I cried like a baby seeing him hold his son for the first time.

I was also knee-deep involved with my sponsor and home group as I attended various group functions to stay busy and off drugs.

Thanksgiving came and changed it all.

Maw-Maw Cruse was walking across the living room floor and turned around too quickly. She suffered a pathological fracture to her hip. She fell to the floor, screaming so pitifully it broke my heart. I called an ambulance, and she was transported to the hospital. She was scared out of her mind as she'd never been to the hospital in her life. She'd only seen a doctor a handful of times in her eighty-six years as it was. They rushed her into surgery almost as soon as she got there. Bless her heart; I felt so bad for her.

It was the beginning of the end for poor Maw-Maw Cruse. She refused all efforts to learn to walk again. She was terrified she'd fall and hurt herself again. What I couldn't get her to understand was that if she didn't learn to walk again, she was gonna die. No matter how hard I tried, she wouldn't listen to me. Nor would she let me out of her sight. I don't know what I would have done without Andy. He was terrific with Maw-Maw and even changed her when she was soiled. It was hard watching my precious Maw-Maw waste away as time went on. It was happening right before my eyes, yet when the end came, I wasn't prepared to say goodbye.

The stress and strain got to Andy and me, and we split up late spring of 1999. Cassie got out of prison not long after and came to stay with me, James, and Maw-Maw. It wasn't long before she moved out to live with her new boyfriend. She seemed to be doing well, so I let James go with her.

Maw-Maw got sick with pneumonia and ended up going to the hospital. While there, she developed septicemia and stayed nearly two-months before the doctors said she had to go into a nursing home to be cared for. Maw-Maw was not a happy camper, and I felt awful cause I promised Momma and Maw-Maw that I'd never let that happen.

I was so worried about Maw-Maw the day I drove off and left her in that place. I can still hear her screaming for me not to leave her there as I walked down the hall away from her room. I vowed to find a way to get her out of there, but first, I had to take care of some outstanding traffic warrants I had out for my arrest. I turned myself into the Seagoville police department to serve out their tickets and waited for transfer to Dallas County to sit those tickets out next. Learning to stay clean meant learning to be responsible and pay your bills. I was working on my program and starting to feel like a productive member of society.

I had over one thousand dollars in warrants and fees in Dallas County, which should have kept me there for at least a week to ten days. I was shocked when I was released the following day right after breakfast. I found a way to my sponsors' house where I was staying temporarily until I got the electric back on at Maw-Maw Cruse's. I remember thinking how blessed I was to have all my warrants dismissed with time served. Little did I know it was a God thing.

Later that afternoon, I got a call at my sponsor's house, saying that Maw-Maw was being rushed to the emergency room with respiratory failure. I got there almost as fast as the ambulance did.

"Yvette, don't let me die," Maw-Maw pleaded with me as we waited for the E.R. doctor to come and discuss the results of the tests they'd run on Maw-Maw.

"Maw-Maw stop talking nonsense, I'd never let you die," I promised.

Famous last words...

"Your grandmother is experiencing respiratory failure and will die within the next six to twelve hours if we don't put her on a ventilator," the young doctor told me.

I was glad I'd asked to speak with him in private. I needed time to figure out what to do, and this was a decision I didn't want to make on my own. I called my Uncle Thomas. I hadn't ever asked his advice before, but this was a time I figured I needed to. He was, after all, Maw-Maw's son.

"Thomas is on a business conference call, and I'm not going to disturb him. You're the one who has cared for her all these years; you make that decision. When she passes, don't make any plans with the funeral home, we'll handle all of that," my aunt stated.

"But...," I started to say something, but before I got another word out of my mouth, my uncle's wife hung up on me.

The myriad of emotions that bombarded me at that moment was overwhelming. All I could do was stare at the phone in my hand with the dial tone in the background.

"Dear Lord, what do I do," I yelled out in a silent prayer. Taking a deep breath, I walked back down the hall and found the young doctor. I needed answers if I was going to make this decision on my own.

"If we put her on a ventilator, can she ever come off of it and go back to normal," I asked.

"Chances are she will have to remain on it until she dies," the doctor replied.

For some reason, I knew I could trust this soft-spoken man.

"If this was your grandmother, what would you do?"

"If my grandmother were eighty-seven years old, she would have lived a pretty full life. I wouldn't want to prolong her suffering by putting her on a machine she would never come off until she died. If she were my grandmother, I'd let her die as peaceful as I could."

"Okay, then. I don't want her put on a ventilator," I barely got out before bursting into tears.

The young doctor put his arms around me and told me how courageous I was being for my grandmother. He said he could give her some medicine to help calm her down, and would send us upstairs to a room so we could have some privacy.

I called the family and explained what was happening before going back in to see Maw-Maw.

"They're putting you in the hospital for a couple of days until you feel better," I said, wishing it was true.

"Are you gonna stay with me, Yvette," Maw-Maw questioned, almost as if she expected me to say no?

"Of course, I am Maw-Maw! I'm not gonna leave your side."

They moved her upstairs shortly after that and gave her some medicine to help her breathe easier. I crawled into bed beside Maw-Maw after the nurse left and laid there holding her. I didn't know what to say and was afraid if I opened my mouth I would start bawling, so I just laid there and held her.

"I'm not gonna make it this time, am I," Maw-Maw asked in a scared, timid voice?

I don't know where I got the courage to answer her, but I looked down at her and responded.

"Maw-Maw, do you remember telling me how happy you was gonna be the day you met your maker," I prayed for God to help me be strong, "and besides, I'm a little jealous, 'cause you're gonna see Momma soon. I love you, Maw-Maw, and I'm gonna miss you more than you'll ever know."

"I love you too, Yvette," Maw-Maw whispered before falling silent.

I laid there and brushed her hair off her forehead with my hand in a soft, comforting manner. I kept praying for Bubba and Shelley to show up soon as I listened to her breathing, which came in the same rhythmic manner.

I soon lost track of time lying there, holding my dear grandmother. A couple of hours later, I was suddenly startled when I heard her take a deep breath in, followed by a long, pronounced exhale. I kept waiting for her to take another breath in, but it didn't come. I think I was in shock knowing what had happened; it was the first time anyone had ever died in my arms.

No telling how long I would have continued to lay there if the phone hadn't rung.

"Yvette! Bubba, Shelley, your Daddy, and Nita ought to be there any minute. Yvette, can you hear me," Na-Ne asked me, "how is Miss Cruse?"

"I don't think she's breathing Na-Ne," I said, barely able to speak.

"Yvette, push the call light for the nurse, now," Na-Ne broke me out of my spell and into action.

When the nurse opened the door, he barely stuck his head in and asked, "Has she expired?"

"No, my Maw-Maw didn't expire. She passed away and went to live with her Savior in heaven!"

Right after he closed the door, it opened again. Everyone had finally made it to the hospital, but not in time to tell Maw-Maw goodbye. I called my uncle to tell him Maw-Maw was gone, and this time he got on the phone with my aunt.

"Your grandmother didn't have a lot of friends, so there's no need to go to a big expense to bury her," my aunt said.

"Well if she's not gonna have some kind of funeral, and I can't honor her wishes, then I'm not gonna give y'all the burial policies me and her been paying, these past several years," I fired back.

"Yvette, meet us at Laurel Land around nine am tomorrow and bring her policies," Uncle Thomas said.

"Thank you, Uncle Thomas, I'll see you in the morning."

I could hear my aunt spewing in the background as he hung up the phone, but I knew my Uncle Thomas understood where I was coming from, and probably, secretly agreed with me.

We came to a compromise the next morning. Maw-Maw's policies weren't much but allowed her to be prepared for a small viewing and graveside service. I prepared a eulogy to read at the graveside to keep from having to pay a minister to do it for us.

So much for what my aunt thought! Maw-Maw had quite a few people show up for her viewing and graveside service. In addition to her eulogy, I wrote a poem for her. The poem spoke of what a humble soul Maw-Maw was and how she didn't have to put on airs and pretend she was someone she wasn't to be loved. Uncle Thomas was standing behind his wife, who never saw the smile he had on his face at the words I spoke of his mother. I believe, in his own way, Uncle Thomas did love Maw-Maw.

I'm not saying that all childhoods are worth remembering, but sometimes folks get so high above their raising that they can't be proud of where they came from. Seems to me they end up losing sight of what mattered most.

Chapter 55

Facebook and Maw-Maws

Sunday, November 3, 2019

IN MY PROFESSION, I AM surrounded by death. Some find it a morbid occupation and often suggest it must be hard to do. I understand why they'd say that, but to me, it's not morbid at all. It's undoubtedly an occupation I feel a calling for. Sitting here this morning, I wonder how long I'll continue this path I'm on.

Stepping outside for a smoke break, I reflect on where my storytelling will lead as well. I tell myself that regardless of all else, I am leaving behind a lifetime of memories for generations yet to come. What I wouldn't give to have a collection of stories from my family who have gone before me. I'm sure some of my stories will be painful for my loved ones to read. Yet, to speak only of happy times would be misleading. If I didn't tell about the hard times, whether by my own hand or not, I couldn't show how my Lord saw me through to the other side.

I was sitting here thinking that my stories won't matter to those who don't know me, but I know it's only the devil putting those thoughts in my mind to keep me from sharing them. Since I began this journey, I have been plagued with self-doubt, but I refuse to give up.

"Don't you dare quit," I hear Daddy saying.

Looking through my phone, a '*sign*' pops up in the form of my daily horoscope. The gist of it is that I have been granted something which may seem to fall short of my expectations. It goes on to say that I shouldn't underestimate the power it holds. Although it may seem insignificant to me, it can bring about a profound, long-lasting change. The last sentence tells me to trust that I have all I need to make it happen.

Some call horoscopes entertainment and hogwash. To each his own I always say. For me, *however* God chooses to get my attention and speak to me, leaves me feeling comforted.

Call me crazy. It doesn't matter to me how others view my relationship with God. His *signs* are everywhere for all who have eyes that will see, and ears that will hear.

February 9, 2020

I've loved Facebook from day one. For me, being able to follow friends and family far away is such a blessing. I have also used Facebook for other reasons over the years, some good, and some not so good. From venting, journaling, and a way to combat loneliness, it has come in handy. When I began this journey, I took all my friends and family along with me. I used them as a sounding board when I needed encouragement and shared a few chapters to see if anyone would actually enjoy reading them. So many times, I wanted to give up, and once I became discouraged and stopped writing for months. It was my friends and family on Facebook who kept asking, "Where's your book?" that kickstarted me back in gear. What started out as a post on Facebook yesterday morning, grew into a chapter.

I've shared my innermost thoughts within the pages of this book. Once they're out there, I can never take them back. As it grows closer to being published, I'm a little bit anxious. Okay, maybe a lot anxious, but how can I tell my story without being transparent?

The only thing I would change about any of my family members would be to take away the pain they've suffered. But we're no different than others; everyone suffers pain in their lives. It's just life.

Anytime I hear the word family, I feel arms wrapped around me. Now that's not to imply we haven't had our times amongst ourselves. Are you kidding me? Never a dull moment was to be had. It warms my heart to think of all the happy times we shared. I smile, thinking 'bout some of the messes we got into as well. I remember how we circled the wagons as a family and got through those tough times together. We might fight amongst ourselves, but let someone mess with one of us and see if we didn't all come a-runnin'?

When I think of my grandmother's, sometimes I want to cry cause I miss them so much! They were as different as night and day, yet alike in many ways. I want to shout to the world how lucky I feel to be their granddaughter! They taught me more 'bout life just being themselves.

I've made much 'bout my little cajun MawMaw, but I only saw her drunker than a skunk a few times in my life. I remember those times being funny. Everyone knew to back up and listen to that little four ft eleven-inch woman cause she'd had her fill of something or else she wouldn't have got herself that way. Maw-Maw indeed drank her beer like most folks drink water, but you'd have never known it if you hadn't seen her with a can in her hand. She always acted 'bout as normal as anyone else.

Now, Maw-Maw Cruse could get you rolling on the floor too. Most times, she was a quiet, timid little woman, but make her mad, she'd get as feisty as Granny on Beverly Hillbillies. Never drank a drop in her life. Well, except for the last year, she lived on her own. She'd gotten to taking Nyquil at night cause she thought she needed it to sleep. When I moved in with her, I asked her one day how come she was going through so much of the stuff? She said she didn't know cause she was only drinking a half a bottle at a time! Once I told her it was helping her sleep cause it was making her drunk, she laid off it for good.

One memory stands out as I remember my precious grandmother's. It's 'bout the only time I recall where we were off together by ourselves.

It started off one morning when I'd stopped by NaNe's to see if they had anything for a toothache. I'd been sitting there talking to Maw-Maw Lummus when Maw-Maw Cruse called 'round looking for me. She needed a ride to the feed store to get her chicken's some feed.

"Wanna ride with me? It'd get you outta the house for a while," I asked. I was 'bout the only one Maw-Maw Lummus trusted riding with, and I always enjoyed getting her out of the house.

"I reckon so. Let me get my shoes on and grab my purse," she answered, and set about getting ready to go.

At the time, I was driving Paw-Paw Roy's Chevy II. It was a small, four-door, box of a car, but I enjoyed driving it. It was very compact. We picked up Maw-Maw Cruse and ran by the Dairy Queen to get something to drink before we set off on our 'rat killing' as Maw-Maw Cruse suggested.

"Ouch!" I cried out after that cold Dr. Pepper hit my bad tooth.

"What's the matter," Maw-Maw Lummus asked 'bout, jumping out of her seat next to me?

"My tooth is killing me," I said, holding my aching jaw.

"Didn't that clove help you none," she asked, referring to the home remedy she'd offered me earlier?

"It did for a little while. Don't worry; I'm gonna smoke a joint after I drop y'all off. It'll stop hurting then."

"Well smoke it now if it'll help you. It won't bother me," looking over her shoulder, Maw-Maw Lummus asked, "will it bother you, Miss Cruse?"

"I don't care what Yvette does long as it helps her," she said, concern in her voice.

The heater in Paw-Paw Roy's little car didn't work very well, and since it was cold outside that morning, I had the windows rolled up tight to keep the warmth in. I started the car and was about to pull out of the parking lot when Maw-Maw Lummus spoke up.

"Just smoke it right here. We're liable get pulled over by the police while your smoking that stuff!"

I finished my joint and off to the feed store we went. I got turned around for a minute, but finally found the feed store. It seems like I remember it being either on or near Military parkway. Anyways, all three of us were quiet and lost in thought, not speaking much 'til we got there. Maw-Maw Cruse sat there a minute, scratching her head before getting out of the car with her purse hanging off her arm, and as always, her scarf tied under her chin. Me and Maw-Maw Lummus sat there for the longest in silence 'til Maw-Maw spoke up.

"Wonder what happened to Miss Cruse? She's been in there quite a while?"

Just about that time, Maw-Maw Cruse came walking out of the store empty-handed, still scratching her head. Walking down the sidewalk toward us. She got in the car with the most bewildered look I ever saw.

"Well, I swanny, I can't for the life of me, 'member what I came here after," Maw-Maw Cruse said, frowning.

I looked at poor Maw-Maw Cruse, then at Maw-Maw Lummus as it dawned on me.

"Oh God forgive me, I done went and got my grandmothers stoned," I thought out loud before I busted out laughing.

Maw-Maw Lummus looked at me like I was crazy before she went to laughing. Not to be left out, Maw-Maw Cruse soon chimed in. I laughed 'til my sides hurt, then I went in the store to get Maw-Maw Cruse's chicken feed. They were still laughing when I got back to the car.

"Hey, why don't we go the diner and get some lunch 'fore we go down on Second," Maw-Maw Cruse suggested.

I smiled and agreed. I didn't want to tell my grandmother's they were having the munchies. A part of me felt bad, but they were so cute, laughing at everything.

We got to the diner, and man were they cutting up. Quiet little Maw-Maw Cruse was having herself a ball. When they brought the food, they went to eating everything in sight. Maw-Maw Cruse finished first and was 'bout to grab Maw-Maw Lummus roll.

"I'll take that if you don't want it," Maw-Maw said, reaching across the table.

Quick as lightning, Maw-Maw Lummus snatched it up.

"Now Miss Cruse, you done ate your'n. This one's mine," Maw-Maw Lummus said before taking a big bite out of the roll. Then she went to laughing so hard she almost choked.

Before I knew it, we were all laughing.

In fact, we laughed all the way to the beer store, and 'til I dropped them both off.

The pot had worn off not long after we left Lake June Cafe, but it seemed to be one of those times when life wasn't so bad.

Boy, did that change when I dropped Maw-Maw Lummus off at Auntie's. She'd just got home from the store and was carrying groceries in.

"You did what," she asked? Each word rising in decibels.

"Yvette, you ought to be ashamed of yourself! What am I gonna do with you," Nane asked, looking at me as though she could pinch my ears off?

"Now wait just a minute here, I'm a grown-ass woman, and I guess I can get stoned if I want too," Maw-Maw said, stepping up and getting in the mix.

Auntie looked at both of us, shook her head, and turned around to put her groceries up. Later, after she cooled off a bit, me and Maw-Maw went to telling her about the day's events, and she laughed 'til she cried. But you can bet, by the time I left, I knew better than to ever do that again.

Years would pass, and God only knows how many times that story got told. Just for the record, I did not coerce my grandmothers to smoke pot with me! My grandmothers got high from secondhand smoke. I'd always heard it could happen, but I never believed it until I saw it happen for myself. I don't give a care what anybody thinks about it, that afternoon with my grandmothers will always be one of my most cherished memories.

This chapter started out as a post to my friends and family here on Facebook. I had been seeking advice as to the question,

"Do my stories seem like I'm insulting my family's memories?"

I've answered my own question. It's the memories that keep them alive.

Chapter 56

Maw-Maw Cruse's Rose Bush

Maw-Maw Cruse never made out a formal Will, but Uncle Thomas honored what Maw-Maw had asked. Everything in the house was to be left to us grandkids, and he was to get the house. When I moved in to take care of Maw-Maw, Uncle Thomas had promised to give me time to find somewhere to live after she passed.

Maw-Maw had been paying on her appliances and things she had bought for me on credit when she died. Her monthly payments also included a fee, which was to pay everything off upon her death. My aunt demanded that all the things she still owed on be returned or paid for immediately. Maw-Maw had also purchased a few things for her best friend up the street, which her friend had been paying each month. I was already upset with my aunt for the way she forced me to decide on my own to let Maw-Maw die. I was still struggling with that decision as I faced cleaning out Maw-Maw's home. I told my aunt about the fee which paid everything off, but she said it didn't. I told her I wasn't 'bout to jerk Maw-Maw's friends' property away from her, and she wasn't getting anything out of Maw-Maw's house either. In the end, my aunt must have gotten to Uncle Thomas. After all the money I'd saved him taking care of Maw-Maw twenty-four seven for the past three years, he gave me two weeks to vacate the property. I never expected anyone to pay me for taking care of Maw-Maw, but I never expected the way he treated me either.

I had no money, no job, and no place to live. I had a garage sale and sold what I could. Then I set about throwing everything away, which didn't hold sentimental value. Maw-Maw was a packrat, and it took every bit of two weeks to finish my chore. Once everything was out of there, I scrubbed that house 'til my fingers were raw. It was the last thing I could do for Maw-Maw.

NaNe let me move in with her and Clinton since I had nowhere to go. I found a job at a printing company as an apprentice and tried to move on with my life. Still, my conscience ate at me for letting Maw-Maw die. I was haunted by the fact that Maw-Maw had died September 9th, 1999, at straight-up nine pm that night. Nine, nine, of ninety-nine at nine. I just knew there had to be something up with all those nines.

A few weeks later, I awoke from a dream in which God had spoken to me. "My precious child," he said, "I chose that specific time and date to call your grandmother home. I wanted you to know that I am the one who was responsible, not you. It was her time, as it will be yours someday. Go, and worry no more."

It took some time, but I finally believed what God had said in my dream.

I've reached out over the years to speak to my Uncle Thomas since he's all I have left of Momma and Maw-Maw Cruse, but my aunt repeatedly told me he doesn't want to talk to me after the shameful way I cost them money. I never really believed her, but after the harsh words she said the last time I called, I have given up.

I drove by Maw-Maw's little house on Ella Ave a few years after she passed. I was in the area and wanted to see if it was still there. Stopping in front of the house, I got the surprise of my life.

Maw-Maw used to take a plant from every funeral she attended and re-plant them in her front yard. She had a whole row of them across the front of her lawn. They were rather gaudy looking since they were different types of flowers and plants without any uniformity. I never understood why, but she'd also planted a rose bush right in the center of her yard. Remember I said she could stick a stick in the ground, cover it with a jar, and it would bloom? Well, that was Maw-Maw. Everything she planted grew. I remember looking at her hodge-podge garden the day I drove away from her house for the last time. I always figured whoever bought the property would get rid of those flowers, and the rose bush right away.

As I sat in my car staring at the yard for so long, an older Hispanic woman stepped out and asked me what I wanted. I got out of the car and walked up to speak to her. I explained that the house used to belong to my grandmother years before. Come to find out, she and her husband were the ones who bought it from Uncle Thomas.

"I was in the area and wanted to drive by here for old times' sake. I knew whoever bought it, would get rid of her row of mismatched plants and figured her rose bush would be long gone as well," I said, pointing at Maw-Maw's beloved rose bush.

The mention of Maw-Maw's rose bush sent the poor woman to speak in Spanish and crossing herself as I've seen many Catholics do. In broken English, she explained.

"Yes, my husband dug those plants up not long after we moved in. He dug up the rose bush too. But it came back," again crossing herself before continuing, "and it grew back after the second time he dug it up. We decided that the rose bush belonged here, and we haven't touched it since."

I tried hard not to smile as I thanked the poor woman for sharing her story and letting me take a rose from the bush. The petals from that rose have long since withered away, but the memory has not.

Chapter 57

Last donut shop, and who's that country singer?

I MISSED ANDY SOMETHING FIERCE and finally convinced him to celebrate New Year's Eve with me at Lynn's house. Her house was the place to be every New Year's Eve, and this year was slated to be the best ever since it was going to be the turn of the century!

I was so excited that Andy was coming that I went out and bought a new pair of jeans to go with my favorite shirt. I had lost so much weight since Maw-Maw died that I had to buy a size five. For the first time in a long time, I had a reason to smile.

Everyone that was expected to show had arrived by ten o'clock, except Andy. Just when I started to give up hope of him coming, he walked in. It was just past eleven. We all shouted in the new century as the clock struck midnight, and the ball dropped at Times Square. Life was good as Andy kissed me for the first time in months. We began dating again, but it wasn't long before he moved in with me. A few months later, he proposed to me sitting on the curb at my job. I can't remember why, but I had been crying.

"What did you say," I asked between sobs?

"If you'd stop crying long enough to hear me, I asked you if you'd marry me," Andy said with a huge grin on his face?

We were married by his boss, who was a minister, on July 17, 2000. It was Maw-Maw Cruses' first birthday in heaven. I just knew she was smiling down on us since we'd chosen her birthday for our special occasion.

A few months passed when Andy changed jobs and went to work for a man; he'd met at the plumbing supply house where he worked. I'd long since given up my job and was no longer working. After spending a weekend in East Texas with his new boss, we decided it would be nice to live out there in the country away from the hustle and bustle of the city. We found a little efficiency not far from his boss and moved right away.

During all this time, we had continued to drive to Ft. Worth and pick up James every other weekend. We always stopped and saw Daddy and the family who lived there as well. We'd often stop in and see Auntie and Clinton when we had the time either coming or going from East Texas so they could see James too.

Months passed until one weekend, Cassie's boyfriend informed me; I could not pick James up as he was being punished for something he had gotten in trouble for at school. An argument ensued between Cassie, her boyfriend, and me. When the next weekend came and went with me still being denied access to James, I took matters into my own hands. I found out where James was, and with custody papers in hand, I went and had the police help me pick James up.

Thus, began a custody battle back and forth between Cassie and me that lasted for quite some time. A lot happened during those months as we battled it out. Circumstances arose that led to my taking a bus to North Carolina, where Patrick was stationed in the Marines to pick up PJ, who was seven months old at the time. He would remain with us for a couple of months until I drove him back to his parents. Not long afterward, PJ came back to stay for another couple of months while his parents continued trying to work on their marriage. Having two small children in an efficiency apartment wasn't working out, so I found a 2-bedroom home in Grand Saline, Texas. We moved there in August 2001.

I clearly remember September 11, 2001.

Bubba and I had driven to another court hearing with Cassie in Ft. Worth that morning. I was so nervous that all I did was discuss our case, not wanting to listen to the radio. Pulling into the Tandy Center parking lot, we noticed everyone standing outside their cars in groups talking among themselves. We walked to the platform where we would catch the subway train over to get to the courthouse. Everyone was talking about one of the Trade Center towers getting hit by a commuter plane. I remember thinking how odd that was, but not paying much attention to it at the time. Settling into our seats in the courtroom to await our lawyer, I noticed an eerie silence all around us. It wasn't until our lawyer came and explained what was happening that the full impact of what had occurred hit me. By this time, the second plane had hit the other tower, and all federal buildings were being closed. By the time our lawyer finished explaining, folks were running out of the courtroom in a panic. We were told to get home as quickly and safely as we could.

America was under attack, and no one knew why.

I don't remember much about the drive back to Grand Saline, but as soon as we got there, I ran in and turned on the television. For the next several days, it was all I could do to make sure we all got fed. All I wanted to do was sit and stare at the tragedy and devastation that had befallen my precious New York and our country. I videotaped everything I could, knowing it was history in the making. I cried for days and days, wondering what was happening to our country and our way of life. I cried for all those that were lost, for the courageous fire-fighters, and policeman and their families who'd lost so much as well. I constantly worried who would be targeted next and wondered if the next target would be near our home. There was so much misinformation flying across the airwaves that it was hard to tell. I was relieved when we were finally told where the threat came from and that the government was working to contain them. Once the ban was lifted, and air travel resumed, I felt safe enough to get back to a normal routine.

Like the rest of the country, I knew our lives would never be the same.

Shortly after 9-11 occurred, my daughter-in-law moved in with us because once again, she and Patrick were at odds with one another. She was pregnant for the second time, and she and PJ needed a place to live. She was expecting a girl this time, and I'd been crocheting my heart out to complete the tiny christening gown my new granddaughter would be wearing home from the hospital. I love to shop at thrift stores, and one store had a ton of baby outfits in good condition. One weekend I bought every girlie outfit on their racks. I think there were close to fifty outfits I brought home to dress a baby girl in. I added them to the other things my daughter-in-law was collecting. We gave her a baby shower at NaNe's house, and everyone showed up. A week before my granddaughter was born, we gave my daughter-in-law a birthday party at the house. Pictures show a very pregnant young woman who looked like she was fixing to pop open any minute. By then, she and Patrick had reconciled and were looking for a house of their own.

Katelyn Renee Stewart was born on December 10th, 2001. It would be many months before we knew she was gonna be a redhead like her mother, but from the first, she stole all whose hearts she touched. The spitting image of her mother from the start, as she grew older, it would be hard to tell their pictures apart. Patrick and his growing family soon moved into a house not far from us in Grand Saline. Christmas 2001 was indeed a time for celebrating. I snapped picture after picture showing Andy climbing a ladder with PJ on his hip to supervise that his Paw-Paw was hanging the lights correctly.

Scuter and his girlfriend spent that Christmas with us as well. By this time, his first marriage had ended in divorce. The son he'd given his name to, my first grandchild Trey, was determined to be someone else's through DNA, but many years later, that would come into question. Another story to be told.

Shortly before my granddaughter was born, an incident occurred which nearly split Andy and me apart. I came home from my job at Wal-Mart early after having a strong feeling that something wasn't right. The details of what I found doesn't matter anymore. After several hours of begging him to be honest, Andy finally admitted that he'd been smoking methamphetamine during the night. He also admitted that he'd been doing it behind my back for quite some time. He begged for another chance, promising he'd never do it again. I was devastated. How could he have continued doing meth, knowing how hard it had been for me to quit? I told him he could stay for the time being, but I needed time to think about things. I quit my job at Wal-Mart since it was an over-night job and started looking for a day-time position so I could keep a close eye on him. He was so sweet and attentive to me that before long, we got caught up in the holiday season, and I forgot I was mad at him.

Christmas came and went, and in the process of looking for another job, I stopped by the little donut shop at the other end of town to grab some breakfast. After talking to the girl at the window, I found out their donuts weren't made there but shipped in from another location. The wheels began turning immediately. You can bet, 'Lucy' was in fine form. By the time I got back home, I'd made up my mind! I would open a donut shop in Grand Saline.

I had opened a shop in Ft. Worth when Andy and I had lived there before moving in with Maw-Maw Cruse in '97, but it bit the dust before we ever got it off the ground. Unbeknownst to me at the time, we had opened up in the middle of a Hispanic neighborhood with a Hispanic bakery just a few doors down from us. We'd been doomed from the start. Since there wasn't an actual donut shop in Grand Saline, we were bound to have a chance this time.

I called Daddy and asked if I could use his equipment to launch another shop. He agreed but said if I didn't make a go of it this time, he was going to sell it all. Next, I had to convince Andy.

"What's Lucy up to this time," he asked as soon as I said I had a perfect idea. He just shook his head when I told him. "You might as well go ahead. I can see you've already made up your mind, and nothing I say will change it,"

The Grand Saline Economic development board was offering funds to help start new businesses in Grand Saline, so I applied. The proposal I put together was a success. I found a financial partner to put up the funds, and I went to work renovating the building, which would become my fourth venture into business for myself. I worked my fingers to the bone on that building. It had been everything from a diner to a pool hall. It took weeks for me to scrape the layers of paint that had covered the entire plate glass windows of the pool hall it had last been. The ceiling had fallen in some areas where you could reach up and touch it. By the time we were through, we essentially gutted the place and started over. The building had been scheduled to be condemned when I took it over, so the city had code officer's checking my progress every step of the way. I'll never forget the three-day weekend we shoveled eighteen truckloads of dirt across a 50 X 30 X 10-foot area to stabilize the pier and beam foundation the building sat on. I lost five pounds and had blisters on my hands even though I wore gloves while shoveling dirt those three days.

One morning when I was at the shop pulling nails from the rafters, an elderly gentleman showed up asking what we were doing with the place. We made introductions and chatted for a while. He said he and his wife attended the big church on Main Street and invited us to come visit sometime. He said he'd be glad to help with the donut shop any way he could, and handing me his telephone number, told me to call any time before heading out the door.

Attending NA had been a spiritual program for me. It had brought me closer to God, but I missed being a part of a church family. It had been over two years since I attended an NA meeting too, come to think about it. I shoved the information to the back of my mind and went back to pulling nails from the rafters. I bet I pulled thousands of nails out by the time I was through.

The lady that babysat James for me asked if James could attend Vacation Bible School with her family that summer. He'd already been going to Sunday school with them, so I said sure, why not. On the last day, the children were encouraged to invite their parents. Dragging Andy with me, we attended. Listening to the children and the workers filled my heart with joy. I remembered a time long ago when I too attended VBS. As I listened to the preacher who was close to my age, talk about the importance of raising our children to know the Lord, I knew it was time. I was fighting for custody of James. If I was going to take responsibility for raising him, I knew I needed to raise him in church. I knew I'd found the perfect church as the kind elderly gentleman I'd met at the donut shop walked up with his wife to shake our hands.

When we attended church services that following Sunday morning, the kind gentleman drug us to his Sunday school class with the seniors. Andy was enthralled by the big ol' man teaching the class and swore he wasn't coming back unless we could go the Seniors class from then on. The big ol' man introduced himself and said that'd be fine with him.

We opened the shop to an overnight success. We were doing so well that the other place had to shut down. Andy was coming up and helping me get started at night, then running home to catch a couple hours of sleep before he had to go to work. My daughter-in-law was helping on the counter, but for the most part, I was on my own. We'd only been open a couple of months when tragedy struck. Andy and I were on our way to some friends of ours when I got sleepy and pulled over for Andy to drive. We'd been burning the candle at both ends for quite some time and should have gone home and slept before going anywhere. Andy said he was fine to drive and took over. Fifteen minutes later, I was awakened to Andy, screaming and looking out the windshield to see that we were flying through the air. I was disoriented and wondered if we were flying off a bridge. I passed out, and the next brief memory I have is being in an ambulance and seeing Andy on a gurney opposite me. The next memory I have was that of my daughter-in-law leaning over me with tears in her eyes, promising me everything was going to be okay.

Sometime the next day, I woke up in a hospital room where I was told I had broken a couple of ribs, but thankfully my lung had not been punctured. When I asked where Andy was, I was told he'd initially been sent to another hospital but had since been released and was at his mother's home. I tried being patient, but a couple of hours later, I demanded to be released. My son picked me up and took me home. I think I was still in shock because a couple of hours after I got home, I couldn't breathe, and they had to call an ambulance. After giving me some oxygen, I felt better and told them I didn't want to go to the hospital. I finally got to talk to Andy, who told me his mother said I could come over there and recover at her house.

Andy explained that he had fallen asleep at the wheel and driven head-on into another vehicle that was driven by a mother and her two children. Luckily, neither one of them was seriously injured. When he asked if I'd paid the insurance, I began crying. I had meant to mail the payment the day we'd gotten in the wreck. It was in an envelope in my purse, wherever that was by now. If it'd been postmarked that day, our insurance wouldn't have expired. Andy lost his license, and we spent the next several years trying to stay current on the payments that the judgment stated.

By the time we healed enough to go back to work, I had lost a great many of the customers I had started with. Andy went back to his job, and I tried to rebuild my business. My business partner began demanding a return on his money around the same time we had to start making payments on the wreck. The kind gentleman and his wife loaned me the money to buy out my partner, but try as I might, I kept ending up in the red each month. Then something happened that took the wind out of my sails.

I was running late one night when I got to the donut shop and realized I'd left the money bag at home. I started the coffee and turned everything on to get things rolling before running home to pick up the bag. When I walked in, there sat Andy. In one hand was a pipe filled with meth, in the other hand, a lighter.

The donuts were very late coming out that morning. I was so furious and hurt that Andy spilled the beans right then and there. He'd never stopped since I'd caught him the last time. The guys he worked with were all meth heads, and he'd been doing it with them all along for the past couple of years. I got James up and carried him to the shop where I made him a pallet. Until I figured out what to do about us, I wasn't letting Andy out of my sight. Later that morning, he called and quit his job. Any trust I'd had for Andy was gone. In its place was nothing but doubts and fear. I'd trusted him over and over despite the lies I kept catching him in. I'd placed more trust in him than I ever had in another human being outside of my father.

As if that wasn't enough, Daddy called and said he needed an equipment payment. I had agreed to purchase the equipment from Daddy this time, so it wouldn't look like he was favoring me over the other kids by giving me his equipment to start a business. Daddy had never asked me for anything, so I knew he must be in deep if he was asking me for anything.

I had to get permission to sell my shop from the economic development board, and they agreed. I'd already convinced the property owner into selling me the property after I'd been open for a year, and my year was almost up. I added the total price of the property to what I had to have for the business to pay off my bills, and I sold it.

I gave Daddy the money he had coming, paid off the kind gentleman and his wife, paid off my other debts, and was left with a couple thousand for all my efforts. I was so disappointed with myself and Andy that I didn't even care anymore. I suggested we take the money to the boats and see what luck we had left. We lost most of it in Shreveport, before heading home.

We made it to Tyler and decided to spend a couple of nights by ourselves. We spent the time talking and trying to figure out how to pick up the pieces and go on with our lives. Andy went out to get us something to eat while I stayed behind, looking for a movie to watch on the television.

Flipping through the channels, I came to stop at a country music channel with a haunting melody playing. It was the beginning of a new video. Intrigued, I sat and watched it all the way through. I'd never seen this country artist before and kept wondering who he was. I tried hard to catch his name at the end of the video, but just as the ending credits popped up, Andy came through the door, distracting me just long enough to keep me from seeing his name.

Little did I know, but that handsome country singer would help change my life forever someday.

Chapter 58

Concerts, grandbabies, and true Christian friends!

ANDY FOUND ANOTHER JOB WITH a new plumbing company, and I stayed at home for a couple of months, trying to figure out what to do next. Summer came, and I decided to take James, PJ, and my sons' half-sister to Disney World. It was quite a ride out there, but we all had a good time. I learned plenty of tips for our next excursion to Orlando, which I was sure would happen again someday. Next time, I told myself, would be a lot cheaper and a whole lot more fun.

We became involved with the church and made sure the kids went with us every time. Now and then, Patrick and his wife would attend as well. Scuter even went when he was out for the weekend.

When I left Oklahoma in 1996, I deliberately stopped listening to country music for a reason. I needed to blot out all memories of a love gone wrong to move on with my life. Every song I heard reminded me of the cowboy who would never be mine. He came back into my life a decade after I left there, but by then it was too late to cross that bridge again. That's all I have to say about that!

I found out the name of the country artist that had caught my attention on the country music channel the weekend after we sold the donut shop. Keith Lionel Urban. He was originally from New Zealand but had grown up in Australia. I was familiar with his first U.S. #1 single, "But For the Grace Of God," but never knew the name or face behind the song. The more I researched the man and his music, the more obsessed I became. I felt a connection to him that I couldn't explain. My cousin suggested I join his fan club if I wanted a chance to meet him someday. So, I did.

April 4th, 2003

The first time I saw him in concert was a fluke.

"Hey, your man is in Dallas. I just heard he's gonna be in concert with Kenny Chesney at Fair Park today at the Smirnoff Music Centre," Andy said.

"My man," I repeated in momentary confusion before it dawned on me who he was talking about. "Oh my God, you can't be serious," I screamed into the phone. I jumped up and ran to my computer as Andy repeated the details of what he'd heard on the radio.

"You have to know I'm going to that concert, with or without you. I'll figure out the details and call you when I have it nailed down. You'll have to meet me there. Goodbye, I love you, you're the greatest," I yelled in a rush before hanging up on him.

I arranged for James to be cared for, got dressed, and out the door I ran. It's a wonder I didn't get a speeding ticket on my way to the ticket broker. It was one-thirty in the afternoon when I left Grand Saline headed for a concert in Dallas that started around six pm.

Kenny Chesney was the headliner, so I knew Keith would be one of the first acts to appear. No way was I gonna let anything stand in the way of my seeing him. I called Andy and told him where to meet me as soon as I got to the venue. He already knew to take off work early, or I would go in without him. Bless his heart; this is one time he didn't let me down. He arrived just after they opened the gates.

I saw the area where fans were going in for Meet and Greets, and I tried to convince the guards that I was Keith's biggest fan. I was a fan club member after all, and even showed them proof of it. Sorry, but no cigar. My ploy didn't work. We went in and found our seats, which were twenty-something rows away from the stage.

I forget which female artist came out first, but I wasn't at all happy that I was so far away from the stage. Looking around, I noticed that the guards weren't paying much attention as the arriving guests made their way down the aisle to their seats. Down near the front of the stage, I saw quite a few chairs that weren't taken, so I assumed it was because they were Kenny Chesney fans who hadn't arrived yet.

"C'mon, go with me," I pleaded with Andy, "the worst thing they can do is make us return to our seats."

"Nope, you go ahead. I'm fine right here," Andy grinned.

Waiting for an opportunity when the guards were distracted, I headed for the closest spot to the stage. It was fifth-row center, and I prayed for God to let me remain there until Keith finished performing without getting caught.

I was so star-struck when he hit that stage that I barely remember that first concert at all. One thing was sure; if I hadn't been hooked before, after that concert, I became obsessed. I wanted to know everything and anything to do with Mr. Keith Urban! I'd had music crushes before in my teen years, but this, I didn't understand at all. It wasn't like I wanted to be a part of his life, or I was in love with him. It was something else that I couldn't put my finger on. I felt a connection, but it would be some time before I understood what it all meant.

I found a job at a telemarketing company in Canton not long after that concert, and life went on. I enjoyed talking to people on the phone and found that I was good at communicating the need for families to plan for their futures. Our company invited folks to come out for a complimentary meal and learn about estate planning regarding wills and trusts. I believed in what I was offering. It wasn't to scam people out of their hard-earned money but to help them protect what they left behind. It also made me wonder what I had to leave behind for my family. Sadly enough, I knew it wasn't much. All I could hope for was to live long enough that I could leave behind a better example of how to live one's life than I had in my past.

I'll be the first to say that I've never read the Bible cover to cover, and I'm not a theologian. I can't quote scripture and verse, but I know enough about my God to say I believe that the words of the good book are true and have meaning. I wish I could say that I've lived my whole life by those words, and in honor to God, but I can't. For those who have, I say that you're fortunate to have avoided some of the roads I've traveled. Knowing that I can't say that I would go back and change anything in my life. Not unless I could keep all my same family members, and still meet all the people I've met on my travels through life. It is a conundrum for me to this day. I'm sorry for the mistakes I made, yet if I hadn't made them, I wouldn't be who I am today.

Of all the regrets I have, not being a better mother for my sons is second only to not honoring God in all that I did. The Bible speaks of *'Sins of the Father'* being revisited upon future generations, but mothers are just as responsible as far as I can tell. If I could change one thing, it would have been to provide my sons with a better upbringing than I did.

Back in 2003…

I became wholeheartedly involved in church. So much so, that the first churchwide Thanksgiving Meal service I attended at the big church on Main Street, I stood when the pastor invited congregation members to share what they were thankful for. I bared my soul and told it all. To say there was a hushed silence across the gymnasium floor is an understatement. Looking back now, I realize some of the things I shared weren't quite appropriate, given the audience in attendance. I know I embarrassed some of my family members that were there. It was never my intention to do so, but I know I did. In a way, I don't regret it because after it was all over, I got to see who my real Christian friends were. It was those individuals who helped me grow closer to God's plan for my life. In all honesty, there were only a handful of members who turned their nose up at me as if I were the devil incarnate. As the years passed, I learned how to share my testimony without offending others.

While I was growing stronger in God's plan for my life, my sons were becoming more involved in the world around them, being adults, there was nothing I could do to stop them. Oh, but I tried. I tried controlling them by any means possible. I was determined to prevent them from going down the roads I'd traveled. I used every trick in the book from withholding financial support if they didn't do what I suggested, to turning them and all their associates into the police if they didn't listen to me. It's a wonder I didn't end up with a bullet in the back of my head, but at that time I couldn't have cared less. The only thing I had in mind was protecting my family. I can recall a few instances where I walked right up to, if not into the homes of drug dealers, and threatened to turn them in to the police if they didn't cut ties with my family members. I wouldn't suggest anyone else try what I did, but there were a few who caught my drift and immediately disassociated themselves. Unfortunately, all I did was alienate and force my family members to find it elsewhere. There's always going to be drugs and drug dealers out there willing to accommodate any poor soul who searches for them.

Any time folks' lives become intertwined; there is a side to every story. In telling the stories of my life, I'm well aware that others saw my life from a different angle and may have plenty to say when I'm done. As I said early on, I can only tell my story as I lived it. I have tried to be as transparent as I could except for respecting others' privacy when necessary. In going forward, it is not for me to delve into my sons' lives and tell their stories. I will not offer up my own opinions regarding who was at fault for relationships that didn't survive, or choices that were made. I have been blamed for many things that happened in their lives, and perhaps some of that blame was justified. What's done is done, and without going back and reliving history, no one will ever know what might have happened if things would have worked out differently. All I can say is that the choices I made were from my heart. To the best of my ability, I made those choices in what I thought was in the best interests for all concerned.

March 26, 2003, my grandson Mason Windell Stewart was born. I remember when they called me in and told me they were giving him his middle name after me. I bawled like a baby. It was an honor I cherish to this day.

Speaking of grandbabies…

Harlie LeeAnn Davidson Haney was born on June 27, 2003. My second granddaughter, and half-sister to PJ, Katelyn, and Mason. I was overjoyed at her birth as well, regardless of the circumstances which brought her into this world. Another story to be told, but not mine to tell.

Time marches on and waits for no one. Scattered as we were, my family was still getting together for holidays and special events as we had before. Gathering at NaNe's since her home was mid-point for us all. As the years passed, fewer and fewer showed up as different families celebrated with in-laws. One Thanksgiving, everyone drove the distance to celebrate Thanksgiving in Grand Saline with us. So many showed up that I had to clear a bedroom and rent tables and chairs to accommodate everyone. Pictures show smiles all around. It is a memory to be remembered.

Chapter 59

Bubba the wild-man, child custody, and Hair Loss

It wasn't very long after I started working as a Telemarketer that Daddy and Shelley showed up at my house with Bubba in tow. Daddy told me that he had brought Bubba to Grand Saline, and he meant for him to stay here. He said he didn't want to see Bubba back in Ft. Worth, or else he was gonna have a mess on his hands. Bubba had gone way off the deep end after getting out of prison and was about to either kill himself doing drugs or end up dead cause someone had killed him. Daddy had issued warnings to everyone Bubba knew, and to all his own personal associates that if they got caught giving, selling, or otherwise enabling Bubba to get drugs, they were going to answer to him personally. No one that knew my father was about to cross him. Daddy was worried for Bubba's life. I wanted to ask Daddy what he thought I could do to stop Bubba's nonsense, but I knew just like Daddy did, Bubba wasn't about to walk to Ft. Worth, and without a ride, he was at the very least stuck here. I felt so bad looking at my brothers' face. He had really upset Daddy this time.

I knew the first thing which had to be done was find Bubba something to do to occupy his time. He needed a job. I remembered that Bubba had been a telemarketer before, and a darn good one as I recall.

I didn't walk around and advertise my past at my job, but I never made a secret of the fact that I was a recovering addict either. You never know when someone can use an encouraging word from someone who's been there, done that. The day after Daddy dropped Bubba off was a Friday. I asked to see the floor manager right before quitting time.

"Dave, I need a huge favor," I began. "I know we're always hiring new help, so I wanted to see if you'd hire my brother. He's done telemarketing before and was really good at it. The problem is, he's detoxing off drugs. If he doesn't find something to do to occupy his time, he's not going to make it."

Dave stared at me for a good long while before responding.

"Do you believe he's ready to give up drugs and straighten out his life," he asked as he twirled a pencil through his fingers?

"I believe at this point; Bubba doesn't have much of a choice since my father dropped him off at my house and banned him from Ft. Worth. He doesn't know anyone out here to get drugs from, and he knows that if he crosses me, he won't have anyone in this world to help him. He'd be riding to work with me every day, so he wouldn't be able to get out of my sight," I replied honestly.

Dave thought about what I said before, responding.

"Tell you what, bring him with you on Monday morning. We'll give him a chance. Make sure he understands that in thirty days, he will be drug tested, and he better be able to pass it. I'm putting my neck on the line, and he better not let me down," winking at me, he stood to shake my hand.

"You have no idea but that you might have just saved my brother's life," I cried as I ran around his desk and threw my arms around him in a hug.

Thinking back to that day, I'm glad that Dave lived long enough to witness the fruits of his labor.

Bubba indeed looked a fright. When we got there Monday morning, folks wanted no part of my brother. He looked like someone's worst nightmare. His first photo badge with the company seemed more like a wanted poster for some deranged criminal.

Dave forewarned the higher-ups, so they all knew he'd probably looked a mess. Laughing to myself, I remember the look on the trainer's face as she followed him into the training room. I just winked at her and gave her a thumbs up that she was safe, and he wasn't gonna hurt her. Thirty days came and went, and he passed his drug screen with flying colors. I was beginning to rethink my strategy when, before long, I had a competitor. I was no longer the top dog of marketing!

Everyone could decorate their cubicle as they saw fit. Most folks had pictures of their family, and witty sayings to help keep themselves motivated. I chose a different motif for each of the three walls of my cubicle. One had pictures of my family. One had all my Keith Urban memorabilia, and one was wall to wall pictures of the man himself. Folks just rolled their eyes when they passed my cubicle. I didn't care; I was the one who had to stare at those walls every day. I surrounded myself with things that made me happy and kept me motivated. Over the months, I sat and crocheted a huge afghan with Keith's name on it while I talked on the phone, knowing someday I would be able to give it to him. If all this didn't bother my husband, I didn't see why it should bother anyone else.

One day I got called from my cubicle for a personal call. It was a call that would change my life forever. I had to leave work immediately and pick up my grandchildren.

The events of that day, and all that occurred afterward, are not up for discussion. They are private details of lives that were torn apart and not all mine to tell. Suffice it to say, my son and his wife would eventually divorce, and I received custody of my grandchildren, PJ, Katelyn, and Mason. Their parents became possessory conservators and remained a big part of their lives.

It took a while to get everything sorted out with the addition of three more children to our household, but things settled down after some time.

June 8th, 2004

I finally had a chance to go to a fan club gathering for Keith in Nashville, Tennessee. I didn't get to meet him personally but had an opportunity to take the afghan I designed for him and set it on the stage in front of him. I was excited that he looked up at me when I snapped his picture.

While I was in Nashville, I found an article on his back story. It spoke of his determination to follow his dreams of being a country music star. From an early age, he had started pursuing his passion in life. His biography mentioned the struggles he had after arriving in Nashville, and how he had hit rock bottom from drug use. Instead of giving up, he got help. His first hit single, 'But For The Grace Of God', came after he turned himself around.

All the way back to Texas, I listened to his music, really listened. One particular song caught my attention, "You Won." It was an AH-HA moment of epic proportions for me. He hadn't walked my road, but he understood what it meant to fall, get back up, and chase his dreams despite the mistakes he'd made. He was my inspiration! If he could do it, so could I! I decided I wanted to meet Keith to thank him for *"lighting a fire in my soul"* through his music and walk in life. How to do it was another matter.

Summer came to a close after camping trips to the lake and outdoor barbeques. I couldn't believe I was starting over with children to raise. I never questioned God's plan but figured he knew better than me. Andy took it all in stride but was not happy about giving up marijuana. No way was I having it around these children. I wanted to give them as healthy a life as possible.

September 27th, 2004

I had just got to work and was turning on my computer when first one person ran up to me, then another.

"Wendeee, you're not gonna believe this. 99.5 the Wolf radio station is giving out chances to meet Keith Urban tomorrow, and have breakfast with him at their radio station," the first person said.

"C'mon hurry," the second girl said, dragging me toward the phone.

I dialed and dialed the radio station's number but kept getting busy signals. My supervisor let me keep dialing until the operator answered and said the contest had ended. Walking back to my desk, I remembered that tomorrow was my 45th birthday. It was a *sign*!!!

My mind was reeling as I sat there, taking calls that morning. No way was I gonna let this chance to meet Keith pass me up. There had to be a way! 'Lucy' came up with all kinds of scenarios. The best idea I could come up with involved me waiting outside the building where the radio station was and catching him as he walked in. Images of being carted off to jail sent that idea to the wastebasket. By the time lunch rolled around, I had an idea.

"99.5 the Wolf, how may I direct your call," the receptionist asked?

"My name is Wende Nabors, and I'd like to speak with your station manager," I asked in my most cheerful voice?

"What is this concerning, ma'am?"

"I know this might sound crazy, but here goes. I am a huge fan of Keith Urban. I'm even a member of his fan club. Tomorrow is my birthday, and I tried so hard to win a chance to have breakfast with him but couldn't get through. I know his favorite charity is St. Jude's Children's hospital. I would be willing to donate all my hair to them for a chance to meet Keith tomorrow morning at y'alls radio station," I blurted out in a nervous rush.

There was a slight pause before the operator continued.

"Are you serious," the receptionist questioned?

"Yes, ma'am. Dead serious."

"Let me speak with the station manager. Give me a number he can call you back at, and I'll give him your message," the receptionist requested.

Giving her my number, I sat the phone in its cradle.

"Oh, sweet Jesus, please let this work. I don't wanna go to jail for stalking," I silently prayed, walking back to my desk.

The floor had just resumed calling when my supervisor told me to log off and take a personal call.

"Who is it," I asked, walking up to my supervisors' podium?

"A radio station manager from 99.5 the Wolf," she said, grinning ear to ear.

Everyone knew the crazy, hair-brained idea I'd offered during lunch to meet Keith.

"Oh my, I think I'm gonna faint," I said, barely able to contain the scream begging to be let loose.

"Here, you'd better hurry before he hangs up," my supervisor urged, handing the phone to me.

"Hello, this is Wende Nabors," I said breathlessly.

"Good afternoon, I'm the radio station manager for the Wolf. I hear you made quite the offer to meet Keith Urban tomorrow. You're really serious, huh?"

"Oh, yes, sir. You have no idea how serious I am," I offered.

"Just how much hair are we talking about," the gentleman asked.

"Well, my hair is long. It goes almost down to my butt. I would say about two to three feet," I guessed.

"Hmm, we'd need to contact a hairstylist to come to the station," the manager stated as if in thought, "Ok, if you're sure this is what you want to do. You can bring one person with you to take pictures. You'll need to be here by seven am sharp. Tell all your friends and family that you'll be live on air with Keith at seven-thirty-five am tomorrow," he laughingly advised.

"You mean you're gonna do it," I yelled?

"Yes, ma'am. See you tomorrow," he answered before hanging up.

Luckily for me, no one got mad after I hung up the phone and released the scream at the back of my throat, "YEE HAW! THANK YOU, SWEET JESUS!"

373

Chapter 60
Meeting Keith Urban

I WOKE UP LATE ON the morning of September 28, 2004. I had driven to Ft. Worth after work the day before to pick up my niece Gracie who I had chosen to go with me. All that afternoon and late into the evening, we listened to 99.5 the Wolf, who kept advertising that, "Wende Nabors of Grand Saline, Texas will be coming in to donate her hair to meet Keith Urban. Listen in for the chance to hear all about it at seven-thirty-five am tomorrow."

"Hurry Gracie, we're late," I yelled as I threw on my favorite concert shirt and grabbed my fan club lanyard to show off to Keith. I wanted to make sure he knew I was his biggest fan.

The drive into Dallas from Grand Saline was bumper to bumper. Listening to the Deejays discuss the details of my meeting, Keith on-air every fifteen or twenty minutes didn't help my nerves either.

"Oh my God, get outta my way," I screamed at the cars around me as if they could hear me!

Poor Gracie was holding on to the dashboard for dear life. I was driving like a madwoman on a mission. I knew that if I didn't get there on time, I would miss my opportunity. To top it off, I hadn't even mapped my route to the radio station until we were on our way that morning. We pulled into the parking lot of the building where the Wolf's suites were when I heard the Deejay ask Keith, who was already in the studio, how he felt about the woman who was donating her Crystal Gayle length hair to meet him.

"Well, it just makes my blue eyes turn brown," Keith laughingly said.

It was at that moment, my throat went dry, and if I hadn't been nervous already, that sent my stomach to doing flip-flops for sure. I was shaking like a leaf standing in front of the elevator that would take us upstairs to the radio station.

"It'll be okay, Aunt Wende. We made it on time, calm down," Gracie laughed as we stepped on the elevator.

Stepping into the conference room where the stylist from the upscale, Dallas salon waited to band my hair, I saw the contestants who'd won the chance to meet Keith. They looked at me as if they all thought I was crazy. It didn't matter to me; all I knew was that I was about to realize my dream. The stylist stepped away and nodded to the young man with the headset on when he finished. The young man stepped up, took me by the elbow, and began leading me out of the window-plated room.

"Where are we going," I asked in a fog?

"You're going into the studio to meet Keith," he acknowledged.

Then it dawned on me. I hadn't thought about the reason the station manager said I was going to be live on air until that very moment. My legs turned to jelly, and I had a hard time keeping up with the assistant who was fast approaching a door with a light above it. Opening the door, he shoved me in.

"Good morning," I vaguely heard someone say. "Did you have a nice drive in?"

I didn't notice who was speaking to me because sitting there, at the end of the long counter and larger than life, sat Keith Urban. I was led around to stand between Keith and a smiling woman, one of the three morning-show hosts. I was so star-struck that I couldn't look at Keith, who was close enough for his shoulder to occasionally brush against my thigh. The main Deejay gave me instructions regarding what was about to happen.

"We're about to go live. When it's your turn, speak clearly into the microphone in front of you," the Deejay said as he held up his fingers, three, two, one.

"We have Wende Nabors here in the studio with us," he said to the listeners, "How are you feeling this morning," he asked before pointing at the microphone in front of me?

"I ugh, ugh, ugh…" I stammered, unable to speak. I would find out later from my husband, and all my co-workers that a ten-second pause filled the airwaves before the main Deejay spoke up.

"Are you more nervous about meeting Keith, or getting all your hair cut off," he asked to fill the void.

"Ugh, both," was all I managed to utter.

I don't remember his reply before going off-air as I was dumbstruck. I will never forget what happened next as Keith stood, took his headset off, and wrapped me in a tight embrace.

"I promise, I won't bite," he said in that adorable accent of his.

I was unaware of the others in the room as Keith sat back down and engaged in a private conversation with me. We spoke a moment about my crazy idea to meet him, and my being a fan club member when I remembered seeing him in Nashville.

"By the way, how do you like the afghan I gave you at the fan club party in Nashville," I asked proud of the work I'd done?

"Afghan," he pondered in apparent confusion, "I don't have a dog." I saw the light come on as he realized what I was referring to. "That was you," he asked incredulously? "You're the afghan lady?"

"Yes, that was me. I designed it myself so that I could put your name on it. I've already started a body pillow that I am crocheting 'Keith' into. I planned to give it to you for your birthday at the Nokia center in Grand Prairie. This time I made sure I would be close enough to the stage to give it to you. I paid over three-hundred dollars to get a seat second-row center," I bragged, pulling out my ticket and holding it in front of him.

"You paid what," Keith asked, dismay flashing across his face. "You've got to be kidding me," he asked, reaching for the ticket I'd purchased from a broker, "may I see it?"

"You need to find out about this," he said handing it to his tour manager he continued, "my fans shouldn't have to be robbed just to get close to the stage," he said with a determined look on his face.

Imagine my delight when seeing that, fan club members had an opportunity to purchase tickets before the public, a short time later, that perhaps my encounter with Keith had influenced that decision.

"I'm sure my tour manager," looking over his shoulder and winking, "can arrange for a backstage pass for you at the concert three weeks from now," Keith stated, handing me back my overpriced ticket.

The assistant walked in and ushered all of us out to the conference room at this time. Walking down the hall in front of Keith, I caught Gracie and the other fans staring in awe as we approached the doorway. The stylist had followed the assistant into the room and stopped me after we all got in, turning me around to face Keith.

"I almost forgot to tell you why I was determined to meet you," I said, looking up at him. "Your walk in life and your music has inspired me to believe I could go back to college and achieve my dream of becoming a nurse. I've attempted college a half dozen times, and each time I made a mess of it. I set my goals too high, got messed up on drugs, and gave up before I ever really got started. Seeing how you overcome your own obstacles, and eventually achieved your dreams has given me the courage to try once more. I believe I can make it this time."

A picture captured the emotions of the moment between Keith and me as his tour manager looked on. I didn't understand what was going on behind me, as Keith stepped up and gripped my shoulders.

"This is such a wonderful thing you are doing for the kids at St. Jude," Keith said. Looking out into the group of people gathered there, he commented, "I think she deserves a round of applause."

Just as the stylist picked my hair up and began to cut, Keith turned and squeezed my shoulders.

"This isn't going to hurt a bit," Keith told me.

When the stylist cut through my ponytail and stepped away, the lightness I felt made my knees weak. Grasping my left shoulder, and taking my right hand in his, Keith said, "Steady there." I remember thinking to myself, "I wish this moment could last forever." The next photo shows me reaching for the back of my head with my mouth wide open as Keith smiled at the camera.

Gracie stepped up and met Keith with more pictures snapped of the three of us together. He autographed the photos I'd brought for him to sign, taking note of the one I'd taken of him at the fan club party earlier in the summer. Next, Keith turned his attention to the other fans there to meet him, taking time to hear what they had to say. It soon came to an end as Keith addressed us all before departing the conference room.

Keith and his entourage were walking back up the hallway when he looked over his shoulder at me through the conference room windows. Pausing briefly, he spoke with his group before turning and walking back into the room.

"Happy birthday, Wende," Keith said as he walked up behind me and embraced me in a hug from behind. "Take this picture," he told the photographer's.

God Bless Gracie's heart! She took her sweet time and fiddled with the camera for a few extra seconds of bliss…

It was a birthday I would never forget!

No one who knew me could believe that I was struck speechless. I mean, c'mon, I talked for a living. Andy was the most surprised of all. He related how his construction crew had stopped working to hear me that morning.

"I can never get her to shut up. Put Keith Urban next to her, and she can't think of a word to say," Andy recalled the conversation with his crew to me.

At work the next day, I was teased and tormented to no end. It didn't matter to me as I floated around on a cloud of blissful memories. Something that had never occurred to me was how many compliments I would get on my new hairstyle. Everyone said it took ten years off my appearance. It made me feel young and carefree.

I worked fast and furious to finish Keith's birthday present as I talked on the phone. I just had to finish it since I'd bragged about it to him. I had a special surprise that I was taking him as well. It was a poem I had written, which everyone said sounded more like a country song than a poem. I typed up and notarized a statement giving Keith all rights to my poetry, title, and any of the words contained therein. A year later, I almost flipped when his first single off his new album was titled very similar to the title of my poem. Coincidence? Maybe, but it made my day just the same.

October 16th, 2004

On the day of the concert at the Nokia Center, I got there early. Through research on the fan club, I found out that Keith often brought his motorcycle on tour with him. I was gonna check it out to see if that was fact or fiction. Sure enough, I scouted out the right vantage point and caught a cool picture of him returning to the venue before the start of the concert. I'd been so busy skulking around to catch him on his motorcycle that I almost missed my Meet and Greet. Wanting to spend more time with him, I asked the tour manager to let me go in last.

"Now that's a cute hairstyle," he said as I walked up to him.

"Yep, and I have you to thank for it," I said, barely containing my glee, "Happy early birthday to you!"

I handed Keith his pillow, and the small bag containing his card and poem. I gave him the photo of the day I met him and asked him to autograph it.

"That's Wende with an *'E'* because you're unique," Keith said, mimicking me from the first time I told him how I spell my name.

"Aww, you remembered. How sweet of you," I replied genuinely.

He posed for another picture with me, and it was over too soon.

After seeing him at Nokia, I saw him at the Houston Rodeo on March 8th, 2005. I couldn't get up close, but I was sitting by the chute area when he entered the arena. I yelled out, "Keith," he looked up and waved, causing everyone around me to freak out cause he'd recognized me.

A few months after the Houston concert, I decided I wanted to get a tattoo. I'd thought long and hard about what I wanted to get but never could make up my mind. One afternoon I was looking through my Keith pictures when I figured it out. I was gonna get his autograph tattooed on one shoulder, and his guitar monkey on the other. I'd always heard you should never tattoo someone's name on your body, it being permanent and all. Yet when I thought about it, I knew in a gazillion years, Keith would never let me down. What I hadn't considered was how painful it was gonna be. Proud of my accomplishment, I posted a picture of it on the fan club website.

"Mother, you've got to be kidding," Patrick stated more than asked. "First, you cut all your hair off to meet this guy, and now you get his autograph and monkey logo tattooed on you! Have you lost your mind? You're a grandmother for crying out loud!"

I just laughed and fired back, "Well, you've got tattoos, and you're a father."

I caught a lot of criticism for my crazy stunts, but Patrick's was the harshest. He soon got over it, referring to me as his *'teeny-bopper'* mother. It was my way of paying tribute to a fantastic artist and human being. No matter where I saw Keith, he was always so attentive and respectful to those around him. He gives so much of his life to his fans and truly cares about them.

Red Rocks Ampitheatre in Denver, Colorado, was my next big concert. I met another fan on the fan club website who offered to pick me up at the airport and give me lodging while I was there. I was so grateful that I bought tickets for us to see him in Rapid City, South Dakota, the night after we saw him in Denver.

September 17th, 2005

On the day of the concert, my friend dropped me off at the venue around five am so I could be sure to be first in line. It was general admission, and I didn't mind sitting there all day to sit in the first couple of rows. Besides, the afghan I had been crocheting for his mother wasn't finished, and it would give me something to do while I waited.

I remember watching for Keith's tour buses to drive into the venue. There was only one way in, and from my vantage point, I had a clear view. By the time they arrived, many other fans were waiting with me. Almost immediately after the buses arrived, two burly gentlemen with heavy accents came up to where I was standing in line and asked me to turn around so they could see my tattoos.

"Do you mind if we videotape them," the man holding the video camera asked?

"Be my guest," I replied.

I could only assume the pictures of my tattoos on Keith's official fan club site had garnered some attention from the website administrator, and these gentlemen wanted to see for themselves.

In any event, time passed, and soon it was time to make a mad dash for the seating area. I ran like the wind, terrified I was gonna trip, but I didn't. I was on the second row, which wasn't bad since the first row was reserved for handicap access.

There were about fifty or so fan club members all wearing matching t-shirts we'd designed and purchased as a group, so we stood out in the crowd. I'd altered mine by cutting off the top portion and sleeves and sewing an elastic band in it to make my tattoos visible. Everyone wanted to take pictures of them. I was happy they had healed and didn't look swollen, so I didn't mind at all.

We'd all been sitting for a while when two band members came out and motioned for me to turn around. They wanted to see my tattoos too. When I turned back to face them, one of the guys shook his head, laughing and spinning his finger in a circle to insinuate how crazy I was. It made me excited cause that had to mean Keith had to know about the tattoos by now for sure.

On this concert tour, Keith would invite a fan onstage to help him sing a song. He chose the fan from the audience by reading signs. I had my sign ready. I just knew I would get on the stage! Unfortunately, I goofed it up.

He read several signs, seemingly ignoring mine as he strutted across the stage. I was just about to give up when halfway across; he turned and looked straight at me.

"I should see your tattoo, huh," he asked in that accent of his?

Instead of allowing him to ask me onstage to see it, I immediately turned around. Everyone around me said that my tattoos were on the overhead screens. Looking over my shoulder, I could see they were visible to the entire venue.

"Wow, you must have gotten those since March," Keith said for all to hear.

I never heard what else he said as I was stunned that he'd remembered when he'd seen me last! I could hear everyone around me, commenting on his statement as well.

"Oh my God, he remembered when he saw you last," one after another was saying.

As exciting as the moment was, Keith moved on and invited another fan to come up. I could have kicked myself for ruining my chance to get on stage, maybe next time, I thought. I will never forget that night as a full moon rose over the stage into the sky. It was magical!

September 18th, 2005

We headed for South Dakota as soon as the concert was over. My friend's husband drove as we slept. We almost had an accident with a big deer on the way, but luckily, he avoided it. After checking in to the motel, we went sight-seeing. We drove through Deadwood, Sturgis, and then headed for Mount Rushmore. I stood there in awe staring at the faces carved in granite. Soon it was time to head back to the motel for the concert.

Arriving at our seats, I was disappointed that we were at the very back of the concert hall, but the small stage not far from us meant we'd get a closer look later. The overhead screens showed what was going on down front, but it's not the same. Still, we were having a blast singing along to the songs we knew. I was glad I wore my *light-up* wedge heels that evening cause I used them to get Keith's attention when he came to the back. Not long after he returned to the front stage, the drummer had a solo, and Keith stepped off stage.

Just as Keith came back out to sing, a man holding a flashlight approached my friend and me.

"Uh oh, looks like I might be in trouble for flashing my heels," I whispered to my friend just as he stepped up to us.

"Ma'am, were you at the concert in Denver last night," asked the man with a crew member badge?

"Ugh, yes, I was," I answered, wondering how he knew.

"He said that was you," he commented, shaking his head and laughing as he walked off.

"HE," me and my friend screamed in unison!

"You got his attention with your heels," my friend squealed!

Leaving the venue, we spotted the tour buses and walked over to see what we could see. Standing outside, one of them was a band member.

"Hey, that was a great concert," I yelled over the fence to get his attention.

"Hey yourself," the guy smiled up at me. "You better watch it, or someone might call you a groupie."

We exchanged a few more pleasantries before locating her husband and heading back to Denver. I spent another night with my friend, and she took me to the airport for my flight home the next morning. Looking out the plane window as it took off, I had the most remarkable view of the city of Denver and the mountains. I stared until it was out of sight. It was a trip I'd never forget.

I would attend three more concerts chasing Keith across the country in 2005. In the next few years, I would attend over twenty-four shows across the United States. I always sat in the first couple of rows as well. From Red Rocks Amphitheater in Denver, Colorado to Gillette Stadium in Foxboro, Massachusetts, and many points in between. I have unique stories from each adventure and have met dozens of amazing people throughout the years. Those stories could fill pages upon pages. My favorite Keith Urban buddy, and monkey sista' would be the one and only Bobbi-Jo Davis! She flew down to Texas from Michigan one summer, and we set out on our K.U.R.T., aka Keith Urban Road Trip. We drove up to Omaha, Nebraska where I gave Keith a personalized baby blanket for his daughter, and followed him back down to Texas, attending three concerts along the way. We almost got ourselves in trouble a time or two cause you're not supposed to follow tour buses.

"I'm gonna get a call someday cause Wende was put in jail for stalking Keith Urban!" Mom Nita used to say.

Bobbi-Jo and I share a special bond. When she first told me about it, she thought I'd be mad at her, but I wasn't. It brought us closer, in fact. She had Keith autograph her right shoulder to have it tattooed. We had ourselves a blast posing for folks at every concert. It made me feel better to know I wasn't the only *crazy* Keith fan out there. We've stayed in touch throughout the years and remain very close to this day.

The last time I saw Keith in concert was a couple of years ago for my birthday. He smiled and winked when I got his attention. I think he just might've remembered this crazy fan of his with the short hair and distinctive tattoos.

Chapter 61
China

Two-thousand five was a busy year for me, but it was also a year of changes that set my life on a new course. Some I never saw coming. Some I'd only dreamed of in my wildest dreams.

Staring at the map of China and the goals to get there, I was startled to hear my Pastor speak behind me.

"You know Wende; I think you ought to go with us this year," Pastor H remarked.

"Me," I questioned as I turned to face him?

"Yes, you! You have a way of getting people's attention. I believe God could use you in a mighty way. There are young people over there who are in need of hearing the Good News. I believe, with your personality, you could make a big difference in their lives," Pastor H stated.

I was humbled to hear the Pastor's words. Listening to him say God could use me, knowing full well my past, was one of the most empowering things I'd ever heard. I'd never considered myself an ambassador for God, but hearing Pastor H's belief that I could stunned me.

"How soon would I have to come up with the money to pay for my trip," I asked?

"We're having fund-raisers to pay for those who need help. I'm sure money won't be an issue. So, what do you think? Would you like to join us" Pastor H asked?

Before I could answer, Andy walked into the room.

"Andy. What better timing? I was telling Wende here that she should come along on our mission trip to China this year. Don't you think she'd be a good one for sharing the Good News about God with others," Pastor H aked as he grabbed Andy's hand and shook it?

"I believe Wende is capable of doing anything she sets her mind to; that's for sure," looking at me, he continued, "you've been everywhere else, why not around the world? I say go for it."

"Okay, I'll go," I answered, looking back at the map on the wall in awe of the new adventure I'd just agreed to go on.

I jumped in and got busy with my part in earning funds for my trip. I don't know where I found the time back then to care for four children, work, participate in fund-raisers, and chase Keith Urban across the country, but I did. It was one of the happiest times of my life.

I attended many planning trips in preparation for the mission trip to China. Pastor H schooled us in the customs, and do's and don'ts of visiting another country. We had to learn to eat with chopsticks since silverware isn't a commodity found in some of the places we would be visiting. We were cautioned about drinking water unless it was bottled and how other countries don't always adhere to strict guidelines regarding food preparation.

"They eat what," I blurted out during one of Pastor H's lectures?

"I know you all might find it disgusting, but they eat all kinds of things we would never consider here in the States, dogs being one of them," Pastor H commented. "This is why it's crucial to study and research the areas where we are traveling. We will be guests in their country. We must be mindful of their customs for the safety of our group, and out of respect for them."

"I can guarantee you one thing. I plan to become a vegetarian on this trip cause I ain't eating no dog," I promised Pastor H, causing everyone around me to break out in laughter.

"Wende, you will undoubtedly break any monotony we encounter on this trip," Pastor H declared, looking out into our group.

I never realized how much planning went into a trip of this magnitude. We had a lot to learn in a short period, but soon the day came for us to leave. Andy, Patrick, and the kids drove me to the church where everyone and their families had gathered to see us off. We all held hands as one of the deacons led everyone in prayer.

Hugging each of my family members goodbye, I pulled Andy to the side to remind him of the promise he'd made me.

"Please, whatever you do, be careful of your actions while I'm away. One wrong move could put my custody of these children in jeopardy. I hope you realize how much I'm counting on you," I pleaded, looking into his eyes for assurance.

"I promise Wende. I will be on my best behavior while you're away."

"You should behave even when I'm here," I teased as the tension left my body.

Waving at my family as the bus pulled from the parking lot, I had no idea how our lives would change when I returned.

My first memory of driving through the city on our way to the hotel where we would spend the first leg of our journey brought tears to my eyes. All my life, I'd tried imagining what being illiterate meant. I'd learned to read at such a young age that it was impossible to fathom.

Staring at the signs and billboards all around me, I finally understood how hard life must have been for Daddy. Navigating life is a challenge in itself. The enormity of the obstacles Daddy had faced all his life, hit me with such an impact, it took my breath away. It must have shown on my face cause the person sitting beside me asked if I was okay. Drying my tears, all I could do was shake my head yes. I would be reminded over and over during this trip, what it meant to view life through my father's eyes.

There are so many stories I could share about my trip to China, but I have a deadline to meet. In the spirit of brevity, I'll only mention a few. I shared my testimony with many students while I was there and led several young women to know the Lord. I stayed in contact with one of them many years before losing touch with her. Last I heard, she had quite a following of other young women who'd come to know the Lord through her and was helping spread God's love. I am humbled knowing how God had used me in such a positive way. I guess Pastor H had been right after all.

After arriving at the hotel, Pastor H passed out business cards from the hotel to each of us.

"I expect each of you to carry these with you at all times. You never know when they might come in handy," he advised us.

Zipping mine into my fanny pack, I thought nothing more of it.

Each day we would gather in groups to attend different functions. There were too many of us to be present at each one. In the evenings, we'd meet to share our experiences of the day and talk about the plans for the following day. We all had opportunities to explore the city for shopping excursions and free time in between our main reason for being there. We were paired with others and not allowed to go out on our own.

I felt like a kid in a candy store trying to take it all in. There was so much to see, and experience that accomplishing it all was impossible. One day I chose to stay behind cause I didn't feel well. I took the nausea medication I'd brought with me and went back to bed. Waking later that morning, I became bored and decided to strike out on my own. How much trouble could I get into I asked myself?

At first, I walked around the neighborhood, careful not to get lost. The traffic laws I was familiar with didn't apply here. Had it not been for an elderly gentleman grabbing my arm as I stepped off a curb to cross the street, I'd have been struck by a fast-moving car.

"Whew," that could've been disastrous, I thought to myself. Handing the man a leaflet about God, and a few bills of currency to thank him, I carried on my way.

I remembered a shopping area I'd visited the day before. My group hadn't had much time when we were there, so I decided I'd go back and look around on my own. I had plenty of time to return before anyone found out I had left. I ignored the voice in my head that said this wasn't a good idea and flagged a taxi down.

I barely told the driver where I wanted to go before he pulled away in a rush. Not paying attention to the direction he went, I sat back to take in the sights. A half-hour later or so, I noticed we were heading out of the city. Looking around, I didn't recognize any of the landmarks I'd seen the day before. It took some time to get the driver's attention as he was talking to someone over the radio, occasionally yelling in his native tongue. Looking at me in his rearview mirror, he turned his attention to me and spoke. He'd never said a word when I got in the taxi and told him where I wanted to go, so I'd just assumed he'd understood me. Now I realized he hadn't at all. I'd gotten in a taxi with someone who didn't speak English!

Frantically, I searched my mind trying to remember the few words we'd learned in Chinese. In my panic, I couldn't remember a single one of them. Still, the driver kept going. He might not have understood what I was saying, but he understood the tears that began pouring down my cheeks. Pulling over, he shut his car off and started talking to the man on the radio.

"Oh God, what am I gonna do now," I thought to myself?

We tried communicating through sign language, but the version we were using wasn't working. I kept trying to explain to the man that I wanted to go back where he'd picked me up, but he kept shrugging his shoulders in obvious confusion. This went on for another half hour, and I could see he was getting frustrated with me by the way he kept looking at his watch.

"Help me, Lord, I promise I won't make this mistake again," I spoke aloud.

At that very moment, I remembered the card I'd hid inside my fanny pack. Retrieving it, I handed it to the driver. I was so relieved I cried tears of joy all the way to the hotel. Pastor H was there when I arrived. I could see by the look on his face he wasn't happy with me. Staring at the mess I was, he softened.

"Do we need to discuss the importance of following rules from now on," he asked?

"No, sir. I'm so sorry," I replied, hanging my head in shame.

"Go wash up. I'm just glad you're safe," Pastor H said, shoving me toward the elevator banks.

The next day, I was assigned to accompany Pastor H and his group for a prayer walk through certain areas of the city. We prayed as we walked along for God to shower his blessings on all. It broke my heart to see how impoverished people lived and made me grateful for the opportunities I'd had in my life.

Coming upon an older woman with a tattered bedsheet spread before her, I walked over to see the items up close. It was a mishmash of empty spools, wire, and junk that looked like it had seen better days. The woman motioned for me to pick things up and get a closer look. When I didn't, she picked up a tortoise-shell hair-comb and handed it to me. It was missing several teeth, but I reached in my pack for money to pay her. Giving the one-hundred Yen to her, and stuffing the comb in my bag, I turned to walk away.

She held it up and began crying out to her husband, who was sitting just inside their shack on the dirt floor. He couldn't stand because both of his legs were amputated below his knees, but I could see the joy that spread across his features.

The woman scooped up the sheet tying it into a knot, and placed it in my hands. I tried giving it back to her, but she wouldn't take it. Dropping to the ground, she wrapped her arms around my legs, hugging with all her might. I looked at Pastor H in confusion as he walked to my side.

"What did I do," I worriedly asked.

"You probably gave her more money just now, than she could scrape together in a whole year. You have to accept the stuff she's giving you; otherwise, she would consider it an insult," Pastor H told me.

Holding the small bundle close, I bowed in thanks to her. Standing, she reached out and pulled my face close and kissed my cheek. I handed her a pamphlet explaining God's love and prayed she could read. Thinking of Daddy, I walked away more determined than ever to help him overcome his disability before it was too late.

Our time here was over before we knew it. I'd grown close to several people and was sad to say goodbye knowing I'd never see them again. One such lady was standing just outside the elevators as I got off with two young girls giggling behind me. It was apparent they were laughing at me.

"I don't understand," I commented to the kind manager of the hotel, "All week, people have laughed at me when I spoke to them."

"What have you said," she questioned?

"Nothing much, besides, hello," I answered, shrugging my shoulders.

"Wende, say "Hello" to me," she prompted with an intense look on her face.

"Niao."

To my dismay, she began laughing so hard; it took her a moment to stop.

"Oh, my dearest friend," she began, "you should have come sooner to me. I could have helped you understand your error. "Hello" in Chinese is "Ni hao." The word you have been saying to everyone, "Niao," means "Bird."

Looking at each other, we both had a good laugh at my expense. It made perfect sense to me. If someone walked up to me and said: "Bird, Bird," I would laugh at them as well.

We left for Beijing that evening, traveling there by train. A new experience for me, it took away some of the sorrow I felt at leaving my new friends behind. Our itinerary for the next few days included visits to Tiananmen Square, The Emperor's Palace located within the Forbidden City, and The Great Wall of China. Drifting off to sleep on my bunk, I was hopeful that being in a more populated area meant I would be able to eat meat without fear of eating a dog.

The next several days went by in a whirlwind as we visited one place after another. I stared in wonder at the many ancient structures and artifacts as we went along. I often found myself overwhelmed with emotion in the realization of how blessed I became the day Pastor H invited me along on this journey.

One evening Pastor H told the group we'd be visiting a popular eatery the next day. I couldn't wait. If it was a popular tourist spot, maybe I could find something to fill my stomach. I'd eaten so many vegetables that week; I just knew I'd lost weight.

Arriving at the restaurant, I noticed a large fenced-in area off to itself away from the main building. There was a man just inside the gate with a sign advertising camel rides for five dollars.

"Pastor H, can I run over there and take a camel ride," I pleaded with my bottom lip stuck out in a pout?

"Go ahead, but don't be long," he grinned.

I was glad I'd worn long pants that day as I climbed on top of the camel's back. At first, it felt awkward as the man led the lumbering animal away from the gate down a row of caged, exotic animals on both sides. Handing the reins to me, he turned and walked back to the gate entrance.

"Heyyy, wait a minute," I called out, "I've never steered a camel before."

Ignoring me, he kept on walking.

I got the hang of it pretty quick as I steered the camel to the end of the row and around the corner to the next one. I felt confident enough to look away from the camel and glance at the animals in the cages. I'd never seen so many different animals in one spot before in my life. The owners of this place must really be animal lover's I thought to myself. Spotting the funny looking dogs playing in one of the pens changed my mind about everyone seeing dogs as food in China.

Jumping off the camel's back when I got back to the front of the enclosure, I hurried in to find Pastor H and the rest of our group sitting at a large, lazy susan table.

"I hoped you washed your hands," one of the ladies from the group commented, "that camel didn't look very clean to me."

"I did after I used the facilities," I replied. (Thinking of facilities made me yearn for a toilet seat. Many facilities in China consisted of holes in the floor where one squats to relieve themselves.)

"Guess what Pastor H, not everyone in China, considers dogs a delicacy. The people who own this place have a whole pen of dogs as pets. As a matter of fact, they have a whole bunch of pets out there in those cages."

It got quiet all around me as Pastor H leaned forward to comment.

"Wende, those animals aren't pets, they're what's on the menu."

Images of those poor dogs playing so fondly together ruined my appetite. It was all I could do not to puke right then and there. I managed to eat a few bites of vegetables and was relieved when it was time to go. I couldn't bring myself to look at the menagerie as we drove away.

Pastor H advised us all to get a good night's sleep since we were visiting The Great Wall of China the next day. He said we were going to need all the rest we could get. I couldn't believe our adventure was nearing an end. We would be traveling home in two days, and as much as I hated to admit it, I was homesick.

It's a good thing Pastor H chose one of the smaller points of the wall to climb. I was aching all over by the time we made it to the top. My legs hurt so much that I dreaded the walk down. We took a break to catch our breath and rehydrate while everyone took pictures of the view and masonry marvels around us. Going down wasn't as difficult as the trip up had been. I couldn't wait to get to the hotel and a nice hot shower.

I was so exhausted climbing into bed later that night that I fell asleep not long after my head hit the pillow. Smiling to myself, I closed my eyes and dreamed of home.

Chapter 62

Broken promises and forgotten dreams...

I'd only talked to Andy a couple of times while I was away. So as soon as I got off the plane in California, I called home. He said everything was going great and they couldn't wait to see me. I told him a few highlights of my trip and that I couldn't wait to see them either.

When we finally pulled into the church parking lot, the same group who'd seen us off was waiting on us. We once again gathered for prayer before retrieving our luggage and heading to our homes. Everyone was so excited to see me that they all started talking at the same time when we got to the house.

"Hey, one at a time," I repeated several times before they listened.

After each one had their say, I gathered up some refreshments from the kitchen and carried them into the living room. It was a rare treat when I let the kids eat anywhere but the kitchen, so they were all on their best behavior. I passed out all their souvenirs taking the time to explain where they'd come from, but they were more interested in hearing my stories. Looking at their eager faces, I took them on a journey to a faraway land as I recalled all that I had seen and done. They sat there wide-eyed through each story, soaking in all I had to say. They had a blast admonishing me for breaking the rules when I left the hotel alone; and laughing at the funny stories of me walking around telling everyone "Bird, Bird." When I'd finished telling my tales, they all wanted more.

"Tell y'all what, when the pictures get developed we'll talk about it some more. It's past bedtime, and I've got jet-lag." Seeing the confusion on their faces, I explained what jet-lag was and herded them off to bed. I was definitely ready to sleep in my own bed, so once everyone was settled, I made a beeline for it.

Andy headed off to work the next morning while I set about getting my house back in order. He'd done a decent job of keeping up with things, but I could see plenty of things that needed my attention. I had just finished unpacking my suitcases and having my morning coffee when I heard a knock on the door.

"Wende, it's me," I heard a familiar voice say as the screen door slammed shut in her wake.

"I'm in here," I hollered, pouring myself another cup of coffee and offering her one when she stepped into the kitchen.

"Naw, I'm good," she answered as she sat down at the table across from me.

The sense of foreboding I felt when I looked over at her worried features startled me.

"What's wrong," I asked, all the while knowing I wasn't gonna like what I heard.

She sat there without saying anything for so long, I asked her again.

"You might as well tell me now," I demanded, "from the looks on your face, I'm not gonna like it, and I'd just as soon hear it from you."

I sat there glued to my seat for so long after she left, I found it hard to stand when the kids came in asking for lunch. I fixed their lunch in a daze before going to sit on my bed.

"You okay, Aunt Wende," I heard James ask from the doorway?

"No. I don't feel good at all. Would you mind keeping the kids occupied while I take a nap."

"Sure, Aunt Wende."

I sat there all day, unable to do more than make sure the kids were okay. I tried to sleep, but my mind wouldn't shut off. I wanted to cry, but the tears wouldn't come. I was numb from the inside out.

"There you are," Andy said, walking into the room. "How was your day?"

When I didn't answer him, he came around the bed to face me. Looking up, at him, the tears finally came.

"How could you?"

Once the words left my mouth, Andy's expression changed as he hung his head in shame.

"I begged you! You knew how much this meant to me! I have given you chance, after chance, after chance!" Despite the anguish he had to know I was suffering, he stood there saying nothing. "Do you even realize what you've done? It was one thing to jeopardize my sobriety by having meth under our roof, but to jeopardize these children's lives and threaten my custody of them, it's… it's…" The magnitude of the situation got the best of me. I was rendered speechless momentarily. My heart was broken as I looked up at the man I'd spent the longest time with, the only man I'd trusted with all my heart besides Daddy. "You've backed me in a corner where I have to choose between you and these babies! Say something, damn you!"

Andy sat down on the side of the bed and held his head in his hands, still refusing to utter a word; it was my undoing. Great wracking sobs tore from my chest, and I began shaking violently. When Andy reached for me, I struck out at him, hitting him repeatedly until he grabbed me in his arms so I couldn't hit him anymore. He held me that way until my anger subsided. I let him continue to hold me once I felt the rage leave my body, knowing it was the last time he'd ever hold me as my husband.

I don't remember the details of what happened past Andy holding me for the last time that night, all I recall is what happened in its wake.

June 2005

I'd only been home from China for two days, yet the exhilaration I'd felt vanished. Daddy couldn't help cause he had his own issues, so I didn't want to burden him with mine. I called my Sunday school teacher, Charlie, and his wife, Barbara, and asked to speak with them. I didn't have a clue which direction to turn but knew in my heart; I had to leave Andy immediately. His actions had put my custody of the children in danger; the longer I stayed, the higher the risk would become. My friends had a studio apartment on their property and agreed to let the four children and me stay there while I gathered my bearings.

Returning to the house, I grabbed a few things to get us by and left.

My friends' property was isolated and very pastoral. Sitting on the swing outside the little studio apartment, I could hear nature all around me. It was comforting to me as I pondered my life and where to go from there. God and

I had many conversations during my time there. It brought peace to my heart, and I will be forever grateful for all my friends' help. They provided refuge, but more importantly, they loved me for who I was and not where I'd been. Sharing my past with them openly, they never judged me. Instead, they spent many hours encouraging me to draw closer to God and gave me examples of how to accomplish it by studying God's word. Charlie was like a father to me, and as such, he and I butted heads from time to time. I always knew his intentions were to help me avoid the pitfalls I had in my past and to help me become a better person.

A few strings were pulled in my favor, and the next thing I knew, the children and I were moving into an apartment in government housing. Things started falling into place so quickly that it could have only come from God.

I'd met Pam at church a couple of years, or so before, and knew from the start she was special. She reminded me of Momma Beatrice and Calvinette. Her love of God is infectious to everyone around her. We talked often, so she was another person I called for guidance. Being friends, she knew my frustrations. I was up a creek, without a paddle, and having someone to talk things through with helped me. Pam asked if it would offend me if she offered me used furniture for my apartment because she and her sister had some they needed to get rid of cause it was taking up storage space. (I would soon find out that was a little white lie she told to help me.) I told her I loved shopping at garage sales and thrift stores, so no, I wouldn't be offended at all. I told her I would appreciate any help she could give me. She told me to meet her at my apartment at a particular time that next morning cause the furniture was being delivered.

She got there a little before the furniture store truck arrived. I was overwhelmed as they filled my entire apartment with furniture. Some pieces were brand new, and you would have had a hard time telling the rest were used. Most of them were better than anything I'd ever had before. I stared in disbelief as they installed a brand-new washer and dryer set. After they left, she brought in bags and bags of things from her car full of items I needed to set up my apartment. She helped me decorate all day long and then sat me down for a serious talk.

"Wende, what are your plans going forward," she asked, looking into my eyes?

"I don't know. It's been all I could do to make another day," sighing deeply,

I continued, "I haven't thought much about the future."

"Have you ever thought about going back to school," was her next question?

"I've tried a half dozen times, but ended up quitting every time."

"What did you want to do" she continued?

"All my life, the only thing I ever wanted to be was a nurse, and I'm pretty sure I messed that up by becoming a felon," I answered near tears.

"How do you know you messed it up? Have you ever looked into it," she wanted to know?

"No. Seemed easier, not knowing for sure than to ask and get my heart broke. If they said no, it would've been one more thing to beat myself up over," I replied honestly. "Lord knows I already have a long list of regrets to deal with."

"Oh, Wende, I'm so sorry. You need to forgive yourself and let it go. Have you asked God to forgive you?"

"Yes, but I keep taking it back. I know that's not the way it's supposed to work, but it's hard sometimes," taking a breath, "I am my own worst enemy sometimes."

"You're already beating yourself up over it. You'll never know if you don't ask," Pam pointed out. "Tyler Junior College has a nursing program, and it wouldn't hurt to find out. Would you be willing to go over there if I go with you?"

At that moment, Keith Urban's smiling face popped into my thoughts. I recalled the bio I had read about him in Nashville and all the struggles he'd faced to chase his dreams of being a country star. He didn't give up and look at him now.

"Okay, okay, okay. You're right, as always, my dearest friend. I can always count on you to point out the obvious and not let me make excuses," seeing the grin on her face, and relenting, "I'll go!"

Pam showed up bright and early the next morning as always, with her optimistic attitude, unwilling to let me back out. We drove the thirty-five miles to Tyler, and finding the right building; Pam parked the car. Sensing my nervousness, she stopped me as I went to open the door. She suggested we say a prayer for God to open doors as only he can do.

We located the nursing administrator's office and asked to speak with an administrator. Sitting at a desk waiting on the woman to join us, Pam made a funny face at me to lighten my tension and assured me everything would be okay no matter what, according to God's plan.

Feeling assured she was right, I took a deep breath and smiled at the woman who sat down in front of us. Here goes, I thought to myself.

"How can I help you," she asked, smiling.

"I have some questions I need answered. All my life, I've wanted to become a nurse, and even made a run at it many years ago. Unfortunately, I made a mess of my life through poor choices and mistakes I can't take back. Some of those poor choices led to my getting in trouble and receiving felonies for my efforts." Breathing deeply to calm my nerves, I carried on, "I've come to find out if having felonies precludes my chances of pursuing a nursing career; now that I have my life straightened out," I stated with more confidence than I felt.

Holding my breath for her answer, I silently prayed for God to help me accept whatever she said with grace and not start bawling all over the place.

The administrator sat in silence, considering what I'd asked. I held my head up and looked her straight in the eyes, willing her to see how much this meant to me.

"Hmm. What were the felonies you received, and how long ago were they," she inquired?

"I have three drug felonies; two for unlawful delivery of marijuana, and one for possession of a controlled substance. I received a five-year sentence. The first six months, I served in the county jail, and the rest I completed on probation in 1996. I also have two misdemeanors for driving under the influence and public intoxication back in the early nineties. I haven't gotten into any more trouble since then."

"If you'll excuse me for a couple of minutes, I want to check something out," dismissing herself, she left the room.

"So far, so good. She hasn't said no yet," Pam winked, "I'm so proud of you! You're doing good, keep it up."

The minutes seemed to drag by as I silently prayed for God to grant me a miracle. I couldn't tell if what she was going to say was good or bad as she walked back into the room, but the sheaf of papers she held in her hands gave me a glimmer of hope. Sitting down, the administrator folded her hands atop the documents that were turned upside down to keep my attention focused on her as she'd seen me staring at them. Looking at me with a stern look on her face, she spoke with conviction.

"There are no clear-cut answers to your question, but having felonies in and of themselves, won't necessarily prohibit you from becoming a nurse. However," pausing and looking at me intently, she stressed, "I can't make any promises that yours won't keep you from it. The Board of Nurses considers each case separately, taking into consideration the individual circumstances surrounding the convictions. I'm not going to lie to you. The process isn't easy by a long shot. It involves miles and miles of red-tape and will be an uphill battle all the way. I don't want to dissuade you or change your mind about trying, but there is the very real possibility that even after you've given it your best shot, you could be denied licensure."

Letting what she'd had to say sink in before continuing, "The Board of Nurses must protect the public by monitoring individuals who they grant licenses' to. The Board is not a group of individuals without heart, and realize that people are human and make mistakes. They aren't there to judge, but are obligated to investigate all applications sent to them." Her features softening, she turned the sheaf of papers over and handed them to me. "If you're up to the task, and sincerely want to be a nurse, here is the paperwork that will get you started. You'll need to go through them carefully and follow all the steps. The Board will not accept incomplete applications. In the meantime, you'll need to enroll in college, and consider taking some core classes while you petition the Board." Handing me a list of prerequisites required for nursing, she went on, "Fall classes are beginning to fill up, but you might have time to get in if you hurry. I wish you all the luck going forward, and if I can help in any way, please let me know." Standing, she shook mine and Pam's hands before walking us out to the front office.

Standing outside the building, Pam let out a praise to God. Grabbing my hand, she pulled me toward another group of buildings instead of the parking lot.

"Where are we going," I asked, trying to keep up with her brisk pace?

"To enroll you in college silly," she said, laughing, but not slowing down.

It was a lengthy process tracking down all the many transcripts I'd accumulated from three different states and over the last twenty-two years, but with Pam beside me every step of the way, I finally got it done. The same afternoon I began the process of enrolling in school. Pam also steered me toward the Financial Aid office to start that ball rolling as well.

A few short weeks later, I had to pinch myself to make sure I wasn't dreaming, as I stood in line to register for the classes I had chosen to begin. Pam had accompanied me with her checkbook in hand.

"Don't worry," she said with a smile, "you can repay me once you receive your financial aid check."

Chapter 63

Flying high and Crashing low

Recalling my college years and all that has occurred since then, I realize there is no way I can share it all in the pages of one book. To try to do so would be an injustice. Perhaps I'll write another one someday and pick up where I left off. For now, I'll do my best to find an ending to this one.

The years I attended school and traversed the many obstacles of petitioning the Nursing Board were filled with many happy memories, but they were also fraught with tragedy. It was during those times, if not for God's love, I would've given up.

No matter how many times I failed to complete whatever I'd undertaken in life, Daddy was always ready to stand behind me and offer encouragement when I was ready to get up and start over. He'd always believed that someday I would get it right. As I began that first semester of college in the Fall of 2005, I promised Daddy, this time, I wouldn't quit.

"I'll make a deal with you Daddy," I began, catching his attention cause he sensed I was up to something, "if you promise to be there when I walk across the stage and get my nursing license no matter what you got going on, I won't quit this time."

Laughing cause I'd caught him off guard, he became serious when he replied, "Nothing in this world would keep me away, are you crazy? I'll even get there early enough to sit in the front row!"

I knew I needn't have asked, but I wanted him to know that of all the people I expected to come, his being there to see me finish this time was what I wanted most.

Christmas 2005 came and went along with the completion of my first semester of college. I made it on the Dean's list and made sure everyone knew it, especially Daddy. I was so proud of myself. I remember Daddy commenting something such as, "You always were book smart, now if you could just work on your common sense you'd have it made." Yet, I could see the pride in his eyes of my accomplishments the day I told him. It was his sixty-ninth birthday, and I'd driven from Grand Saline to Ft. Worth to take him a present.

'Here Daddy, let me read your card to you," I said, pointing out the funny characters as I read.

"That's cute, but it will never beat this one," he laughed as he retrieved a worn card from his top dresser drawer. He kept all sorts of things in that drawer, which held meaning to him, but that card was extra special. As far as I know, it was the only one he ever kept over the years. I'm sure that fact hurt others' feelings from time to time, but if they'd have realized the meaning behind it, it shouldn't have. The joke was on me!

Daddy used to tell me from time to time when I'd go to him to borrow money that he believed I'd take his last dime before I'd learn to manage my money better. He'd be madder than the devil at me, but he always pulled his wallet out and gave me whatever I needed. I would eventually learn to make a budget, so I didn't have to ask as often.

One Father's Day many, many years ago, as I searched for the perfect card for Daddy, I didn't have to look too hard. I busted out laughing so uncontrollably after reading it aloud, that everyone turned to see if someone had gone mad. I couldn't wait to see the expression on Daddy's face when I gave it to him.

I figured everybody would want to see Daddy's expression as well, so I made sure everyone who was at his house that day was standing there when I gave it to him. Daddy laughed so hard when I got through reading it to him that his top denture fell out.

The front of the card showed a man's arm with a suit on, holding up a shiny dime… It said: *"Happy Father's Day to the Dad that would give his last thin dime—"*

The inside read:

"From the daughter who'd probably take it!"

I began the Spring 2006 semester in high hopes. I felt as though nothing could stop me now. I had received correspondence from the Nursing Board and was in the process of gathering the additional information they required to move the process forward. The kids and I had a pretty decent routine down, but Andy was often around to lend a hand. We had worked through the issues that tore our marriage apart, but the deep friendship we had refused to die. Even though our divorce was in the works, Andy swore as my friend; he'd never leave my side.

Mid-semester, I was sitting in my Anatomy and Physiology lab class, looking at sections of lungs blackened from cancer when I got a text from Bubba telling me to call Mom Nita as soon as I could. I wondered why she hadn't texted me herself but figured since she hadn't, it could probably wait until class was over. I'd become so engrossed in my studies that I almost forgot to call her.

Walking into the hallway, I stopped and turned the volume of my phone up since it'd been on vibrate during class. It still showed the message from Bubba when the screen lit up. Looking at the time, I saw it was eight-thirty pm.; and not too late to call Mom Nita. I sat my backpack down and leaning against the wall I dialed her number. She answered right away, and I could tell she'd been crying.

"Wende," I heard her sob before a long pause, the tone of her voice sending chills up my spine as I waited for her to continue, "your Daddy's doctor ran some chest x-rays on him last week. They had him come in yesterday for an MRI and a CT Scan. We went in to get the results from the doctor this afternoon. Wende, your Daddy, has Stage IV Small Cell Carcinoma."

Chapter 64

Waterworks forever...

I told Mom Nita I was on my way, and I'd take a look at the pathophysiology report they'd given Daddy when I got there. Her and Daddy had a hard time understanding everything the doctor had tried to explain in part due to his thick accent. Flying down I-20, the last thing on my mind was a speeding ticket. All I could think about was Daddy, and images of the blackened lungs I'd been studying less than an hour ago. I prayed to God that they'd misunderstood the doctor that afternoon, or better yet, that this was all just a bad nightmare I would soon wake from.

Nightmares. I have been plagued with nightmares all my life. Some of them were actual events from my past that I recalled while dreaming. Some turned out to be visions of what was to come. I've only discussed this ability with a handful of people I trust before now. I don't understand it, and it scares me. I'm afraid folks won't believe me, or worse yet, think I'm crazy.

One nightmare was a recurring one for as long as I can remember. It wasn't frequent, only occurring every few years, but it was the same every time. It was Daddy's funeral. Every time I had that dream, I would wake up in a cold sweat, and so terrified that it would take days for me to banish it from my thoughts.

The nightmare consisted of two picture-like images that were so vivid it felt like I was there. In the first image, I am at the back of a chapel, staring down at the scene below as if I'm floating above them. The pews are filled with people, but I can't tell who they are. Standing at Daddy's casket is Bubba and Shelley. The second image was Daddy lying in his coffin as if I was parallel right above him, looking down into his face.

Thinking of Daddy with Stage IV Small Cell Carcinoma evokes those images as I drive.

Pulling into Daddy's driveway, I took slow deep breaths and tried to calm myself before I went in. No matter what, the last thing I wanted to do was frighten Daddy any more than I knew he must be.

"Hey Daddy," I said as I bent down to hug his neck. He looked up briefly before he went back to fiddling with some gadget in his hands. I knew he was deliberately avoiding looking me in the eye as he often did when he was troubled 'bout something. "Where's Mom Nita at?"

"Probably in the kitchen. Nita," Daddy hollered out.

I heard the toilet flushing right before she stepped into the room.

"I didn't hear you come in," she said to me as she walked into the room. "What did you need, John," worry etched across her features as she stepped up next to Daddy to see what he wanted.

"Nothing. I just wondered where you were," again, only glancing up for a second.

"You want a coke," Mom Nita nodded to the kitchen more interested in getting me out of Daddy's earshot than really wanting to know if I was thirsty?

Handing me the pink carbon copy of Daddy's pathophysiology report once we walked into the kitchen, she sat down and grasped her head in her hands as I silently read the words on the page, not once, but twice. The words blurred in my vision as the tears collected in my eyes. It's a good thing there was a chair in front of me cause in the next instance, my knees buckled out from under me. I managed to slide into the chair before I hit the floor.

"Do you understand what it means," she questioned through red-rimmed eyes?

When I finally let the words slip from my lips, they sounded foreign as I whispered, "Daddy is a dead-man walking."

We sat there without speaking for the next several minutes. The only sound coming from Grandma Georgia Bell's wall clock, tick-tock, tick-tock. When Grandma passed away, Daddy and Mom Nita moved from across the street over here to her house. It still felt awkward to come here and not see Grandma. I guess I was in shock from the numbness I felt all over. The tears pooled in my eyes and slowly made their way down my cheeks one or two at a time. I wanted to cry my heart out; I wanted to scream and shout and curse to the high heavens, but all I could do was sit there in numbed silence.

"You better go see your Daddy for a while before you head back home," Mom Nita suggested, "you got school tomorrow, don't you?"

I'd washed up and put on my best poker face before going back to Daddy's room. I sat down on the side of Daddy's bed and silently prayed for God to give me the courage I needed. I promised myself I could lose it later if I pulled this off.

"How long you been feeling bad, Daddy," trying not to sound frightened as I asked?

He sat there a minute before responding, "I ain't really paid that much attention, but I been havin' a cough for a long time." Concentrating on his gadget a bit before going on, "Seems like this cold won't go away. Did you read that paper Nita has?"

"I did, but I'm not sure I understand what it means," the lie coming out calmer than I thought it would. "Whatever it is, Mom Nita said they want to do some more testing. If it turns out to be cancer for sure, Daddy, there are all kinds of treatments they can use to maybe get rid of it, or slow it down," I lied again.

"You think so," he questioned? Looking over at me for the first time since I'd got here, and seeing the hope in his eyes, felt like I'd just gotten sucker-punched in the gut.

The last thing I wanted to do was leave my Daddy's side, but I knew if I didn't get out of there soon, I was gonna lose my mind. I needed time to process what I'd read, and time to release the raging flood I knew was on its way. Mom Nita came to my rescue as she walked into the room.

"Wende, you better get going if you're gonna make it to school tomorrow."

I leaned over and kissed Daddy on the cheek telling him I loved him, and to try not to worry himself too much. Mom Nita walked out to the porch with me for one more word in private.

"I've never seen your Daddy this afraid of anything in his life. I don't know how I'm gonna keep his hopes up if he finds out he doesn't have long to live."

"Aren't they gonna try to slow it down with Chemo?"

"We're going to see another doctor 'bout that tomorrow," Mom Nita said, opening the screen door to go in. "I love you, have a safe trip home."

"I love you too. Let me know as soon as you find out something. Text me if you can't talk," I hollered over my shoulder as I walked to the car for the long ride home.

Chapter 65

"Revealing Conversations"

I don't remember the drive back home after I left Grandma's house that night. In fact, I don't recall much about anything those first few weeks, except the tears that refused to stop pouring day and night. I cried so much that my eyes always looked like someone had hit me. I can't tell you how I made it through the rest of that semester of school, but I did. I even made the Dean's list, but God only knows how.

I talked Patrick into quitting the job he had with Scuter out in Florida to come home and stay with the kids for the summer so I could live in Ft. Worth and be near Daddy for a while. Daddy's white blood cell count had gotten knocked down so low after only one round of Chemo; that the doctor's said he couldn't take any more. The Chemo also burned Daddy's throat to the point where they had to give Daddy a peg-tube so he could receive nutrition. It was getting harder and harder for Daddy to hold on to even the slightest glimmer of hope. Then one day, a heartless bastard stole that too.

Like a videotape stuck on replay, I'll never forget the morning it happened. An ambulance had transported Daddy to Harris Methodist Hospital the night before cause he'd suffered chest pains. The emergency room doctors had put him in the hospital overnight for observation to make sure it wasn't anything serious. It was late when someone finally called me, so I got up early the next morning and drove over to see what was going on. Mom Nita and a friend of hers from work were there when I arrived.

"Hey Daddy," greeting him, I bent down and gave him a hug and a kiss on the cheek. "How are you feeling this morning?"

"Not too good this morning. I been having pains in my chest all night long. "

Turning to Mom Nita, I asked, "It's nothing serious, is it?"

"The doctors downstairs said it wasn't," she answered.

Just then, a doctor walked through the door with a scowl on his face. It was plain to see he was upset. Wasting no time, he got right to the point.

"Mr. Beaird, The doctors downstairs shouldn't have put you in the hospital. I'm going to discharge you right away." Staring at the chart in his hands, he continued, "There's nothing we can do for you, you're dying. You're a grown man and need to accept that. Go home and stop wasting taxpayer money."

I was staring at my precious Daddy when the doctor began his ugly, verbal attack. The range of emotions that crossed his features kept me from looking away. I watched in horror as the hope faded, and the realization sunk in.

It's a good thing that happened before I was fully aware of HIPPA Laws, cause I would've hired a lawyer and sued that man for all he was worth! He never once asked who any of us were before pronouncing my father's death sentence and taking away the last traces of hope my Daddy had. If it hadn't been for Mom Nita, I would have blasted him right there on the spot, but out of respect for her, I kept my mouth shut. Later that afternoon, when I stopped by NaNe's on my way home to Grand Saline, I sat down and wrote a scathing letter to the administrators of Harris Methodist Hospital describing in detail what had occurred. I never even received so much as an apology on Daddy's behalf.

The minute that man, cause he sure didn't deserve to be called a doctor, left the room; Daddy got out of the hospital bed and dressed to go home.

I told Mom Nita of my plans to move to Ft. Worth for the summer that afternoon while we waited for Daddy's discharge. I told her I was gonna rent an efficiency apartment, and get a waitress job somewhere so I could support myself. I explained that it would enable me to visit Daddy awhile each afternoon.

"I absolutely forbid it!" Momma Nita flatly stated. "I will not have you keeping your father upset by shoving God down his throat on a daily basis. I've got too much on my hands to deal with you bawling all over the place to boot!" Turning beet red in the face, she looked from me to Daddy and stormed out of the room.

"That's not fair, Daddy. I haven't shoved God down your throat, not even once, nor have I broke down in front of you. I want to spend time with you to Daddy," crying as I spoke, and for the first time since this all began, breaking down. "Grand Saline is too far away from here for me to spend much time with you at all." Pleading with Daddy to step in and back me up.

"I'm sorry Yvette, Nita is having a real hard time too. Please, for my sake, respect her wishes."

For the first time in my life, I hated Mom Nita. She allowed Shelley, and my step-sister to come to the house every day to help her and spend time with Daddy, but she forbade my presence! It would be a bitter pill to swallow, but I would've done anything my father asked of me at this point. It would be years down the road before I forgave Mom Nita for taking away precious time I could've spent with Daddy. I had to dig deep into my soul and continuously turn it over to God. It would be hard to accept, but I finally realized that God always knows better than me. It would have been hard to carry memories of watching Daddy's rapid decline right before my eyes.

The few memories I have with Daddy during that time are precious to me. Driving over most weekends and attending church with my father blessed my soul, knowing he finally made peace with God, and one day he will be in heaven waiting on me. I always knew Daddy believed in God, but being illiterate, he never had an opportunity to study God's word and understand God's plan for him.

On one occasion, Mom Nita allowed me to stay all weekend. There was a "Tammy" marathon running with both Debbie Reynolds and Sandra Dee playing the part of Tammy. Me and Daddy watched every show together. I used to love watching the escapades of Tammy Tyree growing up. After that weekend, I can't bring myself to watch them anymore at all. So, yes, maybe it was for my protection that God allowed my time with Daddy to be limited.

My last conversation with Daddy was one of the most important conversations we ever had in our lives. I remember it almost verbatim. The impact it had on my life was immeasurable.

It occurred one Sunday afternoon when I drove over to see him. Me and Daddy were sitting in the living room while his peg tube was running. Mom Nita was in the kitchen, washing dishes. Daddy asked me a question about the Bible. I had no sooner answered Daddy 'til Mom Nita came to stand in the doorway, hands on her hips, with the dishtowel hanging from one of them. The look on her face said it all.

"I thought I told you I wasn't gonna have you shove God down your Daddy's throat," she spat out with such venom I was taken by surprise. I was momentarily speechless, unable to answer her.

She stared at me, waiting for my response when Daddy spoke up.

"I asked her a question 'bout the Bible," Daddy answered for me.

Shooting daggers at me with her eyes, she threw the dishtowel on the back of the couch, "Fine! I'm leaving; you can have your Daddy all to yourself!" Grabbing her purse, she stormed out the front door, slamming it with all her might.

"Thank you, Daddy," his expression saddened by Mom Nita's behavior as I spoke.

Neither one of said much while his feeding came to an end. I unhooked the tubing from the empty bag and helped Daddy back to his bed. When Momma died, I was young and in denial to the last moment of her life. I had no way of knowing I'd wasted any chance of resolving the issues between us. I've lived in torment since Momma's death because so many things were left unsaid and unanswered. I'd been waiting for the right moment to approach Daddy and make sure I didn't make the same mistake twice. Thanks to Mom Nita's anger, I now had that chance.

We talked about so much that afternoon, clearing the air between us. We laughed and cried together as we recalled the history of our family, and spoke of the future without Daddy in it. We'd talked about everything under the sun, as I frantically searched my memory for every last tidbit that might haunt me once Daddy was gone. I'd been lying on the bed next to Daddy when I got up to walk around and stretch my legs. Standing at the foot of the bed, I stared at Daddy, trying to burn his image into my heart so I wouldn't forget one single moment of this magical afternoon I'd spent with him. Feeling confidant that I'd dredged up every last circumstance or memory I could ever need a resolution for, my knees went weak when I realized there was one memory I hadn't thought of amidst the many we'd discussed that day. Gathering my courage, I spoke up.

"Daddy, there is one thing I need answers to," I said. Daddy must have sensed the seriousness in my voice cause he stopped what he was doing and raised his eyes to meet mine, staring intently. "You might not remember it cause it happened so long ago, but do you remember the time when we went to that place called Horseshoe Bend for the weekend?" This was the first time the subject had been brought up since I left my parents room, thirty-six years ago, so I thought Daddy might've forgotten 'bout it.

Immediately, the expression on Daddy's face changed, but he just nodded, never saying a word.

Nervously I went on, "Remember that night when I came and stood by Momma to tell her 'bout that man raping me," I asked. I watched in horror, as the exact expression I'd seen on Daddy's face that night long ago, cloud his features before he hung his head. Dear sweet Jesus, he still thought I had lied to him and Momma.

I began crying deep, gut-wrenching sobs, and barely got the next words out of my mouth, "It's not fair, Daddy! I swear to you, I wasn't lying, Daddy! That man ruined my life and never had to pay for what he'd done to me!"

Daddy sat up in the bed, jerking his head to look me straight in the eyes as if he'd been struck by lightning before he spoke the words that crumpled me to my feet, "What do you mean he never paid for what he did? I beat him so senseless it partially paralyzed him for life!"

The cry that tore from my soul at hearing Daddy's words must've scared him, cause he got up and came to sit at the foot of the bed, reaching out to pat my shoulder. He sat there quietly as I cried a river of tears. Spent, I leaned against Daddy's legs, pulling myself together. Daddy helped me to my feet, then went back to lay against the headboard of his bed.

"How come you never went to jail for paralyzing him," thirsty for knowledge, I needed answers?

"You think he was 'bout to turn me in? He would've gone to prison for raping my daughter, and paralyzed on top of it. Even if he had told on me, I would've got out of it for what he'd done to you!"

"I believed all my life that you thought I was lying. I knew Momma did cause she said so right before she slapped me."

"Your Momma believed you too." Seeing my disbelief, he continued, "Try not to think too harshly 'bout what your Momma did to you." Daddy softly plead. "She knew I was gonna go kill that son-of-a-bitch and was afraid I'd go to prison. Hell, I tried to kill him, and damned near did!"

"But why didn't y'all talk to me and get me some help? I was so scared cause he made me bleed. I didn't know where all that blood came from; I thought I was gonna die, Daddy!"

Daddy hung his head in shame, knowing they had let me down.

"I'm so sorry Yvette, I never thought 'bout how it musta' been for you. Back then, they didn't have all the stuff they have nowadays. Folks just took care of things, and let it go. I guess me and your Momma thought it was better for you to just forget 'bout it 'stead of makin' you remember it all the time."

Seeing the distress it brought Daddy thinking he'd hurt me worse, I went and laid down on the bed next to him. I laid my head on his chest, hugging him with my right arm thrown over his middle. Daddy reached around and hugged me back in a tight squeeze that told how he was feeling.

"It's okay, Daddy; I know now that you did what you thought was right. You telling me what happened has helped me more than you will ever know!"

We'd laid that way for a while when I thought of a few more things I wanted to know. Sitting up, I resumed staring at my father to see his expressions as we talked further.

"Daddy, you asked God to forgive your sins, didn't you?"

"I kinda did," I saw the question in his eyes that he wasn't quite sure he had. "How can I ask the good Lord to forgive me right now before I die when I lived my whole life the way I wanted without giving him the respect he deserved. What kind of man would that make me? It'd be chickenshit of me to ask him now!"

"Oh, Daddy," my poor Daddy didn't understand at all. He thought to ask God to forgive him now, would be to dishonor to him even more than he had all his life. My father had been an honorable man in all he'd ever done if he'd been nothing else. Daddy was prepared to risk going to Hell rather than dishonoring God further. "That's not true, Daddy, and I can prove it. When Jesus was hanging on the cross dying, there were also two other men hanging on crosses that day. One on either side of him. One was a thief, and one was a murderer. Just before the thief died, he spoke to Jesus. He said, 'Remember me to your father.' Immediately Jesus told that thief, 'Today, you will be with me in paradise.' Paradise meant heaven. Daddy, that thief who'd lived his life sinning against God, meant as much to God as anyone of the saints who'd lived their whole life for God."

"You really think so," Daddy asked, hope returning to his beautiful eyes.

"I don't just think so; it says it in black and white right there in that Bible. I know you always said it was hard to believe what the Bible said was true cause mortal men wrote it, but Daddy, it was inspired by God. Even if men didn't get it exactly as God meant it, God's words pour from that book."

Picking up the Bible lying on the dresser, I found the passage 'bout Jesus hanging on the cross and read it to Daddy. Listening intently, I saw the light go on in his eyes, acknowledging his understanding at last.

"Daddy, do you want to ask Jesus to forgive your sins and be your savior for real this time?"

"I'm ready," was all he said.

I led my precious father in the sinner's prayer. I heard him ask in a tearful voice for Jesus to please save his soul. I saw the light shine as my Daddy raised his head, knowing he was truly forgiven at last.

We sat there for a moment before Daddy spoke up and said he wasn't afraid of dying anymore with a genuine smile; I knew he felt in his heart.

"Daddy, what is your biggest regret in life," I wanted to know.

"Selling drugs, and knowing my grandkids will always think that's all I was ever good for."

"No, they won't, Daddy! I won't let them. Someday I'm gonna write a book and tell them all about the man their PaPa really was before he chose the wrong path. I'm also gonna make sure they know it was me who got you involved with drugs to begin with. I'm gonna make sure they understand that you only did it so you could take care of your family the way you always had. Please forgive me, Daddy?'

"I was a grown man and knew better, wasn't nobody's fault but my own. I'm just grateful all my kids are off that dope now!"

I knew Mom Nita would be home any minute, but I had one last question.

"Daddy, is there anything you ever wanted to do in life, but never got the chance to?"

Without hesitation, he answered, "Read a book."

"Guess what Daddy, I got a surprise for you." Hugging his neck, I saw the questioning look in his eyes he got every time I approached him this way, thinking I was up to something. "When we die and go to heaven, we are made perfect. Any imperfections and disabilities we had here on earth are wiped away. Books are one of the pleasures God made sure we had here on earth. It's how we learned 'bout him. I know there will be huge buildings full of books waitin' on us when we get there. You'll be able to read every last one of them!"

"You think so," he said with a smile that lit up his eyes with wonder.

"Where y'all at," I heard Mom Nita call out as she walked in the house?

"I love you, Daddy, more than all the stars in the sky, and blades of grass on the ground. You are the greatest father in the whole world. I wouldn't have traded you for the richest, most educated man if I'd had the chance. You hear me," I asked?

"Course not, you wouldn't been you if you had," he joked, "I love you too. You better go on home and let Nita cool her jets."

"I'll see you later, Daddy," hugging my Daddy and kissing him bye, I left. I told Mom Nita I would see her later as I walked out the door.

Driving home, I felt more at peace with my life since I had as a young girl. I was crushed knowing I was losing my precious Daddy, but smiling to myself, I knew I'd see him again someday.

I had no way of knowing it would be the last time I talked to Daddy as I drove off that evening. Two weeks later, I'd get the call that he'd lapsed into a coma.

Chapter 66

Hit by a train!

I'D PROMISED THE KIDS WE'D go camping before school started back up, but I'd been so busy running back and forth to Ft. Worth to see Daddy, that I hadn't kept my promise, and here it was the first week of August. I finally buckled down and made plans to go camp out at Lake Holdbrook the weekend of August fifth and sixth. My conscience got the best of me out there having fun while Daddy was dying. I called all weekend every few hours, but Mom Nita kept coming up with reasons why Daddy couldn't make it to the phone. I did my best to help the kids have fun, but in the back of my mind, all my thoughts were on Daddy.

Tuesday, August 8th, 2006

I woke up at three am from the recurring nightmare of Daddy's funeral. It was so real it sent shivers up my spine. I couldn't go back to sleep, so I made a pot of coffee, and turned on the TV. I got the kids off to school and had started cleaning the house when the phone rang.

"Wende, you better get over here quick if you want to say goodbye to your Daddy," I heard Mom Nita say.

"Can I talk to him for a minute," I begged as I ran and grabbed my shoes?

"He's lapsed into a coma and is non-responsive."

"I'm on my way."

Driving ninety to nothing, I got there in just over an hour. Sure enough,

Daddy was unconscious as I stepped up to his bedside.

"I love you, Daddy, go on home to Jesus, he's waiting on you with Maw-Maw Lummus and Paw-Paw John. Don't be afraid, Daddy; everything is gonna be alright.

The rest of the day passed in a haze for me with people coming and going. I spent a lot of time sitting out back, remembering my last conversation with Daddy. I was sure gonna dread having to look down at Daddy in his casket, but by then, I knew he'd be at home in heaven. Probably off somewhere reading a book, I thought to myself, smiling.

Around two am in the early morning hours of August 9th, Daddy took Jesus' hand and left this earth behind. I thanked God for having blessed me with such a great man for a father as I kissed his cheek one last time. Shelley left not long after Daddy died, and around four am we got the call saying she had been rushed to the emergency room. Later, we found out she'd been admitted to the telemetry unit for observation.

"That'd be just like Shelley. She's gonna take off with Daddy so she can have him all to herself," I joked to my step-sister Lynn, but I was concerned all the same.

Mom Nita told Lynn to tell me to go on home and get any pictures I wanted of Daddy for the memorial video, but I refused to. I was gonna go to the funeral home to help with Daddy's arrangements come hell, or high water. I made sure Lynn understood, and that she better convince Mom Nita of the same. Must've work cause Mom Nita finally gave in. The funeral home picked up Daddy's body around five am, and I tried to nap for a while 'til it was time to go make Daddy's arrangements, but I couldn't sleep to save my soul.

We arrived at the facility around ten am, and by noon Lynn and I were standing in front of my van, discussing the details of the next couple of days. I promised to be careful and told Lynn I'd be back later that evening.

Clark and Patrick were driving up from New Orleans, where they'd been working the past few weeks, along with my ex-sister-law, my step-sister Renee and her son and husband.

My boys were so afraid I was gonna fall asleep at the wheel and have a fatal accident; that they took turns talking to me on the phone all the way from Ft. Worth to Grand Saline. I admit, I was distraught, but I wasn't sleepy. I humored them and let them talk their hearts out.

I got to Grand Saline and stopped to see if the local mechanic had the time to charge the AC system in my van. The ride from the funeral home after Daddy's service to the cemetery was a long one, and I knew my van would be hot and stuffy as many people were gonna fill it. He was in the middle of a game of pool and on his lunch break. He offered to do it later in the afternoon, but I declined knowing I didn't have time.

Pulling up to the red-light by the Exxon, I realized I wasn't wearing a seat-belt. I briefly considered not putting it on, but then thought to myself it'd be my luck I'd get pulled over between here and my apartment and get a ticket. Not wanting anything to slow me down, I tugged at the belt and clicked it in place. Making a left turn onto Houston Street, I answered the phone. It was the boys again.

"Mom, hurry and get your things together cause we're dropping Patrick off at your house so he can drive you back to Ft. Worth," Clark insisted.

Just as I crossed Frank Street, I saw the warning lights and the arm coming down at the railroad crossing in front of me. Just what I need, I thought. That damn thing had been malfunctioning for over a year. The arm would come down and stay there sometimes for fifteen minutes or longer without a train ever passing. Everyone who lived on Circle Drive, the first street past the tracks, had gotten used to going around the arm to avoid unnecessary delays. Driving up to it, I looked down the tracks toward Brookshires Grocery and didn't see a train in sight. Looking the opposite direction, all I saw was the overgrown shrubbery and grey cinder blocks that cover the mechanism that controls the track. Making a split decision, I backed up and drove around the arm and onto the tracks so I could get home without being delayed.

I always wondered what people are thinking when they know they're fixing to die, such as right before the impact of a deadly collision? Staring at the train bearing down on me, I found out.

I threw my left foot on the brake and shifted the gears into reverse. Looking up, I saw the train as it sped toward me, thinking, "I'm dead!"

"Wende, Wende," I heard someone calling through the fog.

"Where are my babies, where are my babies," I vaguely recall screaming.

The lady standing with her head stuck in the window had seen the collision and had run over to my van while calling 911. She said when I turned to look at her; my eyes were open and as wide as saucers. She said I became zombie-like after I stopped screaming and wasn't responding, I was staring but not seeing.

She heard my phone ringing, but it had stopped before she could answer it. One of the first numbers she tried dialing connected her to my ex-sister-in-law, who pulled her vehicle over and alerted my sons to the accident.

The lady would later describe for the officer who arrived on the scene that the train struck the front of my van, causing it to fly up in the air and spin around in the process. It then collided with the structure which controls the arm, causing my van to turn around again before coming to rest in the ditch.

I was in and out of consciousness and vaguely remember bits and pieces of the period that they used the jaws of life to extricate me from my vehicle. I remember the intense pain I felt when they lifted me out of my van to place me on a stretcher. I later learned that was because ten inches of my tibia had been shattered.

"My Daddy died today," I kept trying to tell everyone. "My Daddy died today."

I guess I repeated that phrase so much that the officer on the scene was said to have asked me if I'd tried to kill myself. He would place a citation on my chest for going around the arm that morning as I was loaded into the helicopter. Months later, I paid the one hundred-eighty dollar fine. That ticket upset Mom Nita to the point she wrote a letter to the Chief of Police in Grand Saline to complain.

The whir of the helicopter blades, and the insistent voice of the medical flight personnel, got a response from me.

"I'm in a helicopter, am I dying," I asked.

That evening, many people from the church came to wish me well. Pastor H, the music minister, and Charlie were the only faces I vaguely recall seeing before darkness overtook me.

I was placed in a drug-induced coma over the next several days for my safety. I had suffered hairline fractures to my C-3 and C-4 vertebrae. I received four broken ribs, which punctured and collapsed my lungs. Then ten inches of bone was shattered to my left lower tibia.

Funny, I had dreaded seeing my Daddy in a casket and having to go to his funeral all my life. I'd even had the nightmare images about it. On the day of his funeral, I was having surgery on my leg. The five-hour-long surgery entailed a titanium rod inserted through my tibia and then connected to the one and a half inches of tibial bone attached to my ankle. It was, for this reason, the doctors told me I'd never walk again without assistance. The doctors said I would probably never walk again without a cane or a walker.

My first clear thoughts upon waking in a regular hospital room were profound. I thought of the train and realized; I'm not dead! I knew I only lived and breathed because God said it was so. When I asked the nurse what day it was, I knew I'd missed Daddy's funeral. As sad as that thought was, it didn't take away the joy I felt at being alive.

The ringing phone brought me out of my reverie.

"Hello," I answered weakly.

"Mom, oh Mom, it's so good to hear your voice," Patrick stated tearfully. "You're not going to believe this, but there are voice messages from all three major news networks out of New York City on your phone. There are numbers they want you to call. Apparently, someone leaked the video footage from the train, which captured the accident, to the news networks as it was being sent to the Union Pacific Offices in St. Louis. I think they want to interview you."

"Is this *the* Windell Nabors from Grand Saline, Texas, whose vehicle was struck by a train," the news anchor inquired.

"Yes, sir, that would be me," I replied.

"Unbelievable," letting out an incredulous gasp, he stated, "We would like to do a fifteen-minute interview with you, live on-air. We would send a remote crew to interview you in your hospital room. Would you be interested?"

I had agreed to the interview, but later that evening, I received a call letting me know it was canceled. The video was the property of Union Pacific Railroad, and they refused to let it be aired due to future legal actions that had yet to be determined.

Everyone who lived on Circle Drive where I lived vowed to stand by me in court based on the malfunctioning arm, but a lawyer friend of mine checked it out and said because the arm was functioning at the time the train hit me, I had no case.

I hadn't really considered suing them in the first place. I was just glad to be alive.

Chapter 67
Inspirations and shocking requests

I didn't have insurance and couldn't afford to go to a rehab when the doctor's released me from the hospital, but I was provided a hospital bed, a walker, and a bedside commode. Patrick's youngest daughter's mother moved into the house with her children and cared for the kids and me while I recuperated.

I had extreme anxiety issues during the first few weeks I was home. The train tracks ran behind my home. Every time the train went past, I would shake uncontrollably, whether I was awake or sleeping. Sometimes I would start trembling for no apparent reason, then seconds later, the train horn could be heard.

A few weeks after I was home, Mom Nita called.

"What do you want that belonged to your Daddy," she asked?

"Nothing of value," I replied, knowing she expected me to ask for more. "All I'd like to have is something Daddy carried in his pocket. Maybe one of his pocket knives or something like that."

The one item I would liked to have had, besides the card I had given Daddy, was the Zippo lighter I'd given Daddy years ago. It had white leather-like material on the outside with a ship engraved on it, similar to a scrimshaw engraving. Daddy carried it around for years and had rubbed his thumb across that lighter to the point that the engraving was faded. Almost none of the boat was left visible. He'd had me go to the drug store and pick him up some flint, and lighter fluid thinking he could make it work, but unable to do so, he tossed it in his dresser well over ten years ago. I figured that lighter was long gone by now.

Shelley came to see me and brought me a small box Mom Nita had sent a couple of days later. Inside were two things: a small pocket knife I'd seen Daddy carry off and on over the years, and a Zippo lighter with a faded ship on it! I felt Daddy's presence surround me at that moment. I carry that lighter in my purse and take it wherever I go to this day!

I'd called the school and managed to get them to drop me from my classes as soon as I'd gotten home from the hospital. They'd tried to make me come to Tyler and do it in person, but once I'd explained the situation to them, they made an exception for me. I was undecided 'bout going back to school since the doctor's said I'd never be able to walk on my own again. I was pretty sure they might be right since I could barely walk even with a walker. The rehab people had worked with me a little bit before I was discharged, but other than that, I was on my own. Every single time I put my left foot on the floor, I felt a shocking sensation that sent pain shooting up my leg. I was almost to the point of quitting school, filing for disability, and accepting defeat. Depressed, I wondered how I would ever be able to raise these kids.

I woke up one morning not long after deciding to throw the towel in; to bright sunlight filling the room.

"Get your butt out of that bed and learn to walk again! I didn't spare your life for you to become crippled," I clearly heard someone say.

"Jessica, you in there," I called out.

I called out several more times but still got no response.

"I said, get up and walk!"

The message was concise and clear, and I'd hear it out loud!

"Is that you God," I asked?

By this time, I was pretty spooked, so much so that I wasn't taking no chances.

My walker was sitting at the end of my bed, and maneuvering a few inches at a time; I was able to drag it forward. Recalling the instructions I'd had, I was able to stand while holding the walker in place. I felt the pain shooting up my leg, but after it subsided, I took a step using the walker. Each time I stepped on my left leg, it hurt. Undaunted, I continued 'til I made it all the way to the front door and then out to the curb. I was exhausted but managed to get back to the hospital bed. It had taken the better part of an hour, but I didn't care. I could walk!

I made a makeshift pouch to hang on my walker to carry a couple of things in, and the next day I began my own version of rehabilitation. On my second day, I walked to the curb but added a huge sidewalk square to the distance. I added a new square every day, increasing my range.

I started and ended each 'rehab' session listening to my favorite Keith song, "You Won." The words spoke to my heart. I was inspired to be the best me I could, and it brought me closer to God every step I took. Listening to Keith's music was almost as if I gained physical strength through the words he sang. I was constantly reminded of how he never gave up despite the odds stacked against him. If he could beat the odds, so could I!

By the time December rolled around, I could walk around Circle Drive and back down Houston Street to where I lived, which was close to an eighth of a mile. I was able to do it in half the time it took from when I first began. I decided it was time to go back to school, and pushing my walker, I showed up for registration.

I'd been back in school for almost two weeks when one of my professors asked me to see her after class.

"Wende, I admire your spunk and determination, but don't you think it would be prudent to change your major, perhaps? I've seen how difficult it is for you to get around, and I'm not sure you'll ever recover well enough to become a nurse."

"I've had a couple of people ask me that question, and briefly wondered if they might be right. But you know what, God spared my life for a reason, and I don't believe he did that for me to settle for second best. I'm not gonna give up 'til I see some kind of sign that it's what God wants. I appreciate your words of advice, though; I know you're only looking out for me," thanking her, I went on to my next class.

May 4th, 2007

It was a Friday morning and less than a week before my Final in Anatomy and Physiology 1. It was also Patrick's twenty-eighth birthday. I'd planned to make him a cake later that afternoon after I'd spent some time studying. I was standing in front of my kitchen sink, having just washed the morning breakfast dishes when the phone rang. The caller ID said it was Shelley.

"Hello," I answered as I rinsed the soap out of the sink.

"What're you doing," my baby sister asked?

"I just finished the dishes, and I'm fixing to sit down and study for a while. How are you feeling," I replied, knowing she was in the hospital.

"Wende, you know how you always stop what you're doing to help Bubba? You've helped Bubba all his life. Now I need you to come help me," Shelley said in her most argumentative voice. Being the baby, she'd always gotten whatever she wanted when she used that avenue. With Shelley, everything was urgent, and she always wanted what she wanted right that minute. Always!

"Shelley, come on now, I just told you I have to study. I have a very important Final next week that is gonna require a lot of studying. Tell you what, give me 'til Sunday, and I promise I'll be over there bright and early to help you do whatever it is you're needing," I all but begged her. She didn't answer for a minute, so I took a deep breath and decided to find out what it was that had her in such a tizzy, "What exactly is it that you are needing me to do," I asked in frustration?

"I need you to come help me die," she said so quietly, I was sure she was messing with me.

I held the phone out and stared at it, not believing what I'd just heard. It angered me that she would say something like that cause death wasn't anything to joke about.

"Shelley, that ain't funny. Don't be fucking with me like that. Just tell me what you need."

"They're sending me home with hospice, and told me I have less than a week to live," again, her voice soft, and not sounding anything like my little sister at all.

The words sank in, and I knew she wasn't joking at all.

"I'm sorry I yelled Shelley. I thought you were messing with me," taking a deep breath, I said, "where are you at now?"

"Nita is fixing to be here to take me home."

"I'll be right there, Shelley. I love you," I promised.

Chapter 68
Daddy Dimes and Little Sister

I'd given up cigarettes a couple of months before I sat out for Ft. Worth that morning when I got off the phone with Shelley. Once again, with my foot in the peddle and not caring if I got pulled over for speeding. Pulling off the freeway, I pulled in the 7-11 to pick up a pack of smokes. I pumped twenty dollars in the gas tank since I was there.

Something shiny caught my attention as I opened the door. Bending down, I saw a dime hanging off the edge of the seat. How in the world did I scoot across the seat without knocking it off, I wondered to myself? From the way it was hanging there, it would have been impossible. Picking it up, I held it close to see the date on it. It was 1965, the year of Shelley's birth!

Immediately I thought of Daddy! Holding the dime as I was right then, it reminded me of the card that was so special to him. The dime tucked tightly in my palm, I closed my eyes and recalled a conversation I'd had with Daddy and Mom Nita where Daddy had said he believed folks could send a sign after they passed to their loved ones to let them know they were near. I could feel Daddy's presence so strong in that moment that I knew it was him!

"Thank you, Daddy, cause if I ever needed you here, it's now," I spoke aloud so he could hear me. Climbing in my car, I sat there quietly, listening with my heart.

"I'm here. I'm gonna take care of everything. It'll be okay," I heard the words in my father's voice just as sure as I'd seen the dime barely hanging off the edge of the seat.

Shelley was sitting on the porch when I pulled up in front of her house.

Hearing the car pull up, she raised her head and gazed out at me. I walked up and sat down beside her, wondering what to say. Shelley and I had never been close as other sisters I knew. We'd always had a love-hate relationship. Not that I'd ever really hated her, but she could get me fired up in a skinny-minute, and she knew it too. I'd always envied sisters who hung out together and were close. I would have given anything to bond with my little sister that way, but Shelley had never been mushy with me. She always challenged me, or it seemed like she wanted to fight. I knew Shelley was always jealous of me trying to get close to Daddy. Especially at family gatherings. She was forever picking fights with me at get-togethers for sure. I'd always hoped that would change someday, and we could build a close relationship. Now I knew someday was never gonna come. Sitting there next to her, I silently begged God to let the time we had left together to be peaceful, and for God to give me the courage to help her like the big sister I'd always wanted to be. Wanting to break the silence between us, I said the first thing that come to my mind.

"You're damn determined to have Daddy all to yourself aren't you," I nudged her shoulder with mine, laughing softly, so she'd know I'd meant it in a joking manner.

Looking up, that smug little grin on her face, I could see she wanted to cry but was being brave.

"What happened, I thought they put you in the hospital to boost up your system?'

"They gave me IV fluids and medicine but said it wasn't helping me the way it used to. They said my liver is really bad this time."

Thinking back to how Shelley's problems started made me furious! She'd been twenty-nine at the time, and none of us knew much 'bout proper medical procedures back then. Going to the dentist with a toothache, the dentist had pulled it out on the spot. Shelley went home, took the pain meds the dentist prescribed, and went to sleep. She woke up the next morning with a fever, and thinking nothing of it, took some ibuprofen. For the next several days, she took ibuprofen for the temperature. By Friday, her temperature had gone so high Daddy took her to the emergency room. Come to find out; the dentist had pulled her tooth while it was abscessed, allowing the infection to go into her bloodstream. The resulting septicemia became so severe it caused her Mitral heart valve to prolapse. At twenty-nine years old, she was having open-heart surgery. They used a pig heart-valve to fix her heart, but she was so sick she had to spend nearly two months in ICU. The doctors told her that so much damage had been done to her heart, she would never be able to work again. Shelley was told to apply for disability, and her doctor agreed to sign off on it. She got denied the first year but was told she could reapply every year. She got jacked around and finally hired an attorney to represent her. Hiring a lawyer didn't seem to make much difference, but every year she kept trying. It wasn't so much the income she needed, but the insurance, which would have allowed for proper medical care.

She went to the county hospital frequently since she didn't have insurance and needed to have labs drawn to maintain the blood thinners she had to take. Somewhere along the way, she acquired Hepatitis C, which was especially hard on her given her circumstances. She asked to receive the treatments which might have cured her Hep C, but they turned her down with the excuse that her condition wouldn't allow it. I'm not sure I ever believed what the doctors told her. I couldn't help but feel if she'd had received the Interferon treatments, she might not be dying right now.

"How come you're sitting out here," I questioned to break the silence.

"They're supposed to deliver my hospital bed any minute now."

Walking around the hedge separating the two houses, her neighbor come up the sidewalk.

"Hey, I haven't seen you for a few days, where you been," the gentleman asked with a smile?

"I was in the hospital, but they sent me home to die," Shelley stated matter of factly.

"Naw man, you're gonna be okay. Don't say that," he replied uncomfortably.

"No, I really am dying. The doctor said I have less than a week to live."

Looking uncomfortable, the man said, "Oh man, you're serious. I'm so sorry. Is there anything I can do for you?"

"You ain't gotta be sorry. We all gotta die someday," Shelley exclaimed while pulling her lips together in a smile.

The man bid a hasty goodbye before disappearing back around the bushes.

The hospital supply company showed up a short time later with her bed. They put it together, leaving Shelley and I alone again. I asked her if she was hungry, but she said she didn't have an appetite. When the delivery guys left, I made the bed so she could lay down.

She'd sent the message out that she was dying and invited her friends to come over and say goodbye to her. One by one, they began showing up. Hovering in the background, I watched as her friends tried comforting her, but in the end, it was Shelley who consoled them. She'd picked out small keepsakes to share with her closest friends.

All evening long, a steady stream of people came to see her, family members included. She held court like that of a brave warrior princess who was going off into battle, exhibiting courage and bravery as I'd never seen before. Never once breaking down, never once bemoaning her lot in life. She'd always been jealous of me, but I wasn't sure it wasn't the other way around. She'd asked me to come and help her, how I wished she could've of known, it was she helping me.

The evening slowly came to a close, and things quieted down. After everyone else who was staying had gone to bed, Shelley asked me to come sit by her side. Pulling a chair up close and sitting down, she grabbed my hand, and we talked way into the early morning hours. Recalling childhood memories, we laughed, and we cried. When the time came for serious discussion, she finally broke down. She wasn't worried for herself. She was tired of all the medical treatments she'd endured, the extended hospital stays, and the pain she'd suffered. She was ready for it all to end.

Shelley's greatest worries concerned her family. She felt bad cause she wasn't gonna be here when they needed her. Her children were just now entering adulthood, a time when they needed guidance and help as only a mother can give. She'd been blessed with three grandchildren so far, but being young, she believed they'd forget her. Not to mention the ones who were to come in the future who'd never even know her. I did my best to reassure her that between Bubba and me, we would always be there for her children and grandchildren. I vowed, that where I would never try to stand in her shoes, I would always treat her babies as if they were my own. I gave her my word that I would move heaven and earth to help them when they needed it. I assured her that no one could, or would ever forget her and that I would make sure the children yet to come would know all about their Guardian Angel, their NaNa.

We discussed other concerns she had, and I did my best to ease them. She got quiet and closed her eyes. I would have thought she was sleeping, but for the firm way, she continued to hold my hand. She hadn't let go of it for hours. I sat and stared at my baby sister, giving her the chance to fall asleep before I moved. The emotions of the day had got the best of me, and I laid my head on the bed. Before long, I was nodding out, unable to remain awake. I decided I would get up and lay down on the couch across from her bed. Trying to ease my hand from hers, she opened her eyes. I told her I was only gonna take a nap on the couch and wasn't going far.

"No, don't," she softly cried. Scooting over in her bed, she pulled back the covers and said, "You can sleep with me."

She turned on her side, facing the windows, and I crawled in beside her. Reaching out with her left hand, she pulled my arm around her. Grasping my hand in hers firmly once again, she got quiet, then whispered, "I'm scared, Wende."

"Me too, little sister, me too," I said, squeezing her hand tighter.

"Please don't leave my side 'til I'm gone," she begged.

"Wild horses couldn't drag me away," I promised.

Just before she fell asleep, she had one more request for me, "Wende, promise me you'll never forget this night and the promises you made?"

"I swear, God as my witness, I won't ever, ever forget this night!"

Little did she know, the memories of that night and all that we shared, were etched in my heart. Every word, every moment, seared so profoundly as never to go away. Her soft snoring let me know she'd finally drifted off to sleep. It would be some time before I too slept. I didn't want to close my eyes; I wanted this night to last forever.

Nothing lasts forever, and time waits for no one. The next few days were a repeat of Friday evening with friends and family arriving non-stop. I never imagined she had so many friends. Sunday was the day she chose to have her oldest grandson brought to her. She was waiting on the sofa when he walked in the door. He had spent much of his young life with his NaNa while his parents worked and was very close to her. Jordan was six, maybe seven years old at the time she died, but he was old enough to understand his NaNa was going away, and he would never see her again. His red-rimmed eyes were proof he was upset.

"Hey baby, I missed you so much," Shelley said, wrapping her arms tightly around him.

"I missed you too, NaNa," Jordan got out between sobs.

They talked about his school and what he'd done the previous week, making small talk as she led him gently toward saying goodbye.

"Do you remember that talk you and me had about me going to live with PaPa and Jesus in heaven," she asked?

"Uh-huh," he muttered.

"Well, I'm gonna be leaving any day now, and I don't want you to be afraid. I want you to know that I'll always be here," placing her hand across his little chest, she continued, "in your heart. You can talk to me anytime you want. I'll always be able to hear you, and even though you can't hear me, I'll always be listening. When you get to missing me, all you have to do is look up at the stars and find the brightest one. That'll be me shining down on you."

Unable to control his grief any longer, he jumped up and threw his little arms around her neck, crying for all his worth.

"Oh, Nana, I'm gonna miss you so much," he cried.

I stepped out of the room at that point, for I too had to cry my heart out.

Her health declined at an alarming rate, and she got to where the simplest task of going to the restroom zapped her strength. By Tuesday, her friends had all came to say goodbye, and all that remained were family. By now, she was sleeping more than she was awake, and we all tried to let her rest. That evening we noticed she was having conversations with Daddy through the bits and pieces she spoke out loud as she slept. Some thought she was dreaming, but I had no doubt Daddy was right there by her side.

Around eleven pm, she woke up and demanded to be carried out to the porch to smoke a cigarette. Leaning forward, she had to be held up to keep her balance. Some of the last words she spoke had us laughing, in a sad kind of way. She'd answered questions those around were asking, and then got quiet.

"Maw-Maw Cruse said y'all better clean up all these cigarettes butts on the porch," she declared.

"When did you talk to Maw-Maw," I questioned, listening carefully for her reply?

"While ago," looking up at me, she went on, "she took me to her house, and guess what, she ain't dead!"

One of my ex-sister-in-laws leaned over and whispered, "If Maw-Maw told Shelley the porch is a mess, then that means she's here with us." A cold shiver ran up my spine as her words sank in.

Shelley passed away early the next morning with her husband and children at her side. Nine months to the day since Daddy died. She was forty-one years old, one year younger than Momma when she passed.

I agreed to stay there with Shelley's body to wait for the funeral home to pick her up so that my brother-in-law and her children could leave to make arrangements. Around nine-thirty, the phone rang.

"Greeson residence," I answered.

"Is Mrs. Greeson there," the cheery voice inquired?

"She's unavailable, but I'm her sister if you'd like to leave a message," I questioned suspiciously?

"This is her attorney's office. Could you please let her know that her disability is approved as well as medicare. They're even going to award her five years retro-pay," the lady exclaimed excitedly.

Gazing over at my baby sister's body, remembering how hard she'd fought for help, and wondering if it might have saved her life, I lost it! The poor woman on the other end of the line didn't deserve the onslaught she received from me as I raged on and on about the governments' injustice toward my sister, but I'm thankful she listened to me. Right that minute, I needed someone to blame and someone to listen.

Of all the deaths I'd had to endure, Shelleys' was the hardest. I never saw it coming. I knew she was sick but didn't understand she was *fixin' to die sick* until she called me that Friday afternoon.

Shelley made good on her threats to haunt me if I fell down on my job of seeing after her children. Though both times she's reached out to me, it was good to hear her voice. One day I was shopping in Wal-Mart when I imagined hearing her voice. Ignoring my imaginings, I continued on until I heard her a second time.

"Wende, call my kids, there's something wrong," her voice clear and persistent.

For giggles and grins, I called my niece Gracie and asked her if they were all okay.

"Tiffany told you, didn't she? She promised not to tell a soul," she cried out tearfully.

"What are you talking 'bout Gracie, I haven't spoken to Tiffany in a hot minute?"

"She had to tell you cause me, and her are the only ones who know."

"Know what baby," feeling the hairs stand up on the back of my neck, I waited for her response?

"I'm pregnant, Aunt Wende, and I'm not ready to be a mother," she bawled.

I could almost see Shelley grinning, "I told you so."

I explained to Gracie how I'd come to call, but I know she didn't buy it. She had her little boy and went on to have a little girl too. She was ready for motherhood by the time it came for her.

Down the road, I got another message from my sister.

"Wende, you'd better call and check on my kids," I heard her demand loud and clear.

This time, I think Gracie believed me when I told her that Shelley had insisted I call cause she knew I couldn't possibly have heard it from somewhere else.

I've kept my word to Shelley. Bubba stepped up too like I always knew he would. We stay in contact with Shelley's kids and grandkids as if they're our own. Her grandchildren that came after know all about their NaNa, who's an angel. They love to hear stories about her and even ask me to repeat them sometimes. The one they enjoy the most was the time she turned thousands of crickets loose in PaPa's donut shop.

Her family makes the trek to the cemetery almost every holiday that rolls around to take fresh flowers and new decorations. While her husband and children decorate, her grandchildren chase each other around and play, their laughter carrying on the wind.

See baby sister, I was right! You always were, and will always be unforgettable!!!

Chapter 69

Promises Kept and Dreams Come True

It took quite a while for me to get over being mad with God over Shelley. I was furious with government policies as well. I took my anger out by using one of my assignments for my Speech class to research America's uninsured. I was saddened to learn that over one-hundred-thousand people died in America the year Shelley died due in part to the fact they were uninsured and lacked proper medical care.

I was mad cause God kept sticking me in front of family members who were dying, and no one but me could care for them cause they couldn't handle it. Why me, I often asked God? It would all make sense someday, but for now, I was angry.

As for Shelley, God finally helped me understand. Even if Shelley had access to medical care, she would have still left us when she did because it was her time to go. End-Stage Liver disease was simply the vehicle she left in.

I threw myself into my studies and my determination to finish what I'd started. Each passing semester I either made the Dean's or President's List. Phi Theta Kappa Honor Society sent me an invitation to join due to my grades, and I did. After years of red-tape, I was approved to become a nurse.

In 2009 I graduated cum laude with two Associate's Degrees: Associate in Arts and Associate in Applied Science. Many of my family members were there to see me walk the stage wearing my yellow honor stole. I was all set to begin my nursing classes.

Scuter and Patrick had stayed in touch with Ted over the years as they never stopped seeing him as their father. I had stayed in touch with Pa, Ted's dad, cause we remained close as well. I got the call that Ted was in the hospital dying from mesothelioma. I went to Grand Prairie to see how Pa was holding up under that news and found out he didn't even know. I drove him down to see Ted one last time, and it was a good thing I did cause it was the last time he talked to his son. We made the trip back down to Houston to say goodbye before they took him off life support. Pa was so devastated that I convinced him to move in with the kids and me. When he got sick with what I thought was a cold, I took him to the emergency room. He was eaten up with mesothelioma as well. They'd worked years in hot tar roofing and had developed cancer as a result. Pa died in my arms in January 2010. I would later have quite the adventure when I drove their ashes to Wisconsin to be buried near Ted's ma. But that's another story.

Spring 2010

I began nursing school with gusto! I felt so proud to be wearing my new scrubs and couldn't wait to go to the hospitals and nursing homes for clinicals. I was on my way, baby!

In the second week of classes, I received a phone call from my step-sister Renee. She needed me to take custody of her two young grandchildren, who were in the care of Child Protective Custody and about to be lost to our family forever. Her daughter and unborn grandchild had died in a car accident years ago, and she'd lost contact with her daughter's other children.

Oh, my God? Which way do I go now?

I didn't have the heart to turn her down, knowing all she'd been through and agreed to talk to the worker. I didn't think I would be placed with two more children since I already had four, was in school, not working, and lived in government housing, but I gave it a shot.

Later that afternoon, the worker called and said I'd been approved.

"When can you pick up the children," the kind worker asked?

I did some quick calculations before replying, "How about Friday?"

"No, I mean, what time today? They have to be picked up by this evening," sounding urgent, he commented.

Thinking back to that day, I laugh to myself and wonder how I managed. When I met him later that evening, I almost fainted! They were babies. Lily was fourteen months old, and Drake was three months old.

It most certainly had been in God's plan for me. The way it all fell in place could never have happened without his divine intervention. When I contacted my nursing administrator and explained the situation that Wednesday afternoon, she had given me the next couple of days off to settle them in. When I picked them up, they had no clothes other than a Wal-Mart bag full of stained items. I had nothing in my home to care for babies at all.

By Friday afternoon, I had childcare and other assistance in place for them. Over the weekend, my friends and some of my church family swooped in and filled my home with everything I needed to care for these two new additions to my family.

We soon settled into a routine those six children and me. We'd hit the floor running at six am to start our day with everyone running around waiting for their chance in our one bathroom. After dropping everyone at school and daycare, I'd make a mad dash to the college thirty-five miles away. Once school was over, I'd rush to pick the babies up at daycare and make it home to the school bus's arrival.

Everyone had a snack while homework was seen to, followed by playtime, and other extracurricular activities such as football and cheerleading practices. Each afternoon after I got the kids working on their homework, I'd start a load of clothes while I began dinner. Baths were synchronized so that everyone was in bed by nine pm. I'd go to sleep with the kids setting my alarm for two am so I could wake up and do my own homework from two to six am. If it wasn't for my granddaughter Katelyn, who at eight was thrilled to have live babydolls to care for, I know beyond a shadow of a doubt I would have never got it all done.

Nursing school was a tough business, and if not for a particular red-headed classmate of mine named Kelly, it would have been harder. We spent many, many nights on the phone all night long grilling each other as we studied.

We had a hectic year, but soon it was time for graduation. Most all of my family showed up to cheer me on as I graduated in the top ten percent of my class. Mom Nita was allowed to sit in the front row since she was in a wheelchair. I'd noticed the empty chair next to her as I sat at the back of the auditorium with my graduating class but thought nothing more of it until it was time for me to cross the stage for my ceremonial pinning.

Holding my head high as I crossed the stage, I looked down at Mom Nita, but what caught my eye was the eight by ten glossy photograph occupying the seat next to her. Smiling up at me from that photo was my Daddy! He'd made it after all…

Chapter 70

Epilogue

March 6th, 2020

When I began my journey to tell the story of my life three years ago, I was going to take it through to the current day. I soon realized it would take more than one book to get the job done in a manner that pleased me. Who knows, maybe I'll write another book someday.

My life has taken many twists and turns since the day I graduated from nursing school, but that doesn't surprise me. Perhaps it's the driver who gets sidetracked, or maybe it's just life. Just when I think I've got it all figured out, something comes along and turns everything upside down again. There would be many more funerals to attend, and obstacles to overcome, but they haven't slowed me down yet.

Come to find out; there's nothing wrong with me at all. Though I grant you some may disagree, but that's on them. I'm just one of the millions of people who've had a hard row to hoe at times in their lives. Life never was meant to be easy; I don't care who you are.

How we view life is the key to understanding. How we react to it will determine the roads we travel. It really is all about choices. We can choose to see that glass as half-empty, or half-full. I have learned that viewing the glass as half-full will take me much further than the alternative.

I no longer harbor resentments toward anyone for the events of my life, cause let me tell you, resentment will tear you up inside. Its destructive nature will steal your peace and make you miserable. It will destroy your life if you let it.

It wasn't cancer, making me so sick. The doctors ran test after test and eventually decided that Hep C was the actual culprit. They gave me the treatment for it, and I am now cured. I'm glad they first thought it was cancer; however, since it was the fear of my life coming to a possible end that pushed me to begin my final bucket list item.

My book may not make the New York Times best-seller list, but that's okay cause I've already reaped my greatest rewards by writing it. I'd always heard if you bring ugliness into the light that it loses its power. It can't hurt you anymore. I can't speak for others, but for me, it's true. This journey has been a healing experience for me of epic proportions.

Bubba now has sixteen years of sobriety, and I'm so proud of him. He's still working at the same place he started when he turned his life around. He's got a whole mess of grandchildren just like me. We see after Shelley's kids and grandchildren the same as we always have.

Scuter gave me several grandchildren over the years. Trey, Skylar, Ashton, Mason James, Jaxon, and of course, his youngest Shelley...

I almost died in twenty thirteen and spent fifty-seven days in ICU. I had a spiritual experience where I went to "God's Waiting Room," as Mason Windell called it. It was during my recovery period that I saw God's plan for me to become a hospice nurse take shape. Morbid as it may seem, I absolutely love it! He'd had it in mind all along I just didn't know it. My job brings me comfort, knowing that I can help folks die with dignity while teaching their family members to let go with love! I've told all of my children that as they contemplate where their lives are headed to choose a career they're passionate about, I promised them if they do, they'll never have to dread going to work again!

Over the years, I feared Jerry would make good his threat, and tried keeping up with his whereabouts. All the charges against him in Midland were dropped; although, I never knew why. He was released from Texas after serving out his time to a half-way house in Houston. I lost track of him for a while and always looked over my shoulder. I could've sworn I saw him lurking around the neighborhood not long before Maw-Maw Cruse died but chalked it up to nerves. I finally found him in early 2010. He was serving time in the J Donovan Correctional Facility in San Diego County, California. Best as I could figure out, he'd joined a traveling carnival in Texas and made his way across the states as a Carny. He was apprehended for the deviant sexual assault on a minor in Ventura, California. I've since learned he was also serving two other sentences for a separate sexual assault and murder of a prison inmate. In September 2013, I made the call, as I did every year, to make sure he hadn't been released. When the voice on the other end of the line questioned my relationship to Jerry, I momentarily became panicked, thinking he'd been released.

After a few moments, the lady continued, "I'm so sorry to inform you that Mr. Ferguson passed away at Ironwood State Prison this past July."

Thanking the lady on the other end of the line, I sank to my knees and cried. The fear I'd carried for so many years slipped away; I knew his reign of terror in my life was over. I prayed to God that his time traveling across the country hadn't left other victims behind, but thinking of the worn, faded-yellow spiral, I doubted it. I prayed for the faceless souls who'd encountered Jerry during his time on earth, but mostly I thanked God that he couldn't hurt anyone anymore.

Yesterday I finally found his daughter, whom I'd begun searching for when I started writing my book. I'd wanted to let her know about it before she possibly found out on her own. She is the spitting image of her father except for one thing; the light that shines in her eyes. We talked for hours filling each other in on all that had transpired over the years since we spoke those brief moments when she was eleven. I was saddened to learn of the hard life she'd lived, but soon realized she is a strong young woman. Unbelievably, we'd crossed paths many times. Even though we'd both lived in different states throughout our lives, we now live a mere thirty miles apart. She told me those few moments she'd spoken with her father and me so long ago was the only time they'd ever spoken, and she had recalled the conversation again and again as she grew up. She'd misunderstood when I told her I had two sons and grew up thinking she had two brothers named Clark and Patrick. She'd been looking for us as well. When she was eighteen, she contacted her father, and they'd exchanged letters for a few years. He never gave her a clear answer about us, only stating he had a wife and two sons. As our conversation grew to a close, she asked if it'd be alright with me if we stayed in touch. I didn't hesitate to tell her, yes. I knew, in my heart, God had planned it this way.

I eventually made it to New York and saw Macy's parade in person, but I wasn't alone. I discovered what all the mystery was about, but that's another story. Maybe I'll tell it someday!

Looking over at the large container of 'Daddy Dimes,' I smile and wonder what God has planned for me next…

SPECIAL MESSAGE JUST FOR YOU!

TO ALL WHO SUFFER IN SILENCE - FOR ANY REASON - THIS MESSAGE IS FOR YOU!!!

I UNDERSTAND! I'VE BEEN THERE! I've done that!

If you, or someone you know, is suffering for any reason, please reach out!

If you've read this book, then you should know by now, it is possible to turn your life around and achieve your wildest dreams.

You are the captain of your ship, and only you can change its course.

Anything worth having is worth the effort it takes to achieve it.

The best advice my Daddy ever gave me is simple but true:

"The only thing standing between you and anything you want in this life is yourself!"

I didn't turn my life around overnight, and it wasn't easy by a longshot. I would have never made it without God, who, by the way, doesn't expect you to become perfect to receive his love. He will love you no matter where you are on your journey!

Take that first step, and never look back!

Listed below are a few numbers in case you need them. There are many more, like the 12-Step Programs, but these will get you started.

LOVE, WENDE

National Prayer 1-800-4-PRAYER (1-800-477-2937)

SAMSHA/Substance Abuse and Mental Health Services 1-800-662-HELP (4357)

United Way Crisis Helpline 1-800-233-HELP (4357)

National Domestic Violence Hotline 1-800-799-SAFE (7233)

Battered Women and their Children 1-800-603-HELP (4357)

National Suicide Prevention Lifeline 1-800-273-8255

National Sexual Assault Hotline 1-800-656-HOPE (4673)

National Child Abuse Helpline 1-800-4-A-CHILD (1-800-422-4453)

Girls and Boys Town 1-800-448-3000

Made in the USA
Monee, IL
20 April 2020